COMPETITION, COMMITMENT, AND WELFARE

COMPETITION, COMMITMENT, AND WELFARE

KOTARO SUZUMURA

CLARENDON PRESS · OXFORD
1995

Oxford University Press, Walton Street, Oxford OX2 6DP
Oxford New York
Athens Auckland Bangkok Bombay
Calcutta Cape Town Dar es Salaam Delhi
Florence Hong Kong Istanbul Karachi
Kuala Lumpur Madras Madrid Melbourne
Mexico City Nairobi Paris Singapore
Taipei Tokyo Toronto
and associated companies in
Berlin Ibadan

Oxford is a trade mark of Oxford University Press

Published in the United States
by Oxford University Press Inc., New York

British Library Cataloguing in Publication Data
Data available

Library of Congress Cataloging in Publication Data
Data available

ISBN 0–19–828914–6

Typeset by Pure Tech Corporation, Pondicherry, India
Printed in Great Britain
on acid-free paper by
Biddles Ltd, Guildford & King's Lynn

PREFACE

This monograph focuses on one of the classical issues in theoretical welfare economics, the effects of increasing interfirm competition on economic welfare. As is often the case in many branches of economic theory, the origin of this central focus can be traced back all the way to Adam Smith's *Wealth of Nations*, according to whom '[i]n general, if any branch of trade, or any division of labour, be advantageous to the public, the freer and more general the competition, it will always be the more so'. Not only is the general validity of this assertion worth theoretical examination in some depth, but also it has an acute relevance to the appropriate design of competition policy *vis-à-vis* industrial policy.

Over the past ten years, a large portion of my theoretical work has centred around this focal issue. This monograph is a modest attempt to synthesize my work along these lines. The analytical framework and scenario of the book are explained in the Prologue, and my previously published articles, which paved the way towards this book, are listed with due gratitude to publishers as well as co-authors in the Acknowledgements section. What remains to be explained in this Preface is the empirical motivation that underlies this theoretical research.

In April 1982, I was offered an excellent opportunity to initiate a new joint research project on the postwar Japanese economy at the Tokyo Centre for Economic Research, which is an inter-university organization promoting interactive research among academically oriented economists. For various reasons, I decided to propose a project on Japanese industrial policy. The first reason was an academic curiosity; despite an upsurge of interest in Japanese industrial policy in the 1980s, serious scholarly studies from the standard economic perspective were surprisingly few, and many interesting issues remained almost unexplored. The second reason was that competition and industrial policies are precisely the arena where welfare economics is set in motion, and pursuing a project on the inter-disciplinary research on industrial policy seemed to provide an excellent opportunity to test the empirical relevance of welfare economics in general, and of theoretical industrial organization in particular.

This project turned out to be very fruitful, and the outcome of our joint efforts was published first in Japanese, and then in English (Komiya *et al.* 1988). Subsequently, those among the participants of this first project who were theoretically inclined continued their joint research, which resulted in a second monograph. It too was published originally in Japanese, and subsequently made available in English translation (Itoh *et al.* 1991).

This book is an outgrowth of my own work in these joint projects. It goes without saying that I am grateful to the participants of the two projects. Above all, my greatest gratitude goes to Professors Ryutaro Komiya and Masahiro Okuno-Fujiwara.

It should be clear by now that this short monograph has had a rather long and tortuous history. I sincerely hope that in its present form it is not hard to follow.

K.S.

Harvard University
November 1993

ACKNOWLEDGEMENTS

This monograph is based partly on my previous articles, some of which were co-authored. I am grateful to the co-authors as well as the publishers of the original articles for their permission to include such material, after substantial revisions, in this monograph. The list of the published articles is as follows.

'Entry Barriers and Economic Welfare', *Review of Economic Studies*, 54 (1987) 157–67. Joint paper with Kazuharu Kiyono.

'Oligopolistic Competition and Economic Welfare: A General Equilibrium Analysis of Entry Regulation and Tax-Subsidy Schemes', *Journal of Public Economics*, 42 (1990) 67–88. Joint paper with Hideki Konishi and Masahiro Okuno-Fujiwara.

'Alternative Firm Objectives and the Welfare Effects of Entry', *Osaka Economic Papers*, 40 (1991) 194–8.

'Taxation and Welfare in an Oligopoly with Strategic Commitment', *International Economic Review*, 33 (1992) 413–31. Joint paper with Timothy Besley.

'Cooperative and Non-Cooperative R&D in an Oligopoly with Spillovers', *American Economic Review*, 82 (1992) 1307–20.

'Symmetric Cournot Oligopoly and Economic Welfare: A Synthesis', *Economic Theory*, 3 (1993) 43–59. Joint paper with Masahiro Okuno-Fujiwara.

'Cooperative and Non-Cooperative R&D in an Oligopoly with Spillovers: Strategic Substitutes versus Strategic Complements', *Hitotsubashi Journal of Economics*, 34 (1993) 1–11. Joint paper with Noriyuki Yanagawa.

Thanks are due to Professors Kenneth Arrow, Kenneth Binmore, Claude d'Aspremont, Louis Gevers, Akira Goto, Murray Kemp, Tetsuya Kishimoto, Sajal Lahiri, Jean-Jacques Laffont, Michio Morishima, Masahiro Okuno-Fujiwara, Prasanta Pattanaik, Andrew Postlewaite, Patrick Rey, Agnar Sandmo, Amartya Sen, David Ulph, and John Vickers for their helpful comments and suggestions on my previous work, which formed the building blocks of this monograph; to Ms Carolyn Dodd for checking and improving my English; and to Ms Keiko Maiwa and Ms Hiromi Nikishima for carefully typing two drafts of this book.

Over the past few years, my research has been generously supported by the Tokyo Centre for Economic Research, the Japan Centre for Economic Research, the Grant-in-Aid for Scientific Research by the Japanese Ministry of Education, the Fulbright Foundation, and the Kikawada Foundation. I am very grateful for the financial help that was kindly extended by these organizations. Needless to say, they cannot be held responsible for any opinion expressed here.

It was in April 1988, when I was staying at All Souls College, Oxford University, as a Visiting Fellow, that the plan of this monograph first began to take shape. I am deeply indebted to the hospitality and excellent academic environment of All Souls College, without which this project may not have got off the ground. The finishing touches to the monograph were applied in the Fall Term of 1993, when I was granted an opportunity to visit the Department of Economics, Harvard University, as Fulbright Senior Fellow. I am extremely grateful to Professor A. K. Sen and the Fulbright Program for their courtesy, without which the completion of this monograph might not have been warranted.

Last but not least, my gratitude goes to my family. Without their moral support, I would not have completed this project.

CONTENTS

III. Generalizations and Qualifications

Appendices

Prologue

You never know what is enough unless
you know what is more than enough.

William Blake, 'Proverbs of Hell',
from *The Marriage of Heaven and Hell*

1. TWO COMMON BELIEFS ABOUT COMPETITION AND ECONOMIC WELFARE

To those who are trained in the tradition of standard economic theory, interfirm competition in pursuit of profit opportunities is nothing other than an efficient allocator of resources in a decentralized economy. It is widely considered that this conventional wisdom on the role of competition in the market-place culminates in the celebrated first fundamental theorem of welfare economics, according to which a perfectly competitive market economy attains a Pareto-efficient resource allocation as long as the existence of a competitive equilibrium is warranted. Since perfect competition is a state in which the number of competitors is so large that each competitor cannot exert recognizable influence on market prices on its own, it is natural, if not compelling, that a widespread belief developed that increasing the number of competing firms, thereby strengthening interfirm competition, improves economic welfare. This belief seems to be underlying the policy prescriptions of traditional literature on industrial organization and competition policy.[1]

In sharp contrast, a second conventional wisdom exists on competition and economic welfare, which has been strenuously held by a large group of people outside the standard academic circle, including people in business and industrial policy authorities. According to this second commonly held belief, the adage 'doing too much is as bad as not doing enough' applies to competition as well, and competition should be duly kept under deliberate public control if it is to function as an efficient allocator of resources. In other words, this second view construes competition as at best a necessary evil, which can serve a socially useful role only when a proper harness is in the dependable grasp of public policy authorities. The infamous concept of 'excessive competition', which appears every so often in the general discussions on competition and industrial policies, is an expression that symbolizes such a view of competition.[2]

Those who are accustomed to the first conventional wisdom would regard the concept of excessive competition simply as self-contradictory. It is true that competition, in the process of weaning out the winners from the losers, may well generate some frictions and waste. However, these frictions and waste are social costs which are unavoidable in the Schumpeterian process of constructive destruction, through which fierce competition eliminates inefficient firms from the market arena and shifts resources away from industries that are less needed socially, and towards industries that are more needed socially. If it were not for this process of competitive elimination of social inefficiency, firms would not be motivated to introduce new innovations for competitive survival and distinction, and widely dispersed private information on demand, technology, and resources might fail to be independently discovered, widely disseminated, and made socially available. Furthermore, government intervention in the name of avoiding these social costs by keeping excessive competition under due control might simply result in an unnecessary delay in adjustment which might be unavoidable after all. Unless the economic analysis within the standard conceptual framework of welfare economics finds a proper meaning in such an esoteric expression as excessive competition, and succeeds in identifying the possible existence of dysfunctions of a competitive mechanism arising from excessive competition in this well defined sense, this notion cannot claim any proper niche whatsoever, and public policy interventions in the name of duly controlling excessive competition have no legitimacy. In a nutshell, this is the state of art that lies behind this monograph.

Thus, the book aims at posing and settling the following two basic questions:

1. Can competition ever be excessive in a well defined welfare-theoretic sense?
2. Can policy intervention in the name of keeping excessive competition under due control always be justified?

2. PLAN OF THE BOOK

This monograph, which is in three parts, is mainly devoted to answering the first basic question.

In Part I, on 'Firm Entry and Economic Welfare', this question is posed in the context of long-run competition in an oligopolistic industry with economies of scale. It is asked whether the entry and exit decisions by individual firms in response to profit incentives can bring about a socially desirable allocation of resources. This investigation culminates in what may be called the *excess entry theorem*. Supposing the existence of an omnipotent 'first-best' government, it is shown that an excessive firm entry occurs at the free-entry Cournot–Nash equilibrium *vis-à-vis* the 'first-best' number of firms. Essentially, the main thrust of this first assertion can be carried over to the down-to-earth 'second-best' government, which lacks the power to enforce the 'first-best' marginal cost pricing. Indeed, we can show that there occurs an excessive firm entry at the free-entry Cournot–Nash equilibrium *vis-à-vis* the 'second-best' number of firms. Furthermore, even when it is not clear where exactly the first-best or second-best number of firms is located *vis-à-vis* the equilibrium number of firms because of the lack of information on the precise nature of demand, technology, and resources, it is still clear that the exit of firms at the free-entry Cournot–Nash equilibrium is welfare-improving at the margin. These claims will be established, first, in the context of a simple partial equilibrium analysis, and their robustness will then be reconfirmed in the context of a two-sector general equilibrium analysis. On the basis of these results, it may be asserted that a welfare-theoretic sense exists in which competition in the long run can be socially excessive. In addition to vindicating this central message, Part I also examines several welfare-improving tax subsidy schemes in a two-sector general equilibrium model of oligopoly.

In Part II, on 'Strategic Commitment and Economic Welfare', the first basic question is posed in the alternative context of oligopolistic competition with strategic commitment, which is captured by a two-stage model of competition.[3] At the first stage, firms make a strategic commitment which irrevocably affects their cost conditions in the second stage. Competition at the second stage is for output levels based on cost conditions emerging from the strategic commitment made at the first stage. Strategic competition may be considered socially excessive (socially insufficient) at the margin if a reduction (increase) in strategic commitment at the subgame-perfect equilibrium of the two-stage game raises economic welfare.[4] Focusing on the welfare effects of strategic commitment with cost-reducing R&D investment, we show that there is a wide range of normal situations in which strategic commitment made on the basis of private incentives is socially excessive at the margin, in both the first-best and the second-best senses, if a sufficient number of competitors exists in the oligopolistic industry. Furthermore, for a wide range of situations it is shown that the number of firms need not be unrealistically large for these results to hold. Thus, we may assert that there is a sense, which is rationalizable within the standard framework of welfare economics, in which the oligopolistic competition with strategic commitment may be socially excessive. In addition to establishing this central message, Part II also examines, first, the welfare impacts of excise tax subsidy in the presence of strategic commitment and, second, the welfare effects of forming a collaborative R&D in the presence of R&D spillovers *vis-à-vis* competitive R&D.

In Part III, 'Generalizations and Qualifications', we examine the robustness of the two basic results established in the previous two parts, the excess entry theorem and the excess investment theorem, from various angles. In the first place, two basic theorems are synthesized and a generalized excess entry theorem is established on the basis of a three-stage model of oligopolistic competition. It is shown that the excess entry theorem remains true even when a firm that decides to enter into the market in the first stage is required to make strategic commitment prior to the commencement of competition in the product market. In the second place, we examine how the two basic theorems are affected if firms are not profit-maximizers pure and simple, if firms form conjectures other than the simple Cournot type, if firms produce differentiated products and consumers have preferences for product diversity, and if firms compete in terms of prices rather than quantities. When it is found that there are exceptions to the two basic theorems, the reasons why these exceptions occur will be identified. Finally, the crucial assumption of identical firms and symmetric equilibria, which has been maintained up to this last stage, will be dispensed with. We show that the central message of the two basic theorems can still be maintained, *mutatis mutandis*.

To sum up, our answer to the first basic question cannot but be in the affirmative. On the one hand, there is a distinct possibility for the number of firms to be socially excessive in that social welfare is higher with free competition among a restricted number of firms than with free competition under unrestricted entry and exit of firms. On the other hand, there is a distinct possibility that competition among oligopolistic firms leads to socially excessive commitment with strategic cost-reducing R&D. In the light of these robust results, the traditional belief that increasing competition raises social welfare cannot but be suspect.

Granted that there exists a sense, which is firmly rooted in the standard conceptual framework of welfare economics, that competition can be socially excessive, the next step of this investigation is to determine if government intervention in the name of keeping excessive competition under due control can be justified. This second basic question will be examined in the Epilogue of this monograph.

For the sake of easy reference, the logical sequence of our exposition is summarized in Fig. 1. Those who are interested only in a portion of the project may choose their own short-cut on the basis of this diagram.

Two appendices at the end of the book are meant to explain the empirical relevance of our theoretical results by expounding Japanese policy contexts in which the problem of excessive competition and the control thereof has persistently surfaced. More specifically, Appendix A provides a succinct overview of the exemption systems from the Anti-Monopoly Law and other anti-competitive policy measures in Japan, while Appendix B presents an account of the Japanese system of collaborative R&D and gauges the empirical relevance of the theory of co-operative versus non-cooperative R&D which is developed in Chapter 6.

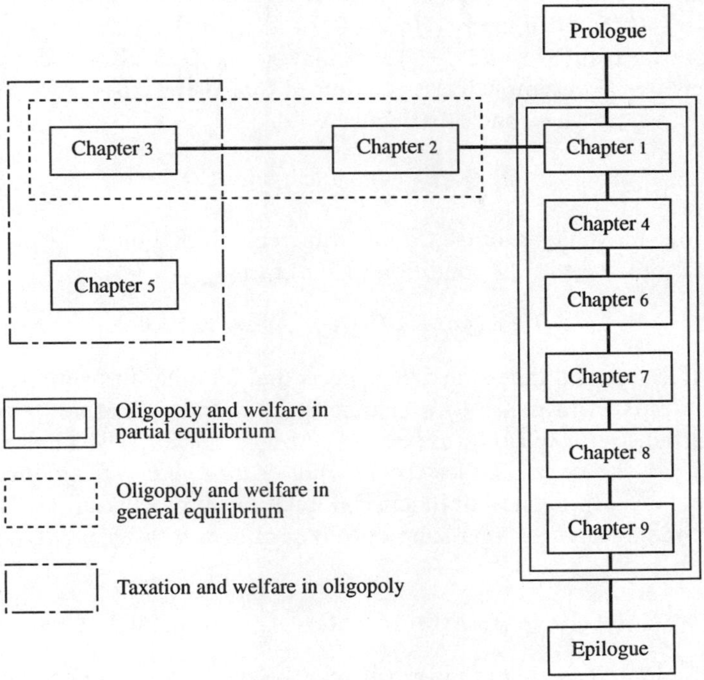

Fig. 1 Logical Sequence of Chapters

3. SYMMETRIC COURNOT–NASH OLIGOPOLY: PRELIMINARY ANALYSIS[5]

3.1 Symmetric Cournot–Nash equilibrium: concept and characterization

Since this monograph makes extensive use of the symmetric Cournot–Nash oligopoly model with a single homogeneous product, it would facilitate readers' understanding if some standard properties of, and useful analytical tools for, this model were succinctly summarized.

Let there be n firms, which are identical and engaging in oligopolistic competition, where $2 \leqslant n < +\infty$. The output produced by firm i is denoted by q_i, and $C(q_i)$ denotes the cost function thereof. The inverse demand function for the product of this industry is denoted by $p = f(Q)$, where p is unit price of the product and $Q = \Sigma_{j=1}^{n} q_j$ is industry output. The profit function of firm i is given by

$$\pi_i(q_i, Q_{-i}) := q_i f(q_i + Q_{-i}) - C(q_i), \tag{1}$$

where $Q_{-i} = \Sigma_{j \neq i} q_j$. Throughout this section, it is assumed that $f(Q)$ is twice continuously differentiable with $f'(Q) < 0$ for all $Q \geqslant 0$ such that $f(Q) > 0$.

It is also assumed that $C(q_i)$ is twice continuously differentiable with $C(q_i) > 0$, $C'(q_i) > 0$, and $C''(q_i) > 0$ for all $q_i \geqslant 0$.

It follows from (1) and $f'(Q) < 0$ that $\pi_i\,(q_i, Q_{-i})$ always decreases as Q_{-i} increases. For simplicity, it is assumed that there exists a constant Q^0_{-i}, where $0 < Q^0_{-i} < +\infty$, such that[6]

$$\max_{q_i > 0} \pi_i(q_i, Q_{-i}) > (<)\ 0 \text{ if and only if } Q_{-i} < (>)\ Q^0_{-i}. \tag{2}$$

The profit-maximizing output q_i of firm i corresponding to Q_{-i} is characterized by the first-order condition $(\partial/\partial q_i)\pi_i(q_i, Q_{-i}) = 0$; i.e.

$$f(q_i + Q_{-i}) + q_i f'(q_i + Q_{-i}) - C'(q_i) = 0, \tag{3}$$

where it is assumed that each firm expects that all other firms do not change their outputs in response to a change in its output (Cournot conjecture). The output vector $\mathbf{q}^N(n) = (q_1^N(n), \ldots, q_i^N(n), \ldots, q_n^N(n))$, which satisfies (3) for all $i = 1, 2, \ldots, n$, is called the *Cournot–Nash equilibrium* among n firms.

Note that (3) defines a functional relationship between Q_{-i} and the corresponding profit-maximizing output q_i of firm i, say $q_i = r_i(Q_{-i})$, which satisfies

$$f(r_i(Q_{-i}) + Q_{-i}) + r_i(Q_{-i})f'(r_i(Q_{-i}) + Q_{-i}) - C'(r_i(Q_{-i})) = 0, \tag{4}$$

by definition. It is clear that $\mathbf{q}^N(n)$ may be equivalently characterized by $q_i^N(n) = r_i(Q^N_{-i}(n))$ for all $i = 1, 2, \ldots, n$, where $Q^N_{-i}(n) = \Sigma_{j \neq i} q_j^N(n)$. In what follows, $r_i(\cdot)$ will be referred to as the *reaction function* of firm i.

Throughout this book, the following two terms will play an essential role:

$$\begin{aligned} \alpha_i(q_i, Q_{-i}) &:= (\partial^2/\partial q_i^2)\pi_i(q_i, Q_{-i}) \\ &= 2f'(q_i + Q_{-i}) + q_i f''(q_i + Q_{-i}) - C''(q_i) \end{aligned} \tag{5}$$

and

$$\begin{aligned} \beta_i(q_i, Q_{-i}) &:= (\partial^2/\partial q_i \partial q_j)\pi_i(q_i, Q_{-i}) \qquad (i \neq j) \\ &= f'(q_i + Q_{-i}) + q_i f''(q_i + Q_{-i}) \end{aligned} \tag{6}$$

for all $(q_i, Q_{-i}) > 0$. Note that the second-order condition for profit maximization requires that $\alpha_i(q_i, Q_{-i}) < 0$. On the other hand, when an inequality $\beta_i(q_i, Q_{-i}) < 0$ is satisfied, we say that the interaction among firms satisfies the assumption of *strategic substitutability*. The meaning of this assumption can be easily understood by computing the slope of reaction function $r_i(\cdot)$. It follows from (4) that

$$r_i'(Q_{-i}) = -\frac{\beta_i(r_i(Q_{-i}), Q_{-i})}{\alpha_i(r_i(Q_{-i}), Q_{-i})}, \tag{7}$$

where

$$\alpha_i(r_i(Q_{-i}), Q_{-i}) := 2f'(r_i(Q_{-i}) + Q_{-i}) + r_i(Q_{-i})f''(r_i(Q_{-i}) + Q_{-i}) - C''(r_i(Q_{-i}))$$

and $\beta_i(r_i(Q_{-i}), Q_{-i}) := f'(r_i(Q_{-i}) + Q_{-i}) + r_i(Q_{-i})f''(r_i(Q_{-i}) + Q_{-i})$. Note also that

$$\alpha_i(r_i(Q_{-i}), Q_{-i}) - \beta_i(r_i(Q_{-i}), Q_{-i}) = f'(r_i(Q_{-i}) + Q_{-i}) - C''(r_i(Q_{-i})) < 0 \quad (8)$$

holds by virtue of the assumption of strategic substitutability. We may now conclude from (5), (6), (7), and (8) that

$$-1 < r_i'(Q_{-i}) < 0, \quad (9)$$

which is the crucial implication of strategic substitutability.

Although the reaction function $r_i(\cdot)$ is useful in characterizing the Cournot–Nash equilibrium $\mathbf{q}^N(n)$ analytically, it is of limited value in describing the equilibrium diagramatically. However, this potential weakness can be easily rectified by introducing the *cumulative reaction function* $q_i = R_i(Q)$. This is an analytical device due originally to McManus (1962), and is defined by

$$q_i = R_i(Q) \text{ if and only if } q_i = r_i(Q - q_i), \quad (10)$$

where $r_i(\cdot)$ is the reaction function defined by (4).[7] By definition, $R_i(Q)$ gives the profit-maximizing output for firm i which is consistent with the *aggregate* output Q. It should be kept in mind that $0 \leqslant Q_{-i} = Q - q_i \leqslant Q^0_{-i}$, so that $R_i(Q)$ can be defined only for $q_i \leqslant Q \leqslant q_i + Q^0_{-i}$. As it follows from (10) that $R_i(Q) = r_i(Q - R_i(Q))$, we obtain

$$R_i'(Q) = \frac{r_i'(Q_{-i})}{1 + r_i'(Q_{-i})} < 0, \quad (11)$$

where the sign of $R_i'(Q)$ is due to (9). It also follows from (4) and (10) that the industry output at the Cournot–Nash equilibrium, $Q^N(n)$, is characterized by

$$Q^N(n) = \sum_{i=1}^{n} R_i(Q^N(n)); \quad (12)$$

that is to say, $Q^N(n)$ is nothing other than the fixed point of the aggregate cumulative reaction function $\Sigma_{i=1}^n R_i(\cdot)$.

In Fig. 2, the line AB represents the cumulative reaction function of firm i, whereas the line CD represents the aggregate cumulative reaction function. The aggregate output at the Cournot–Nash equilibrium, $Q^N(n)$, is determined at point E, where the line CD cuts the 45° line emanating from the origin. The Cournot–Nash equilibrium output of firm i, $q_i^N(n)$, can be determined as $q_i^N(n) = R_i(Q^N(n))$, i.e. at point F, where the line $EQ^N(n)$ cuts

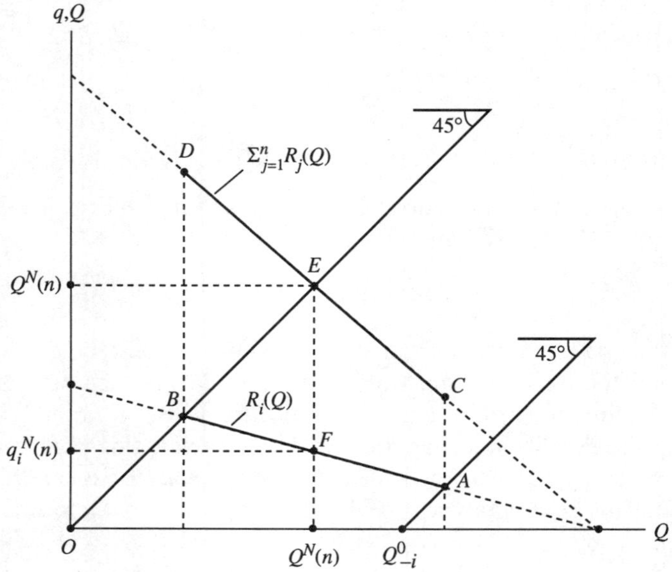

Fig. 2 Cournot–Nash equilibrium

the line *AB*. This is a useful way of representing the Cournot–Nash equilibrium, since we can allow for any number of firms and can still do with a two-dimensional diagram in representing the equilibrium.

Throughout this monograph, we assume that the symmetric Cournot–Nash equilibrium uniquely exists. A simple sufficient condition for this crucial assumption to be sustained may be derived as follows. Let $s_i(\mathbf{q})$ be defined by

$$s_i(\mathbf{q}) = r_i(Q_{-i}) \qquad (i = 1, 2, \ldots, n). \tag{13}$$

For any two output vectors $\mathbf{q}$ and $\mathbf{q}'$, there exists a θ such that

$$s_i(\mathbf{q}) - s_i(\mathbf{q}') = \sum_{j=1}^{n} (\partial/\partial q_j) s_i(\mathbf{q}^{\theta})(q_j - q_j') \tag{14}$$

holds, where $0 < \theta < 1$ and $\mathbf{q}^{\theta} = \theta\mathbf{q} + (1 - \theta)\mathbf{q}'$ by virtue of the mean value theorem. Note that (13) entails $(\partial/\partial q_j)s_i(\mathbf{q}) = r_i'(Q_{-i})$ if $i \neq j$, whereas $(\partial/\partial q_i)s_i(\mathbf{q}) = 0$. Thus, it follows from (14) that

$$|s_i(\mathbf{q}) - s_i(\mathbf{q}')| \leqslant |r_i'(Q_{-i}^{\theta})| \sum_{j \neq i} |q_j - q_j'|, \tag{15}$$

where $Q_{-i}^{\theta} = \Sigma_{j \neq i} q_j^{\theta}$. Let μ be defined by

$$\mu := \max_{1 \leqslant i \leqslant n} \max_{0 \leqslant Q_{-i} \leqslant Q^0_{-i}} |r'(Q_{-i})| > 0. \tag{16}$$

Then we may obtain

$$d(\mathbf{s}(\mathbf{q}) - \mathbf{s}(\mathbf{q}')) \leqslant \mu(n-1)d(\mathbf{q}, \mathbf{q}'), \tag{17}$$

where $\mathbf{s}(\mathbf{q}) = (s_1(\mathbf{q}), \ldots, s_i(\mathbf{q}), \ldots, s_n(\mathbf{q}))$, $d(\mathbf{q}, \mathbf{q}') = \Sigma^n_{i=1} | q_i - q'_i |$, and so forth. It is clear from (17) that $\mathbf{s}(\cdot)$ is a contraction mapping if a crucial inequality,

$$0 < \mu(n-1) < 1, \tag{18}$$

is satisfied, so that the mapping $\mathbf{s}(\cdot)$ has a unique fixed point under (18) (see e.g. Smart 1974: 2). By virtue of (4) and (13), we are now assured that there exists a unique Cournot–Nash equilibrium $\mathbf{q}^N(n)$ under the condition (18).[8]

Note that the crucial condition (18) may be boiled down to

$$|\alpha_i(q_i, Q_{-i})| > (n-1)|\beta_i(q_i, Q_{-i})| \qquad (i = 1, 2, \ldots, n) \tag{19}$$

in view of (7). By virtue of (5) and (6), (19) can be reduced to

$$\alpha_i(q_i, Q_{-i}) - (n-1)\beta_i(q_i, Q_{-i}) < 0 \qquad (i = 1, 2, \ldots, n). \tag{20}$$

For n = 2, (20) is clearly satisfied in view of (8). For larger values of n, (20) may be a severe restriction. However, condition (20) at $\mathbf{q} = \mathbf{q}^N(n)$ is often invoked as '[t]he simplest set of sufficient condition' (Dixit 1986: 117) for the stability of Cournot–Nash equilibrium.[9]

3.2. *Welfare criterion*

In evaluating the welfare performance of the Cournot–Nash equilibrium among n firms, a well defined welfare function which enables one to measure the attained level of economic welfare is required. In order not to smuggle unorthodox results in through the back door, the welfare function mainly invoked is the conventional *net market surplus function* $W(n, \mathbf{q})$, which is defined by

$$W(n, \mathbf{q}) := \left[\int_0^Q f(Z)\mathrm{d}Z - Qf(Q)\right] + \sum_{i=1}^n \left[q_i f(Q) - C(q_i)\right]$$

$$= \int_0^Q f(Z)\mathrm{d}Z - \sum_{i=1}^n C(q_i), \tag{21}$$

i.e. the sum of consumer's surplus and producer's surplus.

The use of this welfare function in measuring economic welfare, and in particular the use of consumer's surplus in measuring consumer's welfare, have been the focus of heated disputes among economists. Two extremes in the wide spectrum of opinions on this issue are represented by Paul Samuelson and Max Corden:[10]

> [A]ny judgement as to the usefulness or lack of usefulness of consumer's surplus has nothing to do with the problem of the admissibility of welfare economics as a significant part of economic theory since nobody has ever argued that the latter subject presupposes the validity of consumer's surplus. . . . It is for these reasons that my ideal Principles would not include consumer's surplus in the chapter on welfare economics except possibly in a footnote, although in my perfect Primer the concept has a limited place, provided its antidote and alternatives were included close at hand. (Samuelson 1947: 195–7)

> [Consumer's Surplus] was a simple intuitively appealing idea, discovered by Dupuit, rediscovered and developed by Marshall, revived by Hicks, and obviously useful. Upon careful examination it turned out to require many assumptions for its validity, and to have several possible meanings. The purists convinced themselves it was unnecessary for dealing with any relevant problem. It was a 'totally useless theoretical toy'. Officially, one might say, it died. And yet it would not stay in its grave. It has such a strong intuitive appeal, and there is nothing better available, so people keep on measuring it. Indeed, with the overwhelming belief, characteristic of modern computer-age economics, in measurement as the proper activity of economists, it has had a revival. One suspects that the perfectionist theorists gave up too quickly. They forget that theory should be the handmaiden of applied economics. Theorists should provide some useful concepts that their practical colleagues, or they themselves, can test and use. (Corden 1971: 242–3)

These sharp differences in opinion notwithstanding, there are many well circumscribed situations where the use of the net market surplus function can be rigorously justified. This is enough for the immediate purpose of this monograph; what is obtained on the basis of this simple welfare criterion may not be universally valid, but it is not altogether pathological either. For the purpose of establishing signposts to further theoretical research, this reassurance seems to be good enough.[11]

NOTES TO PROLOGUE

1. Note, however, that there is in fact a huge logical gap between the intuitive reasoning behind the desirability of competition and the stringent concept of perfect competition. It should be recognized that the concept of perfect competition, interpreted as a state where firms are too small *vis-à-vis* the size of market to affect market prices, differs crucially from the intuitive concept of competition that any profit opportunity, once found, leads to vigorous attempts to exploit it. Indeed, it may well be impossible for an actual firm to gather information on the existence of profit opportunities and exploit such opportunities unless the size of

the firm exceeds a certain minimum level. Those who are interested in the critical examination of the concept of perfect competition are referred to McNulty (1967, 1968). See also Baumol *et al.* (1982), Burke *et al.* (1988), Demsetz (1982), Dennis (1977), Hayek (1948, 1978), Itoh *et al.* (1991), Kirzner (1984, 1989), Nalebuff and Stiglitz (1983), Robinson (1954, 1969), Stigler (1957), and von Weizsäcker (1980*a*, *b*).

2. In Japan this second traditional belief has been quite widely held, and has actually provided a strong support for anti-competitive policies in the form of approving cartels and other government interventions in industrial organization. For factual details, see e.g. Itoh *et al.* (1991), Komiya *et al.* (1988), and Appendix A at the end of this monograph.
3. By 'strategic commitment' we here mean that the firm takes a decision on its choice variable at the first stage in full awareness that it cannot modify or nullify the choice later on. Therefore, the firm must carefully foresee the effect of such choice on the behaviour of other firms at the second stage.
4. Consider a game $\Gamma = [N, \{S_i\}_{i \in N}, \{\omega_i\}_{i \in N}]$, played in two-stages among n players ($2 \leqslant n < +\infty$), where $N = \{1, 2, \ldots, n\}$ is the set of players, $S_i = S_i(1) \times S_i(2)$ and $S_i(\tau)$ is the set of strategies of player $i \in N$ at stage $\tau = 1, 2$, and ω_i is the payoff function of player $i \in N$ which maps each and every strategy $2n$-tuple $(\mathbf{s}(1), \mathbf{s}(2)) \in \{\Pi_{i \in N} S_i(1)\} \times \{\Pi_{i \in N} S_i(2)\}$ into the set of real numbers. Once a strategy n-tuple $\mathbf{s}(1) \in \Pi_{i \in N} S_i(1)$ is specified, it can induce a *subgame* $\Gamma(\mathbf{s}(1)) = [N, \{S_i(2)\}_{i \in N}, \{\omega_i(\mathbf{s}(1), \cdot)\}_{i \in N}]$. Let $\mathbf{s}^N(\mathbf{s}(1)) \in \Pi_{i \in N} S_i(2)$ be the Nash equilibrium of the game $\Gamma(\mathbf{s}(1))$. In what follows, it is assumed for the sake of simplicity that $\mathbf{s}^N(\mathbf{s}(1))$ uniquely exists for each $\mathbf{s}(1)$. Under this crucial assumption, a game $\Gamma^N = [N, \{S_i(1)\}_{i \in N}, \{\Omega_i\}_{i \in N}]$ is now defined, where $\Omega_i(\mathbf{s}(1)) = \omega_i(\mathbf{s}(1), \mathbf{s}^N(\mathbf{s}(1)))$ ($i \in N$) for each $\mathbf{s}(1) \in \Pi_{i \in N} S_i(1)$. Let $\mathbf{s}^N(1) \in \Pi_{i \in N} S_i(1)$ be a Nash equilibrium of the game Γ^N. Then the equilibrium pair $\{\mathbf{s}^N(1), \mathbf{s}^N(\mathbf{s}^N(1))\}$ is nothing other than the *subgame-perfect equilibrium* of the two-stage game Γ. Note that (i) $\{\mathbf{s}^N(1), \mathbf{s}^N(\mathbf{s}^N(1))\} \in \{\Pi_{i \in N} S_i(1)\} \times \{\Pi_{i \in N} S_i(2)\}$ is a Nash equilibrium of the entire two-stage game Γ, and (ii) $\mathbf{s}^N(\mathbf{s}^N(1)) \in \Pi_{i \in N} S_i(2)$ is a Nash equilibrium of the subgame Γ^N. It should be clear how this definition can be extended to a many-stage game.
5. Those who are well acquainted with the standard concepts of, and standard analytical tools for, Cournot–Nash oligopoly theory may wish to skip this section altogether. They can always come back to the relevant part later if necessity dictates.
6. Q^0_{-i} may well depend on the number of firms n, which is fixed throughout this section.
7. To be precise, $R_i(\cdot)$ is what Novshek (1984) christened the *backward reaction mapping*, whereas McManus's cumulative reaction function corresponds to $Q = S_i(Q) := Q_{-i} + r_i(Q_{-i})$. On the history and use of these concepts, see McManus (1962, 1964), Novshek (1984, 1985), Okuno-Fujiwara and Suzumura (1993), and Roberts and Sonnenschein (1976, 1977).
8. More general treatment of the existence issue may be found in Frank and Quandt (1963), Nishimura and Friedman (1981), Novshek (1985), Roberts and Sonnenschein (1976), Suzumura (1971), and Szidarovszky and Yakovitz (1977, 1982). On the uniqueness of the Cournot–Nash equilibrium, see Kolstad and

Mathiesen (1987), Okuguchi and Suzumura (1971), and Szidarovszky and Yakowitz (1977, 1982).

9. On the stability of the Cournot–Nash equilibrium, see S. 2.3 of Ch. 1.
10. For rigorous and critical examination of these concepts, interested readers are referred to Bergson (1979), Bruce (1977), Chipman and Moore (1976, 1980), Dixit and Weller (1979), Harberger (1971), Henderson (1940–1), Hicks (1943, 1945–6, 1956), Just *et al.* (1982), Kokoski and Smith (1987), McKenzie (1983), Seade (1978), Silberberg (1972), Weitzman (1988), Whalley (1975), and Willig (1976).
11. Alternatively, let a representative consumer's utility function $u(x, y)$, where $x(y)$ denotes his consumption of the good x (the numeraire good y), be of the quasi-linear type, viz. $u(x, y) = v(x) + y$. Maximizing this utility function subject to the budget constraint $px + y = M$, where p is the relative price of x and M is his income, we obtain $v'(x) = p$ as the first-order condition for utility maximization. Assume now that M consists of his fixed outside income M_0 and the aggregate profits earned in the industry x, viz. $Qf(Q) - \Sigma_{i=1}^{n} C_i(q_i)$. Then the objective function may be represented by $v(Q) + M_0 - \Sigma_{i=1}^{n} C_i(q_i)$ with $v'(Q) = f(Q)$, which is in effect the same as (21) in the main text. Thus, using the net market surplus function is tantamount to assuming a representative consumer having a quasi-linear utility function and receiving the aggregate profits earned in the industry x.

I

Firm Entry and Economic Welfare

> The basis of comparison, on the grounds of which the achievement of competition ought to be judged, cannot be a situation which is different from the objective facts and which cannot be brought about by any known means. It ought to be the situation as it would exist if competition were prevented from operating. Not the approach to an unachievable and meaningless ideal but the improvement upon the conditions that would exist without competition should be the test.
>
> Friedrich von Hayek, *Individualism and Economic Order*, 1948

Despite the repeated emphasis in the vast literature on the importance of competition in allocating resources efficiently and in making effective use of dispersed information, the mechanism through which competition plays such a vital role has not yet been fully articulated. It is sometimes surmised that the fundamental theorem of welfare economics captures the role of competition as an efficient allocator of resources and also as an effective mechanism of utilizing dispersed information. However, the basic concept of perfect competition, the property of which is precisely characterized by the fundamental theorem, has so little in common with competition in the actual markets that the perfectly competitive equilibrium hardly serves as a useful standard of reference in evaluating the welfare performance of competition in actual (imperfectly competitive) economies.

The purpose of Part I is to analyse an aspect of the classical problem of welfare and competition in an imperfectly competitive economy. Chapter 1 establishes several versions of excess entry theorem to the effect that, left unregulated, there exists a strenuous tendency towards socially excessive firm entry into an oligopolistic market. Since this analysis is based on the framework of partial equilibrium analysis, which has been criticized for its neglect of income and price feedback effects, Chapter 2 shows that one of the excess entry theorems can essentially survive even in the presence of general equilibrium interactions. One of the basic assumptions, upon which this generalization hinges, is that there exists no *capital intensity twist* (in the sense made precise in Chapter 2). As this is a somewhat unfamiliar condition, it is worth while asking how the welfare performance of an oligopolistic economy can be improved if this basic assumption is violated. It is shown in Chapter 3 that there are several tax subsidy schemes that unambiguously improve economic welfare precisely when capital intensity twist occurs.

1 Entry Barriers and Economic Welfare: Partial Equilibrium Approach

1. INTRODUCTION

One of the most deeply rooted and widely held beliefs among economists is the welfare-enhancing effect of increasing competition. Indeed, as Baumol has aptly observed,

> [T]he standard analysis [of industrial organization] leaves us with the impression that there is a rough continuum, in terms of desirability of industry performance, ranging from unregulated pure monopoly as the pessimal [sic] arrangement to perfect competition as the ideal, with relative efficiency in resource allocation increasing monotonically as the number of firms expands (Baumol 1982: 2).

However, recent studies in theoretical industrial organization have uncovered several instances that cast serious doubts on the reasonableness of 'a widespread belief that increasing competition will increase welfare' (Stiglitz 1981: 184). It has been exemplified, e.g. by Schmalensee (1976) and von Weizsäcker (1980*a*; 1980*b*: ch. 4), that there are cases, which are not far-fetched, where social welfare will be increased by strengthening, rather than weakening, the protection of incumbent firms from the threat of potential entry, and this is clearly incompatible with the traditional belief.[1] What is not known, however, is how robust these 'pathologies' in fact are. The purpose of this chapter is to settle this crucial question by proving three excess entry theorems in the symmetric Cournot oligopoly model.

The first approach presupposes the existence of a strong ('first-best') government which can costlessly enforce the marginal cost pricing by firms in an oligopolistic market and regulate entry in pursuit of first-best social welfare optimization. It will be shown that *the number of firms at the free-entry equilibrium exceeds the 'first-best' welfare-optimizing number of firms*. Although this result has already been noted by Schmalensee (1976) and von Weizsäcker (1980*a*; 1980*b*: ch. 4) in terms of numerical examples, the first-best excess entry theorem asserts that it is valid for the whole family of symmetric Cournot oligopoly models at hand. An implication of this result is that the existence of entry barriers, which protect incumbent firms from threats by potential competitors, is not necessarily welfare-decreasing, and this is clearly in sharp contrast with the traditional belief.

An important problem still remains with the first-best excess entry theorem, however, in that an omnipotent 'first-best' government does not exist in reality, and the first-best ideal is unrealizable in the actual government-assisted market economies.[2] Therefore, even if intervention by a first-best government may be welfare-improving, it does not follow that intervention by a 'second-best' government, which lacks the leverage of optimal price regulation, is justified. What is needed is an evaluation of the social gains from alternative *feasible* government actions. This is precisely the task of the second approach, where an explicitly 'second-best' social welfare optimization in an oligopolistic economy is analysed. It will be shown that *the 'second-best' number of firms falls short of the number of firms at the free-entry equilibrium*. Furthermore, *a marginal decrease in the number of firms starting from the free-entry equilibrium level unambiguously improves welfare in terms of the second-best criterion*. It follows that the free-entry equilibrium number of firms is socially excessive at the margin even from the 'second-best' viewpoint, where by 'second-best' it is meant that the oligopolistic (marginal-cost-equals-marginal-revenue) pricing is taken for granted by an entry regulating government that pursues social welfare optimization.

The plan of this chapter is as follows. In Section 2 the symmetric Cournot oligopoly model is formally introduced and the basic assumptions of the analysis explained. Section 3 is devoted to the first-best excess entry theorem, whereas Section 4 establishes two versions of the second-best excess entry theorem. Section 5 makes some clarifying observations on the excess entry theorems, and Section 6 concludes with several remarks on the implications of the analysis.

2. A MODEL OF COURNOT–NASH COMPETITION

2.1. Basic assumptions

This chapter will be concerned with a model of an oligopolistic industry producing a single homogeneous good. All firms are assumed to be identical, both in technology and in behaviour. The number of firms in the industry will be denoted by n, where $2 \leqslant n < +\infty$. The output of the ith firm is q_i ($i = 1, 2, \ldots, n$), and $Q = \Sigma_{j=1}^{n} q_j$ represents the industry aggregate output. The inverse demand function and the cost function of each firm are denoted by $p = f(Q)$ and $C(q_i)$ ($i = 1, 2, \ldots, n$), respectively, where p is unit output price. Firms being assumed to be identical, cost function need not have any firm index.

It will be assumed that:

A1: $f(Q)$ is twice continuously differentiable with $f'(Q) < 0$ for all $Q \geqslant 0$ such that $f(Q) > 0$.

A2: $C(q_i)$ is twice continuously differentiable with $C(q_i) > 0$, $C'(q_i) > 0$ and $C''(q_i) > 0$ for all $q_i \geqslant 0$.

The profit function of firm i is defined by

$$\pi_i(q_i, Q_{-i}) := q_i f(q_i + Q_{-i}) - C(q_i), \tag{1}$$

where Q_{-i} represents the aggregate output of all firms other than i taken together, viz. $Q_{-i} = \Sigma_{j \neq i}\, q_j = Q - q_i$.

Each firm i tries to maximize $\pi_i(q_i, Q_{-i})$ by choosing q_i appropriately, but this choice is necessarily constrained by the behaviour of its rival firms. In the first place, firm i must form its own conjecture as to the extent by which rival firms will adjust their outputs in response to a change in i's choice variable, viz. output q_i. The extent of this interdependence, which is subjective in nature, can be measured in terms of the *coefficient of conjectural variation* $\mu_i := \partial Q/\partial q_i = 1 + \partial Q_{-i}/\partial q_i$. In the second place, firm i's marginal profitability will be affected by the behaviour of its rival firms, the extent of which can be measured by

$$\beta_{ij}(q_i, Q_{-i}) := \frac{\partial^2}{\partial q_i\, \partial q_j}\, \pi_i(q_i, Q_{-i}) \qquad (i \neq j). \tag{2}$$

Unless otherwise specified, it will be assumed throughout this monograph that:

A3: The Cournot conjecture prevails; viz., $\mu_i = 1$ holds for all $i = 1, 2, \ldots, n$.

A4: The strategic substitutability prevails; viz., $\beta_{ij}(q_i, Q_{-i}) < 0$ holds for all i and j such that $i \neq j$ and $i, j = 1, 2, \ldots, n$.[3]

Under A1, A2, A3, and A4, the profit-maximizing output q_i of firm i, corresponding to the output of all other firms taken together, Q_{-i}, will be characterized by

$$f(q_i + Q_{-i}) + q_i f'(q_i + Q_{-i}) - C'(q_i) = 0, \tag{3}$$

viz. by the equality of marginal revenue $f(q_i + Q_{-i}) + q_i f'(q_i + Q_{-i})$ to marginal cost $C'(q_i)$.

2.2. *Some properties of the Cournot–Nash equilibrium*

For each number of firms n, let $\mathbf{q}^N(n) = (q_1^N(n), \ldots, q_i^N(n), \ldots, q_n^N(n))$ be the *Cournot–Nash equilibrium* among n firms, which is defined by

$$f(Q^N(n)) + q_i^N(n) f'(Q^N(n)) - C'(q_i^N(n)) = 0 \qquad (i = 1, 2, \ldots, n), \tag{4}$$

where $Q^N(n) = \Sigma_{j=1}^n q_j^N(n)$. It will be assumed that a symmetric and positive Cournot–Nash equilibrium uniquely exists for each n.[4] To simplify our notation, let $q^N(n)$ denote the individual firm's output at the symmetric Cournot–Nash equilibrium, so that $q_i^N(n) = q^N(n)$ for all $i = 1, 2, \ldots, n$. The crucial equation (4) can then be rewritten as follows:

$$f(nq^N(n)) + q^N(n)f'(nq^N(n)) = C'(q^N(n)). \tag{5}$$

As an auxiliary step in analysing the nature of the Cournot–Nash equilibrium $\mathbf{q}^N(n)$, it is useful to examine the properties of

$$\alpha_i(q_i, Q_{-i}) := \frac{\partial^2}{\partial q_i^2} \pi_i(q_i, Q_{-i}) \tag{6}$$

and $\beta_{ij}(q_i, Q_{-i})$, which is defined by (2), evaluated at $(q_i, Q_{-i}) = (q_i^N(n), Q_{-i}^N(n))$. Note that (1), (2), and (6) yield

$$\alpha_i(q_i, Q_{-i}) = f'(q_i + Q_{-i}) + q_i f''(q_i + Q_{-i}) - C''(q_i) \tag{7}$$

and

$$\beta_{ij}(q_i, Q_{-i}) = f'(q_i + Q_{-i}) + q_i f''(q_i + Q_{-i}). \tag{8}$$

Evaluating (7) and (8) at $(q_i, Q_{-i}) = (q_i^N(n), Q_{-i}^N(n))$, and taking the symmetry of $\mathbf{q}^N(n)$ into consideration, it is verified that

$$\alpha^N(n) = 2f'(nq^N(n)) + q^N(n)f''(nq^N(n)) - C''(q^N(n)) \tag{9}$$

and

$$\beta^N(n) = f'(nq^N(n)) + q^N(n)f''(nq^N(n)), \tag{10}$$

where $\alpha^N(n) := \alpha_i(q_i^N(n), Q_{-i}^N(n))$ and $\beta^N(n) := \beta_{ij}(q_i^N(n), Q_{-i}^N(n))$ for short. By virtue of assumption A4 at $(q_i, Q_{-i}) = (q_i^N(n), Q_{-i}^N(n))$, it follows from (10) that $\beta^N(n) < 0$, whereas A1, A2, and $\beta^N(n) < 0$ imply that $\alpha^N(n) < 0$, where use is made of (9).

How will the individual firm's equilibrium output $q^N(n)$, the industry equilibrium output $Q^N(n) := nq^N(n)$, and the equilibrium price $p^N(n) := f(Q^N(n))$ behave in response to an exogenous change in n? The answer to this question may be summarized as follows.

LEMMA 1. Under A1, A2, A3, and A4,

$$\frac{\mathrm{d}}{\mathrm{d}n} q^N(n) = -\frac{\beta^N(n)}{\alpha^N(n) + (n-1)\beta^N(n)} q^N(n) < 0, \tag{11}$$

$$\frac{\mathrm{d}}{\mathrm{d}n} Q^N(n) = \frac{\alpha^N(n) - \beta^N(n)}{\alpha^N(n) + (n-1)\beta^N(n)} q^N(n) > 0, \tag{12}$$

and

$$\frac{\mathrm{d}}{\mathrm{d}n} p^N(n) = f'(Q^N(n)) \frac{\alpha^N(n) - \beta^N(n)}{\alpha^N(n) + (n-1)\beta^N(n)} q^N(n) < 0 \tag{13}$$

hold for any n.

Proof. Differentiating (5) with respect to n, we may obtain

$$\begin{aligned}(\mathrm{d}/\mathrm{d}n)q^N(n)\,[(n+1)f'(nq^N(n)) + nq^N(n)f''(nq^N(n)) - C''(q^N(n))]\\ = -q^N(n)[f'(nq^N(n)) + q^N(n)f''(nq^N(n))].\end{aligned} \tag{14}$$

Invoking (9) and (10), (14) can be reduced into (11). The negative sign of $(\mathrm{d}/\mathrm{d}n)q^N(n)$ is due to $\alpha^N(n) < 0$ and $\beta^N(n) < 0$.

To obtain (12), we have only to differentiate $Q^N(n) = nq^N(n)$ with respect to n and apply (11). The positive sign of $(\mathrm{d}/\mathrm{d}n)Q^N(n)$ is due to $\alpha^N(n) < 0$ and $\beta^N(n) < 0$.

Finally, to obtain (13), We have only to differentiate $p^N(n) = f(Q^N(n))$ with respect to n and apply (12). The negative sign of $(\mathrm{d}/\mathrm{d}n)p^N(n)$ is once again due to $\alpha^N(n) < 0$ and $\beta^N(n) < 0$. □

According to Lemma 1, the individual output at the Cournot–Nash equilibrium becomes smaller and the aggregate Cournot–Nash output becomes larger as the number of competing firms becomes larger. As a result of the latter assertion, the Cournot–Nash equilibrium price becomes lower as the number of firms becomes larger.

It may help if the assertion of Lemma 1 is illustrated in terms of the cumulative reaction function introduced in Section 3 of the Prologue. For the sake of expositional simplicity, it will be assumed in what follows that Q^0_{-i} is large enough, and neglect the restriction thereby imposed. In Fig. 3, where the horizontal (vertical) axis measures market output (individual firm output as well as market output), the line AB denotes the cumulative reaction function of firm j, i.e. $R_j(Q)$, whereas the line AC denotes the aggregate cumulative reaction function, i.e. $\Sigma^n_{j=1} R_j(Q)$. As was explained in the Prologue, $Q^N(n)$ is determined at point E where the line AC cuts the 45° line emanating from the origin, whereas $q_j^N(n)$ is given by $q_j^N(n) = R_j(Q^N(n))$, i.e. at point F where the line $EQ^N(n)$ cuts the line AB. Suppose that the number of firms undergoes a change from n to $n + \Delta n$, where $\Delta n > 0$. Then the cumulative reaction function shifts up from line AC to line AD, which corresponds to $\Sigma^{n+\Delta n}_{j=1} R_j(Q)$. The equilibrium output of firm j changes accordingly from $q_j^N(n)$ to $q_j^N(n + \Delta n)$, and the equilibrium market output changes from $Q^N(n)$ to $Q^N(n + \Delta n)$. Since the line AB is downward-sloping, which is due to the crucial assumption of strategic substitutability, it is clear that $q_j^N(n) > q_j^N(n + \Delta n)$ and $Q^N(n) < Q^N(n + \Delta n)$. This is precisely what Lemma 1 asserts.

2.3. *On the stability of Cournot adjustment dynamics*[5]

A large literature exists on the stability of the Cournot–Nash equilibrium $\mathbf{q}^N(n)$ for each n, when each firm increases (decreases) its output as positive (negative) marginal profitability prevails.[6] This adjustment mechanism can be formulated by the following differential equation:

$$\dot{q}_i = \sigma(\partial/\partial q_i)\pi_i(q_i, Q_{-i}) \qquad (i = 1, 2, \ldots, n), \tag{15}$$

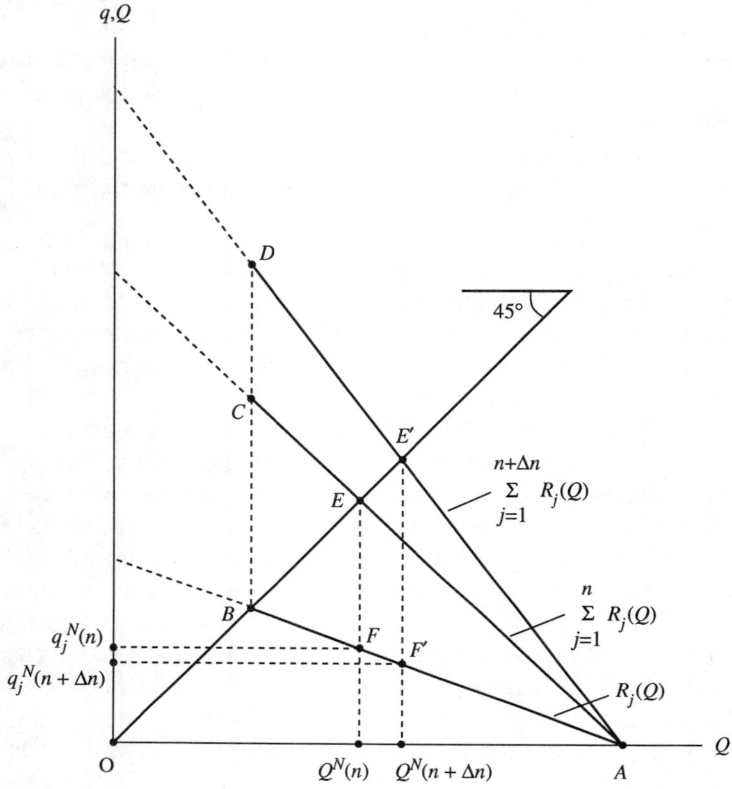

Fig. 3 Effects of change in n on $q^N(n)$

where $\dot{q}_i$ denotes the time derivative of q_i, and $\sigma > 0$ stands for the adjustment coefficient.

With the purpose of analysing the local stability of the Cournot–Nash equilibrium $\mathbf{q}^N(n)$ with respect to the adjustment process (15), let (15) be linearly approximated around $\mathbf{q}^N(n)$ by

$$\dot{\mathbf{q}} = \sigma\boldsymbol{\Omega}(\mathbf{q} - \mathbf{q}^N(n)), \tag{16}$$

where $\dot{\mathbf{q}}$ is an n-dimensional column vector whose ith element is $\dot{q}_i$, and $\boldsymbol{\Omega}$ is an $n \times n$ matrix whose (i, j) element ω_{ij} is given by $\omega_{ii} = \alpha$ and $\omega_{ij} = \beta$ if $i \neq j$, where $\alpha := \alpha^N(n)$ and $\beta := \beta^N(n)$ for short. The dynamic system (16) is locally stable with respect to $\mathbf{q}^N(n)$ if the matrix $\boldsymbol{\Omega}$ is negative definite. It can be verified that this crucial property is in fact guaranteed by assumptions A1 and A4.

To see this, note that $\mathbf{\Omega}$ is negative definite if

$$(-1)^k \det \mathbf{\Omega}_k > 0 \qquad (k = 1, 2, \ldots, n) \tag{17}$$

holds, where $\mathbf{\Omega}_k$ is the $k \times k$ principal submatrix of $\mathbf{\Omega}$. It is easy to verify that (17) is guaranteed by

$$(-1)^k(\alpha - \beta)^{k-1}[\alpha + (k-1)\beta] > 0 \qquad (k = 0, 1, \ldots, n), \tag{18}$$

which holds if, and only if,

$$\alpha + (k-1)\beta < 0 \qquad (k = 0, 1, \ldots, n) \tag{19}$$

is satisfied. It follows from (9) and (10) that $\alpha - \beta = f'(nq^N(n))$, which is negative by assumption A1. Therefore, (19) for $k = 0$ must hold. On the other hand, $\alpha - \beta < 0$ and A4 guarantee that $\alpha < 0$, which is (19) for $k = 1$. Now that $\alpha < 0$ and $\beta < 0$ are assured, (19) for $k = 2, 3, \ldots, n$ must necessarily hold. This completes our proof that the Cournot–Nash equilibrium $\mathbf{q}^N(n)$ is locally stable under A1 and A4 with respect to the dynamic process (15). □

2.4. *Entry dynamics and long-run equilibrium*

Turning to the long-run properties of the Cournot oligopoly model, let $\pi^N(n)$ be the profits of each incumbent firm at the Cournot–Nash equilibrium $\mathbf{q}^N(n)$:

$$\pi^N(n) := q^N(n)f(nq^N(n)) - C(q^N(n)). \tag{20}$$

If $\pi^N(n) > (<)\ 0$ holds, potential competitors (incumbent firms) will be induced to enter into (exit from) this profitable (unprofitable) industry. This classical entry–exit mechanism may be formulated by the following differential equation:

$$\dot{n} = \eta \pi^N(n), \tag{21}$$

where $\dot{n}$ denotes the time derivative of n, and $\eta > 0$ denotes the adjustment coefficient. Let n_e be the *equilibrium number of firms*, which is defined as the stationary point of (21). By definition, it follows that

$$\pi^N(n_e) = 0. \tag{22}$$

It may be verified that the equilibrium number of firms is unique as well as dynamically stable under the imposed assumptions. To verify the uniqueness of n_e, note that

$$\frac{\mathrm{d}}{\mathrm{d}n}\pi^N(n) = (q^N(n))^2 f'(nq^N(n)) \frac{\alpha^N(n)}{\alpha^N(n) + (n-1)\beta^N(n)} < 0 \tag{23}$$

holds by virtue of (11) and assumptions A1 and A4. To verify the dynamic stability of n_e, let $n(t; n_0)$ be the solution path of the differential equation

(21) starting from the initial value $n_0 > 0$. Let the distance between the solution path $n(t; n_0)$ and n_e be defined by $V_t := \frac{1}{2}[n(t; n_0) - n_e]^2$. It then follows that

$$\dot{V}_t = \eta(n(t; n_0) - n_e)\pi^N(n(t; n_0)), \tag{24}$$

which is negative as long as $n(t; n_0) \neq n_e$. Therefore, it may be concluded that $\lim_{t \to \infty} n(t; n_0) = n_e$.

3. FIRST-BEST EXCESS ENTRY THEOREM

3.1. *First-best welfare criterion*

Left unfettered, the equilibrium number of firms n_e will be established through the long-run competitive forces, and the Cournot–Nash equilibrium $\mathbf{q}^N(n_e)$ will result from the oligopolistic competition among n_e firms. Since the equilibrium pair $\{n_e, \mathbf{q}^N(n_e)\}$ is precisely the spontaneous outcome of competition, the traditional belief in the welfare-enhancing effect of competition should have it that the welfare performance of $\{n_e, \mathbf{q}^N(n_e)\}$ is 'optimal' in some well articulated sense. Can this a priori expectation be substantiated?

The first step in examining this question is to specify the criterion that may be used to gauge the welfare performance of this economy. For this purpose, let the *net market surplus function* be defined by

$$W(n, \mathbf{q}) := \int_0^Q f(Z)\mathrm{d}Z - \sum_{j=1}^{n} C(q_j), \tag{25}$$

which is the sum of consumer's surplus and producer's surplus.[7]

As an auxiliary step in defining our first-best welfare criterion, let $\mathbf{q}^F(n)$ be the socially first-best output profile, which is defined by

$$\mathbf{q}^F(n) := \arg\max_{\mathbf{q} > 0} W(n, \mathbf{q}). \tag{26}$$

Assuming interior optimum, $\mathbf{q}^F(n) = (q_1^F(n), \ldots, q_i^F(n), \ldots, q_n^F(n))$ can be characterized by

$$(\partial/\partial q_i)W(n, \mathbf{q}^F(n)) = f(Q^F(n)) - C'(q_i^F(n)) = 0 \qquad (i = 1, 2, \ldots, n), \tag{27}$$

where $Q^F(n) = \Sigma_{j=1}^n q_j^F(n)$.[8] It follows from (27) that each firm produces the same output, say $q^F(n)$, at the socially first-best situation. The *first-best welfare criterion* may be now defined by

$$W^F(n) := W(n, \mathbf{q}^F(n)). \tag{28}$$

By definition, $W^F(n)$ gauges the welfare performance of the number of firms n on the supposition that all firms follow the socially first-best marginal cost principle.

3.2. Some properties of the socially first-best output

Corresponding to Lemma 1 on $\mathbf{q}^N(n)$, it may be asserted that the following propositions hold on $\mathbf{q}^F(n)$.

LEMMA 2. Under A1 and A2,

$$\frac{\mathrm{d}}{\mathrm{d}n} q^F(n) = -\frac{f'(nq^F(n))}{nf'(nq^F(n)) - C''(q^F(n))} q^F(n) < 0, \tag{29}$$

$$\frac{\mathrm{d}}{\mathrm{d}n} Q^F(n) = -\frac{C''(q^F(n))}{nf'(nq^F(n)) - C''(q^F(n))} q^F(n) > 0, \tag{30}$$

and

$$\frac{\mathrm{d}}{\mathrm{d}n} p^F(n) = -\frac{f'(nq^F(n))C''(q^F(n))}{nf'(nq^F(n)) - C''(q^F(n))} q^F(n) < 0 \tag{31}$$

hold for any n, where $p^F(n) := f(q^F(n))$.

Proof. Differentiating (27) with respect to n, we may verify that (29) holds, where the sign is determined by assumptions A1 and A2.

To obtain (30) and (31), we have only to differentiate $Q^F(n) = nq^F(n)$ and $p^F(n) = f(Q^F(n))$ with respect to n and invoke (29) and (30). The sign is again due to A1 and A2. □

How does the socially first-best output $q^F(n)$ fare *vis-à-vis* the Cournot–Nash equilibrium output $q^N(n)$? This important question is answered by the following lemma.

LEMMA 3. Under A1 and A2, $q^F(n) > q^N(n)$ holds for any n.

Proof. Suppose, to the contrary, that $q^F(n) \leqslant q^N(n)$ holds for some n. By virtue of A1, it then follows that

$$\begin{aligned} f(nq^F(n)) &\geqslant f(nq^N(n)) \\ &> f(nq^N(n)) + q^N(n)f'(nq^N(n)). \end{aligned} \tag{32}$$

Thanks to (5) and (27), inequality (32) entails

$$C'(q^F(n)) > C'(q^N(n)). \tag{33}$$

It then follows from A2 and (33) that $q^F(n) > q^N(n)$ holds, which is in direct contradiction with the inequality with which this proof started. Therefore, $q^F(n) > q^N(n)$ must hold for any n. □

3.3. *First-best excess entry theorem: general proof*

The first main theorem of this chapter may now be proved. To begin with, the *first-best number of firms*, n_f, may be defined by

$$n_f := \arg\max_{n>0} W^F(n). \tag{34}$$

By definition, the pair $\{n_f, \mathbf{q}^F(n_f)\}$ represents the optimum optimorum of the Cournot–Nash economy. Assuming interior optimum, the first-best number of firms n_f can be characterized by

$$\begin{aligned}\frac{\mathrm{d}}{\mathrm{d}n} W^F(n_f) &= q^F(n_f)\left[f(Q^F(n_f)) - \frac{C(q^F(n_f))}{q^F(n_f)}\right] \\ &\quad + n_f \frac{\mathrm{d}}{\mathrm{d}n} q^F(n_f)\,\{f(Q^F(n_f)) - C'[q^F(n_f)]\} \\ &= 0.\end{aligned} \tag{35}$$

Invoking (27), condition (35) can be reduced to

$$f(Q^F(n_f)) = \frac{C(q^F(n_f))}{q^F(n_f)}. \tag{36}$$

In words, n_f must be such that $q^F(n_f)$ satisfies the *average cost principle*.[9]

Comparing n_e with n_f, the following theorem can be established.

THEOREM 1 (FIRST-BEST EXCESS ENTRY THEOREM). Suppose that A1, A2, A3, and A4 are satisfied and that the equilibrium number of firms n_e exceeds 1. Then n_e exceeds the socially first-best number of firms n_f as far as $n_f > 1$.

Proof. Suppose that there are n_f firms in this industry, where $n_f > 1$. Since $q^N(n_f)$ is the Cournot–Nash equilibrium output, we have

$$\begin{aligned}\pi^N(n_f) &= q^N(n_f) f(n_f q^N(n_f)) - C(q^N(n_f)) \\ &\geqslant q^F(n_f) f[q^F(n_f) + (n_f - 1) q^N(n_f)] - C(q^N(n_f)) \\ &> q^F(n_f) f(Q^F(n_f)) - C(q^F(n_f)) \\ &= 0,\end{aligned} \tag{37}$$

where the first (weak) inequality is due to the definition of $\mathbf{q}^N(n)$, the second (strict) inequality is due to Lemma 3, A1 and A2, and the last equality is due to (36). By virtue of (23), it follows from $\pi^N(n_f) > \pi^N(n_e)$, which is entailed by (22) and (37), that $n_f < n_e$. This is precisely what we set out to show. □

3.4 First-best excess entry theorem: diagrammatic illustration

Our natural instinct behind Theorem 1 can be suggested by Fig. 4, where the horizontal (vertical) axis measures output (price and cost). Given the market demand curve MM, let $R^N R^N$ be the residual demand curve of a representative incumbent firm which happens to be tangential to the average cost curve at point E^N. Since the marginal cost curve crosses the marginal revenue curve at the output level $q^N(n_e)$, point E^N represents the Cournot–Nash equilibrium where each incumbent firm earns zero profit. Therefore, the number of firms $n_e := Q^N(n_e)/q^N(n_e)$ is nothing other than the equilibrium number of firms defined analytically by (22).

Notice that there exist unexploited economies of scale at point E^N. This being the case, there are several ways in which we can improve the welfare performance of this industry. Of particular interest is decreasing the number of firms from n_e just enough to let the resulting residual demand curve for a representative incumbent firm $R^F R^F$ pass point E^F, where the average cost curve attains its minimum. It is clear that (27) as well as (36) is satisfied at

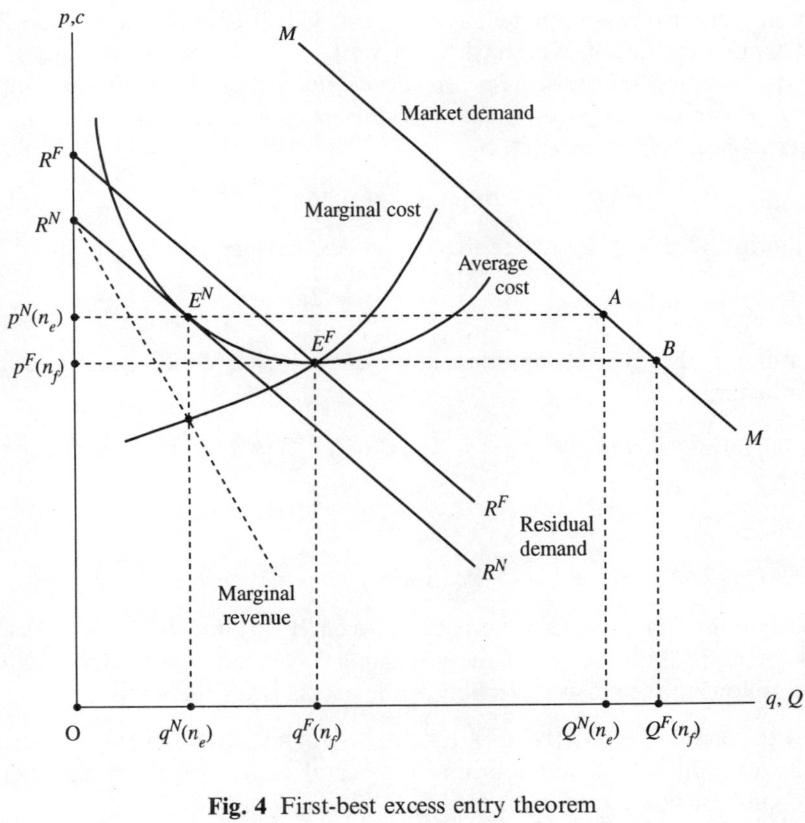

Fig. 4 First-best excess entry theorem

point E^F, where each of $n_f := Q^F(n_f)/q^F(n_f)$ firms produces $q^F(n_f)$. Notice that $n_f > 1$ holds in the described situation, and it is clear that the net market surplus at point E^F exceeds that at point E^N just by the amount measured by the area $Ap^N(n_e)p^F(n_f)B$. As $n_f < n_e$ holds by construction, we have just illustrated the first-best excess entry theorem in this particular setting.

4. SECOND-BEST EXCESS ENTRY THEOREM

4.1. *Second-best welfare criterion*

However desirable the first-best ideal may seem to be, an actual down-to-earth government may be unable to enforce the marginal cost pricing on the incumbent firms as is required by the first-best regulation. This being the case, the bite of the first-best excess entry theorem may be rather small, despite its theoretical appeal.

Let us suppose that the oligopolistic pricing has to be taken for granted by an actual non-omnipotent government which cannot enforce the first-best price regulation. Our task is to verify that the main message of the first-best excess entry theorem can survive under this change in the controlling power of the government. For this purpose, we now introduce the *second-best welfare criterion* by

$$W^S(n) := W(n, \mathbf{q}^N(n)). \tag{38}$$

In terms of $W^S(n)$, we define the *second-best number of firms*, n_s, by

$$n_s := \arg\max_{n>0} W^S(n). \tag{39}$$

Assuming the interior optimum and second-order conditions, n_s can be characterized by

$$\begin{aligned}(\mathrm{d}/\mathrm{d}n)\,W^S(n_s) &= \pi^N(n_s) + n_s\left[f(n_s q^N(n_s)) - C'(q^N(n_s))\right](\mathrm{d}/\mathrm{d}n)q^N(n_s)\\ &= 0.\end{aligned} \tag{40}$$

4.2. *Second-best excess entry theorem: general proof*

Despite the fundamental difference between $W^F(n)$ and $W^S(n)$ with respect to the controlling power of the government, we can nevertheless establish the following second-best version of the excess entry theorem.

THEOREM 2 (SECOND-BEST EXCESS ENTRY THEOREM). Under A1, A2, A3, and A4, the equilibrium number of firms n_e exceeds the socially second-best number of firms n_s.

Proof. Invoking (4), (40) can be reduced into

$$\pi^N(n_s) - n_s q^N(n_s) f'(Q^N(n_s))(\mathrm{d}/\mathrm{d}n) q^N(n_s) = 0. \tag{41}$$

In view of (11), assumption A1, and (22), it follows from (41) that

$$\pi^N(n_s) > 0 = \pi^N(n_e). \tag{42}$$

Since $\pi^N(n)$ is decreasing in n by virtue of (23), it follows from (42) that $n_s < n_e$. This is precisely what we set out to show. □

4.3. *Second-best excess entry theorem: diagramatic illustration*

As in the case of the first-best excess entry theorem, the intuitive meaning of the second-best excess entry theorem can be succinctly illustrated. In Figs. 5 and 6, point E^N represents the Cournot–Nash equilibrium among n_e firms.

Since n_s is the maximizer of $W^S(n)$, we must have $W^S(n_s) \geqslant W^S(n_e)$. Take an arbitrary n which exceeds n_e. In Fig. 5, point E^L denotes the symmetric

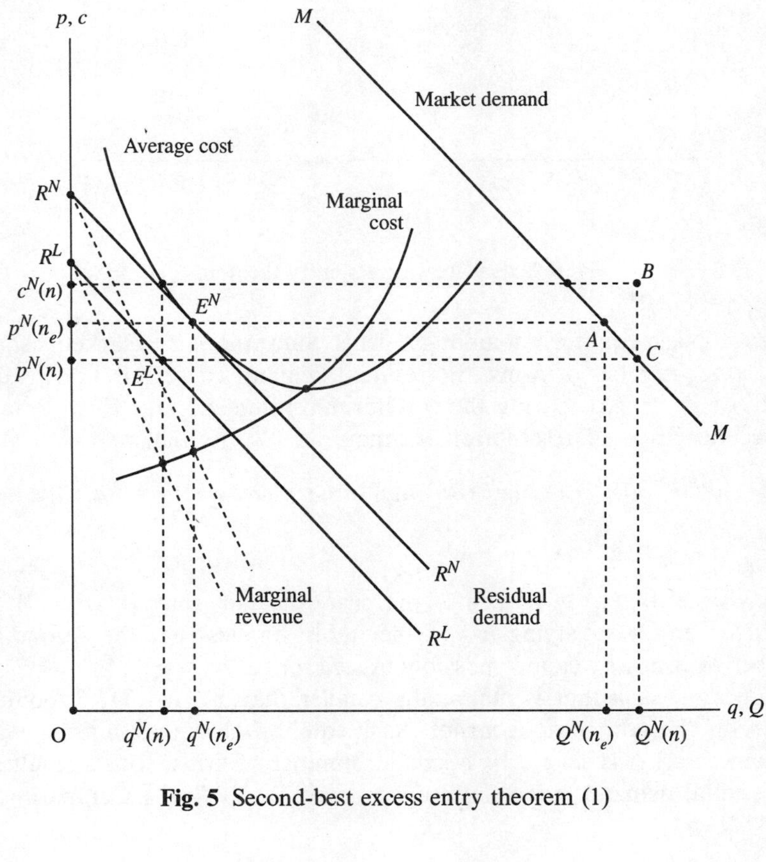

Fig. 5 Second-best excess entry theorem (1)

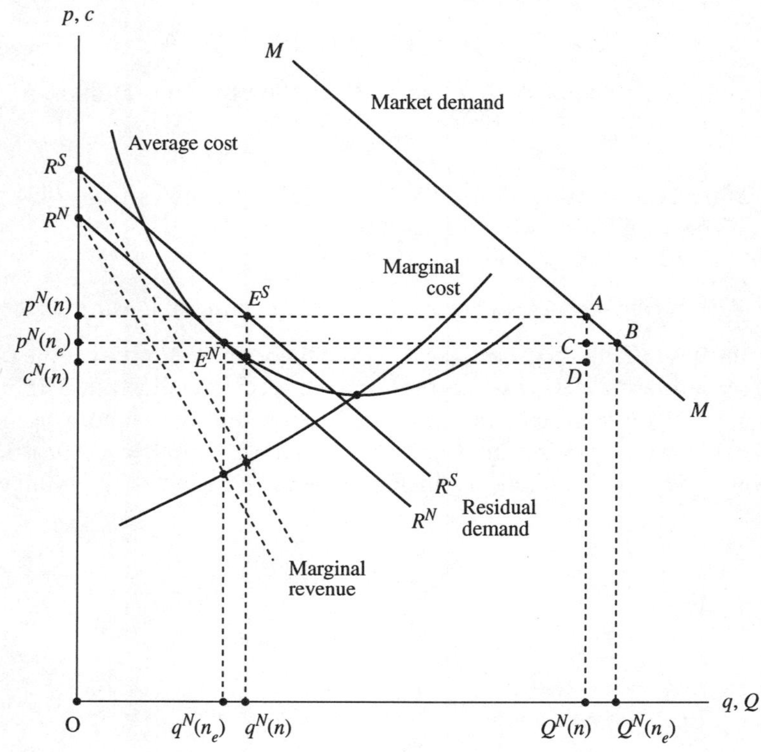

Fig. 6 Second-best excess entry theorem (2)

Cournot–Nash equilibrium among n firms. Since the same market is shared by a larger number of firms, the residual demand curve shifts down from $R^N R^N$ to $R^L R^L$. Comparing the equilibrium points E^N and E^L in terms of the second-best welfare criterion, we may easily verify that

$$W^S(n) = W^S(n_e) - \{[\text{area}\, Bc^N(n)p^N(n)C] - [\text{area}\, Ap^N(n_e)p^N(n)C]\}$$
$$< W^S(n_e)$$

holds. Since $W^S(n_s) \geqslant W^S(n_e)$ is the case, the fact that $W^S(n) < W^S(n_e)$ holds for any n satisfying $n > n_e$ inevitably implies that the second-best number of firms, n_s, cannot possibly exceed n_e; i.e. $n_s \leqslant n_e$.

Take now an n that is marginally smaller than n_e. In Fig. 6, point E^S represents the symmetric Cournot–Nash equilibrium among n firms, where the same market is shared by a smaller number of firms, with a result that the residual demand curve shifts up from $R^N R^N$ to $R^S R^S$. Comparing the equilibrium points E^N and E^S in terms of the second-best welfare criterion, we may immediately verify that

$$\begin{aligned} W^S(n) &= W^S(n_e) + \{[\text{area}\, Ap^N(n)c^N(n)D] - [\text{area}\, Ap^N(n)p^N(n_e)B]\} \\ &= W^S(n_e) + \{[\text{area}\, Cp^N(n_e)c^N(n)D] - [\text{area}\, ACB]\} \\ &> W^S(n_e),^{10} \end{aligned}$$

which suffices to ensure that $n_s < n_e$.

4.4. *Excess entry theorem at the margin*

According to Theorem 1 (Theorem 2), we can improve the welfare performance of our industry by *decreasing* the number of firms from its level at the long-run equilibrium, n_e, to the first-best level n_f (the second-best level n_s). In order to realize this potential welfare improvement, however, the government must be able to compute the value of n_f and/or n_s, which is, in fact, a task far beyond the reach of an actual non-omnipotent government. Indeed, in order to solve the maximization problem (34) and/or (39), it is necessary for the government to have access to detailed information concerning demand and cost characteristics of the industry, which is in fact privately owned either by consumers or by producers.

Note, however, that we can easily circumvent this apparent difficulty by establishing that $W^F(n)$ as well as $W^S(n)$ is decreasing at $n = n_e$ without losing the central message of the excess entry theorems. In the case of $W^F(n)$, we have

$$\frac{\mathrm{d}}{\mathrm{d}n} W^F(n_e) = q^F(n_e)\left[f(Q^F(m_e)) - \frac{C(q^F(n_e))}{q^F(n_e)}\right] + n_e\left[f(Q^F(n_e)) - C'(q^F(n_e))\right]\frac{\mathrm{d}}{\mathrm{d}n}\, q^F(n_e), \tag{43}$$

the second term of the right-hand side (RHS) thereof being 0 by virtue of (27). Besides, the first term of the RHS of (43) is demonstrably negative. To ascertain this fact, we have only to notice that

$$\begin{aligned} f(Q^F(n_e)) - \frac{C(q^F(n_e))}{q^F(n_e)} &= C'(q^F(n_e)) - \frac{C(q^F(n_e))}{q^F(n_e)} \\ &< C'(q^F(n_f)) - \frac{C(q^F(n_f))}{q^F(n_f)} = 0, \end{aligned} \tag{44}$$

where the first equality is due to (27), the strict inequality is due to assumption A2, (29), and Theorem 1, and the last equality follows from (27) and (36).

In the case of $W^S(n_e)$, we have

$$\begin{aligned}(\mathrm{d}/\mathrm{d}n)\, W^S(n_e) &= \pi^N(n_e) + n_e\Big[f(n_e q^N(n_e)) - C'(q^N(n_e))\Big](\mathrm{d}/\mathrm{d}n) q^N(n_e) \\ &= -\, n_e q^N(n_e) f'(Q^N(n_e))(\mathrm{d}/\mathrm{d}n) q^N(n_e) \\ &< 0, \end{aligned} \tag{45}$$

where the second equality is due to (22) and (4), and the last strict inequality is due to assumption A1 and (11).

We have thus verified that the following theorem holds true.

THEOREM 3 (EXCESS ENTRY THEOREM AT THE MARGIN). Suppose that A1, A2, A3, and A4 hold. Then:

(*a*) The equilibrium number of firms n_e is socially excessive at the margin in the first-best sense; that is, a marginal decrease in the number of firms at n_e increases the first-best social welfare.

(*b*) The equilibrium number of firms n_e is socially excessive at the margin in the second-best sense; i.e., a marginal decrease in the number of firms at n_e increases the second-best social welfare.

The thrust of this result lies in that, even if we cannot be sure where n_f and n_s are located exactly (e.g. because of uncertainty on the precise nature of the functions involved), we do know for sure that 'exit' is welfare-improving at the margin. In this sense, Theorem 3 seems to enhance the empirical relevance of the excess entry results rather substantially.

5. CLARIFYING OBSERVATIONS

5.1. Integer problem

Throughout this chapter, we have followed the traditional convention of treating the number of firms as if it were a continuous variable. As a matter of fact, however, it does not make sense to talk about 3.25 firms or $\sqrt{2}$ firms, and the continuous variables n_e, n_f, and n_s are in fact nothing other than continuous proxies to the discrete variables N_e, N_f, and N_s, which are defined by

$$N_e = [n_e], \tag{46}$$

$$N_f = \begin{cases} [n_f] & \text{if } W^F([n_f]) \geqslant W^F([n_f]+1) \\ [n_f]+1 & \text{otherwise,} \end{cases} \tag{47}$$

and

$$N_s = \begin{cases} [n_s] & \text{if } W^S([n_s]) \geqslant W^S([n_s]+1) \\ [n_s]+1 & \text{otherwise,} \end{cases} \tag{48}$$

where $[n]$ for any real number n denotes the greatest integer that does not exceed n, i.e. the *Gauss number* of n. Therefore, a qualification should be placed on the first-best and second-best excess entry theorems to the effect that, although the inequality $n_e > \max\{n_f, n_s\}$ holds quite generally under assumptions A1, A2, A3, and A4, the integer nature of N_e, N_f, and N_s may be such that N_e can still fall short of N_f and/or N_s. It should be noted, however, that the shortfall, if any, of N_e *vis-à-vis* N_f and N_s is at most 1.

This possible discrepancy between the continuous version and the discrete version of the excess entry theorems is generated by the contrast between (46) on the one hand, and (47) and/or (48) on the other. Let us now explain how these definitions are justified.

In Fig. 7, the horizontal axis measures n, whereas the vertical axis measures $\pi^N(n)$ and $W^F(n)$. The continuous proxy of the equilibrium number of firms is given by n_e, where the curve $\pi^N(n)$ cuts the n-axis. $N_1 := [n_e]$ and $N_2 := [n_e] + 1$ are two neighbouring integers of n_e. Since the curve $\pi^N(n)$ is downward-sloping, we have

$$\pi^N(N_1) > \pi^N(n_e) = 0 > \pi^N(N_2),$$

so that N_1 firms are motivated to operate in this industry whereas N_2 firms are not. This justifies the definition (46).

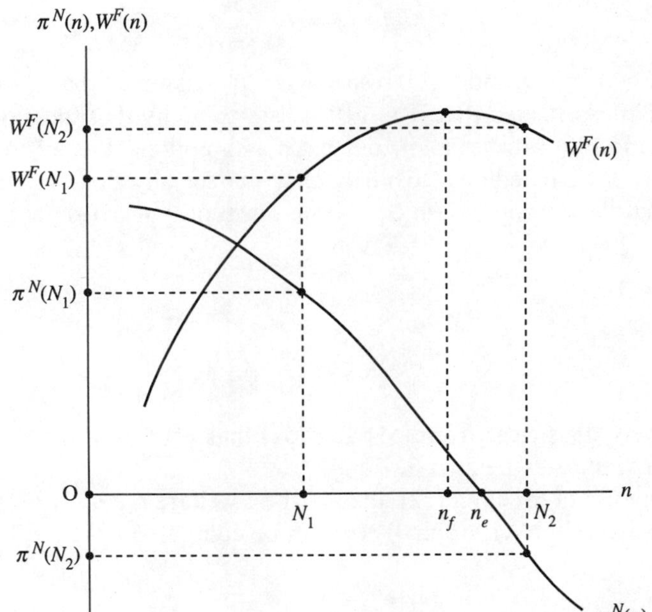

Fig. 7 Equilibrium number of firms and first-best number of firms

Turning to the first-best number of firms, the situation in Fig. 7 is such that $N_1 := [n_f]$ and $N_2 := [n_f] + 1$ are two neighbouring integers of n_f which maximizes $W^F(n)$. Notice that, in the case of social welfare maximization, what matters is the level of social welfare. Since we have $W^F(N_2) > W^F(N_1)$ in Fig. 7, N_2 is identified as the integer version of the first-best number of firms. Besides motivating the definition (47), Fig. 7 also shows the situation where $n_f < n_e$ (in full accordance with Theorem 1), yet we have $N_f = N_e + 1$.

5.2. Numerical illustration

It might help if the first-best and second-best excess entry theorems are illustrated by numerical examples. In so doing, we can also illustrate the relevance of the integer problem we have just identified and the quantitative importance of the welfare losses generated by the 'excessive' firm entry into the symmetric Cournot oligopoly market.

With these purposes in mind, let us specify inverse demand function and cost function by

$$p = A - Q, \tag{49}$$

where $A > 0$, and

$$C(q) = K + aq + \frac{b}{2}q^2, \tag{50}$$

where $K > 0$, $a > 0$, and $b > 0$ respectively. It is assumed that the parameters A and a are so related that $A > a$. It is easy to verify that the model defined by (49) and (50) satisfies all of our basic assumptions A1, A2, A3, and A4. It is also easy, if tedious, to verify that the socially first-best firm output $q^F(n)$ and the Cournot–Nash equilibrium firm output $q^N(n)$ are given by

$$q^F(n) = \frac{A - a}{n + b} \tag{51}$$

and

$$q^N(n) = \frac{A - a}{n + b + 1}, \tag{52}$$

respectively. It is clear from (51) and (52) that $q^F(n) > q^N(n)$ holds for any n, which vindicates Lemma 3.

Making use of (51) and (52), the first-best welfare criterion $W^F(n)$ and the second-best welfare criterion $W^S(n)$ can be computed as

$$W^F(n) = \frac{n}{2(n + b)}(A - a)^2 - nK \tag{53}$$

and

$$W^S(n) = \frac{n(n+b+2)}{2(n+b+1)^2}(A-a)^2 - nK, \tag{54}$$

respectively. Therefore, the first-best number of firms n_f, being the maximizer of (53), may be characterized implicitly by

$$\frac{(n_f+b)^2}{b} = \frac{(A-a)^2}{2K}, \tag{55}$$

whereas the second-best number of firms n_s, being the maximizer of (54), may be implicitly characterized by

$$\frac{(n_s+b+1)^3}{bn_s+(b+1)(b+2)} = \frac{(A-a)^2}{2K}. \tag{56}$$

Finally, the equilibrium number of firms n_e may be implicitly characterized by

$$\frac{(n_e+b+1)^2}{b+2} = \frac{(A-a)^2}{2K}, \tag{57}$$

which follows from the zero profit condition:

$$\pi^N(n) = \left(\frac{A-a}{n+b+1}\right)^2\left(\frac{b}{2}+1\right) - K = 0. \tag{58}$$

Two remarks are due on this parametrized model. First, it follows from (51) and (52) that

$$q^F(n) - q^N(n) = \frac{A-a}{(n+b)(n+b+1)}, \tag{59}$$

which entails $\lim_{n\to\infty}(q^F(n) - q^N(n)) = 0$. This apparently vindicates the famous *Cournot limit theorem*, which asserts the convergence of the Cournot equilibrium output $q^N(n)$ to the first-best (perfectly competitive) output $q^F(n)$ as n tends to infinity. Note, however, that (58) implies $\pi^N(n) > (<)\ 0$ if and only if $n < (>)\ n_e$. Therefore, *in the presence of fixed cost $K > 0$ which generates economies of scale, there exist no private incentives for firm entry beyond n_e*. In other words, the Cournot limit theorem has empirical relevance only when there is no fixed cost in production.

Second, the first-best (second-best) excess entry theorem can be proved in this model by comparing (55) ((56)) with (57). Indeed, by equating the left-hand side (LHS) of (55) with that of (57), we obtain

$$(b+2)(n_f+b)^2 = b(n_e+b+1)^2. \tag{60}$$

If it so happens that $n_e \leqslant n_f$, (60) entails

$$2n_e^2 + 2bn_e - b \leqslant 0, \tag{61}$$

which cannot be true as long as $n_e \geqslant 1$. Therefore, we must have $n_e > n_f$ as long as $n_e \geqslant 1$. Likewise, by equating the LHS of (56) with that of (57), we obtain

$$(b + 2)(n_s + b + 1)^3 = [bn_s + (b + 1)(b + 2)](n_e + b + 1)^2. \tag{62}$$

If it happens to be the case that $n_e \leqslant n_s$, (62) entails

$$2n_s \leqslant 0, \tag{63}$$

which contradicts the positivity of n_s. Therefore, $n_e > n_s$ must hold, as we set out to show.

Let us now define N_e, N_f, and N_s by (46) and (57), (47) and (55), and (48) and (56) respectively. Tables 1 and 2 tabulate (N_e, N_f) and (N_e, N_s) respectively, for alternative values of $[b, (A - a)^2/2K]$, where $(A - a)^2/2K$ can be construed as an index of the size of the Cournot market. Note that the basic message of the excess entry theorems, even after due attention is paid to the qualification necessitated by the integer problem, clearly holds in these tables.

Table 1. (N_e, N_f) for alternative values of $\left[b, \dfrac{(A-a)^2}{2K}\right]$

$\left[b, \dfrac{(A-a)^2}{2K}\right]$	5	10	15	20	25	30	35	40
0.25	(2,1)	(3,1)	(4,2)	(5,2)	(6,2)	(6,3)	(7,3)	(8,3)
0.50	(2,1)	(3,2)	(4,2)	(5,3)	(6,3)	(7,3)	(7,4)	(8,4)
0.75	(1,1)	(3,2)	(4,3)	(5,3)	(6,4)	(7,4)	(8,4)	(8,5)
1.00	(1,1)	(3,2)	(4,3)	(5,3)	(6,4)	(7,4)	(8,5)	(8,5)
1.25	(1,1)	(3,2)	(4,3)	(5,4)	(6,4)	(7,5)	(8,5)	(9,6)
1.50	(1,1)	(3,2)	(4,3)	(5,4)	(6,5)	(7,5)	(8,6)	(9,6)
1.75	(1,1)	(3,2)	(4,3)	(5,4)	(6,5)	(7,6)	(8,6)	(9,7)
2.00	(1,1)	(3,2)	(4,3)	(5,4)	(7,5)	(7,6)	(8,6)	(9,7)

Another use we can make of the parametrized model of oligopoly at hand is to gauge the quantitative importance of the welfare losses involved. For this purpose, let us introduce the *first-best welfare loss measure* by

$$L^F(N_e) := 1 - \frac{W^F(N_e)}{W^F(N_f)} \tag{64}$$

and the *second-best welfare loss measure* by

$$L^S(N_e) := 1 - \frac{W^S(N_e)}{W^S(N_s)}. \tag{65}$$

Notice that $L^F(N_e)$ ($L^S(N_e)$) measures the percentage welfare loss in terms of the first-best (second-best) welfare criterion which is incurred by allowing socially excessive firm entry up to N_e.

Table 2. (N_e, N_s) for alternative values of $\left[b, \dfrac{(A-a)^2}{2K}\right]$

$\left[b, \dfrac{(A-a)^2}{2K}\right]$	5	10	15	20	25	30	35	40
0.25	(2,1)	(3,2)	(4,3)	(5,3)	(6,3)	(6,4)	(7,4)	(8,4)
0.50	(2,1)	(3,2)	(4,3)	(5,3)	(6,4)	(7,4)	(7,4)	(8,5)
0.75	(1,1)	(3,2)	(4,3)	(5,4)	(6,4)	(7,5)	(8,5)	(8,5)
1.00	(1,1)	(3,2)	(4,3)	(5,4)	(6,4)	(7,5)	(8,5)	(8,6)
1.25	(1,1)	(3,2)	(4,3)	(5,4)	(6,5)	(7,5)	(8,6)	(9,6)
1.50	(1,1)	(3,3)	(4,3)	(5,4)	(6,5)	(7,6)	(8,6)	(9,7)
1.75	(1,1)	(3,3)	(4,4)	(5,4)	(6,5)	(7,6)	(8,6)	(9,7)
2.00	(1,1)	(3,3)	(4,4)	(5,5)	(7,5)	(7,6)	(8,7)	(9,7)

Tables 3 and 4 tabulate how the welfare loss measures L^F and L^S behave for alternative values of $[b, (A-a)^2/2K]$. As it should naturally be, L^F is consistently larger than L^S, but even the larger value L^F seems to remain fairly small in percentage terms.

Table 3. L^F for alternative values of $\left[b, \dfrac{(A-a)^2}{2K}\right]$

$\left[b, \dfrac{(A-a)^2}{2K}\right]$	5	10	15	20	25	30	35	40
0.25	0.185	0.110	0.107	0.110	0.110	0.077	0.086	0.092
0.50	0.143	0.071	0.067	0.068	0.073	0.075	0.053	0.060
0.75	0.000	0.052	0.041	0.047	0.049	0.055	0.058	0.041
1.00	0.000	0.036	0.030	0.028	0.036	0.038	0.044	0.027
1.25	0.000	0.023	0.021	0.021	0.024	0.029	0.032	0.036
1.50	0.000	0.013	0.013	0.015	0.016	0.021	0.024	0.027
1.75	0.000	0.005	0.006	0.010	0.012	0.013	0.018	0.020
2.00	0.000	0.000	0.000	0.005	0.032	0.010	0.012	0.016

5.3. Possible generalizations

There are several directions to generalize the excess entry theorems within the partial equilibrium framework. Take, for example, the second-best excess entry theorem at the margin. Let $q(n)$ stand for the firm output at the symmetric oligopoly equilibrium *without specifying the nature of underlying oligopolistic interactions.* Write the second-best welfare criterion as

Table 4. L^S for alternative values of $\left[b, \frac{(A-a)^2}{2K}\right]$

$\left[b, \frac{(A-a)^2}{2K}\right]$	5	10	15	20	25	30	35	40
0.25	0.084	0.054	0.047	0.061	0.067	0.041	0.052	0.060
0.50	0.070	0.037	0.036	0.041	0.047	0.054	0.033	0.042
0.75	0.000	0.023	0.026	0.026	0.034	0.038	0.045	0.029
1.00	0.000	0.012	0.017	0.020	0.023	0.029	0.033	0.020
1.25	0.000	0.003	0.009	0.014	0.016	0.021	0.025	0.029
1.50	0.000	0.000	0.003	0.009	0.012	0.013	0.019	0.021
1.75	0.000	0.000	0.000	0.004	0.008	0.010	0.013	0.017
2.00	0.000	0.000	0.000	0.000	0.026	0.008	0.009	0.013

$$W(n) := \int_0^{Q(n)} f(Z)\mathrm{d}Z - nC(q(n)), \tag{66}$$

where $Q(n) := nq(n)$. Differentiating (66) with respect to n, we obtain

$$(\mathrm{d}/\mathrm{d}n)\,W(n) = [q(n)f(nq(n)) - C(q(n))] + n[f(nq(n)) - C'(q(n))](\mathrm{d}/\mathrm{d}n)q(n). \tag{67}$$

If we evaluate (67) at the free-entry equilibrium number of firms n_e, the first term in the RHS thereof becomes zero by definition, so that we have

$$(\mathrm{d}/\mathrm{d}n)\,W(n_e) = n_e[f(n_e q(n_e)) - C'(q(n_e))](\mathrm{d}/\mathrm{d}n)q(n_e). \tag{68}$$

Since the price $p(n_e) := f(n_e q(n_e))$ exceeds the marginal cost $C'(q(n_e))$ at any oligopolistic equilibrium among profit-maximizing firms, it follows from (68) that

$$\mathrm{sgn}\,(\mathrm{d}/\mathrm{d}n)\,W(n_e) = \mathrm{sgn}\,(\mathrm{d}/\mathrm{d}n)q(n_e). \tag{69}$$

Therefore, *the second-best excess entry theorem at the margin holds if the equilibrium firm output decreases as the number of firms increases.* Viewed from this standpoint, the Cournot–Nash oligopoly model, in the context of which we have established Theorem 3, is nothing other than a concrete example of oligopolistic interactions where the essential property to the effect that $(\mathrm{d}/\mathrm{d}n)q(n) < 0$ naturally holds.

The examination of further generalizations within the partial equilibrium framework will be relegated to Part III. Instead, the next chapter will explore whether the excess entry theorem essentially remains valid even when we pay due attention to the existence of general equilibrium interactions.

6. CONCLUDING REMARKS

In this chapter, three excess entry theorems in the homogeneous output Cournot oligopoly model are established. Presupposing the existence of an omnipotent ('first-best') government, the first theorem asserts that there occurs an 'excessive' entry of firms at the free-entry Cournot–Nash equilibrium *vis-à-vis* the 'first-best' number of firms n_f. The second theorem asserts that the main message of the first theorem is essentially carried over to the down-to-earth ('second-best') government that lacks the leverage of optimal price regulation. In other words, the equilibrium number of firms n_e persistently overshoots the second-best number of firms n_s. The third theorem asserts that a marginal decrease in the number of firms at the free-entry equilibrium unambiguously improves welfare in terms of the first-best as well as the second-best welfare criterion, and it suggests that 'exit' of firms from the free-entry equilibrium is always welfare-improving at the margin even when we do not know where exactly n_f and/or n_s are located *vis-à-vis* n_e.

In concluding this chapter, several remarks are in order.

First, it may be worth while to pinpoint the factors that are crucially responsible for the validity of the excess entry theorems. In the presence of scale economies, entry of too many firms leaves scale economies unexploited, so that it is better, on the basis of *production efficiency* considerations, to have fewer and larger firms than to have more and smaller firms. If there are too few firms, however, *allocative efficiency* of the oligopolistic industry will deteriorate owing to the increased market power of incumbent oligopolistic firms. It is this trade-off between production efficiency on the one hand and allocative efficiency on the other that underlies the excess entry theorems. The assertion of the second-best excess entry theorem is precisely that the improvement of production efficiency, when there are fewer firms, overcompensates the concomitant worsening of allocative efficiency. In contrast, the assertion of the first-best excess entry theorem is due to the fact that the potential worsening of allocative efficiency, when there are fewer firms, is suppressed by the imposition of the socially optimal marginal cost principle.

Secondly, the excess entry theorems are proved on the basis of a standard Cournot oligopoly model satisfying the stability conditions of Hahn (1962), Seade (1980*a*, *b*), and others. This is worth remarking, since several counter-intuitive results on entry into a Cournot market hold true only when the Cournot–Nash equilibrium is unstable. Although the excess entry results go counter to the traditional belief in the welfare-improving effect of increasing competition, this 'pathology' cannot be attributed to unstable equilibria.

Thirdly, Harris (1981) is a rare precursor in the second-best welfare analysis of an oligopolistic economy. However, Harris analysed the welfare effect of direct government control of production decisions by private firms, subject only to the constraint that all firms are assured of making non-negative profits. In contrast, our second-best notion presupposes that the government is deprived of any direct control over the behaviour of oligopolistic firms, leaving them to follow their own private incentives. Care should be taken with this contrast in comparing our results with those of Harris (1981).

Finally, a warning on the policy implications of our analysis may be in order. According to the second-best excess entry theorem at the margin, it is welfare-improving if we marginally decrease the number of firms from its free-entry equilibrium level. However, this result, by itself, does not recommend a rectifying policy to the effect of restricting entry and facilitating exit. Such a policy, if pursued by a down-to-earth government, may bring out distortions of its own. Besides, there are many qualifications on the excess entry theorems which may restrict the direct applicability of our theoretical results. A full discussion on these qualifying considerations will be deferred until the Epilogue.

NOTES TO CHAPTER 1

1. See also Dixit and Stiglitz (1977), Spence (1984), Tandon (1984), and Vickers and Yarrow (1988: ch. 3).
2. This point was strongly made by Schmalensee (1983) in his review of von Weizsäcker (1980*b*).
3. Readers are referred back to Section 3 of the Prologue for the meaning of this crucial strategic assumption.
4. The Cournot–Nash equilibrium $\mathbf{q}^N(n)$ is said to be *symmetric* (*positive*) if $q_i^N(n) = q_j^N(n)$ holds for all $i, j = 1, 2, \ldots, n$ (if $q_i^N(n) > 0$ holds for all $i = 1, 2, \ldots, n$).
5. Our subsequent analysis in no way hinges on the stability result in this subsection. Those who are not interested in minor technicalities may skip this subsection altogether without losing anything of substance.
6. Interested readers are referred to Al-Nowaihi and Levine (1985), Dixit (1986), Furth (1986), Hahn (1962), Okuguchi (1973), and Seade (1980*a*), among many others.
7. Readers are referred back to S. 3 of the Prologue for the rationale of this classical welfare criterion.
8. The second-order condition for net market surplus maximization is given by

$$(\partial^2/\partial q_i^2)\, W(n, \mathbf{q}^F(n)) = f'(Q^F(n)) - C''(q_i^F(n)) < 0 \qquad (i = 1, 2, \ldots, n),$$

which is satisfied in our model by virtue of assumptions A1 and A2.
9. Note that the second-order condition

$$(d^2/dn^2)\,W^F(n_f) = q^F(n_f)\,f'(Q^F(n_f))(\partial/\partial n)\,Q^F(n_f) < 0$$

is guaranteed by virtue of A1 and (30).

10. Note that the area ACB is of higher-order infinitesimal in comparison with the area $Cp^N(n_e)c^N(n)D$.

2 Entry Barriers and Economic Welfare: General Equilibrium Approach

1. INTRODUCTION

In the preceding chapter, we established several versions of excess entry theorem by examining an oligopolistically competitive industry in complete isolation. In so doing, we excluded all potentially important channels through which this industry actively interacts with the rest of the economy. Besides, the welfare criterion of the net market surplus, upon which our analysis in the previous chapter was based, can be a legitimate measure of social welfare only when income effect is of negligible importance.[1]

It is widely recognized that the advantage of using partial equilibrium analysis lies in its simplicity, which may be desirable because it enables us to focus sharply on each new conceptual complication in isolation. In some cases, however, the price and income feedback effects are so essential that the general equilibrium interactions may well qualify, or even nullify, such partial equilibrium conclusions as ours. Indeed, in his paper which examined 'the reliability of partial equilibrium analysis as an approximate solution technique for assessing the impact of changes in the organizational structure of the economy', Whalley (1975) suggested that '[t]he partial equilibrium techniques perform somewhat erratically as approximate methods. . . . [A]lthough there is a considerable gain in computational simplicity in the use of partial equilibrium analysis, the reliability of results using more satisfactory general equilibrium techniques is considerably increased.'

In this chapter, we develop a simple general equilibrium model consisting of two sectors, one being oligopolistic and the other being competitive, with the purpose of examining the robustness of the excess entry theorems in the presence of general equilibrium interactions. This model also serves as the basic framework for our succeeding analysis of welfare-improving tax subsidy schemes, which is presented in the next chapter.

The plan of this chapter is as follows. In Section 2, a simple general equilibrium model of oligopolistic competition is formally introduced and the basic assumptions explained. Section 3 introduces the welfare criterion permitting general equilibrium interactions and obtains the fundamental equation of change. Section 4 establishes the excess entry theorem at the margin in general equilibrium, thus vindicating the fact that the partial equilibrium verdict on the welfare effect of entry regulation in an oligopolistic economy is essentially preserved in a general equilibrium setting. Section 5 concludes with several clarifying remarks.

2. A GENERAL EQUILIBRIUM MODEL OF OLIGOPOLISTIC COMPETITION

2.1. Informal description of the model

We consider a closed economy which produces two goods, X and Y, using two factors of production, capital and labour. The endowment of capital and labour is fixed exogenously, and factors are freely mobile between the two sectors.

Good X is produced under increasing returns to scale owing to the existence of fixed costs, which makes the industrial organization in this industry oligopolistic. For simplicity, we will assume that all firms in the oligopolistic sector are identical, and that they all behave as Cournot–Nash quantity competitors. Thus, we can work with the symmetric Cournot–Nash equilibrium. Good Y, which is competitively produced under constant returns to scale, is the numeraire of our analysis. We also simplify our model by supposing a single representative consumer whose welfare improvement is the central focus of our analysis. Throughout this chapter, we assume that the number of firms in the oligopolistic sector is under government regulation and can be parametrically changed if so desired.

This completes the informal description of our model. Let us now make it more precise.

2.2. Representative consumer

Let $V(p, I)$ be the indirect utility function of the representative consumer, where p and I are the relative price of X in terms of Y and the income of the consumer, respectively. It is assumed throughout that:

A1: $V(p, I)$ is twice continuously differentiable and strictly quasi-convex with respect to $p > 0$ for all $I > 0$. Furthermore,

$$V_p(p, I) := (\partial/\partial p)V(p, I) < 0; \qquad V_I(p, I) := (\partial/\partial I)V(p, I) > 0$$

hold for all $(p, I) > 0$.

The demand function for good X is given by

$$X(p, I) = -V_p(p, I)/V_I(p, I), \tag{1}$$

where use is made of Roy's identity. Assuming that X is a normal good, the inverse demand function

$$p = P(X, I) \tag{2}$$

for good X exists, which satisfies $P_X < 0$ and $P_I > 0$.

2.3. *Industry* X

The industry producing good X (industry X for short) consists of identical and oligopolistically competitive firms. Let the cost function of each firm be

$$C(q; r, w) = c(r, w)q + F(r, w), \tag{3}$$

where q, r, and w are, respectively, the firm's output of good X, the rental rate of capital, and the wage rate. Clearly, $c(r, w)$ and $F(r, w)$ denote, respectively, the marginal cost function and the fixed cost function, which are homogeneous of degree 1. Since we are concerned with the long-run analysis of the oligopolistic economy, where firms enter into and exit from the oligopolistic sector in accordance with its profitability, there is no sunk cost in our economy.

We assume throughout that industry X is engaging in the Cournot–Nash competition in quantities. Suppose that there are n firms in industry X, where $2 \leqslant n < +\infty$, and each firm is producing $\bar{q}$. If one firm deviates from $\bar{q}$ and produces q instead, and all other firms keep on producing $\bar{q}$, the total revenue of the deviant firm becomes

$$R(q, \bar{q}, n, I) = P(q + (n-1)\bar{q}, I)q, \tag{4}$$

so that the best reply function of the deviant firm may be defined by

$$q(\bar{q}; n, I, r, w) = \arg\max_{q>0} [R(q, \bar{q}, n, I) - C(q; r, w)]. \tag{5}$$

Assuming interior optimum, the first-order and the second-order conditions for $q > 0$ to be the best reply for $\bar{q}$ are given by

$$R_q(q, \bar{q}, n, I) = c(r, w) \tag{6}$$

and

$$R_{qq}(q, \bar{q}, n, I) < 0, \tag{7}$$

respectively.

The symmetric Cournot–Nash equilibrium in industry X is nothing other than the fixed point $q^N(n, I, r, w)$ of the mapping $q(\bar{q}; n, I, r, w)$ when (n, I, r, w) is given, i.e.

$$q^N(n, I, r, w) = q(q^N(n, I, r, w); n, I, r, w). \tag{8}$$

2.4. *Industry* Y

The industry producing good Y (industry Y for short) consists of perfectly competitive firms producing Y under constant returns to scale. Let $G(Y; r, w)$ stand for the cost function of the representative firm, so that

$$G(Y; r, w) = g(r, w)Y, \tag{9}$$

where the marginal as well as average cost function $g(r, w)$ is homogeneous of degree 1. Y being the numeraire in our economy, we should have

$$g(r, w) = 1 \tag{10}$$

at equilibrium.

2.5. *Factor supply and demand*

Both factors of production, capital and labour, are in fixed supply at $K > 0$ and $L > 0$, respectively, and freely mobile between sectors. Both factor markets are assumed to be perfectly competitive.

Let K_X denote the demand for capital and L_X the demand for labour, respectively, in industry X. Then we have

$$K_X = nC_r(q; r, w) = n[c_r(r, w)q + F_r(r, w)] \tag{11a}$$

and

$$L_X = nC_w(q; r, w) = n[c_w(r, w)q + F_w(r, w)]. \tag{11b}$$

Likewise, let K_Y denote the demand for capital and L_Y the demand for labour, respectively, in industry Y. Then we have

$$K_Y = G_r(Y; r, w) = g_r(r, w)\,Y \tag{12a}$$

and

$$L_Y = G_w(Y; r, w) = g_w(r, w)\,Y. \tag{12b}$$

2.6. *Income formation*

The income of the representative consumer consists of his factor rewards and profits accruing from industry X:

$$I = rK + wL + n[R(q, q, n, I) - C(q; r, w)], \tag{13}$$

profits in industry Y being driven down to zero by competition. Invoking the implicit function theorem, we may rewrite (13) explicitly for I as follows:

$$I = I(q, r, w, n). \tag{14}$$

To verify how the explicit representation (14) can be obtained from (13), let $E(p, u)$ and $h(p, u)$ be the expenditure function and the compensated demand function for good X of the representative consumer, where u denotes the level of his utility. By definition,

$$p = P(h(p, u), E(p, u)) \tag{15}$$

holds for all $p > 0$ and u. By differentiating (15) with respect to p and invoking Shephard's lemma, we obtain

$$1 - XP_I = \frac{(\partial/\partial p)h(p, u)]_{u=\text{const.}}}{(\partial/\partial p)X(p, I)]_{I=\text{const.}}}. \tag{16}$$

Since good X is normal, we obtain from (16) that $0 < 1 - XP_I < 1$; hence

$$0 < 1 - nR_I < 1, \tag{17}$$

where use is made of $R_I = P_I q$, which is due to (4). In view of (17), we can apply the implicit function theorem to (13) and obtain an explicit representation (14), as we set out to show.

2.7. *General equilibrium*

Putting all the pieces together, let us describe the general equilibrium of our economy.

The profit maximization condition in industry X and that in industry Y are given by

$$R_q(q, q, n, I) = c(r, w) \tag{18}$$

and (10), respectively, where I is specified by (14).

The market for good X is in equilibrium if

$$X(p, I) = nq \tag{19}$$

holds, whereas the market for good Y is in equilibrium if other (goods and factors) markets are.[2]

The market for capital is in equilibrium if

$$n[c_r(r, w)q + F_r(r, w)] + g_r(r, w)\,Y = K \tag{20}$$

holds, whereas the market for labour is in equilibrium if

$$n[c_w(r, w)q + F_w(r, w)] + g_w(r, w)\,Y = L \tag{21}$$

holds.

Our general equilibrium system consists of six equations—(10), (14), (18), (19), (20), and (21)—for six variables—q, r, w, p, Y, and I. Throughout the rest of this chapter, K and L are kept constant, whereas n is assumed to be exogenously determined by the policy choice of regulatory authority. For each set of exogenous variables (n, K, L), it is assumed that our general equilibrium system has a unique solution for the set of endogenous variables (q, r, w, p, Y, I).

3. FUNDAMENTAL EQUATION OF WELFARE CHANGE

3.1. *Welfare criterion*

How will consumer welfare be affected by an exogenous change in n? To answer this question, we must examine how the general equilibrium solution will be disrupted in response to a change in n. With this end in mind, we differentiate $V(P(X, I), I)$ totally to obtain

$$\mathrm{d}V = V_I[-XP_X\,\mathrm{d}X + (1 - XP_I)\mathrm{d}I], \tag{22}$$

where use is made of (1). By totally differentiating (13), we also obtain

$$(1 - nR_I)\mathrm{d}I = (K - nC_r)\mathrm{d}r + (L - nC_w)\mathrm{d}w + n(R_q + R_{\bar{q}} - C_q)\mathrm{d}q + nR_n\mathrm{d}n + (R - C)\mathrm{d}n, \tag{23}$$

whereas total differentiation of (10) yields $g_r\mathrm{d}r + g_w\mathrm{d}w = 0$. In view of (11*a*) and (11*b*), we then obtain $K - nC_r = K_Y$ and $L - nC_w = L_Y$. It then follows that

$$\begin{aligned}(K - nC_r)\mathrm{d}r + (L - nC_w)\mathrm{d}w &= K_Y\,\mathrm{d}r + L_Y\,\mathrm{d}w \\ &= (g_r\mathrm{d}r + g_w\mathrm{d}w)\,Y \text{ by (12a) and (12b)} \\ &= 0, \text{ by (10)},\end{aligned}$$

so that (23) may be reduced to

$$\mathrm{d}I = \frac{1}{1 - nR_I}\{nR_{\bar{q}}\,\mathrm{d}q + [(R - C) + nR_n]\mathrm{d}n\}, \tag{24}$$

where use is also made of (18).

Substituting (24) into (22) and noting that $\mathrm{d}X = q\mathrm{d}n + n\mathrm{d}q$, we obtain

$$\mathrm{d}V = V_I\{n(R_{\bar{q}} - XP_X)\mathrm{d}q + [(R - C) + nR_n - qXP_X]\mathrm{d}n\}, \tag{25}$$

where use is made of

$$R_I = P_I q, \tag{26}$$

which follows from (4). Note that (4) also yields

$$R_{\bar{q}} = (n - 1)qP_X \tag{27}$$

and

$$R_n = q^2 P_X, \tag{28}$$

so that (25) can be reduced further to

$$\mathrm{d}V = V_I\{-XP_X\,\mathrm{d}q + [R(q, q, n, I) - C(q; r, w)\mathrm{d}n]\}, \tag{29}$$

which constitutes the fundamental equation of welfare change in our subsequent analysis.

3.2. Conditions for welfare improvement

Recollect that $V_I > 0$ and $P_X < 0$ hold by assumption. Note also that the second term within the square brackets in (29) is zero if, initially, the number of firms is at the free-entry equilibrium level where each and every oligopolistic firm is earning zero profit. Thus we have the following theorem.

THEOREM 1. Suppose that the initial number of oligopolistic firms is at the free-entry equilibrium level. Then the conditions necessary and sufficient for a change in the number of oligopolistic firms to be welfare-improving are those that induce an increase in the output of each oligopolistic firm.

4. EXCESS ENTRY THEOREM IN GENERAL EQUILIBRIUM

4.1. Derivation of the equations of change

How, then, will the output of each oligopolistic firm be affected by an exogenous change in n? To answer this crucial question, it is helpful to rewrite our general equilibrium system in terms of the relative rates of change. For any variable x, we define $\hat{x} = dx/x$.

To start with, total differentiation of (10) yields

$$\theta_K^Y \hat{r} + \theta_L^Y \hat{w} = 0, \tag{30}$$

where $\theta_K^Y := rg_r/g$ and $\theta_L^Y := wg_w/g$ denote the cost share of capital and the cost share of labour, respectively, in industry Y. Since $g(r, w)$ is homogeneous of degree 1, it is clear that $\theta_K^Y + \theta_L^Y = 1$ holds, so that (30) can be rewritten as

$$\hat{r} = -\theta_L^Y \hat{\omega}; \qquad \hat{w} = \theta_K^Y \hat{\omega}, \tag{31}$$

where $\omega := w/r$ denotes the wage–rental ratio.

We now turn to the profit maximization condition in industry X. Total differentiation of (18) yields

$$A\hat{q} + \theta\hat{\omega} = \gamma\hat{n}, \tag{32}$$

where

$$A := q\left(R_{qq} + R_{q\bar{q}} + \frac{nR_q - R_{qI}}{1 - nR_I}\right),$$

$$\theta := c\left(\theta_K^X \theta_L^Y - \theta_L^X \theta_K^Y\right), \qquad \text{where } \theta_K^X := \frac{rc_r}{c} \text{ and } \theta_L^X := \frac{wc_w}{c},$$

and

$$\gamma := -n\left[R_{qn} + R_{qI}\frac{nR_n + (R - C)}{1 - nR_I}\right],$$

and use is made of (24) and (31). It is clear that θ_K^X and θ_L^X represent the *marginal cost share of capital* and the *marginal cost share of labour*, respectively, in industry X.

It is worth noticing that we may rewrite θ as

$$\theta = \frac{c\theta_L^X\theta_L^Y}{\omega}\left(k_M^X - k^Y\right), \tag{33}$$

where $k_M^X := c_r/c_w$ represents the *marginal capital intensity* of industry X and $k^Y := g_r/g_w$ represents the *marginal as well as average capital intensity* of industry Y.[3] Clearly, $\theta > (<)\ 0$ holds if, and only if, industry X is more (less) capital-intensive than industry Y in the marginal sense.

Next, total differentiation of (20) yields

$$\lambda_K^X\hat{q} + \lambda_K^Y\hat{Y} + \left(\lambda_K^X\theta_L^X\sigma_V^X + \delta_K^X\varepsilon_L^X\sigma_F^X + \lambda_K^Y\theta_L^Y\sigma^Y\right)\hat{\omega} = -\left(\lambda_K^X + \delta_K^X\right)\hat{n}, \tag{34}$$

where

$\lambda_K^X := \dfrac{nqC_r}{K}$ is the share of total capital used as variable input in industry X

$\lambda_K^Y := \dfrac{g_rY}{K}$ is the share of total capital used in industry Y

$\delta_K^X := \dfrac{nF_r}{K}$ is the share of total capital used as fixed input in industry X

$\varepsilon_L^X := \dfrac{wF_w}{F}$ is the share of labour cost in the fixed cost of industry X

$\sigma_V^X := -\dfrac{\hat{c}_w - \hat{c}_r}{\hat{\omega}}$ is the elasticity of substitution between variable inputs in industry X

$\sigma_F^X := -\dfrac{\hat{F}_w - \hat{F}_r}{\hat{\omega}}$ is the elasticity of substitution between fixed inputs in industry X

$\sigma^Y := -\dfrac{\hat{g}_w - \hat{g}_r}{\hat{\omega}}$ is the elasticity of substitution in industry Y.

Similarly, total differentiation of (21) yields

$$\lambda_L^X\hat{q} + \lambda_L^Y\hat{Y} - \left(\lambda_L^X\theta_K^X\sigma_V^X + \delta_L^X\varepsilon_K^X\sigma_F^X + \lambda_L^Y\theta_K^Y\sigma^Y\right)\hat{\omega} = -\left(\lambda_L^Y + \delta_L^X\right)\hat{n}, \tag{35}$$

where

$\lambda_L^X := \dfrac{nqc_w}{L}$ is the share of total labour used as variable input in industry X

$\lambda_L^Y := \dfrac{g_wY}{L}$ is the share of total labour used in industry Y

$\delta_L^X := \dfrac{nF_w}{L}$ is the share of total labour used as fixed input in industry X

$\varepsilon_K^X := \dfrac{rF_r}{F}$ is the share of capital cost in the fixed cost of industry X.

To facilitate subsequent analysis, we eliminate $\hat{Y}$ from (34) and (35) to obtain

$$\lambda\hat{q} + \Lambda\hat{\omega} = -(\lambda + \mu)\hat{n}, \tag{36}$$

where

$$\lambda := \lambda_K^X\lambda_L^Y - \lambda_L^X\lambda_K^Y = \frac{\lambda_L^X\lambda_L^Y L}{K}\left(k_M^X - k^Y\right), \tag{37}$$

$$\Lambda := \Lambda_V + \Lambda_F + \lambda_L^Y\lambda_K^Y\sigma^Y,$$

$$\Lambda_V := \left(\lambda_L^Y\lambda_K^X\theta_L^X + \lambda_K^Y\lambda_L^X\theta_K^X\right)\sigma_V^X,$$

$$\Lambda_F := \left(\lambda_L^Y\delta_K^X\varepsilon_L^X + \lambda_K^Y\delta_L^X\varepsilon_K^X\right)\sigma_F^X,$$

$$\mu := \lambda_L^Y\delta_K^X - \lambda_K^Y\delta_L^X = \frac{\delta_L^X\lambda_L^Y L}{K}\left(k_F^X - k^Y\right),$$

and $k_F^X := F_r/F_w$, which represents the *fixed* capital intensity of industry X.

Comparing (33) and (37), it is clear that θ and λ must always have the same sign, both being the index of relative *marginal* factor intensities. In contrast, μ is the index of how the *fixed* capital intensity in industry X fares *vis-à-vis* the overall capital intensity in industry Y. It is clear that $\mu > (<)\ 0$ holds if and only if the fixed cost part of industry X is more (less) capital-intensive than industry Y.

This completes the derivation of our basic equations of change.

4.2. *Excess entry theorem at the margin*

The system of simultaneous equations of change consisting of (32) and (36), where $\hat{q}$ and $\hat{\omega}$ are endogenous variables and $\hat{n}$ is regarded as being exogenous, can be solved for $\hat{q}$ and $\hat{\omega}$ in terms of $\hat{n}$ as follows:

$$\hat{q} = \frac{\hat{n}}{\Xi}\,[\gamma\Lambda + \theta(\lambda + \mu)] \tag{38}$$

and

$$\hat{\omega} = -\frac{\hat{n}}{\Xi}\,[\gamma\lambda + (\lambda + \mu)A], \tag{39}$$

where $\Xi := A\Lambda - \lambda\theta$. Taking Theorem 1 into consideration, equation (38) helps us ascertain when an exogenous change in the number of firms at the free-entry equilibrium is welfare-improving.

To facilitate our interpretation of the conditions for marginal welfare improvement, let us introduce at this stage the following two additional simplifying assumptions:

A2: The preference of the representative consumer is homothetic.
A3: The outputs of oligopolistic competitors are strategic substitutes; i.e. $R_{q\bar{q}} < 0$ holds.

By virtue of assumption A2, it is clear that demand for good X is proportional to income; that is, there exists a function of p, say $\zeta(p)$, such that $X(p, I) = \zeta(p)I$ holds for all $(p, I) > 0$. It then follows that the inverse demand function for good X takes the following form:

$$p = \rho\left(\frac{X}{I}\right), \quad \text{with } \rho'\left(\frac{X}{I}\right) < 0. \tag{40}$$

Therefore, the total revenue of an oligopolistic firm producing q can be written as

$$R(q, \bar{q}, n, I) = \rho\left(\frac{q + (n-1)\bar{q}}{I}\right)q, \tag{41}$$

where $\bar{q}$ denotes the output of every other firm in industry X.

Differentiating (41) with respect to q and evaluating at $q = \bar{q}$, we obtain

$$R_q = \rho + \frac{q}{I}\rho', \tag{42}$$

$$R_{\bar{q}} = \frac{(n-1)q}{I}\rho', \tag{43}$$

$$R_n = \frac{q^2}{I}\rho', \tag{44}$$

$$R_I = -\frac{nq^2}{I^2}\rho', \tag{45}$$

$$R_{qq} = \frac{1}{I}\left(2\rho' + \frac{q}{I}\rho''\right), \tag{46}$$

$$R_{q\bar{q}} = \frac{n-1}{I}\left(\rho' + \frac{q}{I}\rho''\right), \tag{47}$$

$$R_{qn} = \frac{q}{I}\left(\rho' + \frac{q}{I}\rho''\right), \tag{48}$$

and

$$R_{qI} = -\frac{nq}{I^2}\left(\rho' + \frac{q}{I}\rho''\right) - \frac{q}{I^2}\rho'. \tag{49}$$

By virtue of A3, it follows from (47) that

$$\rho' + \frac{q}{I}\rho'' < 0. \tag{50}$$

Back, then, to (38) and examine how $\text{sgn}\,\hat{q}$ is determined. To begin with, note that $A < 0$ must hold under A2 and A3, where use is made of (17), (43), (46), (47), (49), and (50). Note also that $\Lambda > 0$ by definition, whereas we have already noted that θ and λ must always have the same sign, so that $\lambda\theta \geqslant 0$. Hence $\Xi := A\Lambda - \lambda\theta < 0$.

It remains only to give signs to γ and $\theta(\lambda + \mu)$. If the number of oligopolistic firms is initially at the free-entry equilibrium level, we have $R - C = 0$ by definition. Coupled with (17), (44), (48), and (50), this enables us to conclude that $\gamma > 0$. Finally, it follows from (37) that

$$\lambda + \mu = \frac{\lambda_L^Y(\lambda_L^X + \delta_L^X)L}{K}(k^X - k^Y) \tag{51}$$

holds, where $k^X := (qc_r + F_r)/(qc_w + F_w)$ stands for the *average capital intensity* of industry X. Thus, we can conclude, on the basis of (33) and (51), that $\theta(\lambda + \mu) \geqslant 0$ if, and only if

$$(k_M^X - k^Y)(k^X - k^Y) \geqslant 0 \tag{52}$$

holds. Inequality (52) will be violated only when there is a *capital intensity twist* in the sense that industry X is more (less) capital-intensive than industry Y in the marginal sense, but is less (more) capital-intensive than industry Y in the average sense.

Barring capital intensity twist in this sense, we may now assert on the basis of (38) that $\text{sgn}\,\hat{q} = -\,\text{sgn}\,\hat{n}$. Invoking Theorem 1, we have thus established the following.[4]

THEOREM 2 (EXCESS ENTRY THEOREM IN GENERAL EQUILIBRIUM). Suppose that A1, A2, and A3 are satisfied and there is no capital intensity twist. Then the equilibrium number of oligopolistic firms is socially excessive at the margin in the sense that a decrease at the margin in the number of oligopolistic firms from the free-entry equilibrium level unambiguously improves social welfare.

4.3. *Diagrammatic illustration*

Despite its apparent complexity, our excess entry theorem in general equilibrium, and the role played therein by the somewhat novel condition of no factor intensity twist, can be intuitively understood through the following graphical illustration.

In Figure 8, the horizontal (vertical) axis measures $q(\omega)$. To begin with, consider the case where $\theta > 0$, hence $\lambda > 0$, so that industry X is marginally more capital-intensive than industry Y. The curve *II* (*JJ*) in the figure describes the relationship between q and ω induced by (32) ((36)) when the number of oligopolistic firms is fixed at the free-entry equilibrium level.

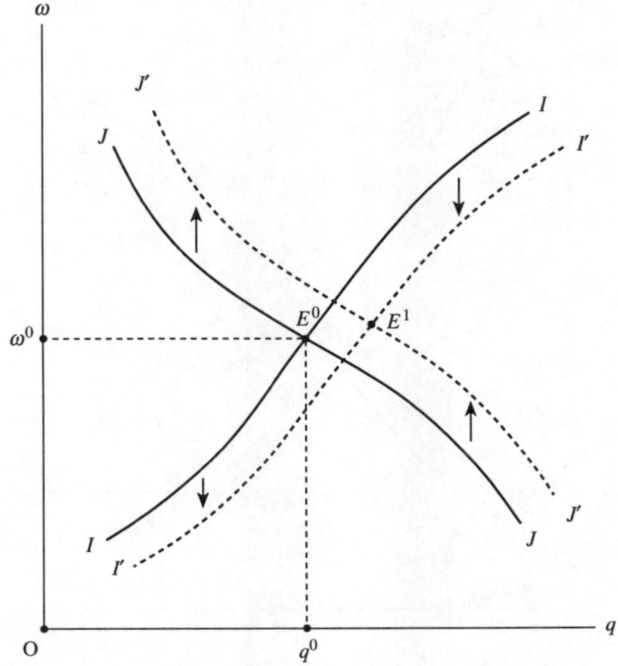

Fig. 8 No factor intensity twist

Since $A < 0$, $\theta > 0$, $\lambda > 0$, $\gamma > 0$, and $\Lambda > 0$ in the case at hand, the curve II (JJ) is upward-(downward-)sloping. The point of intersection E^0 represents the free-entry equilibrium pair (q^0, ω^0).

Suppose that the number of firms is somehow reduced below its free-entry equilibrium level. Since $\gamma > 0$ initially, the curve II shifts down to $I'I'$. If there is no factor intensity twist, we have $\lambda + \mu > 0$ in the case where $\theta > 0$, hence $\lambda > 0$, so that the curve JJ shifts up to $J'J'$. Therefore, the equilibrium point shifts from E^0 to E^1 where the equilibrium output of an oligopolist necessarily increases, thus vindicating the excess entry theorem in view of Theorem 1.

Several remarks are in order here. First, in the absence of factor intensity twist, the effect of a reduction in the number of firms on the wage–rental ratio ω clearly remains ambiguous. Second, in the presence of factor intensity twist, the effect on q becomes ambiguous, whereas the effect on ω becomes unambiguous, which can easily be understood by looking at Fig. 9. Third, the dual case where $\theta < 0$, and hence $\lambda < 0$, can be treated symmetrically and the validity of the excess entry theorem can be verified in the absence of factor intensity twist. Since the discussion of this case is

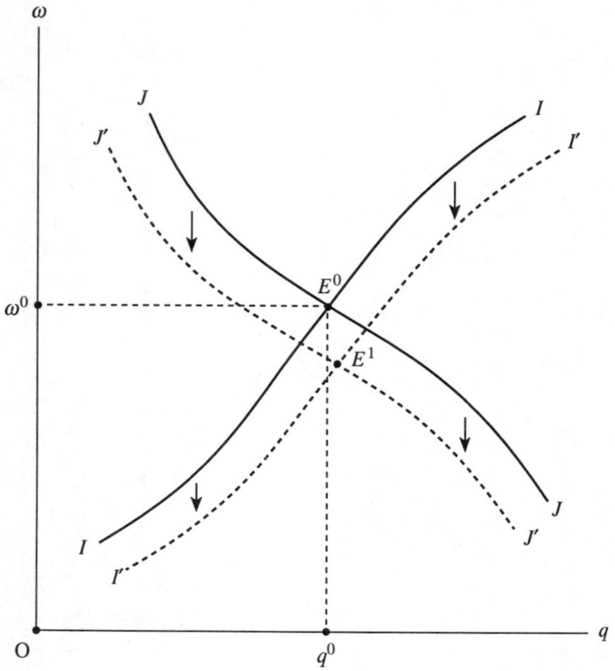

Fig. 9 Factor intensity twist

completely parallel to what we have already presented in detail, we can safely omit it.

5. CONCLUDING REMARKS

In order to gauge how robust the excess entry theorems are in the presence of general equilibrium interactions, we have examined in this chapter a simple two-sector model of general equilibrium consisting of an oligopolistic sector and a competitive sector. It is shown that the excess entry theorem at the margin still holds beyond the narrow confinement of partial equilibrium analysis. Thus, partial equilibrium analysis may be unreliable often enough, but it may not necessarily be so in our present context of the welfare implications of increasing competitiveness.

Among those conditions that support the validity of the excess entry theorem in general equilibrium, the assumption of the strategic substitutability of the competitive strategies of Cournot oligopolists is carried over from partial equilibrium analysis. In the context of quantity competition, this assumption seems to be on safe ground anyway. The second crucial assumption of homothetic preferences also seems to be fairly harmless and standard. The remaining assumption of no capital intensity twist is somewhat novel, but it does not seem to be particularly pathological. At the very least, therefore, we can now assert that there is a non-trivial case where the main thrust of the excess entry theorem is essentially preserved even when we introduce general equilibrium interactions.

An important question still remains. Even though we may, in principle, improve social welfare by marginally restricting the number of firms at the free-entry equilibrium in the absence of factor intensity twist, we do not know how we can improve economic welfare in the presence of factor intensity twist, and the excess entry theorem in general equilibrium remains silent on this point. It is to this question that we now turn.

NOTES TO CHAPTER 2

1. It should also be emphasized that the net market surplus measure of social welfare places equal weights on consumer's surplus and producer's surplus.
2. To see this, let $Y(p, I)$ be the demand for good Y. The budget constraint of the representative consumer requires that

$$\begin{aligned} pX(p, I) + Y(p, I) &= I(q, r, w, n) \\ &= rK + wL + n[R(q, q, n, I) - C(q; r, w)] \qquad \text{(by (13))} \\ &= n\{q[c_r(r, w)r + c_w(r, w)w] + [F_r(r, w)r + F_w(r, w)w]\} \\ &\quad + Y[g_r(r, w)r + g_w(r, w)w] \\ &\quad + n[R(q, q, n, I) - C(q; r, w)] \qquad \text{(by (20) and (21))} \\ &= n[qc(r, w) + F(r, w)] + g(r, w)Y \\ &\quad + n[R(q, q, n, I) - C(q; r, w)] \qquad \text{(by linear homogeneity)} \\ &= nP(nq, I)q + Y \qquad \text{(by (3), (4), and (10))}, \end{aligned}$$

so that (2) and (19) yield $Y = Y(p, I)$, as required. This is nothing other than Walras's law in our present context.
3. The concept of *marginal* and *average* factor intensities was introduced originally by R. W. Jones (1968) in the related but different context. It is clear that the discrepancy between marginal and average factor intensities disappears if there is no fixed cost in production.
4. According to (39), the effect of a change in n on the wage–rental ratio ω is ambiguous in the absence of capital intensity twist. It is left to the interested reader to spell out the unambiguous results that pertain if capital intensity twist does occur.

3 Welfare-Improving Tax Subsidy Schemes with or without Entry Barriers

1. INTRODUCTION

According to the first fundamental theorem of welfare economics, the perfectly competitive economy always attains a Pareto-efficient allocation of resources in the absence of market failures, so that the introduction of a tax subsidy scheme into the perfectly competitive economy cannot but harm at least one economic agent unless it is of the ideal (non-distortionary) lump-sum category. In contrast, the introduction of a tax subsidy scheme can be welfare-improving when the market economy is imperfectly competitive. However, to know that a tax subsidy scheme *can be* welfare-improving is one thing, but to know just when and precisely what type of tax subsidy scheme can be *warranted* as being welfare-improving is quite another. The purpose of this chapter is to examine the conditions under which various tax subsidy schemes are welfare-improving in an oligopolistic economy within the simple general equilibrium framework developed in the previous chapter. This issue does not seem to have received due attention in the existing literature on tax analysis in an imperfectly competitive economy.[1]

As is well known, the allocative inefficiency of the oligopolistically competitive economy results from the oligopolistic behaviour, which sets price above marginal cost with the level of output being less than the socially optimal level. Therefore, the tax subsidy schemes that can induce oligopolists to expand their output can be welfare-improving.[2] Our problem, then, boils down to examining just when the introduction of an infinitesimal tax subsidy scheme can induce oligopolists to increase their output, while paying due attention to the general equilibrium interactions of the whole economy. This is the main task of this chapter.

The plan of the chapter is as follows. Section 2 introduces the two-sector general equilibrium model of an oligopolistic economy with tax subsidy schemes. Since the basic structure of our model remains the same as in Chapter 2, we keep the assumptions A1, A2, and A3 introduced therein intact. Section 3 derives the necessary and sufficient conditions for welfare improvement via the introduction of an infinitesimal tax subsidy scheme. Section 4 identifies welfare-improving tax subsidy schemes in the presence of entry barriers, and Section 5 analyses the case of free entry and exit of firms. Section 6 concludes with several clarifying remarks.

2. A MODEL OF GENERAL EQUILIBRIUM WITH TAX SUBSIDY SCHEMES

2.1. *Tax subsidy schemes*

Throughout this chapter, let $\mathbf{S} = (s, s_r, s_w; t, t_r, t_w)$ denote the tax subsidy scheme that is applied to the oligopolistic industry producing good X, where

s is the production subsidy per unit output

s_r is the rate of subsidy on the capital expenditure component of marginal cost

s_w is the rate of subsidy on the wage expenditure component of marginal cost

t is the lump-sum subsidy

t_r is the rate of subsidy on the capital expenditure component of fixed cost

t_w is the rate of subsidy on the wage expenditure component of fixed cost.

Note that each one of s, s_r, s_w, t, t_r, and t_w can be negative, in which case we are referring to tax, rather than to subsidy.

2.2. *Industry X*

Let the cost function of each firm in industry X in the presence of the tax subsidy scheme $\mathbf{S}$ be

$$C(q; r, w; \mathbf{S}) := c(r, w; \mathbf{S})q + F(r, w; \mathbf{S}), \tag{1}$$

where the *marginal cost function* $c(r, w; \mathbf{S})$ as well as the *fixed cost function* $F(r, w; \mathbf{S})$ is linear homogeneous with respect to r and w. By definition, $c(r, w; \mathbf{S})$ and $F(r, w; \mathbf{S})$ satisfy

$$c(r, w; \mathbf{S}) = c(r - s_r, w - s_w; \mathbf{0}) - s \tag{2}$$

and

$$F(r, w; \mathbf{S}) = F(r - t_r, w - t_w; \mathbf{0}) - t \tag{3}$$

for any (r, w), where $\mathbf{S} = (s, s_r, s_w; t, t_r, t_w)$ and $\mathbf{0} = (0, 0, 0; 0, 0, 0)$.

In what follows, $\mathbf{x} \cdot \mathbf{y}$ denotes the inner product of two vectors of the same size; i.e. for $\mathbf{x} = (x_1, \ldots, x_i, \ldots, x_m)$ and $\mathbf{y} = (y_1, \ldots, y_i, \ldots, y_m)$, $\mathbf{x} \cdot \mathbf{y} = \Sigma_{i=1}^m x_i y_i$. Furthermore, for any function $g(\mathbf{x}; \mathbf{v})$ of $\mathbf{x} = (x_1, \ldots, x_i, \ldots, x_m)$ and $\mathbf{v} = (v_1, \ldots, v_j, \ldots, v_n)$, we denote the gradient vector of $g(\mathbf{x}; \mathbf{v})$ with respect to $\mathbf{v}$ by $\nabla_\mathbf{v} g(\mathbf{x}; \mathbf{v})$; i.e.

$$\nabla_\mathbf{v} g(\mathbf{x}; \mathbf{v}) := [(\partial/\partial v_1)g(\mathbf{x}; \mathbf{v}), \ldots, (\partial/\partial v_j)g(\mathbf{x}; \mathbf{v}), \ldots, (\partial/\partial v_n)g(\mathbf{x}; \mathbf{v})].$$

2.3. *Tax, subsidy, and income*

Note that each firm in industry X whose cost function is specified by (1) will receive $-\nabla_\mathbf{S} C(q; r, w; \mathbf{S})$. $\mathbf{S} = sq + s_r c_r(r, w; \mathbf{S})q + s_w c_w(r, w; \mathbf{S}q) + t +$

$t_r F_r(r, w; \mathbf{S}) + t_w F_w(r, w; \mathbf{S})$ in subsidy if the tax subsidy scheme $\mathbf{S} = (s, s_r, s_w; t, t_r, t_w)$ is in fact applied. In order to support the introduction of this scheme, however, it is necessary to collect tax of the amount

$$T = -n[\nabla_{\mathbf{S}} C(q; r, w; \mathbf{S} \cdot \mathbf{S}] \tag{4}$$

from the representative consumer, where n denotes the number of oligopolistic firms. It follows that the income of the representative consumer is now defined implicitly by

$$I = rK + wL + n[R(q, q, n, I) - C(q; r, w; \mathbf{S})] - T \tag{5}$$

in place of (13) in Chapter 2. Taking (4) into consideration, (5) may be solved explicitly for I to yield

$$I = I(q, r, w, n; \mathbf{S}). \tag{6}$$

2.4. General equilibrium with entry regulation

To begin with, let us consider a situation where the number of firms, n, in industry X is fixed by government regulation. Then the general equilibrium of our economy can be described by the following five equations plus (6), where the endogenous variables of our system are q, r, w, p, Y, and I, whereas n, K, L, and $\mathbf{S}$ are exogenously given parameters:

$$g(r, w) = 1, \tag{7}$$

$$R_q(q, q, n, I) = c(r, w; \mathbf{S}), \tag{8}$$

$$X(p, I) = nq, \tag{9}$$

$$n[c_r(r, w; \mathbf{S})q + F_r(r, w; \mathbf{S})] + g_r(r, w)Y = K, \tag{10}$$

and

$$n[c_w(r, w; \mathbf{S})q + F_W(r, w; \mathbf{S})] + g_w(r, w)Y = L. \tag{11}$$

Recollect that the equation (7) describes the condition for profit maximization in industry Y, (8) the condition for symmetric Cournot–Nash equilibrium in industry X, (9) the equilibrium condition in the market for good X, and (10) ((11)) the equilibrium condition in the capital (labour) market.

2.5. General equilibrium with free entry

When entry and exit of firms in industry X are free, the number of oligopolistic firms, n, becomes an endogenous variable which is to be determined by the zero profit condition in industry X. The general equilibrium of our economy is, then, fully articulated by adding the following equation to the above system:

$$R(q, q, n, I) = c(r, w; \mathbf{S})q + F(r, w; \mathbf{S}). \tag{12}$$

The endogenous variables of our general equilibrium system are now q, r, w, p, Y, I, and n, whereas K, L, and $\mathbf{S}$ are exogenously prescribed parameters.

3. WELFARE CHANGE IN THE PRESENCE OF TAX SUBSIDY SCHEMES

To analyse the impact of introducing a tax subsidy scheme $\mathbf{S} = (s, s_r, s_w; t, t_r, t_w)$ on social welfare, we differentiate $V(P(X, I), I)$ totally to obtain

$$\mathrm{d}V = V_1[-XP_X\mathrm{d}X + (1 - XP_I)\mathrm{d}I]. \tag{13}$$

Note that $\mathrm{d}I$ in (13) should be computed from (5) in the presence of the tax subsidy scheme $\mathbf{S}$. Total differentiation of (5) yields

$$(1 - nR_I)\mathrm{d}I = (K - nC_r)\mathrm{d}r + (L - nC_w)\mathrm{d}w + n(R_q + R_{\bar{q}} - c)\mathrm{d}q$$
$$- n[\nabla_{\mathbf{S}}C(q; r, w; \mathbf{S}) \cdot \mathrm{d}\mathbf{S}] - \mathrm{d}T + nR_n\mathrm{d}n + (R - C)\mathrm{d}n, \tag{14}$$

whereas (4) entails

$$\mathrm{d}T = -[\nabla_{\mathbf{S}}C(q; r, w; \mathbf{S}) \cdot \mathbf{S}]\mathrm{d}n - n\{\nabla_{\mathbf{S}}C(q; r, w; \mathbf{S}) \cdot \mathrm{d}\mathbf{S}$$
$$+ \mathrm{d}[\nabla_{\mathbf{S}}C(q; r, w; \mathbf{S})] \cdot \mathbf{S}\}, \tag{15}$$

which boils down to $\mathrm{d}T = -n[\nabla_{\mathbf{S}}C(q; r, w; \mathbf{S}) \cdot \mathrm{d}\mathbf{S}]$ if we consider only the introduction of an infinitesimal tax subsidy scheme, i.e. $\mathbf{S} = \mathbf{0}$, initially. Taking this fact into consideration, (13), (14), and (15) yield

$$\mathrm{d}V = V_I\{- XP_X\mathrm{d}q + [R(q, q, n, I) - C(q; r, w; \mathbf{S})]\mathrm{d}n\}, \tag{16}$$

as in the previous chapter.

Note that the second term in braces in (16) is 0 in the case of fixed n (where $\mathrm{d}n = 0$), as well as in the case of free entry and exit (where we have (12)). Since $P_X < 0$ by assumption, we have the following.

THEOREM 1. The introduction of an infinitesimal tax subsidy scheme is welfare-improving if and only if it induces an increase in the output of each oligopolistic firm, irrespective of whether entry and exit are regulated or unregulated.

4. WELFARE-IMPROVING TAX SUBSIDY SCHEMES: THE CASE OF ENTRY REGULATION

4.1. *Equations of change*

Let us now rewrite our general equilibrium equations in terms of the relative rate of change of each variable. To begin with, total differentiation of (8) yields

$$A\hat{q} + \theta\hat{\omega} = \nabla_{\mathbf{S}} c(r, w; \mathbf{S}) \, . \, \mathrm{d}\mathbf{S}, \tag{17}$$

where $\mathrm{d}\mathbf{S} = (\mathrm{d}s, \mathrm{d}s_r, \mathrm{d}s_w; \mathrm{d}t, \mathrm{d}t_r, \mathrm{d}t_w)$, A and θ are defined in Chapter 2, and

$$\nabla_{\mathbf{S}} c(r, w; \mathbf{S}) = -\,(1, c_r, c_w; 0, 0, 0),$$

which follows from (2).

Turning to (10) and (11), and noting that the introduction of an infinitesimal tax subsidy scheme modifies the effective wage rate and rental rate in the variable cost part and the fixed cost part of industry X discriminatively, we obtain[3]

$$\lambda_K^X \hat{q} + \lambda_K^Y \hat{Y} - \left(\lambda_K^X \theta_L^X \sigma_V^X + \delta_K^X \varepsilon_L^X \sigma_F^X + \lambda_K^Y \theta_L^Y \sigma^Y\right) \hat{\omega} = \lambda_K^X \theta_L^X \sigma_V^X \left(\frac{\mathrm{d}s_w}{w} - \frac{\mathrm{d}s_r}{r}\right) + \delta_K^X \varepsilon_L^X \sigma_F^X \left(\frac{\mathrm{d}t_w}{w} - \frac{\mathrm{d}t_r}{r}\right) \tag{18}$$

and

$$\lambda_L^X \hat{q} + \lambda_L^Y \hat{Y} - \left(\lambda_L^X \theta_K^X \sigma_V^X + \delta_L^X \varepsilon_K^X \sigma_F^X + \lambda_L^Y \theta_K^Y \sigma^Y\right) \hat{\omega} = -\,\lambda_L^X \theta_K^X \sigma_V^X \left(\frac{\mathrm{d}s_w}{w} - \frac{\mathrm{d}s_r}{r}\right) - \delta_L^X \varepsilon_K^X \sigma_F^X \left(\frac{\mathrm{d}t_w}{w} - \frac{\mathrm{d}t_r}{r}\right). \tag{19}$$

Eliminating $\hat{Y}$ from (18) and (19), we obtain

$$\lambda\hat{q} + \Lambda\hat{\omega} = \boldsymbol{\eta}\ \mathrm{d}\mathbf{S}, \tag{20}$$

where λ, Λ, Λ_V, and Λ_F are defined as in the previous chapter, and

$$\boldsymbol{\eta} := \left(0, -\frac{\Lambda_V}{r}, \frac{\Lambda_V}{w}; 0, -\frac{\Lambda_F}{r}, \frac{\Lambda_F}{w}\right).$$

4.2. *Welfare-Improving Tax Subsidy Schemes*

We are now ready to determine the conditions for welfare-improving tax subsidy schemes in the case of a fixed number of firms. Solving our equations of change (17) and (20) for $\hat{q}$, we obtain

$$\hat{q} = \frac{\Lambda}{\Xi}\left[\nabla_{\mathbf{S}} c(r, w; \mathbf{S}) - \frac{\theta}{\Lambda}\boldsymbol{\eta}\right] \cdot \mathrm{d}\mathbf{S}, \tag{21}$$

where $\Xi := A\Lambda - \lambda\theta < 0$ under A2, i.e. homothetic preferences, and A3, i.e. strategic substitutability. It follows that $\hat{q} > 0$ holds if and only if

$$\Phi := \left[\nabla_{\mathbf{S}} c(r, w; \mathbf{S}) - \frac{\theta}{\Lambda}\boldsymbol{\eta}\right] \cdot \mathrm{d}\mathbf{S} < 0 \tag{22}$$

holds. Invoking Theorem 1, we can now assert the following.

THEOREM 2. Suppose that A2 and A3 are valid. Suppose also that the number of oligopolistic firms is held constant for whatever reason. Then:

(*a*) The introduction of an infinitesimal production subsidy is unambiguously welfare-improving;
(*b*) the introduction of an infinitesimal and uniform wage (capital) subsidy is welfare-improving if industry X is more (less) capital-intensive than industry Y in the marginal sense.
(*c*) the introduction of an infinitesimal subsidy (tax) on the capital expenditure component of fixed cost, which is accompanied by taxation (subsidization) on the wage expenditure component of fixed cost at the same absolute rate, is welfare-improving if industry X is less (more) capital-intensive than industry Y in the marginal sense.

Proof. (*a*) Let $\mathrm{d}\mathbf{S} = (\mathrm{d}s, 0, 0; 0, 0, 0)$ with $\mathrm{d}s > 0$. Then $\Phi = -\,\mathrm{d}s < 0$.

(*b*) In the case of an infinitesimal and uniform wage subsidy, let $\mathrm{d}\mathbf{S} = (0, 0, \mathrm{d}s_w; 0, 0, \mathrm{d}s_w)$ with $\mathrm{d}s_w > 0$. Then we obtain

$$\Phi = -\left[c_w + \frac{\theta}{w\Lambda}(\Lambda_V + \Lambda_F)\right]\mathrm{d}s_w, \tag{23}$$

which is negative if $\theta > 0$. In the case of an infinitesimal and uniform capital subsidy, let $\mathrm{d}\mathbf{S} = (0, \mathrm{d}s_r, 0; 0, \mathrm{d}s_r, 0)$ with $\mathrm{d}s_r > 0$. Then we obtain

$$\Phi = -\left[c_r - \frac{\theta}{r\Lambda}(\Lambda_V + \Lambda_F)\right]\mathrm{d}s_r, \tag{24}$$

which is negative if $\theta < 0$.

(*c*) Consider an infinitesimal tax-subsidy scheme $\mathrm{d}\mathbf{S} = (0, 0, 0; 0, \mathrm{d}s, -\,\mathrm{d}s)$. Then we obtain

$$\Phi = \frac{\theta\Lambda_F}{\Lambda}\left(\frac{1}{r} + \frac{1}{w}\right)\mathrm{d}s, \tag{25}$$

which is negative if (i) $\mathrm{d}s > 0$ and $\theta < 0$, or (ii) $\mathrm{d}s < 0$ and $\theta > 0$ hold. □

5. WELFARE-IMPROVING TAX SUBSIDY SCHEMES: THE CASE OF FREE ENTRY

5.1. *Stability of free-entry equilibrium*

Before introducing an infinitesimal tax subsidy scheme which displaces the free-entry equilibrium, let us examine the stability condition for the dynamic adjustment process defined by

$$\dot{q} = \kappa\left[R_q(q, q, n, I) - c(r, w; \mathbf{0})\right] \tag{26}$$

and

$$\dot{n} = \mu\,[R(q, q, n, I) - C(r, w; \mathbf{0})], \tag{27}$$

where $\dot{q}$ and $\dot{n}$ denote the time derivative of q and n, respectively, and $\kappa > 0$ and $\mu > 0$ are adjustment coefficients.[4] Note that the critical point of the dynamic system defined by (26) and (27) is precisely the free-entry equilibrium.

Linearly approximating (26) and (27) around the free-entry equilibrium, we observe that the free-entry equilibrium is locally stable if the matrix

$$\begin{bmatrix} \kappa & 0 \\ 0 & \mu \end{bmatrix} \begin{bmatrix} R_{qq} + R_{q\bar{q}} + R_{qI}\dfrac{\partial I}{\partial q} & R_{qn} + R_{qI}\dfrac{\partial I}{\partial n} \\ R_q + R_{\bar{q}} + R_I\dfrac{\partial I}{\partial q} - C_q & R_n + R_I\dfrac{\partial I}{\partial n} \end{bmatrix} \tag{28}$$

is negative definite, which is the case if, and only if,

A4: $A < 0$; $AM - BN > 0$

holds, where

$$B := qR_{\bar{q}}\left(1 + \frac{n}{1 - nR_I}\right),$$

$$M := nR_n\left(1 + \frac{n}{1 - nR_I}\right),$$

and

$$N := n\left(R_{qn} + \frac{nR_nR_{qI}}{1 - nR_I}\right).$$

Throughout the rest of this chapter, we require that the stability condition A4 holds, which is essential for the validity of our comparative statics. Note that each one of A, B, M, and N is unambiguously negative under A2 and A3. However, these assumptions, powerful though they are, do not by themselves imply the second inequality in A4. This is why we should assume the stability condition A4 in addition to our standard assumptions A1, A2, and A3.

5.2. Equations of change

Let us now analyse the welfare effect of introducing an infinitesimal tax subsidy scheme in the absence of entry barriers. Totally differentiating (8), we obtain

$$A\hat{q} + N\hat{n} + \theta\hat{\omega} = \nabla_{\mathbf{S}} c(r, w; \mathbf{S}) \cdot \mathrm{d}\mathbf{S}, \tag{29}$$

where $\mathrm{d}\mathbf{S} = (\mathrm{d}s, \mathrm{d}s_r, \mathrm{d}s_w; \mathrm{d}t, \mathrm{d}t_r, \mathrm{d}t_w)$, and n is now treated as an endogenous variable.

Likewise, total differentiation of (10) yields

$$\lambda_K^X\hat{q} + \zeta_K^X\hat{n} + \lambda_K^Y\hat{Y} - \left(\lambda_K^X\theta_L^X\sigma_V^X + \delta_K^X\varepsilon_L^X\sigma_F^X + \lambda_K^Y\theta_L^Y\sigma^Y\right)\hat{\omega} = \lambda_K^X\theta_L^X\sigma_V^X\left(\frac{\mathrm{d}s_w}{w} - \frac{\mathrm{d}s_r}{r}\right) + \delta_K^X\varepsilon_L^X\sigma_F^X\left(\frac{\mathrm{d}s_w}{w} - \frac{\mathrm{d}s_r}{r}\right), \tag{30}$$

where $\zeta_K^X := \lambda_K^X + \delta_K^X$ denotes the share of total capital used in industry X, whereas total differentiation of (11) yields

$$\lambda_L^X\hat{q} + \zeta_L^X\hat{n} + \lambda_L^Y\hat{Y} - \left(\lambda_L^X\theta_K^X\sigma_V^X + \delta_L^X\varepsilon_K^X\sigma_F^X + \lambda_L^Y\theta_K^Y\sigma^Y\right)\hat{\omega} = -\lambda_L^X\theta_K^X\sigma_V^X\left(\frac{\mathrm{d}s_w}{w} - \frac{\mathrm{d}s_r}{r}\right) - \delta_L^X\varepsilon_K^X\sigma_F^X\left(\frac{\mathrm{d}t_w}{w} - \frac{\mathrm{d}t_r}{r}\right), \tag{31}$$

where $\zeta_L^X := \lambda_L^X + \delta_L^X$ denotes the share of total labour used in industry X.

Finally, total differentiation of (12) yields

$$B\hat{q} + M\hat{n} + \phi\hat{\omega} = \nabla_{\mathbf{S}} C(q; r, w; \mathbf{S}) \cdot \mathrm{d}\mathbf{S}, \tag{32}$$

where

$\phi_K^X := \dfrac{r(c_r q + F_r)}{C}$ is the cost share of capital in industry X,

$\phi_L^X := \dfrac{w(c_w q + F_w)}{C}$ is the cost share of labour in industry X,

$$\phi := C\left(\phi_K^X\theta_L^Y - \phi_L^X\theta_K^Y\right) = \frac{\phi_L^X\theta_L^Y C}{\omega}\left(k^X - k^Y\right),$$

and

$$\nabla_{\mathbf{S}} C(q; r, w; \mathbf{S}) = -(q, qc_r, qc_w; 1, F_r, F_w),$$

which follows from (1), (2), and (3).

The derivation of our equations of change in the absence of entry barriers is now complete.

5.3. *Welfare-improving tax subsidy schemes*

Eliminating $\hat{Y}$ from (30) and (31), we obtain

$$\lambda\hat{q} + \zeta\hat{n} + \Lambda\hat{\omega} = \boldsymbol{\eta}\cdot \mathrm{d}\mathbf{S}, \tag{33}$$

where

$$\zeta := \zeta_K^X\lambda_L^Y - \zeta_L^X\lambda_K^Y = \frac{\zeta_L^X\lambda_L^Y L}{K}(k^X - k^Y).$$

Consider the system of simultaneous equations for $(\hat{q}, \hat{n}, \hat{\omega})$ defined by (29), (32), and (33), which can be summarized by

$$\begin{bmatrix} A & M & \theta \\ \lambda & \zeta & \Lambda \\ B & M & \phi \end{bmatrix}\begin{bmatrix} \hat{q} \\ \hat{n} \\ \hat{\omega} \end{bmatrix} = \begin{bmatrix} \nabla_{\mathbf{S}} c(r, w; \mathbf{S})\cdot \mathrm{d}\mathbf{S} \\ \boldsymbol{\eta}\cdot \mathrm{d}\mathbf{S} \\ \nabla_{\mathbf{S}} C(q; r, w; \mathbf{S})\cdot \mathrm{d}\mathbf{S} \end{bmatrix} \tag{34}$$

Let Γ denote the determinant of the coefficient matrix in (34). By rearranging the terms appropriately, we can verify that

$$\Gamma = A\phi\zeta - (AN - BN)\Lambda + M\lambda\theta - B\theta\zeta - N\lambda\phi. \tag{35}$$

Recollect that $\lambda\theta \geqslant 0$ and $\phi\zeta \geqslant 0$ hold by definition, whereas $A < 0$, $B < 0$, $M < 0$, and $N < 0$ hold under A2 and A3. Invoking the stability condition A4, we know that the first three terms in the RHS of (35) must be non-positive, if not negative. Note also that the remaining two terms are negative if $\theta\zeta < 0$; hence $\lambda\phi < 0$ holds. Therefore, if the capital intensity twist to the effect that $\theta\zeta < 0$, hence $\lambda\phi < 0$, holds, we know that $\Gamma < 0$.

Solving (34) for $\hat{q}$, we obtain[5]

$$\hat{q} = \frac{\phi\zeta - N\Lambda}{\Gamma}\left[\nabla_{\mathbf{S}} c(r, w; \mathbf{S}) + \frac{M\phi - N\theta}{\phi\zeta - N\Lambda}\boldsymbol{\eta} + \frac{M\Lambda - \theta\zeta}{\phi\zeta - N\Lambda}\nabla_{\mathbf{S}} C(q; r, w; \mathbf{S})\right]\cdot \mathrm{d}\mathbf{S}, \tag{36}$$

which is positive if and only if

$$\Phi := \frac{1}{\Gamma}\left[\nabla_{\mathbf{S}} c(r, w; \mathbf{S}) + \frac{M\phi - N\theta}{\phi\zeta - N\Lambda}\boldsymbol{\eta} + \frac{M\Lambda - \theta\zeta}{\theta\zeta - N\Lambda}\nabla_{\mathbf{S}} C(q; r, w; \mathbf{S})\right]\cdot \mathrm{d}\mathbf{S} > 0 \tag{37}$$

holds.

Invoking Theorem 1, we may now assert the following.

THEOREM 3. If A2, A3, and A4 are satisfied, then:

(*a*) the introduction of an infinitesimal production subsidy, which is accompanied by the self-financing lump-sum tax, is welfare-improving if capital intensity twist occurs;

(*b*) the introduction of an infinitesimal and uniform wage (capital) subsidy, which is accompanied by the self-financing lump-sum tax, is welfare-improving if industry X is less (more) capital-intensive in the marginal sense, but more (less) capital-intensive in the average sense, than industry Y.

Proof. (*a*) Let $\mathrm{d}\mathbf{S} = (\mathrm{d}s, 0, 0; -\mathrm{d}t, 0, 0)$ with $\mathrm{d}s > 0$ and $\mathrm{d}t > 0$. It follows from (37) that

$$\Phi = \frac{1}{\Gamma}\left[-\mathrm{d}s + \frac{M\Lambda - \theta\zeta}{\phi\zeta - N\Lambda}(\mathrm{d}t - q\mathrm{d}s)\right], \tag{38}$$

where $\mathrm{d}t = q\mathrm{d}s$ holds by virtue of the requirement of the self-financing tax subsidy scheme whereas capital intensity twist ensures that $\Gamma < 0$. It then follows from (38) that $\Phi > 0$, as required for welfare improvement.

(*b*) In the case of an infinitesimal and uniform wage subsidy, let $\mathrm{d}\mathbf{S} = (0, 0, \mathrm{d}s_w; -\mathrm{d}t, 0, \mathrm{d}s_w)$ with $\mathrm{d}s_w > 0$ and $\mathrm{d}t > 0$. By virtue of (37),

$$\Phi = \frac{1}{\Gamma}\left\{-\mathrm{d}s_w\left(c_w - \frac{M\phi - N\theta}{\phi\zeta - N\Lambda}\frac{\Lambda_V + \Lambda_F}{w}\right) + \frac{M\Lambda - \theta\zeta}{\phi\zeta - N\Lambda}[-\mathrm{d}s_w(qc_w + F_w) + \mathrm{d}t]\right\}, \tag{39}$$

the second term in the RHS thereof being zero by virtue of the requirement of the self-financing tax subsidy scheme. Thanks to the assumed capital intensity condition, we have $\theta < 0$ and $\phi > 0$, so that (39) ensures $\Phi > 0$, as required.

Similarly, in the case of an infinitesimal and uniform capital subsidy, let $\mathrm{d}\mathbf{S} = (0, \mathrm{d}s_r, 0; -\mathrm{d}t, \mathrm{d}s_r, 0)$ with $\mathrm{d}s_r > 0$ and $\mathrm{d}t > 0$. Then we have

$$\Phi = \frac{1}{\Gamma}\left\{-\mathrm{d}s_r\left(c_r - \frac{M\phi - N\theta}{\theta\zeta - N\Lambda}\frac{\Lambda_V + \Lambda_F}{r}\right) + \frac{M\Lambda - \theta\zeta}{\phi\zeta - N\Lambda}[-\mathrm{d}s_r(qc_r + F_r) + \mathrm{d}t]\right\}, \tag{40}$$

the second term in the RHS thereof being 0 by virtue of the requirement of the self-financing tax subsidy scheme. The assumed capital intensity condition asserts that $\theta > 0$ and $\phi < 0$, so that (40) ensures $\Phi > 0$ and we are home. □

It is required in Theorem 3 that each and every type of infinitesimal subsidy is accompanied by the self-financing lump-sum tax. What if the accompanying self-financing tax is not of the lump-sum category? In answering this question, a richer class of welfare-improving tax subsidy schemes can be identified. Indeed, we can establish the following.

THEOREM 4. Suppose that A2, A3, and A4 are satisfied. Then:

(*a*) the introduction of an infinitesimal production subsidy, which is accompanied by the self-financing tax on the wage (capital) expenditure component of fixed cost, is welfare-improving if industry X is more (less) capital-intensive in the marginal sense, but is less (more) capital-intensive in the average sense, than industry Y;

(*b*) the introduction of an infinitesimal subsidy on the wage (capital) expenditure component of marginal cost, which is accompanied by the self-financing tax on the capital (wage) expenditure component of fixed cost, is welfare-improving if industry X is less (more) capital-intensive in the marginal sense, but is more (less) capital-intensive in the average sense, than industry Y;

(*c*) the introduction of an infinitesimal subsidy on the capital (wage) expenditure component of fixed cost, which is accompanied by the self-financing tax on the wage (capital) expenditure component of fixed cost, is welfare-improving if industry X is more (less) capital-intensive in the marginal sense, but is less (more) capital-intensive in the average sense, than industry Y;

(*d*) the introduction of an infinitesimal subsidy on the capital (wage) expenditure component of marginal cost, which is accompanied by the self-financing tax on the wage (capital) expenditure component of marginal cost, is welfare-improving if industry X is more (less) capital-intensive in the marginal sense, but is less (more) capital-intensive in the average sense, than industry Y.

Proof. (*a*) Let $\mathrm{d}\mathbf{S} = (\mathrm{d}s, 0, 0; 0, 0, -\mathrm{d}t_w)$ with $\mathrm{d}s > 0$ and $\mathrm{d}t_w > 0$. Then we have

$$\Phi = \frac{1}{\Gamma}\left[-\mathrm{d}s + \frac{M\phi - N\theta}{\phi\zeta - N\Lambda}\left(-\frac{\Lambda_F}{w}\,\mathrm{d}t_w\right) + \frac{M\Lambda - \theta\zeta}{\phi\zeta - N\Lambda}(-q\mathrm{d}s + F_w\mathrm{d}t_w)\right], \qquad (41)$$

where the third term within brackets is 0 by virtue of the condition required for self-financing tax subsidy scheme. Therefore, $\Phi > 0$ holds if $\theta > 0$ and $\phi < 0$.

If $\mathrm{d}\mathbf{S} = (\mathrm{d}s, 0, 0; 0, -\mathrm{d}t_w, 0)$ with $\mathrm{d}s > 0$ and $\mathrm{d}t_w > 0$, we obtain

$$\Phi = \frac{1}{\Gamma}\left[-c_w\mathrm{d}s_w + \frac{M\phi - N\theta}{\phi\zeta - N\Lambda}\left(\frac{\Lambda_V}{w}\,\mathrm{d}s_w + \frac{\Lambda_F}{r}\,\mathrm{d}t_r\right)\right.$$

$$+ \frac{M\Lambda - \theta\zeta}{\phi\zeta - N\Lambda} (-qc_w \mathrm{d}s_w + F_r \mathrm{d}t_r) \Big], \tag{42}$$

where the third term within the parentheses disappears by virtue of the condition of self-financing tax-subsidy scheme. Therefore, $\Phi > 0$ holds if $\theta < 0$ and $\phi > 0$.

The case of capital subsidy (case (*b*)) can be treated similarly.

(*c*) Consider an infinitesimal tax subsidy scheme $\mathbf{dS} = (0, 0, 0; 0, \mathrm{d}s, -\mathrm{d}t)$ with $\mathrm{d}s\,\mathrm{d}t > 0$. Then we obtain

$$\Phi = \frac{1}{\Gamma}\left[-\Lambda_F \frac{M\phi - N\theta}{\theta\zeta - N\Lambda}\left(\frac{\mathrm{d}s}{r} + \frac{\mathrm{d}t}{w}\right) + \frac{M\Lambda - \theta\zeta}{\phi\zeta - N\Lambda}(-F_r \mathrm{d}s + F_w \mathrm{d}t)\right], \tag{43}$$

the second term within the parentheses being 0 by virtue of the self-financing requirement. Then $\Phi > 0$ holds if (i) $\mathrm{d}s > 0$, $\theta > 0$, and $\phi < 0$, or (ii) $\mathrm{d}s < 0$, $\theta < 0$, and $\phi > 0$.

(*d*) Consider an infinitesimal tax subsidy scheme $\mathbf{dS} = (0, \mathrm{d}s, -\mathrm{d}t; 0, 0, 0)$ with $\mathrm{d}s\,\mathrm{d}t > 0$. We then obtain

$$\Phi = \frac{1}{\Gamma}\Big[(-c_r \mathrm{d}s + c_w \mathrm{d}t) - \Lambda_V \frac{M\phi - N\theta}{\phi\zeta - N\Lambda}\left(\frac{\mathrm{d}s}{r} + \frac{\mathrm{d}t}{w}\right)$$

$$+ \frac{M\Lambda - \theta\zeta}{\phi\zeta - N\Lambda} q(-c_r \mathrm{d}s + c_w \mathrm{d}t)\Big], \tag{44}$$

the first and the third term within the parentheses being 0 by virtue of the condition of self-financing tax subsidy scheme. It follows that $\Phi > 0$ holds if (i) $\mathrm{d}s > 0$, $\theta > 0$, and $\phi < 0$, or (ii) $\mathrm{d}s < 0$, $\theta < 0$, and $\phi > 0$. □

6. CONCLUDING REMARKS

In this chapter we have identified several conditions for tax subsidy schemes in an oligopolistic economy to be welfare-improving. Our results in the case of entry regulation are summarized in Table 5 whereas those in the case of free entry are summarized in Table 6. Note that Table 6 keeps complete silence when the sign pattern of (λ, ϕ) is either (+, +) or (–, –). This is precisely where the excess entry theorem, established in the previous chapter, becomes relevant. In the absence of capital intensity twist, a marginal decrease in the number of oligopolistic firms unambiguously improves economic welfare irrespective of how such a decrease is brought about in the first place.

In concluding this chapter, some remarks on the implications of this analysis seem to be in order.

Table 5. Welfare-improving schemes in the case of entry regulation

λ	Welfare-improving tax subsidy schemes[a]
+	• Production subsidy • Uniform wage subsidy • Subsidy on wage expenditure component of fixed cost accompanied by tax on capital expenditure component of fixed cost
–	• Production subsidy • Uniform capital subsidy • Subsidy on capital expenditure component of fixed cost accompanied by tax on wage expenditure component of fixed cost

[a] λ: Index of relative capital intensity in the marginal sense.

Table 6. Welfare-improving schemes in the case of free entry

(λ, ϕ)	Welfare-improving tax subsidy schemes[a]
(+, –)	• Production subsidy • Uniform capital subsidy accompanied by self-financing lump-sum tax • Production subsidy accompanied by self-financing tax on wage expenditure component of fixed cost • Subsidy on capital expenditure component of marginal cost accompanied by self-financing tax on wage expenditure component of fixed cost • Subsidy on capital expenditure component of fixed cost accompanied by self-financing tax on wage expenditure component of fixed cost • Subsidy on capital expenditure component of marginal cost accompanied by self-financing tax on wage expenditure component of marginal cost
(–, +)	• Production subsidy • Uniform wage subsidy accompanied by self-financing lump-sum tax • Production subsidy accompanied by self-financing tax on capital expenditure component of fixed cost • Subsidy on wage expenditure component of marginal cost accompanied by self-financing tax on capital expenditure component of fixed cost • Subsidy on wage expenditure component of fixed cost accompanied by self-financing tax on capital expenditure component of fixed cost • Subsidy on wage expenditure component of marginal cost accompanied by self-financing tax on capital expenditure component of marginal cost

[a] λ: Index of relative capital intensity in the marginal sense.
ϕ: Index of relative capital intensity in the average sense.

First, it goes without saying that the first-best policy in an oligopolistic economy such as ours enforces the marginal cost principle on the incumbent firms while controlling the number of firms with a view to optimizing the welfare performance of the whole economy. Even when the first-best policy is beyond the reach of the actual imperfect government—for lack of enforcing power or otherwise—there may still remain room for the second-best policy by which the government, which is unable to control prices optimally, can nevertheless control the number of firms from the point of view of social welfare. This is where our analysis of the preceding two chapters is relevant. The situation with which we are concerned in this chapter is where the government lacks the leverage even to pursue the second-best policy and has to have recourse to the incentive-providing tax subsidy schemes. The relevance of such an analysis seems to be obvious in view of the weakening leverage of government *vis-à-vis* private economic agents in the government-assisted market economies.

Second, care should be taken in interpreting the policy implications of our results. Recollect that our model is based on several drastically simplifying assumptions, such as the Cournot–Nash quantity competition in the oligopolistic industry, the single consumer (in total neglect of equity issues), and the simple form of increasing returns through the existence of fixed cost. It should also be mentioned that the distinction between the capital and wage expenditure components of marginal cost and those of fixed cost is conceptually simple but is far from being simple in reality. The robustness and relevance of our results should be carefully examined before extracting any serious policy implications from our theoretical analysis.

NOTES TO CHAPTER 3

1. Recent studies on tax analysis in an imperfectly competitive economy are vast and include Anderson and Ballentine (1976), Atkinson and Stiglitz (1980: lect. 7), Besley (1989), Besley and Suzumura (1992), Katz and Rosen (1985), Konishi (1990), Konishi *et al.* (1990), Seade (1985), Stern (1987), and Willig (1983), among many others.
2. This is essentially what Th. 1 in Ch. 2 asserts.
3. Let the wage rate in the marginal cost component (the fixed cost component) of industry X be w_M^X (w_F^X). Likewise, let the rental rate of capital in the marginal cost component (the fixed cost component) of industry X be r_M^X (r_F^X). The wage rate and the rental rate of capital in industry Y are w and r, respectively. In the presence of an infinitesimal tax subsidy scheme, w_M^X (r_M^X) diverges from $w(r)$, and we have

$$\hat{w}_M^X - \hat{r}_M^X = \frac{\mathrm{d}w_M^X}{w_M^X} - \frac{\mathrm{d}r_M^X}{r_M^X} = \frac{\mathrm{d}w - \mathrm{d}s_w}{w} - \frac{\mathrm{d}r - \mathrm{d}s_r}{r} = \hat{\omega} - \frac{\mathrm{d}s_w}{w} + \frac{\mathrm{d}s_r}{r}. \qquad (1^*)$$

Similarly, w_F^X (r_F^X) diverges from $w(r)$, and we have

$$\hat{w}_F^X - \hat{r}_F^X = \hat{\omega} - \frac{\mathrm{d}t_w}{w} + \frac{\mathrm{d}t_r}{r}. \qquad (2^*)$$

Equations (1*) and (2*) are utilized in deriving (18) in the text.

4. The dynamic adjustment process defined by (26) and (27) represents the idea that price variables (p, r, w) adjust instantaneously, whereas the oligopolistic output, q, and the number of oligopolistic firms, n, adjust over time in response to the *marginal* profitability and the *overall* profitability, respectively.
5. We can also solve (34) for $\hat{n}$ and $\hat{\omega}$ and examine the effects of introducing an infinitesimal tax subsidy scheme on the equilibrium number of firms, on the one hand, and the effect thereof on the factor reward ratio, on the other. Since our focus in this chapter is on the welfare impact of tax subsidy schemes, the exploration of these issues is left to the interested reader.

II

Strategic Commitment and Economic Welfare

> If the essence of a game of strategy is the dependence of each person's proper choice of action on what he expects the other to do, it may be useful to define a 'strategic move' as follows: A strategic move is one that influences the other person's choice, in a manner favourable to one's self, by affecting the other person's expectations on how one's self will behave.
>
> Thomas Schelling, *The Strategy of Conflict*, 1960

One of the few important aspects of competition to which our analysis in Part I (where we focused on the welfare effects of long-run competitive forces) did not pay due attention is that each competitor can, and indeed often does, make a strategic move with a view to securing a competitive edge over rival firms. The purpose of Part II is to crystallize the welfare implications of this important aspect of competition among the few.

Examples of such strategic moves abound, but it should suffice to focus on what seems to be the most interesting case of cost-reducing R&D investment. The method of analysis developed will be applicable in analysing the welfare effects of many other types of strategic commitment in oligopoly.

Throughout Part II, the focus is on a two-stage model of oligopolistic competition where firms compete in R&D investments (quantities) in the first-stage game (the second-stage game). It is assumed that the R&D investment made in the first stage constitutes the strategic commitment on the part of an investing firm which cannot be rectified or nullified in the second stage. Assuming that the second-stage strategies, i.e. quantities, are strategic substitutes, we examine the subgame-perfect equilibrium of this two-stage game from the viewpoint of social welfare.

Chapter 4 shows that there is a wide range of cases where the strategic commitment is socially excessive at the margin if there are sufficiently many competitors. In Chapter 5, the welfare impact of excise tax subsidy in the presence of strategic commitment is examined. In Chapter 6 we expand our basic two-stage model of oligopolistic competition by introducing the spillover effects of cost-reducing R&D investment, the analytical focus of which is the comparison between non-co-operative and co-operative R&D from the viewpoint of social welfare.

4 Strategic R&D and Economic Welfare

1. INTRODUCTION

In Part I we focused on the welfare effects of long-run competitive forces and established that socially excessive firm entry robustly occurs in the unregulated Cournot oligopolistic markets. This happens because entry is sometimes more desirable to the entrant than to society, as new entry creates an incentive for incumbent firms to reduce their output. It follows that the long-run competitive forces are not to be blindly relied on as *the* efficient allocator of resources. How about the welfare effects of shorter-run competitive forces? Will competition among the fixed number of firms rehabilitate the welfare-improving efficacy of increasing competitiveness? This chapter will attempt to answer these questions.

The focus of our analysis is the strategic aspect of irrevocable cost-reducing R&D investment, which may create a socially inadequate commitment of economic resources. To summarize the impact of this strategic aspect of oligopolistic competition as succinctly as possible, we assume that the oligopolistic competition occurs in two stages. In the first stage, firms make an irrevocable decision on the level of cost-reducing R&D which, in turn, affects the production cost in the second stage of competition in the homogeneous product market. Since the cost-reducing R&D is a fixed commitment made in advance, firms' investment decisions are affected by strategic considerations, and we explore their welfare implications by examining the welfare performance of subgame-perfect equilibrium in the two-stage game.

It was Brander and Spencer (1983) who first analysed the subgame-perfect equilibrium of the two-stage game in the Cournot *duopolistic* market. Capitalizing partly on their seminal attempt, we show that there is a strong tendency towards socially excessive R&D at the margin. The crucial step in our analysis is the decomposition of the marginal welfare effects of additional R&D into what we may christen the *commitment effect* and the *distortion effect*. This decomposition helps us provide a clear economic interpretation of what lies behind the excess investment theorem we are going to establish in this chapter. Unlike Brander and Spencer, who analysed only the duopoly case, we allow an arbitrary number of firms. In fact, the effect of an increase in the number of firms on the likelihood of excessive R&D is one of our major concerns. Under fairly unrestrictive conditions, we show that there exists a critical number of firms above which strategic cost-reducing R&D becomes socially excessive at the margin if the second-stage strategic variables, i.e. outputs, are strategic substitutes.

The plan of this chapter is as follows. Section 2 introduces our basic model of the homogeneous product Cournot oligopoly game played in two stages. Sections 3 and 4 are devoted to the derivation of our *first-best excess investment theorem* and *second-best excess investment theorem*, respectively. Section 5 introduces product differentiation and shows that the second-best excess investment theorem is essentially preserved as far as firms compete in terms of quantities in the second-stage game. Section 6 concludes with several clarifying remarks.

2. TWO-STAGE MODEL OF OLIGOPOLISTIC COMPETITION

2.1. Basic assumptions

Consider an oligopolistic industry with n firms ($2 \leqslant n < +\infty$) producing a single homogeneous product. Throughout Part II, n is assumed to be fixed. The firms are engaging in a two-stage competition. In the first stage, each firm makes a strategic commitment to cost-reducing R&D investment in full anticipation of the equilibrium in the second stage, where firms compete in terms of quantities. Throughout our analysis the equilibrium concept is that of Nash, so that the equilibrium in the second-stage game is the Cournot–Nash equilibrium in quantities, and that of the entire game is the subgame-perfect equilibrium.

Let $p = f(Q)$ be inverse demand function for the product of this industry, where p and Q are, respectively, price and aggregate output of this product. Throughout this chapter, we assume that f satisfies the following assumption.

A1: $f(Q)$ is twice continuously differentiable and $f'(Q) < 0$ holds for all $Q \geqslant 0$ with $f(Q) > 0$. Furthermore, there exists a constant $\delta_0 > -\infty$ such that

$$\delta(Q) := Qf''(Q)/f'(Q) \geqslant \delta_0 \text{ for all } Q \geqslant 0 \text{ with } f(Q) > 0 \tag{1}$$

holds.

Note that the crucial second part of A1 is always satisfied by inverse demand functions which are constantly elastic. It is also clearly satisfied by concave (hence, *a fortiori*, linear) inverse demand functions. It is worth recalling that the concavity of inverse demand functions has been frequently assumed in the proof of the existence of a Cournot–Nash equilibrium (see e.g. Szidarovszky and Yakowitz 1977).

Turning to the supply side of our economy, let x_i and q_i denote, respectively, the cost-reducing R&D investment chosen by firm i in the first-stage game, and the output level chosen by firm i in the second-stage game. Let the second-stage variable cost function of firm i be $C(q_i; x_i)$, which is common for all firms. For simplicity, we make the following assumption.

A2: $C(q_i; x_i)$ is twice continuously differentiable for all $q_i > 0$ and $x_i > 0$, and it satisfies $C(q_i; x_i) := c(x_i)q_i$ with $c(x_i) > 0$ and $c'(x_i) < 0$ for all $x_i > 0$.

Clearly, $c(x_i)$ denotes the marginal as well as the average variable cost function of firm i, which is lower if firm i invests more in the first-stage game. In the second stage, however, x_i is the fixed commitment made in the past, and this cannot be nullified or rectified under any circumstance.

Given the R&D profile $\mathbf{x} = (x_1, \ldots, x_i, \ldots, x_n)$ chosen in the first-stage game, the second-stage payoff (profit) function of firm i is shown by

$$\pi_i(q_i, Q_{-i}; x_i) := [f(q_i + Q_{-i}) - c(x_i)]q_i - x_i, \tag{2}$$

where R&D level x_i is measured by the expenditure for equipment installation.

As an auxiliary step in introducing our strategic assumption in the second-stage game, let us define

$$\alpha_i(q_i, Q_{-i}; x_i) := \frac{\partial^2}{\partial q_i^2} \pi_i(q_i, Q_{-i}; x_i) \qquad (i = 1, 2, \ldots, n) \tag{3}$$

and

$$\beta_{ij}(q_i, Q_{-i}; x_i) := \frac{\partial^2}{\partial q_i \, \partial q_j} \pi_i(q_i, Q_{-i}; x_i) \qquad (i \neq j;\, i, j = 1, 2, \ldots, n). \tag{4}$$

Throughout this chapter, we will assume the following.

A3: The second-stage strategies are strategic substitutes: i.e.

$$\beta_{ij}(q_i, Q_{-i}; x_i) < 0 \qquad (i \neq j;\, i, j = 1, 2, \ldots, n)$$

holds for any $(q_i, Q_{-i}; x_i)$.

2.2. *Equilibrium concepts*

We are now at the stage of defining our equilibrium concepts. For each specified R&D profile $\mathbf{x}$, $\mathbf{q}^N(\mathbf{x}) = (q_1^N(\mathbf{x}), \ldots, q_i^N(\mathbf{x}), \ldots, q_n^N(\mathbf{x}))$ denotes the Cournot–Nash equilibrium of the second-stage game corresponding to the specified R&D profile $\mathbf{x}$. Throughout this chapter, we assume that $\mathbf{q}^N(\mathbf{x})$ is unique, symmetric, and positive if $\mathbf{x}$ is symmetric and positive.

Using the Cournot–Nash equilibrium of the second-stage game $\mathbf{q}^N(\mathbf{x})$, the first-stage payoff (profit) function of firm i is defined by

$$\Pi_i(\mathbf{x}) := \pi_i(q_i^N(\mathbf{x}), Q_{-i}^N(\mathbf{x}); x_i) \qquad (i = 1, 2, \ldots, n), \tag{5}$$

where $Q_{-i}^N(\mathbf{x}) = \Sigma_{j \neq i}\, q_j^N(\mathbf{x})$.
Let $\mathbf{x}^N = (x_1^N, \ldots, x_i^N, \ldots, x_n^N)$ denote the Cournot–Nash equilibrium of the first-stage game. In what follows, it is assumed that $\mathbf{x}^N$ is unique, symmetric, and positive.

Since the first-stage payoff functions are defined on the supposition that firms foresee what would happen at the second-stage Cournot–Nash equilibrium if they committed themselves to the R&D profile in the first-stage game, the pair $\{\mathbf{x}^N, \mathbf{q}^N(\mathbf{x}^N)\}$ is nothing other than the subgame-perfect equilibrium of the entire game.

2.3. Some properties of the second-stage Cournot–Nash equilibrium

Assuming interior optimum and second-order conditions, the second-stage Cournot–Nash equilibrium $\mathbf{q}^N(\mathbf{x})$ can be characterized by

$$f(Q^N(\mathbf{x})) + q_i^N(\mathbf{x})f'(Q^N(\mathbf{x})) = c(x_i) \qquad (i = 1, 2, \ldots, n), \tag{6}$$

where $Q^N(\mathbf{x}) = q_i^N(\mathbf{x}) + Q_{-i}^N(\mathbf{x})$. Furthermore, evaluating (3) and (4) at $\mathbf{q} = \mathbf{q}^N(\mathbf{x})$, we obtain

$$\alpha_i(q_i^N(\mathbf{x}), Q_{-i}^N(\mathbf{x}); x_i) = 2f'(Q^N(\mathbf{x})) + q_i^N(\mathbf{x})f''(Q^N(\mathbf{x})) \tag{7}$$

and

$$\beta_{ij}(q_i^N(\mathbf{x}), Q_{-i}^N(\mathbf{x}); x_i) = f'(Q^N(\mathbf{x})) + q_i^N(\mathbf{x})f''(Q^N(\mathbf{x})), \tag{8}$$

which imply that α_i and β_{ij} are independent of the indices of the firms if the R&D profile $\mathbf{x}$ is symmetric. Noting this fact, and invoking (1), we can rewrite (7) and (8) for symmetric $\mathbf{x}$ as follows:

$$\alpha(\mathbf{x}) = n^{-1}f'(Q^N(\mathbf{x}))[2n + \delta(Q^N(\mathbf{x}))] \quad . \tag{9}$$

and

$$\beta(\mathbf{x}) = n^{-1}f'(Q^N(\mathbf{x}))[n + \delta(Q^N(\mathbf{x}))], \tag{10}$$

where $\alpha(\mathbf{x}) := \alpha_i(q_i^N(\mathbf{x}), Q_{-i}^N(\mathbf{x}); x_i)$ and $\beta(\mathbf{x}) := \beta_{ij}(q_i^N(\mathbf{x}), Q_{-i}^N(\mathbf{x}); x_i)$ for short under the assumption of symmetry. It follows from A1, A3, (9) and (10) that $\alpha(\mathbf{x}) < \beta(\mathbf{x}) < 0$ and

$$n + \delta(Q^N(\mathbf{x})) > 0 \tag{11}$$

for any symmetric $\mathbf{x} > 0$ and the number of firms n.

In what follows it is crucially important to know how the Cournot–Nash equilibrium output $q_i^N(\mathbf{x})$ behaves in response to a change in x_i and x_j, where $i \neq j$. Since $q^N(\mathbf{x})$ is assumed symmetric if $\mathbf{x}$ is symmetric, we have only to examine the following two terms:

$$\omega(\mathbf{x}) := \frac{\partial}{\partial x_i} q_i^N(\mathbf{x}) \tag{12}$$

and

$$\theta(\mathbf{x}) := \frac{\partial}{\partial x_i} q_j^N(\mathbf{x}) \qquad (i \neq j)\ . \tag{13}$$

It will become clear that the following simple result plays an important role throughout our analysis in Part II.

LEMMA 1. For each symmetric R&D profile $\mathbf{x}$,

$$\omega(\mathbf{x}) = \frac{c'(x_i)}{\Delta(\mathbf{x})} [\alpha(\mathbf{x}) + (n-2)\beta(\mathbf{x})] > 0 \tag{14}$$

and

$$\theta(\mathbf{x}) = -\frac{c'(x_i)}{\Delta(\mathbf{x})} \beta(\mathbf{x}) < 0 \tag{15}$$

hold, where

$$\Delta(\mathbf{x}) := [\alpha(\mathbf{x}) - \beta(\mathbf{x})][\alpha(\mathbf{x}) + (n-1)\beta(\mathbf{x})] > 0. \tag{16}$$

Proof. Differentiating the first-order condition $(\partial/\partial q_i)\pi_i(q_i^N(\mathbf{x}), Q_{-i}^N(\mathbf{x}); x_i) = 0$ with respect to x_i and $x_h (h \neq i)$, we obtain

$$\sum_{j=1}^{n} \frac{\partial^2}{\partial q_i\, \partial q_j} \pi_i(q_i^N(\mathbf{x}), Q_{-i}^N(\mathbf{x}); x_i) \frac{\partial}{\partial x_i} q_j^N(\mathbf{x}) + \frac{\partial^2}{\partial q_i\, \partial x_i} \pi_i(q_i^N(\mathbf{x}), Q_{-i}^N(\mathbf{x}); x_i) = 0 \tag{17}$$

and

$$\sum_{j=1}^{n} \frac{\partial^2}{\partial q_i\, \partial q_j} \pi_i (q_i^N(\mathbf{x}), Q_{-i}^N(\mathbf{x}); x_i) \frac{\partial}{\partial x_h} q_j^N(\mathbf{x}) = 0 \qquad (h \neq i). \tag{18}$$

Rewriting (17) and (18) in terms of $\omega(\mathbf{x})$ and $\theta(\mathbf{x})$, we obtain

$$\begin{bmatrix} \alpha(\mathbf{x}) & (n-1)\beta(\mathbf{x}) \\ \beta(\mathbf{x}) & \alpha(\mathbf{x}) + (n-2)\beta(\mathbf{x}) \end{bmatrix} \begin{bmatrix} \omega(\mathbf{x}) \\ \theta(\mathbf{x}) \end{bmatrix} = \begin{bmatrix} c'(x_i) \\ 0 \end{bmatrix}, \tag{19}$$

which can be solved for $\omega(\mathbf{x})$ and $\theta(\mathbf{x})$ to obtain (14) and (15).

Positivity (negativity) of $\omega(\mathbf{x})(\theta(\mathbf{x}))$ follows from $\alpha(\mathbf{x}) < \beta(\mathbf{x}) < 0$ under A1 and A3. □

How about the effect of a change in x_i on the aggregate output at the second-stage Cournot–Nash equilibrium, i.e. $Q^N(\mathbf{x})$? It follows from (14) and (15) that we have

$$\frac{\partial}{\partial x_i} Q^N(\mathbf{x}) = \omega(\mathbf{x}) + (n-1)\theta(\mathbf{x})$$

$$= \frac{c'(x_i)}{\Delta(\mathbf{x})} [\alpha(\mathbf{x}) - \beta(\mathbf{x})]$$

$$> 0. \tag{20}$$

To summarize, we have shown that a marginal increase in firm i's cost-reducing R&D in the first-stage game increases (decreases) i's own output (i's rival's output) at the Cournot–Nash equilibrium in the second-stage game. It also increases the aggregate output at the second-stage Cournot–Nash equilibrium.

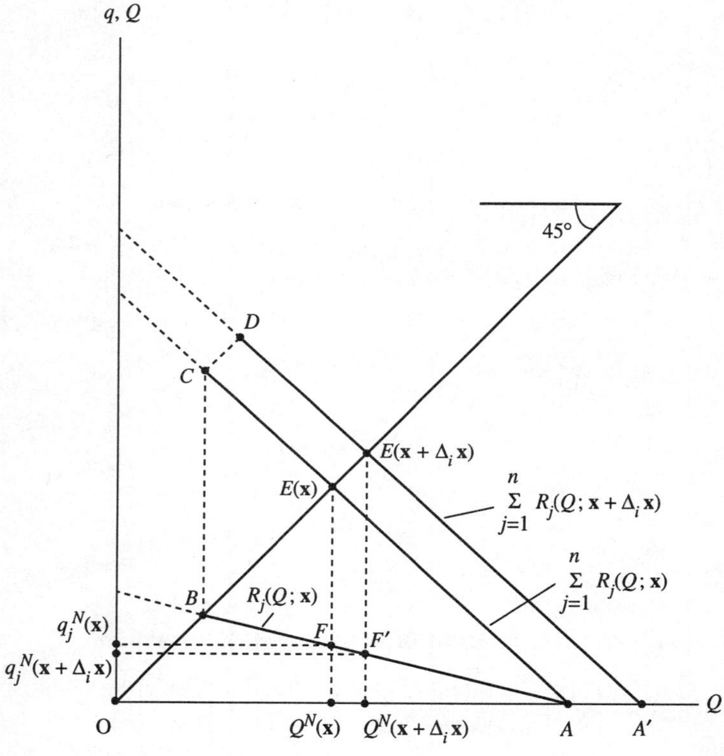

Fig. 10 Effects of a change in x_i on $q^N(\mathbf{x})$

These assertions can be easily illustrated in terms of the cumulative reaction function. In Fig. 10, where the horizontal (vertical) axis measures industry output (individual firm output as well as industry output), the curve $R_j(Q; \mathbf{x})$ denotes the cumulative reaction function of firm j when the first-stage R&D commitment is specified by $\mathbf{x}$. The point $E(\mathbf{x})$ at which the aggregate cumulative reaction curve $\Sigma_{j=1}^{n} R_j(Q; \mathbf{x})$ cuts the 45° line emanating from the origin determines the second-stage Cournot–Nash equilibrium $\mathbf{q}^N(\mathbf{x})$.

Suppose that the first-stage R&D commitment is changed by $\Delta_i\mathbf{x}$, where $\Delta_i x_i > 0$ and $\Delta_i x_j = 0$ for all $j \neq i$. This change in $\mathbf{x}$ shifts up firm i's cumulative reaction curve from $R_i(Q; \mathbf{x})$ to $R_i(Q; \mathbf{x} + \Delta_i\mathbf{x})$, whereas firm j's cumulative reaction curve remains intact for all $j \neq i$ in the absence of R&D spillovers. The second-stage Cournot–Nash equilibrium will change in response to this change in $\mathbf{x}$, and the equilibrium output of firm j (the equilibrium market output) will change from $q_j^N(\mathbf{x})$ to $q_j^N(\mathbf{x} + \Delta_i\mathbf{x})$ (from $Q^N(\mathbf{x})$ to $Q^N(\mathbf{x} + \Delta_i\mathbf{x})$. It is clear from Fig. 10 that $q_j^N(\mathbf{x}) > q_j^N(\mathbf{x} + \Delta_i\mathbf{x})$ and $Q^N(\mathbf{x}) < Q^N(\mathbf{x} + \Delta_i\mathbf{x})$, which in turn implies that $q_i^N(\mathbf{x}) < q_i^N(\mathbf{x} + \Delta_i\mathbf{x})$. This is precisely what we have asserted above.

3. FIRST-BEST EXCESS INVESTMENT THEOREM

3.1. First-best welfare criterion

How can we gauge the welfare performance of the subgame-perfect equilibrium $\{\mathbf{x}^N, \mathbf{q}^N(\mathbf{x}^N)\}$ which will be the spontaneous outcome of our two-stage competition? To begin with, we examine this problem from the viewpoint of the first-best government.

For each prescribed symmetric R&D profile $\mathbf{x} = (x_1, \ldots, x_i, \ldots, x_n)$, we define the *first-best output profile* $\mathbf{q}^F(\mathbf{x}) = (q_1^F(\mathbf{x}), \ldots, q_i^F(\mathbf{x}), \ldots, q_n^F(\mathbf{x}))$ by

$$f(Q^F(\mathbf{x})) = c(x_i) \qquad (i = 1, 2, \ldots, n), \tag{21}$$

where $Q^F(\mathbf{x}) = \Sigma_{j=1}^n q_j^F(\mathbf{x})$. Clearly, (21) is nothing other than the marginal cost principle in the model at hand. Comparing $\mathbf{q}^N(\mathbf{x})$ with $\mathbf{q}^F(\mathbf{x})$, we obtain the following useful property.

LEMMA 2. For each symmetric $\mathbf{x} > 0$, $q_i^F(\mathbf{x}) > q_i^N(\mathbf{x})$ $(i = 1, 2, \ldots, n)$ holds.

Proof. By virtue of the symmetry of $\mathbf{x}$, $\mathbf{q}^N(\mathbf{x})$ as well as $\mathbf{q}^F(\mathbf{x})$ is symmetric. Let $q^N(\mathbf{x})$ and $q^F(\mathbf{x})$ be the components of $\mathbf{q}^N(\mathbf{x})$ and $\mathbf{q}^F(\mathbf{x})$, respectively, which are common for all firms. By virtue of (6) and (21), we obtain

$$f(nq^F(\mathbf{x})) - f(nq^N(\mathbf{x})) = q^N(\mathbf{x})f'(nq^N(\mathbf{x})). \tag{22}$$

By virtue of the mean value theorem, there exists an $\eta(\mathbf{x})$ such that $0 < \eta(\mathbf{x}) < 1$, which satisfies

$$\begin{aligned} &f(nq^F(\mathbf{x})) - f(nq^N(\mathbf{x})) \\ &= n[q^F(\mathbf{x}) - q^N(\mathbf{x})]f'\{n[\eta(\mathbf{x})q^F(\mathbf{x}) + (1 - \eta(\mathbf{x}))q^N(\mathbf{x})]\}. \end{aligned} \tag{23}$$

It follows from A1, (22), and (23) that $q^F(\mathbf{x}) > q^N(\mathbf{x})$. □

Let us now define the net market surplus function in our present context by

$$W(\mathbf{x}, \mathbf{q}) := \int_0^Q f(Z)\mathrm{d}Z - \sum_{j=1}^{n} [c(x_j)q_j + x_j]. \tag{24}$$

In terms of $W(\mathbf{x}, \mathbf{q})$, the *first-best welfare criterion* can be defined by

$$W^F(\mathbf{x}) := W(\mathbf{x}, \mathbf{q}^F(\mathbf{x})), \tag{25}$$

the meaning of which should be clear by now.

3.2. *First-best excess investment theorem at the margin*

The first-best government, which seeks for the optimum optimorum, will try to implement a pair $\{\mathbf{x}^F, \mathbf{q}^F(\mathbf{x}^F)\}$, where $\mathbf{x}^F$ will be defined by

$$\mathbf{x}^F := \arg\max_{\mathbf{x} > 0} W^F(\mathbf{x}). \tag{26}$$

How will the subgame-perfect equilibrium $\{\mathbf{x}^N, \mathbf{q}^N(\mathbf{x}^N)\}$, which will be the outcome when there is no interference in the competitive forces, fare *vis-à-vis* the socially first-best pair $\{\mathbf{x}^F, \mathbf{q}^F(\mathbf{x}^F)\}$ in terms of social welfare? Our answer to this first question can be unambiguous if we are ready to strengthen A3 into the following.

A3*: $f(Q)$ is concave; i.e. $f''(Q) \leqslant 0$ holds for all $Q \geqslant 0$ such that $f(Q) > 0$.

THEOREM 1 (FIRST-BEST EXCESS INVESTMENT THEOREM AT THE MARGIN). Under A1, A2, and A3*, the subgame-perfect level of R&D is socially excessive at the margin with respect to the first-best welfare criterion as long as $n \geqslant 3$.

Proof. Differentiating (25) with respect to x_i and invoking (21), we obtain

$$\frac{\partial}{\partial x_i} W^F(\mathbf{x}) = -q_i^F(\mathbf{x})c'(x_i) - 1. \tag{27}$$

By definition, $\mathbf{x}^N$ is characterized by

$$\sum_{j=1}^{n} \frac{\partial}{\partial q_j} \pi_i (q_i^N(\mathbf{x}^N), Q_{-i}^N(\mathbf{x}^N); x_i^N) \frac{\partial}{\partial x_i} q_j^N(\mathbf{x}^N) + \frac{\partial}{\partial x_i} \pi_i(q_i^N(\mathbf{x}^N), Q_{-i}^N(\mathbf{x}^N); x_i^N) = 0 \quad (i = 1, 2, \ldots, n) \tag{28}$$

which can be reduced into

$$-q_i^N(\mathbf{x}^N)c'(x_i^N) - 1 = -(n-1)f'(Q^N(\mathbf{x}^N))q_i^N(\mathbf{x}^N)\theta(\mathbf{x}^N). \tag{29}$$

Evaluating (27) at $\mathbf{x} = \mathbf{x}^N$ and invoking (22), (23), and (29), we obtain

$$\frac{\partial}{\partial x_i} W^F(\mathbf{x}^N) = q^N(\mathbf{x}^N) f'(Q^N(\mathbf{x}^N)) \left[-\frac{c'(x_i^N)}{nf'(Q(\eta))} - (n-1)\theta(\mathbf{x}^N) \right], \tag{30}$$

where $Q(\eta) := n\{\eta(\mathbf{x}^N)q^F(\mathbf{x}^N) + [1 - \eta(\mathbf{x}^N)]q^N(\mathbf{x}^N)\}$ for short.

Invoking Lemma 2 and A3*, we can ascertain that $f'(Q(\eta)) < f'(Q^N(\mathbf{x}^N))$, so that we have

$$-\frac{c'(x_i^N)}{nf'(Q(\eta))} - (n-1)\theta(\mathbf{x}^N) > -\frac{c'(x_i^N)}{nf'(Q^N(\mathbf{x}^N))} \left[1 - (n-1)\frac{n + \delta(Q^N(\mathbf{x}^N))}{1 + n + \delta(Q^N(\mathbf{x}^N))} \right], \tag{31}$$

where use is made of (9), (10), and (15). It follows from (30) and (31) that $(\partial/\partial x_i) W^F(\mathbf{x}^N) < 0$ holds if

$$1 < (n-1)\frac{n + \delta(Q^N(\mathbf{x}^N))}{1 + n + \delta(Q^N(\mathbf{x}^N))}. \tag{32}$$

Thanks to A1 and A3*, we have $\delta(Q^N(\mathbf{x}^N)) \geqslant 0$, so that (32) can be reduced to

$$n^2 + [\delta(Q^N(\mathbf{x}^N)) - 2]n - 2\delta(Q^N(\mathbf{x}^N)) - 1 > 0, \tag{33}$$

which is satisfied irrespective of the value of $\delta(Q^N(\mathbf{x}^N))$ if $n > 1 + \sqrt{2}$. Therefore, $(\partial/\partial x_i) W^F(\mathbf{x}^N) < 0$ holds as long as $n \geqslant 3$. □

4. SECOND-BEST EXCESS INVESTMENT THEOREM

4.1. *Second-best welfare criterion*

According to Theorem 1, the subgame-perfect level of cost-reducing R&D investment is socially excessive at the margin with respect to the first-best welfare criterion in the sense that a small decrease of R&D investment by firm i from x_i^N unambiguously increases the first-best social welfare if the stipulated conditions are satisfied. Although this welfare verdict at the margin is neat and informative, an exclusive reliance on the first-best welfare criterion may be rather questionable, as any government would be unable in practice to enforce the first-best marginal cost principle. At the very least, it is worth while examining the robustness of this first-best welfare verdict by analysing the second-best welfare performance of the subgame-perfect level of R&D. In so doing, we can also liberate our analysis from the rather restrictive assumption of concave inverse demand functions, i.e. A3*. With this objective in mind, let us define the *second-best welfare criterion* in our present context as

$$W^S(\mathbf{x}) := W(\mathbf{x}, \mathbf{q}^N(\mathbf{x})). \tag{34}$$

It is worth while explaining the rationale for invoking this second-best criterion, at the risk of slight repetition. Recollect that the first-best policy prescription requires the government to control the level of R&D investment as well as the level of output of each firm. Realistically, however, this is difficult to implement; and, if ever it is implemented, it is likely to create additional distortions of its own. For one thing, marginal cost pricing, which is required by the first-best output control, necessitates additional tax revenue for the purpose of making up for firms' deficits, and this will inevitably create tax distortions unless an ideal lump-sum tax is available. For another thing, controlling the number of firms within an industry by regulating entry and exit of firms may slacken long-run competitive pressure, thereby creating organizational inefficiencies within incumbent firms. In contrast, the second-best policy starts from the recognition either that the government lacks the power to enforce the first-best policy or that such a policy creates a prohibitive amount of distortion. Instead, it is assumed that controlling the level of cost-reducing R&D investment is possible by means of tax subsidy or other measures, and it does not create any extra distortion. This is the modest requirement of an actual government which our second-best welfare criterion tries to formulate.

4.2. Decomposition of the marginal welfare effect

Invoking the second-best welfare criterion, we can gauge the second-best performance of the subgame-perfect equilibrium $\{\mathbf{x}^N, \mathbf{q}^N(\mathbf{x}^N)\}$ by evaluating the partial derivative $(\partial/\partial x_i)\, W^S(\mathbf{x})$ at $\mathbf{x} = \mathbf{x}^N$.

By differentiating (34) with respect to x_i, and evaluating the outcome at $\mathbf{x} = \mathbf{x}^N$, we obtain

$$\frac{\partial}{\partial x_i} W^S(\mathbf{x}^N) = \gamma_i(\mathbf{x}^N) + \delta_i(\mathbf{x}^N), \tag{35}$$

where

$$\gamma_i(\mathbf{x}^N) := -q_i^N(\mathbf{x}^N)c'(x_i^N) - 1 \tag{36}$$

and

$$\delta_i(\mathbf{x}^N) := \sum_{j=1}^{n} \left[f(Q^N(\mathbf{x}^N)) - c(x_j^N)\right] \frac{\partial}{\partial x_i} q_j^N(\mathbf{x}^N). \tag{37}$$

The term $\gamma_i(\mathbf{x}^N)$ is what we call the *commitment effect* of a change in x_i, and the term $\delta_i(\mathbf{x}^N)$ may be christened the *distortion effect* of a change in x_i. Throughout this Part of the book, the decomposition of the marginal welfare effect into these economically meaningful terms plays an important role.

To understand the meaning of the commitment effect, let us consider the auxiliary problem of social welfare maximization *in the absence of strategic commitment*, which takes the following form:

$$(\mathbf{x}^*, \mathbf{q}^*) = \arg \max_{(\mathbf{x}, \mathbf{q}) > 0} W(\mathbf{x}, \mathbf{q}). \tag{38}$$

Clearly, $(\mathbf{x}^*, \mathbf{q}^*)$ is characterized by

$$f(Q^*) = c(x_i^*) \qquad (i = 1, 2, \ldots, n) \tag{39}$$

and

$$-q_i^* c'(x_i^*) - 1 = 0 \qquad (i = 1, 2, \ldots, n), \tag{40}$$

where $Q^* = \Sigma_{i=1}^n q_i^*$. Comparing (36) with (40), it is clear that $\gamma_i(\mathbf{x}^N)$ can be different from 0 only by the presence of strategic commitment. Hence the term 'commitment effect'. Note also that we may utilize two first-order conditions, one characterizing $\mathbf{q}^N(\mathbf{x}^N)$ and another characterizing $\mathbf{x}^N$, to rewrite $\gamma_i(\mathbf{x}^N)$ as follows:[1]

$$\gamma_i(\mathbf{x}^N) = (n-1)\mu(\mathbf{x}^N)\theta(\mathbf{x}^N), \tag{41}$$

where $\mu(\mathbf{x}^N)$ denotes the *marginal distortion* at the subgame-perfect equilibrium $\{\mathbf{x}^N, \mathbf{q}^N(\mathbf{x}^N)\}$; i.e.

$$\mu(\mathbf{x}^N) := f(Q^N(\mathbf{x}^N)) - c(x_i^N), \tag{42}$$

which is positive by virtue of (6) and (27).

On the other hand, the meaning of the distortion effect $\delta_i(\mathbf{x}^N)$ is easy to understand. When a marginal change in x_i takes place, a marginal change in firm j's output by the amount of $(\partial/\partial x_i)q_j^N(\mathbf{x}^N)$, i.e. $\omega(\mathbf{x}^N)$ if $i = j$ and $\theta(\mathbf{x}^N)$ if $i \neq j$, will be thereby induced and this will create a distortional impact on social welfare in proportion to the marginal distortion $\mu(\mathbf{x}^N)$. Our distortion effect simply adds together these distortional impacts over all firms. It is clear that $\delta_i(\mathbf{x}^N)$ can be rewritten as follows:

$$\delta_i(\mathbf{x}^N) = \mu(\mathbf{x}^N)[\omega(\mathbf{x}^N) + (n-1)\theta(\mathbf{x}^N)]. \tag{43}$$

4.3. *Second-best excess investment theorem at the margin*

Substituting (41) and (43) into (35) we obtain

$$\frac{\partial}{\partial x_i} W^S(\mathbf{x}^N) = \mu(\mathbf{x}^N)\,[\omega(\mathbf{x}^N) + 2(n-1)\theta(\mathbf{x}^N)]. \tag{44}$$

Invoking Lemma 1, (44) can be further reduced to

$$\frac{\partial}{\partial x_i} W^S(\mathbf{x}^N) = \frac{c'(x_i^N)\mu(\mathbf{x}^N)}{\Delta(\mathbf{x}^N)}\,[\alpha(\mathbf{x}^N) - n\beta(\mathbf{x}^N)]. \tag{45}$$

Under A1, A2, and A3, (45) clearly implies that $\operatorname{sgn}(\partial/\partial x_i) W^S(\mathbf{x}^N)$ is determined by the sign of $[n\beta(\mathbf{x}^N) - \alpha(\mathbf{x}^N)]$, i.e. by the sign of the quadratic form $\{-[n^2 + \delta(Q^N(\mathbf{x}^N))(n-1) - 2n]\}$. Recollect now that, by virtue of the latter part of A1, we have $\delta(Q^N(\mathbf{x}^N)) \geqslant \delta_0$. It then follows that $(\partial/\partial x_i) W^S(\mathbf{x}^N) < 0$ if

$$\phi(n{:}\ \delta_0) := n^2 + (n-1)\delta_0 - 2n > 0. \tag{46}$$

Let $N(\delta_0)$ be the largest real root of the quadratic equation $\phi(n{:}\ \delta_0) = 0$.[2] It is clear that $N(\delta_0) > 0$, and we obtain

$$\frac{\partial}{\partial x_i} W^S(\mathbf{x}^N) < 0 \qquad \text{holds if} \qquad n > N(\delta_0). \tag{47}$$

We have thus established the following.

THEOREM 2 (SECOND-BEST EXCESS INVESTMENT THEOREM AT THE MARGIN). Under A1, A2, and A3, there exists a critical number of firms $N(\delta_0)$ such that the subgame-perfect level of R&D is socially excessive at the margin with respect to the second-best welfare criterion if $n > N(\delta_0)$ holds.

An important question in relation to Theorem 2 still remains: how large is the critical number of firms $N(\delta_0)$? If $N(\delta_0)$ turns out to be unrealistically large, say 1,000,000 or even 1,000, the relevance of our Theorem 2 will be lost completely. Fortunately, we can actually compute the value of $N(\delta_0)$ for some relevant class of inverse demand functions. In the case of concave inverse demand functions, i.e. under A3*, we may always set $\delta_0 = 0$, so that $N(\delta_0)$ turns out to be exactly 2. Therefore, in this case the conclusion of Theorem 2 applies to *all* oligopoly models where $3 \leqslant n < +\infty$.

Let us consider now the case of inverse demand functions where $\delta(Q) = \delta$ (constant), which can be represented as

$$f(Q) = \begin{cases} a - bQ^{\delta+1} & \text{if } \delta \neq -1 \\ a - b\log Q & \text{if } \delta = -1, \end{cases} \tag{48}$$

where a is a non-negative constant and b is another constant such that $b > 0$ ($b < 0$) if $\delta \geqslant -1$ ($\delta < -1$). In this case, the critical number of firms $N(\delta_0)$, where $\delta_0 = \delta$, depends on the value of δ, but it remains fairly small for a wide variation of the values of δ (see Table 7).

4.4 Diagrammatical illustration

Why should the commitment effect dominate the distortion effect as the number of firms becomes larger? To throw some light on the intuition behind Theorem 2, let us rewrite (35) by using (37) and (41) as follows:

$$\frac{\partial}{\partial x_i} W^S(\mathbf{x}^N) = \mu(\mathbf{x}^N)\frac{\partial}{\partial x_i} Q^N(\mathbf{x}^N)\left[1 - (n-1)\frac{-(\partial/\partial x_i)q_j^N(\mathbf{x}^N)}{(\partial/\partial x_i)Q^N(\mathbf{x}^N)}\right], \tag{49}$$

where $i \neq j$. Since $\mu(\mathbf{x}^N)(\partial/\partial x_i)Q^N(x^N) > 0$, the sign of the LHS is determined by the sign of the term within the square brackets in (49). To understand how this crucial terms behaves as n increases, let us have another look at Fig. 10, which describes the second-stage Cournot–Nash equilibrium $E(\mathbf{x})$ as a point where the aggregate cumulative reaction curve $\Sigma_{j=1}^{n} R_j(Q; \mathbf{x})$ cuts the 45° line emanating from the origin. Suppose now that firm i unilaterally increases R&D marginally, changing $\mathbf{x}$ into $\mathbf{x} + \Delta_i\mathbf{x}$, where $\Delta_i\mathbf{x} := (0, \ldots, 0, \overset{(i)}{\varepsilon}, 0, \ldots, 0)$ and $\varepsilon > 0$. Then the aggregate cumulative reaction curve shifts up to $\Sigma_{j=1}^{n} R_j(Q; \mathbf{x} + \Delta_i\mathbf{x})$, where $R_j(Q; \mathbf{x} + \Delta_i\mathbf{x}) = R_j(Q; \mathbf{x})$ for all $j \neq i$. As a result, the aggregate output increases by $Q^N(\mathbf{x} + \Delta_i\mathbf{x}) - Q^N(\mathbf{x})$, whereas the output of firm j, where $j \neq i$, decreases by $q_j^N(\mathbf{x}) - q_j^N(\mathbf{x} + \Delta_i\mathbf{x})$. The ratio between the two output changes, which closely approximates the crucial term $-(\partial/\partial x_i)q_j^N(\mathbf{x})/(\partial/\partial x_i)Q^N(\mathbf{x})$ if $\varepsilon > 0$ is sufficiently small, is given by the absolute slope of $R_j(Q; \mathbf{x})$, which is independent of n. Therefore, as n increases, $(\partial/\partial x_i)W^S(\mathbf{x})$ for $\mathbf{x} = \mathbf{x}^N$ becomes negative, as we set out to show.

Table 7. Critical number of firms[a]

δ	$N(\delta_0)$
− 5	6.19
− 4	5.24
− 3	4.30
− 2	3.41
− 1	2.62
0	2
1	1.62
2	1.41
3	1.30
4	1.24
5	1.19

[a] For each value of $\delta = \delta_0$, $N(\delta_0)$ is computed in accordance with the formula $N(\delta_0) = \frac{1}{2}[2 - \delta + \sqrt{(4 + \delta^2)}]$.

5. COURNOT–NASH COMPETITION WITH PRODUCT DIFFERENTIATION

5.1. Demand side of a Cournot market with product differentiation

Up to this point, our analysis has presupposed that firms produce identical products. In order to demonstrate that our excess investment theorem is not squarely contingent on the homogeneity of industry output, let us briefly examine the welfare performance of a Cournot market with differentiated products.

To start with, we assume that the utility function of a representative consumer is given by

$$U(\mathbf{q}, r) = u(\mathbf{q}) + r, \tag{50}$$

where $\mathbf{q} = (q_1, \ldots, q_i, \ldots, q_n)$ is a profile of differentiated products and r is the numeraire good, both consumed by the representative consumer. The budget constraint of the representative consumer is given by

$$\sum_{i=1}^{n} p_i q_i + r = M, \tag{51}$$

where p_i is price of the ith product and M is income of the consumer. Let $(\mathbf{q}^*, r^*)$ be the optimal consumption plan that maximizes $U(\mathbf{q}, r)$ subject to (51). It is easy to verify that $\mathbf{q}^*$ is independent of M by virtue of the quasi-linearity of $U(\mathbf{q}, r)$, so that we may write $\mathbf{q}^* := \mathbf{q}(\mathbf{p}) = (q^1(\mathbf{p}), \ldots, q^i(\mathbf{p}), \ldots, q^n(\mathbf{p}))$ and $r^* := r(\mathbf{p}, M)$, where $\mathbf{p} = (p_1, \ldots, p_i, \ldots, p_n)$ is a profile of prices.

Let the indirect utility function be defined by

$$\begin{aligned} V(\mathbf{p}, M) &:= U(\mathbf{q}(\mathbf{p}), r(\mathbf{p}, M)) \\ &= u(\mathbf{q}(\mathbf{p})) - \sum_{i=1}^{n} p_i q^i(\mathbf{p}) + M, \end{aligned} \tag{52}$$

where use is made of (51). To simplify our notation, let us define

$$v(\mathbf{p}) := u(\mathbf{q}(\mathbf{p})) - \sum_{i=1}^{n} p_i q^i(\mathbf{p}). \tag{53}$$

It is assumed that $u(\mathbf{q})$ and $v(\mathbf{p})$ satisfy the following:

A4: $u(\mathbf{q})$ and $v(\mathbf{p})$ are symmetric functions which are twice continuously differentiable; $u(\mathbf{q})$ is concave and $v(\mathbf{p})$ is convex; demand curves are downward-sloping and products are ordinary substitutes; i.e.

$$\begin{aligned} q^i_i(\mathbf{p}) &:= (\partial/\partial p_i) q^i(\mathbf{p}) < 0 \qquad (i = 1, 2, \ldots, n) \\ q^i_j(\mathbf{p}) &:= (\partial/\partial p_j) q^i(\mathbf{p}) > 0 \qquad (i \neq j;\ i, j = 1, 2, \ldots, n). \end{aligned} \tag{54}$$

Note that Roy's identity entails

$$v_i(\mathbf{p}) := (\partial/\partial p_i) v(\mathbf{p}) = -q^i(\mathbf{p}) \qquad (i = 1, 2, \ldots, n), \tag{55}$$

whereas the first-order condition for utility maximization is given by

$$u_i(\mathbf{q}(\mathbf{p})) := (\partial/\partial q_i)u(\mathbf{q}(\mathbf{p})) = p_i \qquad (i = 1, 2, \ldots, n). \tag{56}$$

Differentiating (56) with respect to p_i and p_j $(i \neq j)$, we obtain

$$\sum_{k=1}^{n} u_{ik}(\mathbf{q}(\mathbf{p}))q_i^k(\mathbf{p}) = 1 \tag{57}$$

and

$$\sum_{k=1}^{n} u_{ik}(\mathbf{q}(\mathbf{p}))q_j^k(\mathbf{p}) = 0 \qquad (i \neq j), \tag{58}$$

where $u_{ik}(\mathbf{q}(\mathbf{p})) := (\partial^2/\partial q_i\, \partial q_k)u(\mathbf{q}(\mathbf{p}))$ and $q_j^k(\mathbf{p}) := (\partial/\partial p_j)q^k(\mathbf{p})$. Suppose that $\mathbf{p}$ and $\mathbf{q}$ are symmetric, so that $p_i = p_j$ and $q_i = q_j$ $(i, j = 1, 2, \ldots, n)$ are satisfied. Then (57) and (58) can be reduced to

$$\begin{bmatrix} u_{ii} & (n-1)u_{ik} \\ u_{ik} & u_{ii} + (n-2)u_{ik} \end{bmatrix} \begin{bmatrix} q_i^i \\ q_i^k \end{bmatrix} = \begin{bmatrix} 1 \\ 0 \end{bmatrix} \qquad (i \neq k), \tag{59}$$

where we have omitted independent variables of all functions for notational simplicity. Solving (59) for q_i^i and $q_i^k (i \neq k)$, we obtain

$$q_i^i = \frac{1}{\Theta}[u_{ii} + (n-2)u_{ik}] \tag{60a}$$

$$q_k^i = -\frac{u_{ik}}{\Theta} \qquad (i \neq k), \tag{60b}$$

where $\Theta := (u_{ii} - u_{ik})\,[u_{ii} + (n-1)u_{ik}]$. In order that (54) holds for any n, it is necessary and sufficient that

$$u_{ii} < u_{ik} < 0 \qquad (i \neq k;\ i, k = 1, 2, \ldots, n) \tag{61}$$

is satisfied.

5.2. *Supply side of a Cournot market with product differentiation*

There are n firms $(2 \leqslant n < +\infty)$ in the industry which are producing related but differentiated products. They engage in the two-stage game of oligopolistic competition, where the strategic variable of firm i in the first (or the second) stage is the cost-reducing R&D investment x_i (or the level of output q_i). Let the cost function of firms i be $C(q_i; x_i)$, which is identical for all firms. The following assumption is made.

A5: $C(q; x)$ is twice continuously differentiable and its partial derivatives $C_q(q; x) := (\partial/\partial q)C(q; x)$, $C_x(q; x) := (\partial/\partial x)C(q; x)$, $C_{qq}(q; x) :=$

$(\partial^2/\partial q^2)C(q; x)$, $C_{xx}(q; x) := (\partial^2/\partial x^2)C(q; x)$ and $C_{qx}(q; x) := (\partial^2/\partial q\, \partial x)$ $C(q; x)$ satisfy

$$\left.\begin{array}{lll} C_q(q; x) \geqslant 0, & C_x(q; x) < 0, & C_{qq}(q; x) \geqslant 0, \\ C_{xx}(q; x) > 0, & \text{and } C_{qx}(q; x) < 0 & \end{array}\right\} \tag{62}$$

for all $(q; x) > 0$.

Thus, marginal cost is always non-negative and non-decreasing in output. The R&D investment is cost-reducung at a decreasing rate, and R&D investment always decreases the marginal cost of production.

5.3. Subgame-perfect equilibrium

Given the R&D profile $\mathbf{x} = (x_1, \ldots, x_i, \ldots, x_n)$ chosen in the first-stage game, the second-stage payoff function of firm i is defined by

$$\pi_i(\mathbf{q}; x_i) := q_i u_i(\mathbf{q}) - C(q_i; x_i). \tag{63}$$

Assuming interior optimum and second-order conditions, the second-stage Cournot–Nash equilibrium $\mathbf{q}^N(\mathbf{x}) = (q_1^N(\mathbf{x}), \ldots, q_i^N(\mathbf{x}), \ldots, q_n^N(\mathbf{x}))$ can be characterized by

$$\frac{\partial}{\partial q_i}\pi_i(\mathbf{q}^N(\mathbf{x}); x_i) = u_i(\mathbf{q}^N(\mathbf{x})) + q_i^N(\mathbf{x})u_{ii}(\mathbf{q}^N(\mathbf{x})) - C_q(q_i^N(\mathbf{x}); x_i)$$

$$= 0 \qquad (i = 1, 2, \ldots, n). \tag{64}$$

It is assumed that $\mathbf{q}^N(\mathbf{x})$ is unique, symmetric, and positive if the R&D profile $\mathbf{x}$ is symmetric and positive.

Using $\mathbf{q}^N(\mathbf{x})$, the first-stage payoff function of firm i can be defined by

$$\Pi_i(\mathbf{x}) := \pi_i(\mathbf{q}^N(\mathbf{x}); x_i) \qquad (i = 1, 2, \ldots, n). \tag{65}$$

Assuming interior optimum and second-order conditions, the first-stage Cournot–Nash equilibrium $\mathbf{x}^N = (x_1^N, \ldots, x_i^N, \ldots, x_n^N)$ can be characterized by

$$\frac{\partial}{\partial x_i}\Pi_i(\mathbf{x}^N) = [u_i(\mathbf{q}^N(\mathbf{x}^N)) - C_q(q_i^N(\mathbf{x}^N); x_i^N)]\frac{\partial}{\partial x_i}q_i^N(\mathbf{x}^N)$$

$$+ q_i^N(\mathbf{x}^N)\sum_{j=1}^{n} u_{ij}(\mathbf{q}^N(\mathbf{x}^N))\frac{\partial}{\partial x_i}q_j^N(\mathbf{x}^N) - C_x(q_i^N(\mathbf{x}^N); x_i^N)$$

$$= 0. \tag{66}$$

In what follows, the focus of our analysis is the welfare performance of the subgame-perfect equilibrium $\{\mathbf{x}^N, \mathbf{q}^N(\mathbf{x}^N)\}$ in terms of the second-best market surplus function:

$$W^S(\mathbf{x}) := u(\mathbf{q}^N(\mathbf{x})) - \sum_{i=1}^{n} C(q_i^N(\mathbf{x}); x_i). \tag{67}$$

5.4. *Displacement of the second-stage Cournot–Nash equilibrium*

To see how the second-stage Cournot–Nash equilibrium $\mathbf{q}^N(\mathbf{x})$ responds to a change in x_i and x_h $(h \neq i)$, we define $\alpha(\mathbf{x}) := (\partial^2/\partial q_i^2)\pi_i(\mathbf{q}^N(\mathbf{x}); x_i)$; $\beta(\mathbf{x}) := (\partial^2/\partial q_i\, \partial q_j)\pi_i(\mathbf{q}^N(\mathbf{x}); x_i)$; $\omega(\mathbf{x}) := (\partial/\partial x_i)q_i^N(\mathbf{x})$; and $\theta(\mathbf{x}) := (\partial/\partial x_i)\, q_j^N(\mathbf{x})$ $(i \neq j)$; where $\mathbf{x}$ is a specified symmetric R&D profile.[3]

Differentiating (64) with respect to x_i and $x_h(h \neq i)$, we may obtain the following equations system for $\omega(\mathbf{x})$ and $\theta(\mathbf{x})$:

$$\begin{bmatrix} \alpha(\mathbf{x}) & (n-1)\beta(\mathbf{x}) \\ \beta(\mathbf{x}) & \alpha(\mathbf{x}) + (n-2)\beta(\mathbf{x}) \end{bmatrix} \begin{bmatrix} \omega(\mathbf{x}) \\ \theta(\mathbf{x}) \end{bmatrix} = -\begin{bmatrix} \gamma(\mathbf{x}) \\ 0 \end{bmatrix}, \tag{68}$$

where

$$\gamma(\mathbf{x}) := -C_{qx}(q_i^N(\mathbf{x}); x_i) > 0 \tag{69}$$

by virtue of assumption A5. Solving (68) for $\omega(\mathbf{x})$ and $\theta(\mathbf{x})$, we obtain

$$\begin{aligned} \omega(\mathbf{x}) &= -\frac{\gamma(\mathbf{x})}{\Delta(\mathbf{x})}[\alpha(\mathbf{x}) + (n-2)\beta(\mathbf{x})] \\ \theta(\mathbf{x}) &= \frac{\gamma(\mathbf{x})}{\Delta(\mathbf{x})}\beta(\mathbf{x}), \end{aligned} \tag{70}$$

where $\Delta(\mathbf{x}) := [\alpha(\mathbf{x}) - \beta(\mathbf{x})]\,[\alpha(\mathbf{x}) + (n-1)\beta(\mathbf{x})]$.

To give definite sign to (70), we now introduce the following strategic and stability assumptions.[4]

A6: The second-stage strategies are strategic substitutes; i.e. $\beta(\mathbf{x}) < 0$ hold for any symmetric x.

A7: $\alpha(\mathbf{x}) + (k-1)\beta(\mathbf{x}) < 0$ holds for any $k = 0, 1, \ldots, n$ and any symmetric $\mathbf{x}$.

It is clear now that $\omega(\mathbf{x}) > 0$ and $\theta(\mathbf{x}) < 0$ hold for any symmetric $\mathbf{x}$. It is also clear that

$$\begin{aligned} \frac{\partial}{\partial x_i} Q^N(\mathbf{x}) = \omega(\mathbf{x}) + (n-1)\theta(\mathbf{x}) &= \frac{\gamma(\mathbf{x})}{\Delta(\mathbf{x})}[\alpha(\mathbf{x}) - \beta(\mathbf{x})] \\ &> 0. \end{aligned} \tag{71}$$

holds for any symmetric x. It would be unnecessary to reiterate the meaning of (70) and (71).

5.5. Second-best excess investment theorem under product differentiation

We are now in the stage of examining if the second-best excess investment theorem can be carried over to the case of Cournot oligopoly with product differentiation. With this purpose in mind, we differentiate (67) with respect to x_i and evaluate at $\mathbf{x}^N$ to obtain

$$\frac{\partial}{\partial x_i} W^S(\mathbf{x}^N) = \gamma_i(\mathbf{x}^N) + \delta_i(\mathbf{x}^N), \tag{72}$$

where the *commitment effect* $\gamma_i(\mathbf{x}^N)$ is defined by

$$\gamma_i(\mathbf{x}^N) = -C_x(q_i^N(\mathbf{x}^N); x_i^N), \tag{73}$$

whereas the *distortion effect* $\delta_i(\mathbf{x}^N)$ is defined by

$$\delta_i(\mathbf{x}^N) = \sum_{j=1}^{n} [u_j(\mathbf{q}^N(\mathbf{x}^N)) - C_q(q_j^N(\mathbf{x}^N); x_j^N)] \frac{\partial}{\partial x_i} q_j^N(\mathbf{x}^N). \tag{74}$$

Invoking (64) at $\mathbf{x} = \mathbf{x}^N$ and (66), $\gamma_i(\mathbf{x}^N)$ may be reduced to

$$\begin{aligned}\gamma_i(\mathbf{x}^N) &= -q_i^N(\mathbf{x}^N) \sum_{j \neq i} u_{ij}(\mathbf{q}^N(\mathbf{x}^N)) \frac{\partial}{\partial x_i} q_j^N(\mathbf{x}^N) \\ &= [u_i(\mathbf{q}^N(\mathbf{x}^N)) - C_q(q_i^N(\mathbf{x}^N); x_i^N)] \sum_{j \neq i} \frac{u_{ij}(\mathbf{q}^N(\mathbf{x}^N))}{u_{ii}(\mathbf{q}^N(\mathbf{x}^N))} \theta(\mathbf{x}^N). \end{aligned} \tag{75}$$

Note that the assumption of symmetry enables us to rewrite (74) and (75) as follows:

$$\delta_i(\mathbf{x}^N) = [u_i(\mathbf{q}^N(\mathbf{x}^N)) - C_q(q_i^N(\mathbf{x}^N); x_i^N)] [\omega(\mathbf{x}^N) + (n-1)\theta(\mathbf{x}^N)] \tag{76}$$

and

$$\gamma_i(\mathbf{x}^N) = (n-1)[u_i(\mathbf{q}^N(\mathbf{x}^N) - C_q(q_i^N(\mathbf{x}^N); x_i^N)] \frac{u_{ij}(\mathbf{q}^N(\mathbf{x}^N))}{u_{ii}(\mathbf{q}^N(\mathbf{x}^N))} \theta(\mathbf{x}^N). \tag{77}$$

By virtue of assumption A4 and (64) at $\mathbf{x} = \mathbf{x}^N$, the marginal distortion of firm i, viz. $u_i(\mathbf{q}^N(\mathbf{x}^N)) - C_q(q_i^N(\mathbf{x}^N); x_i^N)$, must be positive, so that we can conclude from (72), (76), and (77) that $(\partial/\partial x_i) W^S(\mathbf{x}^N) > (<) \; 0$ if and only if

$$\omega(\mathbf{x}^N) + (n-1)\theta(\mathbf{x}^N)\left[1 + \frac{u_{ij}(\mathbf{q}^N(\mathbf{x}^N))}{u_{ii}(\mathbf{q}^N(\mathbf{x}^N))}\right] > (<) \; 0. \tag{78}$$

Invoking (70) at $\mathbf{x} = \mathbf{x}^N$, (78) can be reduced to

$$\frac{\alpha(\mathbf{x}^N) - \beta(\mathbf{x}^N)}{\beta(\mathbf{x}^N)} > (<)\ (n-1)\,\frac{u_{ij}(\mathbf{q}^N(\mathbf{x}^N))}{u_{ii}(\mathbf{q}^N(\mathbf{x}^N))}, \tag{79}$$

where use is also made of (69), and assumptions A6 and A7. It follows from (79) that *the subgame-perfect R&D investment* $\mathbf{x}^N$ *is likely to become socially excessive at the margin as the term* $\alpha(\mathbf{x}^N)/\beta(\mathbf{x}^N)$ *becomes smaller, and the term* $(n-1)u_{ij}(\mathbf{q}^N(\mathbf{x}^N))$ *becomes larger.*

Note that the term

$$\frac{\alpha(\mathbf{x}^N)}{\beta(\mathbf{x}^N)} = \frac{(\partial^2/\partial q_i^2)\pi_i(\mathbf{q}^N(\mathbf{x}^N);\, x_i^N)}{(\partial^2/\partial q_i\,\partial q_j)\pi_i(\mathbf{q}^N(\mathbf{x}^N);\, x_i^N)}, \tag{80}$$

which may duly be christened the *degree of strategic insusceptibility*, is inversely related to the absolute slope of the reaction function of a representative firm.[5] As $\alpha(\mathbf{x}^N)/\beta(\mathbf{x}^N)$ becomes larger, a change in a firm's strategic variable (output) induces smaller response from other firms. On the other hand, when $u_{ij}(\mathbf{q}^N(\mathbf{x}^N))$ becomes larger (in absolute value) *vis-à-vis* $u_{ii}(\mathbf{q}^N(\mathbf{x}^N))$, products become closer ordinary substitutes.[6]

To sum up our analysis so far, we have established the following.

THEOREM 3. Under A4, A5, A6, and A7, the subgame-perfect level of R&D is more likely to be socially excessive at the margin with respect to the second-best welfare criterion as

(*a*) the degree of strategic insusceptibility becomes smaller,
(*b*) the products become closer ordinary substitutes, and
(*c*) the number of firms *n* becomes larger.

In order to bring the message of Theorem 3 into clearer relief, let us consider a special case where demand functions are linear, hence $u_{ii}(\mathbf{q}^N(\mathbf{x}^N))$ and $u_{ij}(\mathbf{q}^N(\mathbf{x}^N))$ are constant—say u_{ii}^0 and u_{ij}^0, respectively. In this case, it is readily verified that $\alpha(\mathbf{x}^N) = 2u_{ii}^0 - C_{qq}(q_i^N(\mathbf{x}^N);\, x_i^N)$ and $\beta(\mathbf{x}^N) = u_{ij}^0$. Defining $\rho := u_{ij}^0/u_{ii}^0$, we are now assured that $(\partial/\partial x_i)W^S(\mathbf{x}^N) > (<)\ 0$ if and only if

$$-\frac{C_{qq}(q_i^N(\mathbf{x}^N);\, x_i^N)}{u_{ii}^0} > (<)\ (n-1)\rho^2 + \rho - 2, \tag{81}$$

which enables us to assert the following.

THEOREM 4. Suppose that assumptions A4, A5, and A7 hold.[7] Suppose further that the demand functions are linear, and that there exists a constant c_0, $0 \leqslant c_0 < +\infty$ such that $C_{qq}(q;\, x) \leqslant c_0$ holds for any $(q;\, x) > 0$. Then there exists a positive number $M(c_0;\, \rho)$ such that $(\partial/\partial x_i)W^S(\mathbf{x}^N) < 0$ holds; hence the subgame-perfect level of R&D investment is socially excessive at the margin with respect to the second-best welfare criterion, if $n > M(c_0;\, \rho)$ holds.

Proof. Let $M(c_0; \rho)$ be defined by[8]

$$M(c_0; \rho) := 1 + \frac{1}{\rho^2}\left(2 - \rho - \frac{c_0}{u_{ii}^0}\right) > 0. \tag{82}$$

Suppose that $n > M(c_0; \rho)$. Then we have

$$(n-1)\rho^2 + \rho - 2 > -\frac{c_0}{u_{ii}^0} \geqslant -\frac{C_{qq}(q_i^N(\mathbf{x}^N); x_i^N)}{u_{ii}^0}, \tag{83}$$

so that (81) entails $(\partial/\partial x_i) W^S(\mathbf{x}^N) < 0$. □

If, in particular, $C(q; x) = c(x)q + x$ holds, we have $C_{qq}(q; x) = 0$, so that $c_0 = 0$ will suffice. Then the critical number of firms becomes $M(0; \rho) = 1 + (2 - \rho)/\rho^2$. Clearly, $M(0; \rho)$ decreases as ρ increases. Even when ρ is as small as 0.5, however, the critical number of firms remains as small[9] as $M(0; 0.5) = 7$.[10]

6. CONCLUDING REMARKS

In this chapter we have identified several conditions, which are not altogether unlikely, under which socially excessive R&D investment might occur at the subgame-perfect equilibrium in a two-stage model of oligopolistic competition. As far as the homogeneous product Cournot oligopoly is concerned, there exists a robust tendency towards socially excessive R&D investment, in both the first-best and the second-best sense, as long as the number of firms is sufficiently large. Moreover, for several important special cases we have shown that the number of firms above which socially excessive R&D investment is created does not seem to be too large. We have also shown that this tendency towards socially excessive commitment with R&D investment will not be lost altogether in the presence of product differentiation so long as the firms compete in terms of quantities in the product market. The crucial message of these results seems simply to be as follows: even in the context of shorter-run competition among the fixed number of firms, the welfare-improving efficacy of unregulated competitive forces cannot be blindly relied upon.

Given this persistent tendency towards socially excessive cost-reducing R&D investment, what is a welfare-improving policy measure that does not take recourse to directly interventionist regulation of R&D activities? The exploration of this important question is the task we assign to Chapter 5.

NOTES TO CHAPTER 4

1. Note that the first-order condition $(\partial/\partial q_i)\pi_i(q_i^N(\mathbf{x}^N), Q_{-i}^N(\mathbf{x}^N); x_i) = 0$ implies

$$f(Q^N(\mathbf{x}^N)) + q_i^N(\mathbf{x}^N))f'(Q^N(\mathbf{x}^N)) = c(x_i^N) \tag{1*}$$

which is nothing other than (6) in the text at $\mathbf{x} = \mathbf{x}^N$, whereas the first-order condition $(\partial/\partial x_i)\Pi_i(\mathbf{x}^N) = 0$ implies

$$-q_i^N(\mathbf{x}^N)c'(x_i^N) - 1 = -[f(Q^N(\mathbf{x}^N)) - c(x_i^N)]\frac{\partial}{\partial x_i}q_i^N(\mathbf{x}^N)$$

$$- q_i^N(\mathbf{x}^N)f'(Q^N(\mathbf{x}^N))\frac{\partial}{\partial x_i}Q^N(\mathbf{x}^N). \tag{2*}$$

Substituting (1*) and (2*) into (36) in the text, we are home.

2. Since $D := (\delta_0 - 2)^2 + 4\delta_0 = \delta_0^2 + 4 > 0$, it is clear that $\phi(n\colon \delta_0) = 0$ must have two real roots.
3. Thanks to the assumption of symmetric equilibria, $\alpha(\mathbf{x})$, $\beta(\mathbf{x})$, $\omega(\mathbf{x})$, and $\theta(\mathbf{x})$ need not be suffixed by firm indices.
4. Recollect that the stability condition need not be explicitly assumed in the case of homogeneous output Cournot oligopoly as it is implied by other (more basic) assumptions; see S. 2 in Ch. 1 and S. 2.2 in the present chapter.
5. Let $q_i = r_i(Q_{-i}; \mathbf{x})$ be the reaction function of firm i, which is defined by

$$\frac{\partial}{\partial q_i}\pi_i(r_i(Q_{-i}; \mathbf{x}), Q_{-i}; \mathbf{x}) = 0. \tag{3*}$$

Then we have $(\partial/\partial q_j)r_i(Q_{-i}^N(\mathbf{x}^N); \mathbf{x}^N) = -\beta(\mathbf{x}^N)/\alpha(\mathbf{x}^N)$.

6. By virtue of assumption A4, it follows from (61) that $u_{ij}(\mathbf{q}^N(\mathbf{x}^N))/u_{ii}(\mathbf{q}^N(\mathbf{x}^N))$ has an upper bound 1. When this upper bound is actually attained, products become perfect substitutes and our criterion (79) for socially excessive or insufficient R&D investment boils down to the criterion (45) for the case of homogeneous output Cournot oligopoly.
7. If demand functions are linear, we are assured that $\beta(\mathbf{x}^N) = u_{ij}^0 < 0$, so that we need not require A6 as an independent assumption.
8. In view of (61), it is clear that $0 < \rho < 1$.
9. Although it is perfectly natural to require the assumption of strategic substitutability (A6) in our present context of quantity competition in the product market, it is not inconceivable that outputs are strategic complements. If this happens to be the case, i.e. if $\beta(\mathbf{x}) > 0$ holds for any symmetric $\mathbf{x}$, it follows from (70) and A7 that $\omega(\mathbf{x}) > 0$ and $\theta(\mathbf{x}) > 0$ for any symmetric $\mathbf{x}$. Therefore, (78) entails an unambiguous conclusion that $(\partial/\partial x_i)W^S(\mathbf{x}^N) > 0$; that is, *the subgame-perfect level of R&D investment is socially insufficient at the margin with respect to the second-best welfare criterion if the strategic complementarity prevails.*
10. The case where firms compete in terms of prices rather than quantities in the second stage of our two-stage game will be treated in a generalized context later on; see S. 7 in Ch. 8.

5 Taxation and Welfare with Strategic Commitment

1. INTRODUCTION

There are many distinct contexts in which understanding the effects of a cost change in an oligopolistic industry is of crucial importance. Despite the recent upsurge of interest in this class of problems, however, the situation where firms compete in more than one stage—competition with strategic commitment—has not yet been properly worked out. The aim of this chapter is to examine systematically the positive as well as normative effects of a cost change in an oligopoly model with strategic commitment. Although our analysis is conducted in terms of a cost change induced by the introduction of tax subsidy scheme, our method of analysis certainly has wider applicability.

As in the previous chapter, our analytical framework is a two-stage game of oligopolistic competition, and our equilibrium concept is that of subgame-perfect equilibrium. In the first stage of this game, firms compete by making a strategic commitment with cost-reducing R&D investment.[1] At the second stage they engage in Cournot–Nash quantity competition. Within this analytical framework, we can pose, and settle, several interesting questions concerning comparative statics.

Our first main result is a version of the Le Chatelier–Samuelson principle for a wide range of cases.[2] This principle says that a shift of the second-stage tax subsidy rate to a change in output always has the same sign when the strategic commitment is brought in as when it is ignored, but the former effect is strictly greater in absolute value than the latter effect. The second main result of our analysis is concerned with the welfare effects of a change in the second-stage tax subsidy scheme in an oligopoly model with strategic commitment. Although the comparative statics of the subgame-perfect equilibrium adds significantly to analytical complexity, our welfare verdicts are strikingly thorough and simple. It is shown that an excise tax (excise subsidy) always decreases (increases) welfare in what we shall refer to as 'normal' cases.

Besides these main results, this chapter explores the possibility of oligopolistic price overshifting and of profitable cost increase in the presence of strategic commitment. Furthermore, it compares the effect of capital taxation, which shifts the first-stage strategic variables, and that of commodity taxation, which shifts the second-stage strategic variables.

Despite the growing interest in tax analysis when competition is less than perfect, the existing literature does not include strategic commitment made by competing firms.[3] Nor does it consider the comparative statics of the subgame-perfect equilibrium.[4] Hence our analysis represents the first systematic investigation of the normative as well as positive consequences of commodity taxation when oligopolists commit themselves to cost-reducing R&D prior to the output levels being determined by Cournot–Nash competition.

The structure of the chapter is as follows. Section 2 reviews the two-stage model of oligopolistic competition with a tax subsidy scheme. In Section 3 we explore the possibility of price overshifting and profitable cost increase, and establish the Le Chatelier–Samuelson principle in our game-theoretic context. Section 4 turns to the question of oligopoly and welfare. For expositional simplicity, some technical details are relegated to Section 5, and conclusions are drawn in Section 6.

2. TWO-STAGE MODEL OF OLIGOPOLY WITH TAXATION

2.1. Basic assumptions on the second-stage game

Our model is essentially the same as in Chapter 4 save for the introduction of a tax subsidy scheme. Thus, we examine an oligopolistic industry involving n firms, where $2 \leqslant n < +\infty$, which produce a single homogeneous product. In this chapter we assume that n is fixed.[5] The firms compete in two stages. In the first stage, each firm chooses its strategic cost-reducing R&D investment, while in the second stage each firm chooses its output. The choice in the first stage is a commitment made prior to the commencement of production, which cannot be modified or nullified in the second stage. The inverse demand function $p = f(Q)$, where p is price and Q is industry output, is assumed to satisfy the following.

A1: The inverse demand function $f(Q)$ is three times continuously differentiable and satisfies $f'(Q) < 0$ for all $Q \geqslant 0$ such that $f(Q) > 0$.

Firm i's cost function is assumed to take the form $c(x_i; \xi)q_i + x_i$, where q_i and x_i represent, respectively, firm i's output and its cost-reducing R&D investment, which is measured, as in Chapter 4, in terms of the expenditure for equipment installation. We use ξ to denote a shift parameter that is common for all firms. The following is assumed.

A2: The average variable cost function $c(x_i; \xi)$ is twice continuously differentiable and satisfies $c(x_i; \xi) = \phi(x_i) + \psi(\xi)$ with $\phi'(x_i) < 0$ and $\phi''(x_i) > 0$.

Hence the R&D investment x_i is cost-reducing at a decreasing rate, and the shift parameter ξ, which affects the marginal cost positively (as in the case of excise tax) or negatively (as in the case of excise subsidy), does not alter the marginal efficiency of cost-reducing investment. Note that it is assumed that the shape of the cost function is the same for all firms, and that there exist no R&D spillovers.[6]

Let $\mathbf{x} = (x_1, \ldots, x_i, \ldots, x_n)$ denote an R&D profile. The second-stage payoff function of firm i is then given by

$$\pi_i(q_i, Q_{-i}, x_i; \xi) := \{f(q_i + Q_{-i}) - c(x_i; \xi)\}q_i - x_i. \tag{1}$$

Assuming interior optimum and second-order conditions, the Cournot–Nash equilibrium of the second-stage game corresponding to a specified R&D profile $\mathbf{x}$ and a shift parameter ξ, to be denoted by $\mathbf{q}^N(\mathbf{x}; \xi) = (q_1^N(\mathbf{x}; \xi), \ldots, q_i^N(\mathbf{x}; \xi), \ldots, q_n^N(\mathbf{x}; \xi))$, is characterized by

$$f(Q^N(\mathbf{x}; \xi)) + q_i^N(\mathbf{x}; \xi)f'(Q^N(\mathbf{x}; \xi)) = c(x_i; \xi) \qquad (i = 1, 2, \ldots, n), \tag{2}$$

where $Q^N(\mathbf{x}; \xi) = \Sigma_{j=1}^n q_j^N(\mathbf{x}; \xi)$. Throughout, we shall focus on the symmetric equilibrium; i.e. $q_i^N(\mathbf{x}; \xi) = q_j^N(\mathbf{x}; \xi) = q^N(\mathbf{x}; \xi)$, say, for all i, j as far as $\mathbf{x}$ is in itself symmetric, viz. $x_i = x_j$ for all i, j.

As an auxiliary step in introducing our strategic assumption on the second-stage game, let us define $\alpha_i(q_i, Q_{-i}, \mathbf{x}; \xi) := (\partial^2/\partial q_i^2)\pi_i(q_i, Q_{-i}, x_i; \xi)$ and $\beta_{ij}(q_i, Q_{-i}, \mathbf{x}; \xi) := (\partial^2/\partial q_i\, \partial q_j)\pi_i(q_i, Q_{-i}, x_i; \xi)$ $(i \neq j;\ i, j = 1, 2, \ldots, n)$, which help us introduce the following standard strategic assumption.

A3: The strategic variables in the second-stage game are strategic substitutes; i.e. $\beta_{ij}(q_i, Q_{-i}, \mathbf{x}; \xi) < 0$ $(i \neq j)$ holds for any $(q_i, Q_{-i}, \mathbf{x}; \xi)$.

As in Chapter 4, we can verify that

$$\alpha_i(q_i^N(\mathbf{x}; \xi), Q_{-i}^N(\mathbf{x}; \xi), \mathbf{x}; \xi) = 2f'(Q^N(\mathbf{x}; \xi)) + q_i^N(\mathbf{x}; \xi)f''(Q^N((\mathbf{x}; \xi)) \tag{3}$$

and

$$\beta_{ij}(q_i^N(\mathbf{x}; \xi), Q_{-i}^N(\mathbf{x}; \xi), \mathbf{x}; \xi) = f'(Q^N(\mathbf{x}; \xi)) + q_i^N(\mathbf{x}; \xi)f''(Q^N(\mathbf{x}; \xi)) \tag{4}$$

hold, so that the index of firms can be dropped altogether from α and β as far as $\mathbf{x}$ is symmetric. Since $Q^N(\mathbf{x}; \xi) = nq^N(\mathbf{x}; \xi)$ holds for symmetric $\mathbf{x}$, we can rewrite (3) and (4) under the assumption of symmetric equilibrium as follows:

$$\alpha(q_i^N(\mathbf{x}; \xi), Q_{-i}^N(\mathbf{x}; \xi), \mathbf{x}; \xi) = f'(Q^N(\mathbf{x}; \xi))\,[2 + n^{-1}\delta(Q^N(\mathbf{x}; \xi))] \tag{5}$$

and

$$\beta(q_i^N(\mathbf{x}; \xi), Q_{-i}^N(\mathbf{x}; \xi), \mathbf{x}; \xi) = f'(Q^N(\mathbf{x}; \xi))\,[1 + n^{-1}\delta(Q^N(\mathbf{x}; \xi))], \tag{6}$$

where $\delta(Q) := Qf''(Q)/f'(Q)$ is the elasticity of slope of the inverse demand function. It follows from (6) and A1 that A3 holds for symmetric $\mathbf{x}$ if and only if

$$n + \delta(Q^N(\mathbf{x}; \xi)) > 0. \tag{7}$$

It is also worth noticing that $\alpha(q_i^N(\mathbf{x}; \xi), Q_{-i}^N(\mathbf{x}; \xi), \mathbf{x}; \xi) < 0$ holds for symmetric x under A1 and A3. Furthermore, we can show that the symmetric Cournot–Nash equilibrium $\mathbf{q}^N(\mathbf{x}; \xi)$, where $\mathbf{x}$ is a symmetric R&D profile, is locally stable under the myopic adjustment process *à la* Cournot which is specified by $\dot{q}_i = \sigma(\partial/\partial q_i)\pi_i(q_i, Q_{-i}, x_i; \xi)$ $(i = 1, 2, \ldots, n)$, where $\dot{q}_i$ is the rate of change in q_i and $\sigma > 0$ is the adjustment coefficient in the presence of A1 and A3.[7]

2.2. *Basic assumptions on the first-stage game*

Turning to the first-stage game, let the first-stage payoff function of firm i be defined by

$$\Pi_i(\mathbf{x}; \xi) := \pi_i(q_i^N(\mathbf{x}; \xi), Q_{-i}^N(\mathbf{x}; \xi), x_i; \xi)$$

$$= [f(Q^N(\mathbf{x}; \xi)) - c(x_i; \xi)]\, q_i^N(\mathbf{x}; \xi) - x_i. \tag{8}$$

Assuming interior optimum and second-order conditions, the first-stage Cournot–Nash equilibrium $\mathbf{x}^N(\xi)$ can be characterized by

$$f'(Q^N(\mathbf{x}^N(\xi); \xi))\, q_i^N(\mathbf{x}^N(\xi); \xi) \sum_{j \neq i} (\partial/\partial x_i)\, q_j^N(\mathbf{x}^N(\xi); \xi)$$

$$-\phi'(x_i^N(\xi))\, q_i^N(\mathbf{x}^N(\xi); \xi) - 1 = 0 \qquad (i = 1, 2, \ldots, n). \tag{9}$$

In what follows it is assumed that $\mathbf{x}^N(\xi)$ is symmetric, i.e. that $x_i^N(\xi) = x_j^N(\xi) = x^N(\xi)$, say, for all i, j. The equilibrium of the whole game, which is nothing but the subgame-perfect equilibrium of the two-stage game, is defined by $\{\mathbf{x}^N(\xi), \mathbf{q}^N(\mathbf{x}^N(\xi); \xi)\}$ for each ξ. In what follows we shall focus on the displacement of this subgame-perfect equilibrium in response to a change in the second-stage shift parameter ξ.

As an auxiliary step in introducing the strategic assumption on the first-stage game, let us define

$$\lambda_i(\mathbf{x}; \xi) := \frac{\partial^2}{\partial x_i^2} \Pi_i(\mathbf{x}; \xi) \qquad (i = 1, 2, \ldots, n) \tag{10}$$

and

$$\mu_{ij}(\mathbf{x}; \xi) := \frac{\partial^2}{\partial x_i\, \partial x_j} \Pi_i(\mathbf{x}; \xi) \qquad (i \neq j;\ i, j = 1, 2, \ldots, n). \tag{11}$$

As in the second-stage game, we require that the following strategic assumption is satisfied in the first-stage game.

A4: The strategic variables in the first-stage game are strategic substitutes; i.e. $\mu_{ij}(\mathbf{x}; \xi) < 0 (i \neq j)$ holds for any $(\mathbf{x}; \xi)$.

To bring an important implication of the assumption A4 into clearer relief, note that a simple computation yields

$$\lambda(\xi) := \lambda_i(\mathbf{x}^N(\xi); \xi)$$

$$= -\frac{(\phi')^2 q_i^N \nu^N(\xi)}{f'[1 + n + \delta^N(\xi)]} - \eta^N(\xi) \left\{ \phi'' q_i^N + \frac{(\phi')^2 \left[n + \frac{n-1}{n} \delta^N(\xi) \right]}{f'[1 + n + \delta^N(\xi)]} \right\} \tag{12}$$

and

$$\mu(\xi) := \mu_{ij}(\mathbf{x}^N(\xi); \xi)$$

$$= \frac{(\phi')^2}{f'[1 + n + \delta^N(\xi)]} \left\{ -q_i^N \nu^N(\xi) + \eta^N(\xi) \left[1 + \frac{\delta^N(\xi)}{n} \right] \right\}, \tag{13}$$

where $\delta^N(\xi) := \delta(Q^N(\mathbf{x}^N(\xi); \xi))$,

$$\eta(Q) := 1 + \frac{n-1}{n} \frac{n + \delta(Q)}{1 + n + \delta(Q)}, \tag{14}$$

$\eta^N(\xi) := \eta(Q^N(\mathbf{x}^N(\xi); \xi))$, and $\nu^N(\xi) := \eta'(Q^N(\mathbf{x}^N(\xi); \xi))$, and all functions appearing in (12) and (13), are evaluated at the subgame-perfect equilibrium $\{\mathbf{x}^N(\xi), \mathbf{q}^N(\mathbf{x}^N(\xi); \xi)\}$. For the sake of avoiding lengthy expressions, we have omitted arguments from many functions. We have also omitted the firm indices from $\lambda(\xi)$ and $\mu(\xi)$ by virtue of the assumption of symmetric equilibria. Invoking A1 and A3, it follows from A4 and (13) that

$$\eta^N(\xi)[n + \delta^N(\xi)] > \nu^N(\xi) Q^N(\mathbf{x}^N(\xi); \xi) \tag{15}$$

holds, which proves crucially important in our subsequent analysis.

At this juncture, it is worth while clarifying the relationship between (7) and (15). Note that (7) ((15)) is the crucial implication of strategic substitutability in the second-stage game (in the first-stage game). Consider now an interesting example where $\delta(Q)$ remains constant, i.e. the case where the inverse demand function is in the class defined by (49) in Chapter 4. This class of inverse demand functions, which includes the constant elasticity and linear inverse demand functions as two important special cases, is the most general class permitting the constancy of $\delta(Q)$.[8] Since $\nu^N(\xi) = 0$ holds for this class of inverse demand functions, (7) for $\mathbf{x} = \mathbf{x}^N(\xi)$ and (14) for $Q = Q^N(\mathbf{x}^N(\xi); \xi)$ entail that (15) must necessarily hold. This is reassuring, since (49) in Chapter 4 subsumes quite a wide class of regularly used inverse demand functions.

As a final preliminary step, we introduce an assumption that guarantees the local stability of the symmetric Cournot–Nash equilibrium $\mathbf{x}^N(\xi)$ under the myopic adjustment process $\dot{x}_i = \tau(\partial/\partial x_i)\Pi_i(\mathbf{x};\xi)(i = 1, 2, \ldots, n)$, where $\dot{x}_i$ denotes the rate of change in x_i and $\tau > 0$ denotes the adjustment coefficient. In Section 5.1 we show that the following assumption serves to guarantee this stability.

A5: For any second-stage shift parameter ξ,

$$\Theta(\xi) := \phi''(x_i^N(\xi))q_i^N(\mathbf{x}^N(\xi);\xi) + \frac{[\phi'(x_i^N(\xi))]^2}{f'(Q^N(\mathbf{x}^N(\xi);\xi))} > 0 \tag{16}$$

holds.

This completes the description of our two-stage game. We are now ready to proceed to the comparative statics of our model.

3. LE CHATELIER–SAMUELSON PRINCIPLE, PRICE OVERSHIFTING, AND PROFITABLE COST INCREASES

3.1 Short-run effects on output

We begin our comparative statics analysis by examining the dependence of equilibrium output level on the second-stage shift parameter ξ, while holding the first-stage R&D investment level fixed. We refer to this as the *short-run* effect of a change in ξ.

By differentiating equation (2) for firm i with respect to ξ and evaluating the result at the symmetric second-stage equilibrium $\mathbf{q}^N(\mathbf{x};\xi)$, we may obtain

$$[(n+1)f'(Q^N(\mathbf{x};\xi)) + nq_i^N(\mathbf{x};\xi)f''(Q^N(\mathbf{x};\xi))]\frac{\partial}{\partial\xi}q_i^N(\mathbf{x};\xi) = \psi'(\xi), \tag{17}$$

where the expression within the square brackets can be reduced to

$$\alpha^N(\mathbf{x};\xi) + (n-1)\beta^N(\mathbf{x};\xi) = f'(Q^N(\mathbf{x};\xi))\,[1 + n + \delta(Q^N(\mathbf{x};\xi))], \tag{18}$$

where $\alpha^N(\mathbf{x};\xi) := \alpha(q_i^N(\mathbf{x};\xi), Q_{-i}^N(\mathbf{x};\xi);\xi)$ and $\beta^N(\mathbf{x};\xi) := \beta(q_i^N(\mathbf{x};\xi), Q_{-i}^N(\mathbf{x};\xi);\xi)$ for short. Since (18) is negative by virtue of A1 and A3, we can assert that the following theorem is true.

THEOREM 1. Under A1 and A3, a cost-reducing (cost-increasing) shift in ξ increases (decreases) output at a second-stage Cournot–Nash equilibrium.

3.2. Long-run effects: the Le Chatelier–Samuelson principle

To consider the long-run impact of a change in ξ, we start with the effect of a change in ξ on the equilibrium R&D investment level of firm i, $x_i^N(\xi)$. By differentiating (2) for i and j $(i \neq j)$ with respect to x_i, and defining $\omega(\mathbf{x};\xi) := (\partial/\partial x_i)q_i^N(\mathbf{x};\xi)$ and $\theta(\mathbf{x};\xi) := (\partial/\partial x_i)q_j^N(\mathbf{x};\xi)$ $(i \neq j)$, we obtain

$$\alpha^N(\mathbf{x};\xi)\omega(\mathbf{x};\xi) + (n-1)\beta^N(\mathbf{x};\xi)\theta(\mathbf{x};\xi) - \phi'(x_i) = 0 \tag{19}$$

and

$$\beta^N(\mathbf{x};\xi)\omega(\mathbf{x};\xi) + [\alpha^N(\mathbf{x};\xi) + (n-2)\beta^N(\mathbf{x};\xi)]\theta(\mathbf{x};\xi) = 0, \tag{20}$$

which can be solved for $\omega(\mathbf{x};\xi)$ and $\theta(\mathbf{x};\xi)$ to yield

$$\omega(\mathbf{x};\xi) = \phi'(x_i)\frac{\alpha^N(\mathbf{x};\xi) + (n-2)\beta^N(\mathbf{x};\xi)}{[\alpha^N(\mathbf{x};\xi) + \beta^N(\mathbf{x};\xi)]\,[\alpha^N(\mathbf{x};\xi) + (n-1)\beta^N(\mathbf{x};\xi)]}, \tag{21}$$

$$\theta(\mathbf{x};\xi) = -\phi'(x_i)\frac{\beta^N(\mathbf{x};\xi)}{[\alpha^N(\mathbf{x};\xi) + \beta^N(\mathbf{x};\xi)]\,[\alpha^N(\mathbf{x};\xi) + (n-1)\beta^N(\mathbf{x};\xi)]}, \tag{22}$$

and

$$\begin{aligned}(\partial/\partial x_i)Q^N(\mathbf{x};\xi) &= \omega(\mathbf{x};\xi) + (n-1)\theta(\mathbf{x};\xi)\\ &= \phi'(x_i)\frac{1}{\alpha^N(\mathbf{x};\xi) + (n-1)\beta^N(\mathbf{x};\xi)}.\end{aligned} \tag{23}$$

Putting these together with (5), (6), and (11), we obtain the following basic equation for our subsequent analysis:

$$-\phi'(x_i^N(\xi))\eta^N(\xi)q_i^N(\mathbf{x}^N(\xi);\xi) - 1 = 0. \tag{24}$$

By differentiating (24) with respect to ξ and invoking symmetry, we obtain

$$\begin{aligned}&\left\{-\phi''\eta^N(\xi)q_i^N - \frac{(\phi')^2}{f'\{1+n+\delta^N(\xi)\}}[\eta^N(\xi) + Q^N\nu^N(\xi)]\right\}\frac{\mathrm{d}}{\mathrm{d}\xi}x_i^N(\xi)\\ &= \frac{\phi'\,[\eta^N(\xi) + Q^N\nu^N(\xi)]\psi'(\xi)}{f'[1+n+\delta^N(\xi)]} \qquad (i = 1, 2, \ldots, n).\end{aligned} \tag{25}$$

By virtue of A1, A2, A3, and A4, we may use (25) to conclude that

$$\operatorname{sgn}(\mathrm{d}/\mathrm{d}\xi)x_i^N(\xi) = \operatorname{sgn}\{-[\eta^N(\xi) + Q^N\nu^N(\xi)]\psi'(\xi)\} \qquad (i = 1, 2, \ldots, n). \tag{26}$$

This result suggests that some of our comparative statics will hinge upon whether $\varepsilon^N(\xi) := \eta^N(\xi) + Q(\mathbf{x}^N(\xi);\xi)\nu^N(\xi) > 0$, which we refer to as 'case 1', or $\varepsilon^N(\xi) < 0$, referred to as 'case 2'.[9]

In what follows, we maintain that $\varepsilon^N(\xi) > 0$ is the 'normal' case in our economy, since it is always satisfied in the interesting case where $\delta(Q)$ and hence $\eta(Q)$ are constant, i.e. where the inverse demand function is in the class (48) in Chapter 4. As this class of inverse demand functions is quite often assumed in the literature, it seems rather natural to regard case 1 as normal.

Returning to (26), we have the following.

THEOREM 2. Suppose that a shift in ξ is cost-reducing (cost-increasing). Then $(d/d\xi)x_i^N(\xi) < (>) 0$ holds; i.e. the subgame-perfect equilibrium investment increases (decreases) at the stable first-stage equilibrium in the normal case where $\varepsilon^N(\xi) > 0$.

Turning next to the long-run effect on output of a change in ξ, note first that (2) holds at $\mathbf{x}^N(\xi)$, so that we have

$$f(Q^N(\mathbf{x}^N(\xi); \xi)) + q_i^N(\mathbf{x}^N(\xi); \xi)f'(Q^N(\mathbf{x}^N(\xi); \xi)) = c(x_i^N(\xi); \xi) \quad (i = 1, 2, \ldots, n). \tag{27}$$

By differentiating (27) with respect to ξ and simplifying by invoking symmetry, we obtain

$$f'(Q^N(\mathbf{x}^N(\xi); \xi)) [1 + n + \delta^N(\xi)] (d/d\xi)\, q_i^N(\mathbf{x}^N(\xi); \xi) = \phi'(x_i^N(\xi))(d/d\xi)x_i^N(\xi) + \psi'(\xi) \quad (i = 1, 2, \ldots, n). \tag{28}$$

Combining (17) for $\mathbf{x} = \mathbf{x}^N(\xi)$ with (28), and taking (18) for $\mathbf{x} = \mathbf{x}^N(\xi)$ into consideration, we obtain

$$\frac{(\partial/\partial\xi)q_i^N(\mathbf{x}^N(\xi); \xi)}{(d/d\xi)q_i^N(\mathbf{x}^N(\xi); \xi)} = \frac{\psi'(\xi)}{\psi'(\xi) + \phi'(x_i^N(\xi))(d/d\xi)x_i^N(\xi)}, \tag{29}$$

which proves one of the main findings in this chapter, i.e. Theorem 3.

THEOREM 3 (LE CHATELIER–SAMUELSON PRINCIPLE). In the normal case where $\varepsilon^N(\xi) > 0$,

$$(d/d\xi)q_i^N(\mathbf{x}^N(\xi); \xi) > (<) (\partial/\partial\xi)q_i^N(\mathbf{x}^N(\xi); \xi) > (<) 0$$

holds if the shift in ξ is cost-reducing (cost-increasing).

This result is the analogue for the model presented here of the well-known Le Chatelier–Samuelson principle (Samuelson 1947; 1960). It states that *in the normal case, the absolute magnitude of the adjustment to a change in the cost shift parameter is greater in the long-run than in the short run.*

3.3. *Price overshifting and profitable cost increases*

Another interesting question of comparative statics is how the equilibrium price of output $p^N(\xi) := f(Q^N(\mathbf{x}^N(\xi); \xi))$ will be affected by a shift in ξ. If a shift in ξ is cost-reducing (cost-increasing), the market output in equilibrium, $Q^N(\mathbf{x}^N(\xi); \xi)$, increases (decreases) in the normal case; hence the equilibrium price $p^N(\xi)$ goes down (goes up). This much is rather obvious. It is interesting to see, however, under what conditions taxes are under- or over-shifted, meaning whether prices go down (go up) by less than or more than 100 per cent of the cost decrease (increase).

Simple, although tedious, calculations yield that

$$\frac{1}{\psi'(\xi)}\frac{\mathrm{d}}{\mathrm{d}\xi}f(Q^N(\mathbf{x}^N(\xi);\xi)) = \frac{\phi''\eta^N(\xi)Qf'}{\phi''\eta^N(\xi)q_if'[1+n+\delta^N(\xi)]+(\phi')^2\varepsilon^N(\xi)}, \tag{30}$$

where all the functional expressions are evaluated at the subgame-perfect equilibrium $\{\mathbf{x}^N(\xi), \mathbf{q}^N(\mathbf{x}^N(\xi);\xi)\}$. On the basis of (30), we can assert the following.

THEOREM 4. In the normal case where $\varepsilon^N(\xi) > 0$, the overshifting of a change in cost into price occurs if and only if

$$\phi''\eta^N(\xi)q_if'[1+\delta^N(\xi)]+(\phi')^2\varepsilon^N(\xi) > 0 \tag{31}$$

holds.

Within the context of Cournot competition without strategic commitment, Seade (1985) found that $1 + \delta^N(\xi) < 0$ is necessary and sufficient for the occurrence of overshifting. Our Theorem 4 shows that the same condition is sufficient, but not necessary, in the presence of strategic commitment. This result suggests a greater presumption in favour of overshifting in a model with strategic commitment which ties in with the Le Chatelier–Samuelson type finding. If this holds, the greater response of output to the shift parameter makes overshifting more likely.

It is worth noting that in the special, yet commonly invoked, case of linear inverse demand functions, the necessary and sufficient condition for overshifting given in (31) boils down to a simple inequality,

$$\phi''q_if' + (\phi')^2 > 0. \tag{32}$$

Note, however, that this condition *cannot* be satisfied along with A1 and (16). Therefore, *the price overshifting result can never occur in a model of oligopoly with strategic commitment when the inverse demand function is linear.*

Another interesting question we may ask is how profits will behave in the face of a shift in cost. In parallel with our previous result, we can show that Seade's necessary and sufficient condition for a profitable cost increase is a sufficient, but not necessary, condition in our two-stage model. Indeed, we may assert the following result, the proof of which will be relegated to Section 5.2 for expositional simplicity.

THEOREM 5. If $2 + \delta^N(\xi) \leqslant 0$ holds in the normal case where $\varepsilon^N(\xi) > 0$, then

$$(\mathrm{d}/\mathrm{d}\xi)\Pi_i(\mathbf{x}^N(\xi); \xi) < (>)\ 0 \tag{33}$$

holds if and only if a shift in ξ is cost-reducing (cost-increasing).

Although this partial vindication of Seade's result on profitable cost increase in the presence of strategic commitment is not without interest, we should note that it is quite likely that the crucial condition $2 + \delta^N(\xi) \leqslant 0$ will be violated. To illustrate this fact, let

$$N_+(\xi) := \{n \in N_+ \mid \Pi_i(\mathbf{x}^N(\xi); \xi) \geqslant 0 \text{ for all } i = 1, 2, \ldots, n\}, \tag{34}$$

where N_+ stands for the set of positive integers. Suppose that A3 holds for $2 \in N_+(\xi)$. Then $2 + \delta(Q^N(\mathbf{x}; \xi)) > 0$ holds for any $\mathbf{x}$, so that $2 + \delta^N(\xi) > 0$ must hold by setting $\mathbf{x} = \mathbf{x}^N(\xi)$. It follows that *Seade's condition for profitable cost increase cannot be satisfied if the duopoly subgame-perfect equilibrium is profitable and if strategic substitutability holds in the second stage duopoly game.*

This completes our analysis of comparative statics.[10] For inverse demand functions in the constant δ class given by (48) in Chapter 4, the results are particularly straightforward. Our most striking finding is that a type of Le Chatelier–Samuelson principle holds. More generally, our results are also straightforward in the normal case where $\varepsilon^N(\xi) > 0$, which includes the constant δ class. Indeed, all the comparative statics derived for the constant δ class of inverse demand functions are preserved in this case.

4. COMMITMENT, TAXATION, AND WELFARE

4.1. *Welfare effect of excise tax subsidy*

How will a shift in tax parameter affect the welfare performance of the subgame-perfect equilibrium? To answer this problem, we shall again adopt the second-best net market surplus function as our welfare criterion, which is defined by

$$W^S(\mathbf{x}; \xi) := \int_0^{Q^N(\mathbf{x};\, \xi)} f(Z)\mathrm{d}Z - \sum_{i=1}^{n} [c(x_i; \xi)q_i^N(\mathbf{x}; \xi) + x_i] + \kappa(\xi)Q^N(\mathbf{x}; \xi), \tag{35}$$

where

$$\kappa(\xi) := \psi(\xi) - \psi(0) \tag{36}$$

for all ξ. The interpretation is that $\kappa(\xi) = \xi\ (-\xi)$ if ξ represents the rate of excise tax (excise subsidy), so that the last term in (35), that is to say, $\kappa(\xi)Q^N(\mathbf{x}; \xi)$, represents the government's tax revenue (subsidy expenditure).

Hence $W^S(\mathbf{x}; \xi)$ represents the sum of consumer's surplus, profits, plus tax revenue or minus subsidy expenditure of the government. Our focus in the following analysis will be the sign of $(\mathrm{d}/\mathrm{d}\xi) W^S(\mathbf{x}^N(\xi); \xi)$ at $\xi = 0$, i.e. whether the introduction of a marginal tax subsidy scheme will be welfare-improving or -worsening.

In Section 5.3 we shall demonstrate that

$$\operatorname{sgn}\,[(\mathrm{d}/\mathrm{d}\xi) W^S(\mathbf{x}^N(\xi); \xi)]_{\xi=0} = \operatorname{sgn}\,[-\kappa'(0)] \tag{37}$$

holds if either $\{\varepsilon^N(0) > 0$ *and* $\nu^N(0) \leqslant 0\}$ or $\varepsilon^N(0) < 0$ is satisfied. Noting that $-\kappa'(\xi) = -1$ or 1 according to whether ξ denotes the rate of excise tax or excise subsidy, we may summarize our results as follows.

THEOREM 6.

(*a*) In the normal case where $\varepsilon^N(0) > 0$, an excise tax (excise subsidy) decreases (increases) welfare if $\nu^N(0) \leqslant 0$ holds.

(*b*) In the complementary case where $\varepsilon^N(0) < 0$, an excise tax (excise subsidy) always decreases (increases) welfare.

In particular, if inverse demand functions are in the class given by (48) in Chapter 4, $\varepsilon^N(0) > 0$ and $\nu^N(0) \leqslant 0$ are both satisfied, and we have the following clear-cut result.

COROLLARY. If the inverse demand function is such that δ is constant, an excise tax (excise subsidy) always decreases (increases) welfare.

The assumption that $\nu^N(0) \leqslant 0$ may seem rather inexplicable. To understand what is involved, we define firm i's reaction function $r_i(Q_{-i}, \mathbf{x}; \xi)$, where $Q_{-i} = \Sigma_{j \neq i}\, q_j$, by

$$f(r_i(Q_{-i}, \mathbf{x}; \xi) + Q_{-i} + r_i(Q_{-i}, \mathbf{x}; \xi) f'(r_i(Q_{-i}, \mathbf{x}; \xi) + Q_{-i}) - c(x_i; \xi) = 0. \tag{38}$$

By differentiating (38) with respect to Q_{-i}, we obtain

$$\frac{\mathrm{d}}{\mathrm{d}Q_{-i}} r_i(Q_{-i}, \mathbf{x}; \xi) = -\frac{n + \delta(Q)}{2n + \delta(Q)}, \tag{39}$$

where $Q = Q_{-i} + r_i(Q_{-i}, \mathbf{x}; \xi)$, which is negative if and only if A3 holds. By differentiating (39) with respect to Q, we obtain

$$\frac{\mathrm{d}}{\mathrm{d}Q}\left[\frac{\mathrm{d}}{\mathrm{d}Q_{-i}} r_i(Q_{-i}, \mathbf{x}; \xi)\right] = -\frac{n\delta'(Q)}{[2n + \delta(Q)]^2}, \tag{40}$$

where $\delta'(Q)$ is related to $\eta'(Q)$ by

$$\eta'(Q) = \frac{n-1}{n} \frac{\delta'(Q)}{[1 + n + \delta(Q)]^2}, \tag{41}$$

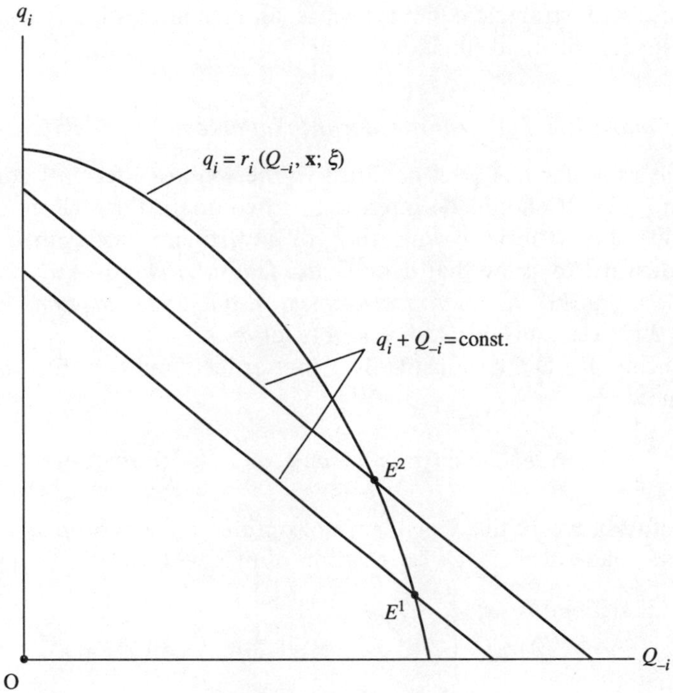

Fig. 11 The meaning of $\nu^N(0) \leqslant 0$

which follows from (14). Since (39) implies $0 > (\mathrm{d}/\mathrm{d}Q_{-i})r_i(Q_{-i}, \mathbf{x}; \xi) > 1$, it follows that the reaction function $q_i = r_i(Q_{-i}, \mathbf{x}; \xi)$ cuts the locus $q_i + Q_{-i}$ = a constant from above (see Fig. 11). In view of (40), it is now clear that the assumption that $\eta'(Q) \leqslant 0$, which implies that $\nu^N(0) \leqslant 0$ and is equivalent to $\delta'(Q) \leqslant 0$ in view of (41), holds if and only if the slope of the reaction function becomes larger as we move from E^1 to E^2.

It is also interesting to compare our welfare conclusions with those obtained in models of taxation in oligopoly without strategic commitment. Recollect that, in the absence of strategic commitment, a small tax (subsidy) raises welfare if and only if it increases (decreases) output per firm. (This can be seen in Besley (1989), within a partial equilibrium framework, and in Theorem 1 of Chapter 3, within a simple two-sector general equilibrium framework.) It is also known that the introduction of an infinitesimal production subsidy to an oligopolistic producer is always welfare-improving (see e.g. Tables 5 and 6 in Chapter 3). Theorem 6 in the present chapter states the conditions for this result to hold even if there is strategic commitment, whereas the corollary thereof shows that it holds for all inverse demand functions in the constant δ class. The extension of this result to the case with strategic commitment is another interesting feature of this class of inverse demand functions.

4.2. Comparison between investment taxation and commodity taxation

Our analysis so far has been confined to the welfare effects of commodity tax or subsidy. It should be interesting to compare the welfare effects of commodity tax (subsidy) with that of investment tax (subsidy). It is straightforward to show that *a small tax* (*subsidy*) *on cost-reducing investment lowers* (*raises*) *the level of investment at all stable stage-one equilibria.* To see this, we consider the example of a tax at rate ρ per unit of cost-reducing R&D investment. The first-order condition for the choice of x_i is now

$$-\frac{\partial}{\partial x_i} c(x_i^N(\xi, \rho); \xi, \rho)\eta\,(Q^N(\mathbf{x}^N(\xi, \rho); \xi, \rho))\, q_i^N(\mathbf{x}^N(\xi, \rho); \xi, \rho) = 1 + \rho \qquad (42)$$

instead of (24), where the dependence of optimal choices on ρ as well as on ξ has been made explicit. Differentiation of (42) with respect to ρ yields

$$\begin{aligned}\lambda(\xi, \rho)(\partial/\partial\rho)x_i^N(\xi, \rho)&\\ +\,(n-1)\,\eta(Q^N(\mathbf{x}^N(\xi, \rho); \xi, \rho))\,(\partial/\partial\rho)x_j^N(\xi, \rho) - 1 = 0,&\end{aligned} \qquad (43)$$

which implies that $(\partial/\partial\rho)x_i^N(\xi, \rho)$ is negative after invoking symmetry and the stability condition.

Recollect that the second-best welfare level is decreasing in x_i at the subgame-perfect equilibrium if the number of firms in the industry is sufficiently large.[11] Thus, whether the equilibrium level of R&D is greater than, or less than, its second-best level depends crucially upon the number of firms. It follows that whether a small tax or subsidy to cost-reducing investment increases or decreases welfare depends also upon the number of firms, and this is the case even if inverse demand functions are confined to the constant δ class. Hence the introduction of commodity tax is more likely to have an unambiguous effect on welfare than the introduction of tax on cost-reducing R&D investment, the incidence of which is contingent on the number of firms.

5. PROOFS

5.1. Local stability of the first-stage equilibrium

The symmetric Cournot–Nash equilibrium $\mathbf{x}^N(\xi)$ is locally stable under the myopic adjustment process

$$\dot{x}_i = \tau \frac{\partial}{\partial x_i} \Pi_i(\mathbf{x}; \xi) \qquad (i = 1, 2, \ldots, n) \tag{44}$$

if

$$\lambda(\xi) + (k-1)\mu(\xi) < 0 \qquad (k = 0, 1, \ldots, n) \tag{45}$$

holds, where $\lambda(\xi)$ and $\mu(\xi)$ are defined by (12) and (13), respectively. Note that (12) and (13) imply

$$\lambda(\xi) - \mu(\xi) = -\eta^N(\xi)\Theta(\xi), \tag{46}$$

where $\Theta(\xi)$ is defined by (16). If A5 is assumed, (46) and $H(\xi) > 0$ imply that $\lambda(\xi) < \mu(\xi)$ holds, which is (45) for $k = 0$. By virtue of A4 and $\lambda(\xi) < \mu(\xi)$, we obtain $\lambda(\xi) < 0$, which is (45) for $k = 1$. Now that we have verified $\lambda(\xi) < 0$ and $\mu(\xi) < 0$, the validity of (45) for all $k = 2, 3, \ldots, n$ is guaranteed. □

5.2. *Proof of Theorem 5*

Firm i's first-stage profit function is defined formally by

$$\Pi_i(\mathbf{x}^N(\xi); \xi) := [f(Q^N(\mathbf{x}^N(\xi); \xi)) - c(x_i^N(\xi); \xi)]\, q_i^N(\mathbf{x}^N(\xi); \xi) - x_i^N(\xi). \tag{47}$$

By differentiating (47) with respect to ξ, we obtain

$$\begin{aligned}(\mathrm{d}/\mathrm{d}\xi)\Pi_i = {} & q_i^N f' \left[\sum_{j=1}^{n} (\partial/\partial x_j)\, Q^N (\mathrm{d}/\mathrm{d}\xi) x_j^N + (\partial/\partial\xi) Q^N\right] \\ & + (f - C)\left[\sum_{j=1}^{n} (\partial/\partial x_j) q_i^N (\mathrm{d}/\mathrm{d}\xi) x_j^N + (\partial/\partial\xi) q_i^N\right] \\ & - \left[\phi'(x_i^N)(\mathrm{d}/\mathrm{d}\xi) x_i^N + \psi'(\xi)\right] q_i^N - (\partial/\partial\xi) x_i^N,\end{aligned} \tag{48}$$

omitting the arguments of all functions for convenience. Invoking symmetry and using the first-order conditions for the choice of q_i and x_i, this becomes

$$\begin{aligned}(\mathrm{d}/\mathrm{d}\xi)\Pi_i = {} & -\psi'(\xi) q_i^N + (n-1) f' q_i^N \left\{(\partial/\partial\xi) q_i^N \right. \\ & \left. + (\mathrm{d}/\mathrm{d}\xi) x_i^N \left[\omega(\mathbf{x}^N; \xi) + (n-2)\,\theta(\mathbf{x}^N; \xi)\right]\right\},\end{aligned} \tag{49}$$

which, after employing (21), (22), and (25), yields

$$\frac{\mathrm{d}}{\mathrm{d}\xi}\Pi_i = -\psi'(\xi) q_i^N \left\{1 - \frac{n-1}{1+n+\delta^N(\xi)}\left[1 + \frac{(\phi')^2}{\Gamma(\xi) f'(1+n+\delta^N(\xi))}\left(2 + \frac{\delta^N(\xi)}{n}\right)\right]\right\}, \tag{50}$$

where

$$\Gamma(\xi) := -\phi''\eta^N(\xi)q_i^N - \frac{(\phi')^2}{f'[1+n+\delta^N(\xi)]}\,\varepsilon^N(\xi) < 0.$$

Invoking the stability conditions, we observe that the term in braces in (50) is less than $[2+\delta^N(\xi)]/[1+n+\delta^N(\xi)]$, so that

$$\frac{\mathrm{d}}{\mathrm{d}\xi}\,\Pi_i(\mathbf{x}^N(\xi);\,\xi) > (<) -\psi'(\xi)q_i^N\,\frac{2+\delta^N(\xi)}{1+n+\delta^N(\xi)} \tag{51}$$

holds if and only if $-\psi'(\xi) < (>)\ 0$, supposing that $2+\delta^N(\xi) \leqslant 0$. This proves Theorem 5. □

5.3. Derivation of (37)

By differentiating $W^S(\mathbf{x}^N(\xi);\,\xi)$ with respect to ξ, we obtain

$$\begin{aligned}(\mathrm{d}/\mathrm{d}\xi)\,W^S(\mathbf{x}^N(\xi);\,\xi) &= \sum_{i=1}^{n}(\partial/\partial x_i)\,W^S(\mathbf{x}^N(\xi);\,\xi)(\mathrm{d}/\mathrm{d}\xi)x_i^N(\xi)\\ &\quad + (\partial/\partial\xi)\,W^S(\mathbf{x}^N(\xi);\,\xi).\end{aligned} \tag{52}$$

Note first that the partial differentiation of (35) with respect to ξ yields

$$\begin{aligned}(\partial/\partial\xi)\,W^S(\mathbf{x};\,\xi) &= [f(Q^N(\mathbf{x};\,\xi)) + \kappa(\xi)](\partial/\partial\xi)Q^N(\mathbf{x};\,\xi)\\ &\quad - \sum_{i=1}^{n} c(x_i;\,\xi)(\partial/\partial\xi)q_i^N(\mathbf{x};\,\xi),\end{aligned} \tag{53}$$

so that we have

$$\begin{aligned}(\partial/\partial\xi)\,W^S(\mathbf{x}^N(\xi);\,\xi) &= [\kappa(\xi) - f'(Q^N(\mathbf{x}^N(\xi);\,\xi))q_i^N(\mathbf{x}^N(\xi);\,\xi)]\\ &\quad (\partial/\partial\xi)Q^N(\mathbf{x}^N(\xi);\,\xi),\end{aligned} \tag{54}$$

where use is made of (9). Invoking (17), and noting that $\kappa(0)=0$ by (36), it follows from (54) that

$$\frac{\partial}{\partial\xi}\,W^S(\mathbf{x}^N(0);\,0) = -\,\frac{\kappa'(0)Q^N(\mathbf{x}^N(0);\,0))}{1+n+\delta^N(0)}, \tag{55}$$

whereas (25) yields

$$\frac{\mathrm{d}}{\mathrm{d}\xi}\,x_i^N(0) = \frac{\kappa'(0)\phi'\varepsilon^N(0)}{-\phi''\eta^N(0)q_i^N f'[1+n+\delta^N(0)] - (\phi')^2\varepsilon^N(0)}. \tag{56}$$

Finally, note that

$$(\partial/\partial x_i)\,W^S(\mathbf{x};\,\xi) = [f(Q^N(\mathbf{x};\,\xi)) + \kappa(\xi)]\,(\partial/\partial x_i)Q^N(\mathbf{x};\,\xi)$$

$$-\sum_{j=1}^{n} c(x_j; \xi)(\partial/\partial x_i) q_j^N(\mathbf{x}; \xi) - \phi'(x_i) q_i^N(\mathbf{x}; \xi) - 1 \tag{57}$$

holds, so that we have

$$(\partial/\partial x_i) W^S(\mathbf{x}^N(0); 0) = -q_i^N(\mathbf{x}^N(0); 0) f'(Q^N(\mathbf{x}^N(0); 0)) [\omega(\mathbf{x}^N(0); 0) + 2(n-1)\theta(\mathbf{x}^N(0); 0)]. \tag{58}$$

Invoking (22) and (23), we may now reduce (58) to

$$\frac{\partial}{\partial x_i} W^S(\mathbf{x}^N(0); 0) = \frac{\phi'(x_i^N(0)) q_i^N(\mathbf{x}^N(0); 0)}{1 + n + \delta^N(0)} \left\{1 - \frac{n-1}{n} [n + \delta^N(0)]\right\}. \tag{59}$$

Combining (55), (56), and (59), we obtain

$$\frac{\mathrm{d}}{\mathrm{d}\xi} W^S(\mathbf{x}^N(0); 0) = -\frac{\kappa'(0) Q^N(\mathbf{x}^N(0); 0)}{1 + n + \delta^N(0)} \Omega(0), \tag{60}$$

where

$$\Omega(\xi) := \frac{-\phi'' \eta^N(\xi) q_i^N f'[1 + n + \delta^N(\xi)] - (\phi')^2 \varepsilon^N(\xi) \dfrac{n-1}{n} [n + \delta^N(\xi)]}{-\phi'' \eta^N(\xi) q_i^N f'[1 + n + \delta^N(\xi)] - (\phi')^2 \varepsilon^N(\xi)}. \tag{61}$$

Note that the denominator of (61) is positive by virtue of A5. On the other hand, the numerator of (61) is positive if $\varepsilon^N(\xi) < 0$. Moreover, in the normal case, where $\varepsilon^N(\xi) > 0$, (9) guarantees that

$$\begin{aligned} &\text{the numerator of } \Omega(0) \\ &\geqslant \eta^N(0) \left\{\phi'' q_i^N f'[1 + n + \delta^N(0)] - (\phi')^2 \frac{n-1}{n} [n + \delta^N(0)]\right\} \\ &> \eta^N(0)(\phi')^2 \left[1 + \left(1 + \frac{n+1}{n}\right)\left(1 + \frac{\delta^N(0)}{n}\right)\right] \\ &> 0 \end{aligned}$$

if $\nu^N(0) \leqslant 0$, as we set out to show. □

6. CONCLUDING REMARKS

The analysis presented in this chapter can be justified in two main ways.

In the first place, it illustrates the possibility of obtaining some clear-cut comparative statics from a two-stage model of oligopolistic competition. It has also illustrated the limits to the generality of results that can be obtained by assuming an unrestricted form of inverse demand functions. The analysis has further served to bring to the fore a class of inverse demand functions whose general merits seem to have gone unnoticed previously, i.e. those given by (48) of Chapter 4. If inverse demand functions are in this class, we can claim a number of relevant findings, among them a variant of the Le Chatelier–Samuelson principle. Just what general features of a game-theoretic framework permit this principle to hold would seem to be an interesting topic for further research.

In the second place, the above tax analysis is also of interest in its own right. We have shown just when a small subsidy to oligopolistic competitors remains welfare-improving under the addition of a further stage of strategic interactions. Our results seem to be quite encouraging, since there are some interesting conditions under which this result is preserved. Since much of the recent literature in oligopoly theory has stressed the role of strategic commitment in oligopolistic interactions, there is great relevance in understanding the incidence of, and impact of taxation on, welfare in the presence of strategic commitment.

Finally, note that our analysis has neglected many important aspects, including distributional equity considerations, general equilibrium consequences of subsidizing oligopolists, and R&D spillovers. This being the case, yet another warning to the effect that care should be taken in extracting policy conclusions from our theoretical analysis may be needed.

NOTES TO CHAPTER 5

1. For simplicity, our strategic choice variable in the first-stage game is assumed to be the cost-reducing R&D investment. It is clear, however, that the demand-creating R&D investment could be used instead without any further complication.
2. For a discussion of this principle in a non-game-theoretic setting, see Samuelson (1947, 1960).
3. See e.g. Anderson and Ballentine (1976), Besley (1989), Katz and Rosen (1985), Konishi (1990), Konishi *et al.* (1990), Stern (1987), Willig (1983), and Chapter 3 above.
4. See e.g. Brander and Spencer (1983), Okuno-Fujiwara and Suzumura (1993), and Suzumura (1992).
5. In Ch. 7 we examine an oligopoly model with strategic commitment and an endogenously determined number of firms. The excess entry theorem of Part I and the excess investment theorem of Part II are going to be synthesized in this extended framework.
6. See Ch. 6 for the effects of R&D spillovers within the framework of two-stage model of oligopolistic competition.
7. The proof of this result is basically the same as in Ch. 1 and need not be repeated here.
8. This class of inverse demand functions played an important role in Katz's (1986) analysis of co-operative R&D. See also Suzumura (1992).

9. We deliberately neglect considerations of the knife-edge case in which $\varepsilon^N(\xi) = 0$ for the sake of brevity of exposition. Needless to say, the findings that follow can be easily altered to accommodate this case if it is found necessary.
10. Let us briefly summarize our analysis in the complementary case where $\varepsilon^N(\xi) < 0$. To begin with, we obtain from (26) that

$$(\mathrm{d}/\mathrm{d}\xi)x_i^N(\xi) < (>)\ 0 \text{ as } \psi'(\xi) < (>)\ 0. \tag{1*}$$

Concerning $(\partial/\partial\xi)q_i^N(\mathbf{x}^N(\xi);\xi)$ and $(\mathrm{d}/\mathrm{d}\xi)q_i^N(\mathbf{x}^N(\xi);\xi)$, we obtain

$$(\partial/\partial\xi)q_i^N(\mathbf{x}^N(\xi);\xi) > (<)\ 0 \text{ as } \psi'(\xi) < (>)\ 0 \tag{2*}$$

and

$$(\mathrm{d}/\mathrm{d}\xi)q_i^N(\mathbf{x}^N(\xi);\xi) > (<)\ 0 \text{ as } \psi'(\xi) < (>)\ 0 \tag{3*}$$

from (17) and from

$$\frac{\mathrm{d}}{\mathrm{d}\xi}q_i^N(\mathbf{x}^N(\xi);\xi) = \psi'(\xi)\left\{1 + \frac{(\phi')^2\varepsilon^N(\xi)}{f'[1+n+\delta^N(\xi)]}\right\}, \tag{4*}$$

respectively, where (4*) is obtained by combining (25) with (28). Note that we cannot in this case compare the size of $(\partial/\partial\xi)q_i^N(\mathbf{x}^N(\xi);\xi)$ with that of $(\mathrm{d}/\mathrm{d}\xi)q_i^N(\mathbf{x}^N(\xi);\xi)$, and the Le Chatelier–Samuelson result fails to hold in general. However, note also that (4*) implies that

$$(\mathrm{d}/\mathrm{d}\xi)p^N(\xi) < (>)\ 0 \text{ if and only if } \psi'(\xi) < (>)\ 0, \tag{5*}$$

so that (31) remains necessary and sufficient for the occurrence of overshifting. Nevertheless, Seade's condition, $1 + \delta^N(\xi) < 0$, is no longer sufficient, although it is necessary, for overshifting. Finally, Th. 5 continues to hold in the complementary case where $\varepsilon^N(\xi) < 0$ as well.
11. This follows from Th. 2 in Ch. 4.

6 Co-operative and Non-Cooperative R&D with Spillovers

1. INTRODUCTION

In the preceding two chapters we examined the positive as well as normative effects of strategic commitment to cost-reducing R&D investment. However, we have neglected one crucial aspect of R&D in general: R&D spillovers, whereby cost-reducing benefits will diffuse to rival firms without payment. Since the incentives for a firm to undertake R&D on its own depend on there being a sufficient degree of appropriability of the research outcomes—hence a limited diffusion of knowledge—it is of particular interest to see how the existence of R&D spillovers affects the welfare effects of strategic commitment to R&D investment.

The purpose of this chapter is to answer this important question. To add a new dimension to our analysis of strategic commitment, we will examine the effects of co-operative R&D (wherein member-firms commit themselves to a joint profit-maximizing level of R&D in a 'pre-competitive stage' but remain fierce competitors in the product market), along with non-cooperative R&D, socially first-best R&D, and socially second-best R&D.[1] The analysis is conducted in terms of the two-stage model of oligopolistic competition which we have examined throughout Part II, except that we now allow for the existence of R&D spillovers. In the first stage firms choose their cost-reducing R&D either co-operatively or non-cooperatively, whereas in the second stage they engage in quantity competition in the product market.

The plan of this chapter is as follows. Section 2 introduces the model and explains our basic assumptions. Section 3 examines the output response to a marginal change in R&D in the presence of R&D spillovers. Sections 4 and 5 are devoted to the first-best welfare analysis and the second-best welfare analysis, respectively, of co-operative and non-cooperative R&D. Some of the complicated reasoning is relegated to Section 6 for the sake of expositional convenience, and Section 7 considers a case that is excluded from our analysis in Sections 4 and 5, viz. the case of 'small' spillovers. Finally, Section 8 offers conclusions.

2. OLIGOPOLY MODEL WITH R&D SPILLOVERS

2.1. Basic assumptions

Consider an industry where n firms, where $2 \leqslant n < +\infty$, are producing a single homogeneous product. Let $p = f(Q)$ be inverse demand function, where p and Q denote, respectively, price and industry output of this product. Let x_i and q_i denote, respectively, the amount of R&D and the output of firm i. The cost of production and of R&D are assumed to be $c(x_i; \mathbf{x}_{-i})q_i$ and x_i, respectively, where $\mathbf{x}_{-i} = (x_1, \ldots, x_{i-1}, x_{i+1}, \ldots, x_n)$ is the R&D profile of firms other than i. Diminishing returns on R&D can be introduced without affecting any of the results in this chapter.

Throughout, we will assume the following.

A1: $f(Q)$ is twice continuously differentiable and $f'(Q) < 0$ holds for all $Q \geqslant 0$ with $f(Q) > 0$.

A2: The average variable cost function $c(x_i; \mathbf{x}_{-i})$ is twice continuously differentiable and satisfies $c(x_i; \mathbf{x}_{-i}) > 0$, $(\partial/\partial x_i)c(x_i; \mathbf{x}_{-i}) < 0$ and $(\partial/\partial x_j)c(x_i; \mathbf{x}_{-i}) \leqslant 0$ $(i \neq j)$ for any $\mathbf{x} = (x_1, \ldots, x_i, \ldots, x_n) > 0$. Furthermore, for any symmetric profile $\mathbf{x} = (x_1, \ldots, x_i, \ldots, x_n) > 0$, $(\partial/\partial x_i)c(x_i; \mathbf{x}_{-i}) < (\partial/\partial x_j)c(x_i; \mathbf{x}_{-i})(i \neq j)$ holds.

The standard assumption A1 requires no further account. According to A2, a firm's R&D is cost-reducing and can benefit other firms without payment. However, the cost-reducing effect of a firm's own R&D outweighs the benefit accruing freely from other firms when all firms are spending the same amount on R&D.

As in the previous two chapters, firms engage in two-stage competition. In the first stage, firms make an irrevocable commitment to a level of R&D in full anticipation of the equilibrium that will be established in the second stage, where firms compete in the product market. The second-stage strategic variable is assumed to be the level of output.

We will examine two concepts of equilibrium in relation to this model. The first equilibrium concept is non-cooperative throughout both stages; that is, the equilibrium of the second stage is a Cournot–Nash equilibrium, and that of the entire game is a subgame-perfect equilibrium. In contrast, the second equilibrium concept is a mixed co-operative and non-cooperative equilibrium; firms are supposed to co-ordinate their R&D in the first stage so as to maximize joint profits with the understanding that they engage in non-cooperative competition in the second stage.

2.2. *Subgame-perfect equilibrium*

Let us begin with the first type of equilibrium. To characterize the second-stage equilibrium, let an R&D profile $\mathbf{x} = (x_1, \ldots, x_i, \ldots, x_n)$ be parametrically given. Then the profits of firm i in the second-stage game is defined by

$$\pi_i(q_i, Q_{-i}; \mathbf{x}) := [f(Q) - c(x_i; \mathbf{x}_{-i})]q_i - x_i \qquad (i = 1, 2, \ldots, n), \tag{1}$$

where $Q = q_i + Q_{-i}$. Let $\mathbf{q}^N(\mathbf{x}) = (q_1^N(\mathbf{x}), \ldots, q_i^N(\mathbf{x}), \ldots, q_n^N(\mathbf{x}))$ stand for the Cournot–Nash equilibrium of the second-stage game corresponding to the parametrically given R&D profile $\mathbf{x} = (x_1, \ldots, x_i, \ldots, x_n)$. Assuming interior optimum and second-order conditions, $\mathbf{q}^N(\mathbf{x})$ can be characterized by the first-order condition $(\partial/\partial q_i)\pi_i(q_i^N(\mathbf{x}), Q_{-i}^N(\mathbf{x}); \mathbf{x}) = 0$ $(i = 1, 2, \ldots, n)$; i.e.

$$f(Q^N(\mathbf{x})) + q_i^N(\mathbf{x})f'(Q^N(\mathbf{x})) - c(x_i; \mathbf{x}_{-i}) = 0 \qquad (i = 1, 2, \ldots, n), \tag{2}$$

where $Q^N(\mathbf{x}) = \Sigma_{j=1}^n q_j^N(\mathbf{x})$. As usual, we focus on the symmetric equilibrium, so that $q_i^N(\mathbf{x}) = q_j^N(\mathbf{x}) = q^N(\mathbf{x})$, say, for all $i, j = 1, 2, \ldots, n$ if $x_i = x_j = x$, say, for all $i, j = 1, 2, \ldots, n$.

To lend substance to the oligopolistic interactions in our model, we now introduce our standard strategic assumption. Let $\alpha_i(q_i, Q_{-i}; \mathbf{x})$ and $\beta_{ij}(q_i, Q_{-i}; \mathbf{x})$ be defined by $\alpha_i(q_i, Q_{-i}; \mathbf{x}) := (\partial^2/\partial q_i^2)\pi_i(q_i, Q_{-i}; \mathbf{x})$ and $\beta_{ij}(q_i, Q_{-i}; \mathbf{x}) := (\partial^2/\partial q_i\, \partial q_j)\pi_i(q_i, Q_{-i}; \mathbf{x})$ $(i \neq j;\ i, j = 1, 2, \ldots, n)$, respectively. Since firms are assumed to compete in terms of quantities in the second-stage game, it is natural that we adopt the following second-stage strategic assumption.

A3: The strategic variables in the second-stage game are strategic substitutes; i.e. $\beta_{ij}(q_i, Q_{-i}; \mathbf{x}) < 0 (i \neq j;\ i, j = 1, 2, \ldots, n)$ holds for any $\mathbf{x}$.

Turning to the first-stage game, let us define the first-stage payoff function of firm i by

$$\Pi_i(\mathbf{x}) := \pi_i(q_i^N(\mathbf{x}), Q_{-i}^N(\mathbf{x}); \mathbf{x}) \qquad (i = 1, 2, \ldots, n). \tag{3}$$

Then the Nash equilibrium of the first-stage game, denoted by $\mathbf{x}^N = (x_1^N, \ldots, x_i^N, \ldots, x_n^N)$, is characterized under the assumption of interior optimum and second-order conditions by the first-order condition $(\partial/\partial x_i)\Pi_i(\mathbf{x}^N) = 0$ $(i = 1, 2,, \ldots, n)$; i.e.

$$\sum_{j=1}^{n} \frac{\partial}{\partial q_j} \pi_i(q_i^N(\mathbf{x}^N), Q_{-i}^N(\mathbf{x}^N); \mathbf{x}^N) \frac{\partial}{\partial x_i} q_j^N(\mathbf{x}^N)$$
$$+ \frac{\partial}{\partial x_i} \pi_i\,(q_i^N(\mathbf{x}^N), Q_{-i}^N(\mathbf{x}^N); \mathbf{x}^N) = 0 \qquad (i = 1, 2, \ldots, n). \tag{4}$$

Throughout this chapter, we focus on the symmetric $\mathbf{x}^N$; i.e. $x_i^N = x_j^N = x^N$, say, for all $i, j = 1, 2, \ldots, n$.

It is clear that $\{\mathbf{x}^N, \mathbf{q}^N(\mathbf{x}^N)\}$ is precisely the *subgame-perfect equilibrium* of our two-stage game which will be the central focus of our analysis to follow.

Although A1, A2, and A3 will be kept throughout most of the present chapter, there will be several occasions where we must replace A3 by the following assumption for the sake of obtaining an unambiguous result.

A3*: $f(Q)$ is concave; i.e. $f''(Q) \leqslant 0$ holds for all $Q \geqslant 0$ with $f(Q) > 0$.

Note that A3* is the condition that guarantees the concavity of profit function $\pi_i(q_i, Q_{-i}; \mathbf{x})$ with respect to q_i, and is clearly satisfied by the class of *linear* inverse demand functions. In the presence of A1, A3* implies A3, so that the set of assumptions A1, A2, and A3* is collectively stronger than the set A1, A2, and A3. Finally, note that $\alpha_i(q_i, Q_{-i}; \mathbf{x})$ and $\beta_{ij}(q_i, Q_{-i}; \mathbf{x})$ become independent of the firm indices i and j $(i \neq j;\ i, j = 1, 2, \ldots, n)$ if they are evaluated at any symmetric $\mathbf{q}$ and $\mathbf{x}$. In such a case, we can denote them simply as $\alpha(q_i, Q_{-i}; \mathbf{x})$ and $\beta(q_i, Q_{-i}; \mathbf{x})$.

2.3. *Mixed co-operative and non-cooperative equilibrium*

Let us now turn to the second equilibrium, i.e. mixed co-operative and non-cooperative equilibrium. Suppose that firms co-ordinate their R&D in the first-stage game in order to maximize their joint profits, whereas they compete non-cooperatively in the second-stage quantity game.

The co-operative equilibrium $\mathbf{x}^C = (x_1^C, \ldots, x_i^C, \ldots, x_n^C)$ of the first-stage game can be characterized by $(\partial/\partial x_i)\ \Sigma_{j=1}^n\ \Pi_j(\mathbf{x}^C) = 0 (i = 1, 2, \ldots, n)$ with the proviso that $x_1 = x_2 = \ldots = x_n$ under the assumption of interior optimum and second-order conditions. It is easy, if tedious, to reduce this first-order condition to the following:

$$q_i^N(\mathbf{x}^C)\left\{(n-1)f'(Q^N(\mathbf{x}^C))\,[\omega(\mathbf{x}^C) + (n-1)\theta(\mathbf{x}^C)] - \left[\frac{\partial}{\partial x_i}c(x_i^C; \mathbf{x}_{-i}^C) + (n-1)\frac{\partial}{\partial x_j}c(x_i^C; \mathbf{x}_{-i}^C)\right]\right\} - 1 = 0$$

$$(i \neq j;\ i, j = 1, 2, \ldots, n) \qquad (5)$$

where $\omega(\mathbf{x}) := (\partial/\partial x_i)q_i^N(\mathbf{x})$ and $\theta(\mathbf{x}) := (\partial/\partial x_i)q_j^N(\mathbf{x})$, where $i \neq j$ and $i, j = 1, 2, \ldots, n$. As before, $\omega(\mathbf{x})(\theta(\mathbf{x}))$ represents the effect of a marginal change in the first-stage R&D expenditure x_i by firm i on the second-stage equilibrium output of firm i (firm j), where $i \neq j$. The equilibrium of the whole game is represented by $\{\mathbf{x}^C, \mathbf{q}^N(\mathbf{x}^C)\}$, which is also assumed to be symmetric. This mixed co-operative and non-cooperative equilibrium is meant to capture the idea of collaborative R&D wherein member-firms commit themselves to a joint profit-maximizing level of R&D in a pre-competitive stage but remain fierce competitors in the product market.

3. R&D SPILLOVERS AND OUTPUT RESPONSE

3.1. *Impact of a marginal increase in R&D*

Before setting about comparing the performance of the subgame-perfect equilibrium $\{\mathbf{x}^N, \mathbf{q}^N(\mathbf{x}^N)\}$ with the mixed co-operative and non-cooperative equilibrium $\{\mathbf{x}^C, \mathbf{q}^N(\mathbf{x}^C)\}$ from the point of view of social welfare, let us analyse how the individual firm's output and the industry output at the second-stage Nash equilibrium react to a change in a firm's R&D expenditure in the first-stage game.

By virtue of the symmetry of $\mathbf{x}$, $\omega(\mathbf{x})$ and $\theta(\mathbf{x})$ are independent of the firm indices i and j ($i \neq j$; $i, j = 1, 2, \ldots, n$). Furthermore, the effect of a change in x_i on the equilibrium industry output $Q^N(\mathbf{x})$, i.e. $(\partial/\partial x_i)Q^N(\mathbf{x})$, is given by $\Psi(\mathbf{x}) := \omega(\mathbf{x}) + (n-1)\theta(\mathbf{x})$.

In Section 6 below, we show that $\omega(\mathbf{x})$ and $\theta(\mathbf{x})$ can be calculated as

$$\omega(\mathbf{x}) = \frac{1}{\Delta(\mathbf{x})}\left\{[\alpha(\mathbf{x}) - \beta(\mathbf{x})]\frac{\partial}{\partial x_i}c(x_i; \mathbf{x}_{-i}) + (n-1)\beta(\mathbf{x})\left[\frac{\partial}{\partial x_i}c(x_i; \mathbf{x}_{-i}) - \frac{\partial}{\partial x_j}c(x_i; \mathbf{x}_{-i})\right]\right\} \tag{6}$$

and

$$\theta(\mathbf{x}) = \frac{1}{\Delta(\mathbf{x})}\left\{\alpha(\mathbf{x})\left[\frac{\partial}{\partial x_j}c(x_i; \mathbf{x}_{-i}) - \frac{\partial}{\partial x_i}c(x_i; \mathbf{x}_{-i})\right] + [\alpha(\mathbf{x}) - \beta(\mathbf{x})]\frac{\partial}{\partial x_i}c(x_i; \mathbf{x}_{-i})\right\} \quad (i \neq j), \tag{7}$$

where $\alpha(\mathbf{x}) := \alpha(q_i^N(\mathbf{x}), Q_{-i}^N(\mathbf{x}); \mathbf{x})$ and $\beta(\mathbf{x}) := \beta(q_i^N(\mathbf{x}), Q_{-i}^N(\mathbf{x}); \mathbf{x})$ for notational brevity, and $\Delta(\mathbf{x}) := [\alpha(\mathbf{x}) - \beta(\mathbf{x})]\,[\alpha(\mathbf{x}) + (n-1)\beta(\mathbf{x})]$. We can then obtain

$$\Psi(\mathbf{x}) = \frac{\alpha(\mathbf{x}) - \beta(\mathbf{x})}{\Delta(\mathbf{x})}\left[\frac{\partial}{\partial x_i}c(x_i; \mathbf{x}_{-i}) + (n-1)\frac{\partial}{\partial x_j}c(x_i; \mathbf{x}_{-j})\right]. \tag{8}$$

It is easy to verify that

$$\alpha(\mathbf{x}) = 2f'(Q^N(\mathbf{x})) + q_i^N(\mathbf{x})f''(Q^N(\mathbf{x})) \tag{9}$$

and

$$\beta(\mathbf{x}) = f'(Q^N(\mathbf{x})) + q_i^N(\mathbf{x})f''(Q^N(\mathbf{x})) \tag{10}$$

hold, so that $\alpha(\mathbf{x}) - \beta(\mathbf{x}) = f'(Q^N(\mathbf{x})) < 0$ by virtue of A1. It follows from A3 that $\alpha(\mathbf{x}) < 0$ holds, which in turn assures us that $\Delta(\mathbf{x}) > 0$. Therefore, $\omega(\mathbf{x}) > 0$ follows from (6) and assumptions A2 and A3. In other words, *an increase in cost-reducing R&D by a firm unambiguously increases the equilibrium output of that firm.*

So far, our story should be a very familiar one. Note, however, that an increase in cost-reducing R&D by firm i exerts two distinct effects on the equilibrium output of its rival firm j ($i \neq j$) in the presence of the R&D spillovers. On the one hand, it tends to increase j's output by bringing j's cost down through spillovers of cost-reducing benefits. On the other hand, it tends to decrease j's output by strengthening i's competitive edge against j. Let us say that *the R&D spillovers are sufficiently large if the former effect outweighs the latter so that* $\theta(\mathbf{x}) > 0$ *holds.*

Finally, it follows from (8) that *the industry output at the Cournot–Nash equilibrium always increases when one of the firms increases its cost-reducing R&D irrespective of whether the R&D spillovers are large or small.*

3.2. *Diagrammatic illustration*

In the case of duopoly ($n = 2$), we can illustrate these results by a simple diagram. In so doing, we can highlight the role of R&D spillovers.

In Fig. 12, where the horizontal (vertical) axis measures firm 1's (firm 2's) output, R_1R_1 (R_2R_2) denotes firm 1's (firm 2's) reaction curve when an R&D profile $\mathbf{x}^0 = (x_1^0, x_2^0) > 0$ is specified. The point $E(\mathbf{x}^0)$ represents the second-stage Cournot–Nash equilibrium corresponding to $\mathbf{x}^0$.

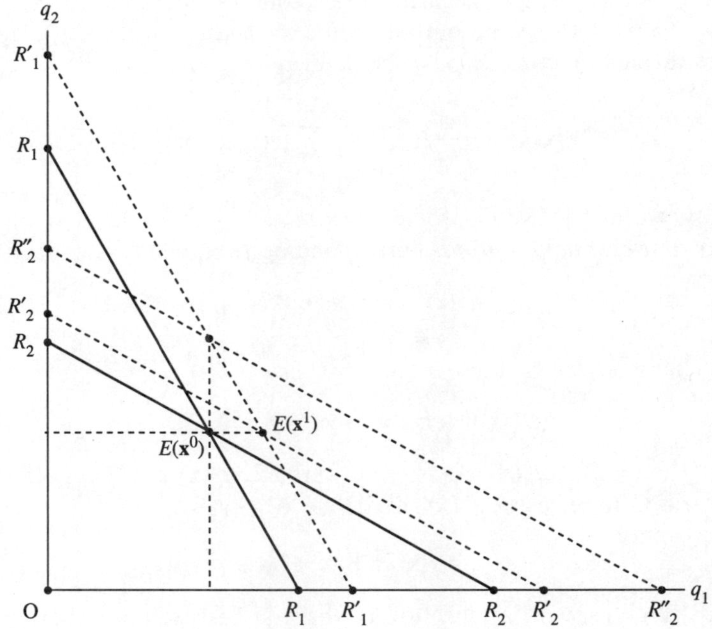

Fig. 12 Shift of the Cournot–Nash equilibrium under R&D spillovers

Suppose that a change in R&D from $\mathbf{x}^0$ to $\mathbf{x}^1 := (x_1^0 + \varepsilon, x_2^0)$, where $\varepsilon > 0$, takes place. The reaction curve of firm 1 shifts up; so does that of firm 2, by virtue of R&D spillovers. If the resulting reaction curve of firm 2 lies above $R_2'R_2'$, it is clear that firm 2's equilibrium output increases as a result of an increase in firm 1's R&D. This has been the case with the sufficiently large spillovers that we have identified. However, if R&D spillovers are too large and the resulting reaction curve of firm 2 lies above $R_2''R_2''$, firm 1's equilibrium output will become smaller than the level at $E(\mathbf{x}^0)$ as a result of the firm increasing its own R&D. But this pathological possibility is prevented from occurring by the latter part of A2. Given our assumptions, therefore, we have $\omega(\mathbf{x}^0) > 0$, $\theta(\mathbf{x}^0) > 0$, and, as a result, $\Psi(\mathbf{x}^0) > 0$.

4. FIRST-BEST WELFARE ANALYSIS

4.1. *First-best welfare criterion*

The welfare performance of $\mathbf{x}^N$ and $\mathbf{x}^C$ can be gauged and compared in terms of several alternative criteria. To begin with, let us put ourselves in the omnipotent government's position and invoke the *first-best welfare criterion* $W^F(\mathbf{x})$, which is defined as follows. For any R&D profile $\mathbf{x} = (x_1, \ldots, x_i, \ldots, x_n)$ and output profile $\mathbf{q} = (q_1, \ldots, q_i, \ldots, q_n)$, let the net market surplus function $W(\mathbf{x}, \mathbf{q})$ be defined by

$$W(\mathbf{x}, \mathbf{q}) := \int_0^Q f(Z)\mathrm{d}Z - \sum_{j=1}^{n} [c(x_j, \mathbf{x}_{-j})q_j + x_j]. \tag{11}$$

For any symmetric R&D profile $\mathbf{x} = (x_1, \ldots, x_i, \ldots, x_n)$, let $\mathbf{q}^F(\mathbf{x})$ be the *socially first-best output profile* corresponding to $\mathbf{x}$, which is defined by

$$\mathbf{q}^F(\mathbf{x}) := \arg \max_{\mathbf{q} > 0} W(\mathbf{x}, \mathbf{q}) \tag{12}$$

and is characterized by the *marginal cost principle*:

$$f(Q^F(\mathbf{x})) = c(x_i; \mathbf{x}_{-i}) \qquad (i = 1, 2, \ldots, n), \tag{13}$$

where $Q^F(\mathbf{x}) = \Sigma_{j=1}^{n} q_j^F(\mathbf{x})$. As is easily verified, $q_i^F(\mathbf{x}) > q_i^N(\mathbf{x})$ holds for any symmetric $\mathbf{x}$. In terms of $\mathbf{q}^F(\mathbf{x})$, we define $W^F(\mathbf{x})$ by

$$W^F(\mathbf{x}) := W(\mathbf{x}, \mathbf{q}^F(\mathbf{x})). \tag{14}$$

One straightforward application of the first-best welfare criterion $W^F(\mathbf{x})$ is to compare $\mathbf{x}^N$ and $\mathbf{x}^C$ directly with the socially first-best R&D, $\mathbf{x}^F$, which is defined by

$$\mathbf{x}^F := \arg \max_{\mathbf{x} > 0} W^F(\mathbf{x}). \tag{15}$$

However, unless we define our model further in terms of details so that we can in fact compute $\mathbf{x}^N$, $\mathbf{x}^C$, and $\mathbf{x}^F$, such a direct use of $W^F(\mathbf{x})$ is hard to achieve.

An alternative feasible way to proceed, which we have used extensively in this monograph, is to evaluate the partial derivative $(\partial/\partial x_i) W^F(\mathbf{x})$ at $\mathbf{x}^N$ and $\mathbf{x}^C$, and determine if $(\partial/\partial x_i) W^F(\mathbf{x}^N) < (>) 0$ holds. If this crucial partial derivative is negative (positive), we are in the position to assert that the cost-reducing R&D at $\mathbf{x}^N$ is socially excessive (insufficient) at the margin in terms of the first-best welfare criterion $W^F(\mathbf{x})$. Similarly, we can gauge the marginal social excessiveness or insufficiency of the cost-reducing R&D at $\mathbf{x}^C$ by evaluating the sign of $(\partial/\partial x_i) W^F(\mathbf{x})$ at $\mathbf{x}^C$. Let us follow this familiar line of reasoning once again.

4.2. *Welfare verdicts in the case of sufficiently large R&D spillovers*

It is easy to verify that the crucial derivative to be evaluated, i.e. $(\partial/\partial x_i) W^F(\mathbf{x})$, consists of two terms: the *commitment effect*:

$$\gamma^F(\mathbf{x}) := -q_i^F(\mathbf{x}) \frac{\partial}{\partial x_i} c(x_i; \mathbf{x}_{-i}) - 1 \tag{16}$$

and the *spillover effect*:

$$\sigma^F(\mathbf{x}) := -\sum_{j \neq i} q_j^F(\mathbf{x}) \frac{\partial}{\partial x_i} c(x_j, \mathbf{x}_{-j}). \tag{17}$$

The spillover effect $\sigma^F(\mathbf{x})$ is easy to interpret. An increase in x_i reduces the marginal cost $c(x_j; \mathbf{x}_{-j})$ of firm j $(i \neq j)$ through the spillover of cost-reducing benefits which will increase the first-best social welfare in proportion to j's output $q_j^F(\mathbf{x})$. Adding the absolute values of these effects over all $j \neq i$, we immediately obtain $\sigma^F(\mathbf{x})$. On the other hand, the motivation behind our commitment effect $\gamma^F(\mathbf{x})$ is the same as in Chapter 4, and need not be repeated here.

It is shown in Section 6 that both $(\partial/\partial x_i) W^F(\mathbf{x}^N) > 0$ and $(\partial/\partial x_i) W^F(\mathbf{x}^C) > 0$ hold in the presence of sufficiently large R&D spillovers. Thus we have the following.

THEOREM 1. Suppose that A1, A2, and A3 hold. Then:

(*a*) the non-cooperative equilibrium R&D level is socially insufficient at the margin in terms of the first-best welfare criterion if R&D spillovers are sufficiently large;

(*b*) the co-operative equilibrium R&D level is socially insufficient at the margin in terms of the first-best welfare criterion irrespective of whether R&D spillovers are large or small.

According to Theorem 1, both x_i^N and x_i^C are socially insufficient at the margin in terms of the first-best welfare criterion. How, then, does x_i^N fare *vis-à-vis* x_i^C? To settle this question, we note that $\mathbf{x}^C$ is the maximizer of

$\Sigma_{j=1}^{n} \Pi_j(\mathbf{x})$ and then compute $(\partial/\partial x_i) \Sigma_{j=1}^{n} \Pi_j(\mathbf{x}^N)$. If we assume A3* instead of A3, we can verify that $(\partial/\partial x_i) \Sigma_{j=1}^{n} \Pi_j(\mathbf{x}^N) > 0$ holds in the presence of sufficiently large R&D spillovers, so that we may assert the following.

THEOREM 2. Suppose that A1, A2, and A3* hold. Then a small increase in R&D level at the non-cooperative equilibrium increases firms' joint profits in the presence of sufficiently large R&D spillovers.

Proof. See Section 6. □

4.3. *Welfare verdicts in the case of no R&D spillover*

To highlight the role played by large R&D spillovers in our results, let us briefly examine the other extreme case of no R&D spillover.

By definition, we have $(\partial/\partial x_j)c(x_i; \mathbf{x}_{-i}) = 0$ $(i \neq j;\ i, j = 1, 2, \ldots, n)$ and $\theta(\mathbf{x}) < 0$ in the absence of R&D spillovers; hence the term $(\partial/\partial x_i) W^F(\mathbf{x}^N)$ remains of ambiguous sign in general. However, we have already proved in Chapter 4 that $(\partial/\partial x_i) W^F(\mathbf{x}^N) < 0$ holds if A3* and $n \geqslant 3$ are satisfied. On the other hand, we know that $(\partial/\partial x_i) W^F(\mathbf{x}^C) > 0$ holds regardless of the extent of R&D spillovers. Furthermore, it is shown in Section 6 that we have $(\partial/\partial x_i) \Sigma_{j=1}^{n} \Pi_j(\mathbf{x}^N) < 0$ in the case of no R&D spillover. Combining these results, we obtain the following.

THEOREM 3. Suppose that A1, A2, and A3 hold and there is no R&D spillover. Then:

(*a*) if A3* is satisfied in place of A3, the non-cooperative equilibrium R&D level is socially excessive at the margin in terms of the first-best welfare criterion when $n \geqslant 3$;

(*b*) the co-operative equilibrium R&D level is socially insufficient at the margin in terms of the first-best welfare criterion;

(*c*) a small decrease in R&D level at the non-cooperative equilibrium increases firms' joint profits.

5. SECOND-BEST WELFARE ANALYSIS

5.1. *Decomposition of the marginal welfare effect*

If we leave the utopian first-best policy arena and invoke the down-to-earth *second-best welfare criterion*,

$$W^S(\mathbf{x}) := W(\mathbf{x}, \mathbf{q}^N(\mathbf{x})), \tag{18}$$

in place of the first-best criterion, $W^F(\mathbf{x})$, the crucial derivative to be evaluated, $(\partial/\partial x_i) W^S(\mathbf{x})$, should be broken down into three, rather than two, terms. In addition to the *commitment effect*,

$$\gamma^S(\mathbf{x}) := -\, q_i^N(\mathbf{x})\,(\partial/\partial x_i)\,c(x_i; \mathbf{x}_{-i}) - 1, \tag{19}$$

and the *spillover effect*,

$$\sigma^S(\mathbf{x}) := -\sum_{j \neq 1} q_j^N(\mathbf{x})\,(\partial/\partial x_i) c(x_j; \mathbf{x}_{-j}), \tag{20}$$

we now have an additional term, which may be called, as in Chapter 4, the *distortion effect*:

$$\delta^S(\mathbf{x}) := \sum_{j=1}^{n} \left[f(Q^N(\mathbf{x})) - c(x_j, \mathbf{x}_{-j}) \right] (\partial/\partial x_i) q_j^N(\mathbf{x}). \tag{21}$$

Clearly, the distortion effect is nothing other than the sum of marginal distortions generated by a marginal change in x_i.

5.2. *Welfare verdicts in the case of sufficiently large R&D spillovers*

If we evaluate $\gamma^S(\mathbf{x})$, $\sigma^S(\mathbf{x})$, and $\delta^S(\mathbf{x})$ at $\mathbf{x} = \mathbf{x}^N$, we obtain

$$\gamma^S(\mathbf{x}^N) = -\,(n-1) f'(Q^N(\mathbf{x}^N))\, q_i^N(\mathbf{x}^N)\, \theta(\mathbf{x}^N), \tag{22}$$

$$\sigma^S(\mathbf{x}^N) = -\,(n-1)\, q_i^N(\mathbf{x}^N)\,(\partial/\partial x_j) c(x_i^N; \mathbf{x}_{-i}^N) \qquad (i \neq j), \tag{23}$$

and

$$\delta^S(\mathbf{x}^N) = [f(Q^N(\mathbf{x}^N)) - c(x_i^N; \mathbf{x}_{-i}^N)]\; \Psi(\mathbf{x}^N). \tag{24}$$

It is clear that all terms are positive under A1, A2, and A3 in the presence of sufficiently large R&D spillovers. Thus, $(\partial/\partial x_i)\, W^S(\mathbf{x}^N) = \gamma^S(\mathbf{x}^N) + \sigma^S(\mathbf{x}^N) + \delta^S(\mathbf{x}^N) > 0$.

On the other hand, evaluating $\gamma^S(\mathbf{x})$, $\sigma^S(\mathbf{x})$, and $\delta^S(\mathbf{x})$ at $\mathbf{x} = \mathbf{x}^C$, we obtain

$$\begin{aligned} \gamma^S(\mathbf{x}^C) = &-\,(n-1)\, q_i^N(\mathbf{x}^C) f'(Q^N(\mathbf{x}^C))\, \Psi(\mathbf{x}^C) \\ &+ (n-1)\, q_i^N(\mathbf{x}^C)(\partial/\partial x_j) c(x_i^C; \mathbf{x}_{-i}^C), \end{aligned} \tag{26}$$

and

$$\delta^S(\mathbf{x}^C) = [f(Q^N(\mathbf{x}^C)) - c(x_i^C; \mathbf{x}_{-i}^C)]\; \Psi(\mathbf{x}^C). \tag{27}$$

Since $\sigma^S(\mathbf{x}^C)$ cancels the second component of $\gamma^S(\mathbf{x}^C)$, we obtain

$$\begin{aligned} (\partial/\partial x_i)\, W^S(\mathbf{x}^C) = \Big\{ &-\,(n-1)\, q_i^N(\mathbf{x}^C) f'(Q^N(\mathbf{x}^C)) \\ &+ \left[f(Q^N(\mathbf{x}^C)) - c(x_i^C; \mathbf{x}_{-i}^C) \right] \Big\}\; \Psi(\mathbf{x}^C), \end{aligned} \tag{28}$$

which is unambiguously positive under A1, A2, and A3 irrespective of whether R&D spillovers are large or small.

We have thus established the following theorem, which asserts, in effect, that the social insufficiency of the amount of co-operative as well as non-cooperative equilibrium R&D at the margin, when the R&D spillovers are sufficiently large, remains intact even if the utopian first-best welfare criterion is replaced by the more realistic second-best welfare criterion.

THEOREM 4. Suppose that A1, A2, and A3 hold. Then:

(*a*) the non-cooperative equilibrium R&D level is socially insufficient at the margin in terms of the second-best welfare criterion if the R&D spillovers are sufficiently large;
(*b*) the co-operative equilibrium R&D level is socially insufficient at the margin in terms of the second-best welfare criterion irrespective of whether R&D spillovers are large or small.

5.3. *Welfare verdicts in the case of no R&D spillover*

In order to crystallize the role played by the assumption of sufficiently large R&D spillovers, let us examine the opposite polar case, i.e. the case of no R&D spillover.

To begin with, the case of non-cooperative equilibrium is already covered by Chapter 4. On the other hand, in the case of co-operative equilibrium, we have $\gamma^S(\mathbf{x}^C) > 0$, $\sigma^S(\mathbf{x}^C) = 0$, and $\delta^S(\mathbf{x}^C) > 0$ from (25), (26), and (27) in the absence of R&D spillover, so that $(\partial/\partial x_i) W^S(\mathbf{x}^C)$ is unambiguously positive.

In summary, we can assert the following.

THEOREM 5. Suppose that A1, A2, and A3 hold and there exists no R&D spillover. Then:

(*a*) if there is a sufficiently large number of firms in the industry, the non-cooperative equilibrium R&D level will always be socially excessive at the margin in terms of the second-best welfare criterion;
(*b*) the co-operative equilibrium R&D level is socially insufficient at the margin in terms of the second-best welfare criterion.

6. PROOFS

Derivation of the formulas for $\omega(\mathbf{x})$ and $\theta(\mathbf{x})$

To derive formulas (6) and (7), we differentiate the first-order condition $(\partial/\partial q_i)\pi_i(q_i^N(\mathbf{x}), Q_{-i}^N(\mathbf{x}); \mathbf{x}) = 0$ characterizing $\mathbf{q}^N(\mathbf{x})$ with respect to x_i and x_h $(h \neq i)$ and use symmetry to obtain the following simultaneous equations for $\omega(\mathbf{x})$ and $\theta(\mathbf{x})$:

$$\alpha(\mathbf{x})\,\omega(\mathbf{x}) + (n-1)\beta(\mathbf{x})\theta(\mathbf{x}) = (\partial/\partial x_i)c(x_i, \mathbf{x}_{-i}) \tag{29}$$

and

$$\beta(\mathbf{x})\,\omega(\mathbf{x}) + [\alpha(\mathbf{x}) + (n-2)\beta(\mathbf{x})]\theta(\mathbf{x}) = (\partial/\partial x_j)c(x_i; \mathbf{x}_{-i}), \tag{30}$$

where $i \neq j$. Solving (29) and (30) for $\omega(\mathbf{x})$ ($\theta(\mathbf{x})$) and rearranging terms appropriately, we obtain (6) (7) in the main text. □

6.2. *Proof of Theorem 1*

Taking the first-order condition (2) characterizing $q_i^N(\mathbf{x})$ and the symmetry of $\mathbf{x}^N$ into consideration, we can rewrite the first-order condition (4) characterizing $\mathbf{x}^N$ as follows:

$$-q_i^N(\mathbf{x}^N)(\partial/\partial x_i)c(x_i^N; \mathbf{x}_{-i}^N) - 1 = -(n-1)f'(Q^N(\mathbf{x}^N))q_i^N(\mathbf{x}^N)\theta(\mathbf{x}^N)$$
$$(i = 1, 2, \ldots, n) \tag{31}$$

Comparing (16) at $\mathbf{x} = \mathbf{x}^N$ with (31), we may obtain

$$\begin{aligned}\gamma^F(\mathbf{x}^N) = &-(n-1)f'(Q^N(\mathbf{x}^N))q_i^N(\mathbf{x}^N)\theta(\mathbf{x}^N)\\ &+ [q_i^N(\mathbf{x}^N) - q_i^F(\mathbf{x}^N)](\partial/\partial x_i)c(x_i^N; \mathbf{x}_{-i}^N),\end{aligned} \tag{32}$$

which is positive in the presence of sufficiently large R&D spillovers where use is made of $q_i^F(\mathbf{x}) > q_i^N(\mathbf{x})$, A1 and A2. On the other hand, (17) evaluated at $\mathbf{x} = \mathbf{x}^N$ can be reduced to

$$\sigma^F(\mathbf{x}^N) = -(n-1)q_i^F(\mathbf{x}^N)(\partial/\partial x_j)c(x_i^N; \mathbf{x}_{-i}^N) \qquad (i \neq j), \tag{33}$$

which is non-negative by virtue of A2. It then follows that $(\partial/\partial x_i)W^F(\mathbf{x}^N) = \gamma^F(\mathbf{x}^N) + \sigma^F(\mathbf{x}^N) > 0$.

Turning to the co-operative equilibrium R&D $\mathbf{x}^C$, we may invoke (5) to obtain

$$\begin{aligned}\gamma^F(\mathbf{x}^C) = &-(n-1)f'(Q^N(\mathbf{x}^C))q_i^N(\mathbf{x}^C)\Psi(\mathbf{x}^C)\\ &+ [q_i^N(\mathbf{x}^C) - q_i^F(\mathbf{x}^C)](\partial/\partial x_i)c(x_i^C; \mathbf{x}_{-i}^C)\\ &+ (n-1)q_i^N(\mathbf{x}^C)(\partial/\partial x_i)c(x_i^C; \mathbf{x}_{-i}^C) \qquad (i \neq j).\end{aligned} \tag{34}$$

Coupling (34) with $\sigma^F(\mathbf{x}^C)$, which can be reduced to

$$\sigma^F(\mathbf{x}^C) = -(n-1)q_i^F(\mathbf{x}^C)(\partial/\partial x_j)c(x_i^C; \mathbf{x}_{-i}^C) \qquad (i \neq j), \tag{35}$$

we obtain

$$\begin{aligned}(\partial/\partial x_i)W^F(\mathbf{x}^C) = &-(n-1)f'(Q^N(\mathbf{x}^C))q_i^N(\mathbf{x}^C)\Psi(\mathbf{x}^C) + [q_i^N(\mathbf{x}^C) - q_i^F(\mathbf{x}^C)]\\ &[(\partial/\partial x_i)c(x_i^C; \mathbf{x}_{-i}^C) + (n-1)(\partial/\partial x_j)c(x_i^C; \mathbf{x}_{-i}^C)],\end{aligned} \tag{36}$$

where $i \neq j$, which is positive by virtue of $\Psi(\mathbf{x}^C) > 0$, $q_i^F(\mathbf{x}) > q_i^N(\mathbf{x})$, and A2 irrespective of the extent of the R&D spillovers. □

6.3. *Proof of Theorem 2*

Invoking (31), we can compute that

$$(\partial/\partial x_i) \sum_{j=1}^{n} \Pi_j(\mathbf{x}^N) = (n-1) q_i^N(\mathbf{x}^N) \{ f'(Q^N(\mathbf{x}^N)) \, [\omega(\mathbf{x}^N) + (n-2)\,\theta(\mathbf{x}^N)] - (\partial/\partial x_j) c(x_i^N; \mathbf{x}_{-i}^N) \} \tag{37}$$

holds where $i \neq j$. Having recourse to (6) and (7), we are assured that

$$\operatorname{sgn}(\partial/\partial x_i) \sum_{j=1}^{n} \Pi_j(\mathbf{x}^N) = \operatorname{sgn} \{ [-(n-3)\,\alpha(\mathbf{x}^N) + 2(n-1)\,\beta(\mathbf{x}^N)](\partial/\partial x_j) c(x_i^N; \mathbf{x}_{-i}^N) - \alpha(\mathbf{x}^N)(\partial/\partial x_j) c(x_i^N; \mathbf{x}_{-i}^N) \}, \tag{38}$$

so that $(\partial/\partial x_i) \Sigma_{j=1}^{n} \Pi_j(\mathbf{x}^N) > (<)\ 0$ holds if and only if

$$\Omega_i(\mathbf{x}^N) := \alpha(\mathbf{x}^N) + [(n-3)\,\alpha(\mathbf{x}^N) - 2(n-1)\,\beta(\mathbf{x}^N)] \frac{(\partial/\partial x_j) c(x_i^N; \mathbf{x}_{-i}^N)}{(\partial/\partial x_i) c(x_i^N; \mathbf{x}_{-i}^N)} > (<)\ 0 \tag{39}$$

holds where $i \neq j$. Under the assumption of sufficiently large R&D spill-overs,

$$\frac{(\partial/\partial x_j) c(x_i^N; \mathbf{x}_{-i}^N)}{(\partial/\partial x_i) c(x_i^N; \mathbf{x}_{-i}^N)} > \frac{\beta(\mathbf{x}^N)}{\alpha(\mathbf{x}^N)} \tag{40}$$

obtains where $i \neq j$. Note that an inequality $(n-3)\,\alpha(\mathbf{x}) - 2(n-1)\,\beta(\mathbf{x}) > 0$ is valid for any symmetric R&D profile $\mathbf{x} = (x_1, \ldots, x_i, \ldots, x_n)$. To verify this statement, let us introduce $\delta^N(\mathbf{x}) := Q^N(\mathbf{x}) f''(Q^N(\mathbf{x}))/f'(Q^N(\mathbf{x}))$, which enables us to rewrite (8) and (9) as

$$\alpha(\mathbf{x}) = f'(Q^N(\mathbf{x})) \left[2 + \frac{\delta^N(\mathbf{x})}{n} \right] \tag{41}$$

and

$$\beta(\mathbf{x}) = f'(Q^N(\mathbf{x})) \left[1 + \frac{\delta^N(\mathbf{x})}{n} \right]. \tag{42}$$

It follows that

$$(n-3)\,\alpha(\mathbf{x}) - 2(n-1)\,\beta(\mathbf{x}) = \frac{\alpha(\mathbf{x})}{2n + \delta^N(\mathbf{x})} \{ -[\delta^N(\mathbf{x}) + 4]\, n - \delta^N(\mathbf{x}) \} > 0, \tag{43}$$

whose sign is due to $\alpha(\mathbf{x}) < 0$ and $\delta^N(\mathbf{x}) \geqslant 0$, which follows from A3*.

Putting (39), (40), and (43) together and having recourse to A3*, we obtain

$$\Omega_i(\mathbf{x}^N) > \alpha(\mathbf{x}^N) + \frac{\beta(\mathbf{x}^N)}{\alpha(\mathbf{x}^N)}\,[(n-3)\,\alpha(\mathbf{x}^N) - 2(n-1)\,\beta(\mathbf{x}^N)]. \tag{44}$$

Using (41) and (42), we can verify that

$$\alpha(\mathbf{x}^N) + (n-3)\,\beta(\mathbf{x}^N) - 2(n-1)\,\frac{[\beta(\mathbf{x}^N)]^2}{\alpha(\mathbf{x}^N)} = -\frac{f'(Q^N(\mathbf{x}^N))\,\delta^N(\mathbf{x}^N)}{2n + \delta^N(\mathbf{x}^N)}\,[\delta^N(\mathbf{x}^N) + n + 1]$$
$$\geqslant 0. \tag{45}$$

We are thus led to conclude that $(\partial/\partial x_i)\,\Sigma_{j=1}^n\,\Pi_j(\mathbf{x}^N) > 0$. □

6.4. *Proof of Theorem 3*

In the case of no R&D spillover, we have $(\partial/\partial x_i)\,W^F(\mathbf{x}^N) = \gamma^F(\mathbf{x}^N)$, which has an ambiguous sign in general. However, if A3* is assumed additionally, it enables us to obtain

$$\frac{\partial}{\partial x_i}\,W^F(\mathbf{x}^N) = \frac{\partial}{\partial x_i}c(x_i^N;\,\mathbf{x}_{-i}^N)\left[\frac{n + \delta^N(\mathbf{x}^N)}{n + 1 + \delta^N(\mathbf{x}^N)}\,\frac{n-1}{n}\,q_i^N(\mathbf{x}^N) + q_i^N(\mathbf{x}^N) - q_i^F(\mathbf{x}^N)\right]$$
$$\leqslant q_i^N(\mathbf{x}^N)\left[\frac{n + \delta^N(\mathbf{x}^N)}{n + 1 + \delta^N(\mathbf{x}^N)}\,\frac{n-1}{n} - \frac{1}{n}\right]\frac{\partial}{\partial x_i}\,c(x_i^N;\,\mathbf{x}_{-i}^N), \tag{46}$$

where use is made of (23) in Chapter 4, plus (32) and (41). Note that the expression within the brackets in the final line is positive when $n \geqslant 3$. It then follows from (46) that $(\partial/\partial x_i)\,W^F(\mathbf{x}^N) < 0$ when $n \geqslant 3$. This proves the part (*a*) of Theorem 3. Part (*b*) of the theorem does not need any further proof, and the part (*c*) follows from (39) by simply substituting $(\partial/\partial x_j)c(x_i^N;\,\mathbf{x}_{-i}^N) = 0$ $(i \neq j)$. □

7. THE CASE OF SMALL R&D SPILLOVERS

7.1. *Simplifying assumptions*

We have so far analysed the situations of 'large' spillovers and 'no' spillover, thus leaving in between a wide grey zone of 'small' spillovers. Note also that some of our results require the number of firms to be 'large', so that we are left in the dark when the number of firms is 'small'. In order to fill in these lacunae to some extent, let us now specify our inverse demand function and cost-reducing technology as follows:

$$f(Q) = a - bQ, \qquad a > 0, b > 0, \tag{47}$$

for all $Q \geqslant 0$ such that $f(Q) > 0$, and

$$(\partial/\partial x_i)c(x_j; \mathbf{x}_{-j}) = \zeta(\partial/\partial x_i)c(x_i; \mathbf{x}_{-i}), \qquad 0 < \zeta < 1 \qquad (i \neq j), \tag{48}$$

for all $\mathbf{x} > 0$ such that $c(x_i; \mathbf{x}_{-i}) > 0$. It is clear that (47) ((48)) are consistent with A1 and A3 (A2).

In this simple parametric model, we can actually compute the Cournot–Nash equilibrium $\mathbf{q}^N(\mathbf{x})$ and the socially first-best output profile $\mathbf{q}^F(\mathbf{x})$. Indeed, it is easy to verify that

$$q_i^N(\mathbf{x}) = \frac{1}{b(n+1)}\,[a - nc(x_i; \mathbf{x}_{-i}) + \sum_{j \neq i} c(x_j; \mathbf{x}_{-j})] \tag{49}$$

and

$$q_i^F(\mathbf{x}) = \frac{1}{bn}\,[a - nc(x_i; \mathbf{x}_{-i}) + \sum_{j \neq i} c(x_j; \mathbf{x}_{-j})] \tag{50}$$

hold, so that we have $q_i^N(\mathbf{x}) < q_i^F(\mathbf{x})$ for any n, which vindicates the general result we have established between $q^N(\mathbf{x})$ and $\mathbf{q}^F(\mathbf{x})$. It is not difficult to check that the industry output $Q^N(\mathbf{x})$ is positive if and only if we have $a > c(x_i; \mathbf{x}_{-i})$ $(i = 1, 2, \ldots, n)$. It is also easy to verify that

$$\frac{\partial}{\partial x_j} q_i^N(\mathbf{x}) = \frac{1 - 2\zeta}{b(n+1)} \frac{\partial}{\partial x_j} c(x_j; \mathbf{x}_{-j}) \tag{51}$$

holds, so that the R&D spillovers are large (small) if and only if we have $\zeta > (<) \frac{1}{2}$.

7.2. *First-best welfare analysis*

Let us begin with the first-best welfare analysis of the non-cooperative equilibrium $\mathbf{x}^N$. It is simple, if tedious, to verify that

$$\begin{aligned} \frac{\partial}{\partial x_i} W^F(\mathbf{x}^N) = &- (n-1) q_i^F(\mathbf{x}^N) \frac{\partial}{\partial x_i} c(x_j^N; \mathbf{x}_{-j}^N) \\ &+ [q_i^N(\mathbf{x}^N) - q_i^F(\mathbf{x}^N)] \frac{\partial}{\partial x_i} c(x_i^N; \mathbf{x}_{-i}^N) \\ &+ \frac{n-1}{n+1} q_i^N(\mathbf{x}^N) \left[\frac{\partial}{\partial x_i} c(x_i^N; \mathbf{x}_{-i}^N) - 2 \frac{\partial}{\partial x_i} c(x_j^N; \mathbf{x}_{-j}^N)\right] \end{aligned} \tag{52}$$

holds. Clearly, the first term in the RHS is non-negative by virtue of A2 and the second term thereof is positive in view of $q_i^N(\mathbf{x}^N) < q_i^F(\mathbf{x}^N)$ and A2, whereas the third term can be rewritten as

$$b(n+1)\frac{n-1}{n+1}\, q_i^N(\mathbf{x}^N)\frac{\partial}{\partial x_j}\, q_i^N(\mathbf{x}^N) \qquad (i \neq j), \tag{53}$$

where use is made of (49). Since (53) is positive in the presence of large R&D spillovers, it follows from (52) that $(\partial/\partial x_i)\, W^F(\mathbf{x}^N) > 0$, thus vindicating the fact that the non-cooperative R&D is socially insufficient at the margin. On the other hand, in the case of no R&D spillover, (52) is reduced to

$$\frac{\partial}{\partial x_i} W^F(\mathbf{x}^N) = q_i^N(\mathbf{x}^N)\frac{n^2-2n-1}{n(n+1)}\frac{\partial}{\partial x_i} c(x_i^N; \mathbf{x}_{-i}^N), \tag{54}$$

which is negative (positive) if $n = 2$ $(n \geqslant 3)$. It is worth noticing that the performance of duopoly and that of oligopoly are in sharp contrast here.

To consider the situation of small spillovers $(0 < \zeta < \frac{1}{2})$, we can rewrite (52) by invoking (49), (50), (51), and symmetry to obtain

$$\frac{\partial}{\partial x_i} W^F(\mathbf{x}^N) = -\frac{a - c(x_i^N; \mathbf{x}_{-i}^N)}{b}\frac{n^2-2n-1}{n(n+1)^2}\,\phi(n\colon \zeta)\frac{\partial}{\partial x_i} c(x_j^N\colon \mathbf{x}_{-j}^N), \tag{55}$$

where

$$\phi(n\colon \zeta) := \frac{(n-1)(n^2+4n+2)}{n^2-2n-1} - \frac{1}{\zeta}. \tag{56}$$

Therefore, $(\partial/\partial x_i)\, W^F(\mathbf{x}^N) > 0$ clearly holds if $n = 2$. On the other hand, if $n \geqslant 3$, (55) entails

$$\operatorname{sgn}(\partial/\partial x_i)\, W^F(\mathbf{x}^N) = \operatorname{sgn}\phi(n\colon \zeta). \tag{57}$$

Note that $\operatorname{sgn}\phi(n\colon \zeta)$ coincides with the sign of

$$\chi(n\colon \zeta) := (n-1)\,[n^2 + (4-\zeta^{-1})n + (2+\zeta^{-1})]. \tag{58}$$

Let $n^*(\zeta)$ be the largest real root of $\chi(n\colon \zeta) = 0$ for given ζ. It is easy to verify that

$$n^*(\zeta) = \begin{cases} 1 & \text{if } (3-\sqrt{7})/4 < \zeta < 1/2 \\ [\zeta^{-1} - 4 + \sqrt{D(\zeta)}]/2 & \text{if } 0 < \zeta \leqslant (3-\sqrt{7})/4 \end{cases} \tag{59}$$

holds, where $D(\zeta) := (\zeta^{-1} - 6)^2 - 28$. We can then assert that:

(*a*) if $(3-\sqrt{7})/4 < \zeta < 1/2$, $(\partial/\partial x_i)\, W^F(\mathbf{x}^N) > 0$ for all $n \geqslant 3$;
(*b*) if $0 < \zeta \leqslant (3-\sqrt{7})/4$, $(\partial/\partial x_i)\, W^F(\mathbf{x})^N > (<)\ 0$ whenever $n > n^*(\zeta)$ $(3 \leqslant n < n^*(\zeta))$.

In the case of co-operative equilibrium $\mathbf{x}^C$, Theorems 1 and 3 have already illustrated that $\mathbf{x}^C$ is socially insufficient at the margin in terms of the first-best welfare criterion irrespective of whether the R&D spillovers and the number of firms are large or small.

7.3. *Second-best welfare analysis*

Let us now turn to the second-best welfare analysis. In this case, also, we have only to consider the non-cooperative equilibrium $\mathbf{x}^N$ when the R&D spillovers are small.

It is easy, if tedious, to derive

$$\frac{\partial}{\partial x_i} W^S(\mathbf{x}^N) = -\frac{[f(Q^N(\mathbf{x}^N)) - c(x_i^N; \mathbf{x}_{-i}^N)]}{b(n+1)} \xi(n\colon \zeta) \frac{\partial}{\partial x_i} c(x_i; \mathbf{x}_{-i}), \tag{60}$$

where

$$\xi(n\colon \zeta) := \zeta(n^2 + 3n - 4) - (n - 2). \tag{61}$$

It is clear that

$$\operatorname{sgn}(\partial/\partial x_i) W^S(\mathbf{x}^N) = \operatorname{sgn}[-\xi(n\colon \zeta)(\partial/\partial x_i)c(x_i; \mathbf{x}_{-i})] \tag{62}$$

holds. If $n = 2$, it follows from (62) that $(\partial/\partial x_i) W^S(\mathbf{x}^N) > (=)\ 0$ if $(\partial/\partial x_i)c(x_j; \mathbf{x}_{-j}) < (=)\ 0$.

Consider now the situation where $n \geqslant 3$ and spillovers are small. It is clear that $\operatorname{sgn}(\partial/\partial x_i) W^S(\mathbf{x}^N) = \operatorname{sgn} \xi(n\colon \zeta)$ holds in this case. Let $\mathrm{d}(\zeta) := (3\zeta - 1)^2 - 8\zeta(1 - 2\zeta)$. Then we have $(\partial/\partial x_i) W^S(\mathbf{x}^N) > 0$ if $\mathrm{d}(\zeta) \leqslant 0$ or $\mathrm{d}(\zeta) > 0$ and $n > n^{**}(\zeta)$, where $n^{**}(\zeta) := (1/2\zeta)[1 - 3\zeta + \sqrt{\mathrm{d}(\zeta)}]$.

In order to understand how $\operatorname{sgn}(\partial/\partial x_i) W^S(\mathbf{x}^N)$ depends on the extent of R&D spillovers, let $\zeta = 0.5$, 0.4, 0.3, 0.2, 0.1, and 0.05. We can easily check that $\mathrm{d}(\zeta) < 0$ for $\zeta = 0.5$, 0.4, 0.3, 0.2, and 0.1. Therefore, for this range of values of ζ, $(\partial/\partial x_i) W^S(\mathbf{x}^N) > 0$ holds for any $n \geqslant 3$. For $\zeta = 0.05$, however, we get $\mathrm{d}(\zeta) = 139/400$ and $n^{**}(\zeta) = (17 + \sqrt{139})/2 = 14.39$, so that we have $(\partial/\partial x_i) W^S(\mathbf{x}^N) > 0$ only when the number of firms n is no less than 15.

8. CONCLUDING REMARKS

To begin with, a few remarks on the literature related to the analysis of this chapter are in order.

Models of two-stage oligopolistic competition with R&D commitment in the absence of R&D collaboration and R&D spillovers have been studied by Besley and Suzumura (1992), Brander and Spencer (1983), Okuno-Fujiwara and Suzumura (1993), and Spencer and Brander (1983), whereas Dasgupta and Stiglitz (1980), Leven and Reiss (1988), and Spence (1984) have analysed models of oligopolistic competition without strategic commitment to R&D. It was d'Aspremont and Jacquemin (1988) who presented a pioneering analysis of co-operative and non-cooperative R&D in terms of a two-stage model of *duopoly* with R&D spillovers. They made the interesting point that co-operative R&D between otherwise competing firms may increase the R&D expenditure level relative to the fully non-cooperative case, provided that the R&D spillovers are sufficiently large, although the co-operative R&D may fall short of the socially first-best level.[2]

For at least two reasons, the robustness of d'Aspremont and Jacquemin's results is questionable. First, they presented their results as surprising on the basis that co-operation should reduce excessive duplication of R&D efforts in the presence of sufficiently large spillovers.[3] However, the R&D incentive of a single firm hinges squarely on the extent of appropriability of the R&D benefits, so that the presence of large R&D spillovers may drastically reduce the incentives for cost reduction; hence the R&D commitment made voluntarily by a firm tends to be socially too small. From this viewpoint, if an enforceable agreement on co-operative R&D efforts is made, it may well facilitate more commitments. The result of the net effect of the R&D co-operation hinges on the relative strength of these two competing forces. This chapter has shown that the latter force dominates the former one, not only in the example of a duopoly with linear inverse demand function and linear marginal cost function, which was assumed by d'Aspremont and Jacquemin, but also in a much wider class of oligopolistic industries, thus supporting the robustness of their results. Second, d'Aspremont and Jacquemin invoked the first-best welfare function as their welfare criterion, but the relevance of this utopian convention may be disputed. What is needed is a comparison of the social gains from co-operative R&D and non-cooperative R&D within the alternative feasible arrangements. This chapter has shown that their results can be extended and made more relevant by invoking a second-best welfare function as an alternative welfare criterion.

Table 8. The case of large R&D spillovers

	$\mathbf{x}^N$	$\mathbf{x}^C$
$\frac{\partial}{\partial x_i} W^F(\mathbf{x})$	+	+
$\frac{\partial}{\partial x_i} W^S(\mathbf{x})$	+	+
$\frac{\partial}{\partial x_i} \Sigma_{j=1}^n \Pi_j(\mathbf{x})$	+[a]	0

[a] This requires assumption A3*.

The main results of our analysis are succinctly summarized in tables 8 (large-spillover case), 9 (no-spillover case), and 10 (small-spillover case), where '+', '0', or '–' in any cell means that the partial derivative in the corresponding row is 'positive', 'zero', or 'negative' when evaluated at the R&D profile in the corresponding column. When the validity of the given sign requires more than just our standard assumptions A1, A2, and A3, this fact is indicated in the table footnote. These marginal conclusions on the performance of $\mathbf{x}^N$ and $\mathbf{x}^C$ can be converted into global conclusions; that is, the ranking among x_i^N, x_i^C, x_i^F, and x_i^S on the one hand, and the ranking among $Q^N(\mathbf{x}^N)$, $Q^N(\mathbf{x}^C)$, $Q^N(\mathbf{x}^S)$, and $Q^F(\mathbf{x}^F)$ on the other, can be obtained if the relevant welfare or joint profit function is guaranteed to be single-peaked.[4]

Table 9. The case of no R&D spillovers

	$\mathbf{x}^N$	$\mathbf{x}^C$
$\frac{\partial}{\partial x_i} W^F(\mathbf{x})$	$-$[a]	+
$\frac{\partial}{\partial x_i} W^S(\mathbf{x})$	$-$[b]	+
$\frac{\partial}{\partial x_i} \Sigma_{j=1}^n \Pi_j(\mathbf{x})$	$-$	0

[a] This requires assumption A3* and $n \geqslant 3$.
[b] This requires that the number of firms is sufficiently large.

Table 10. The case of small R&D spillovers[a]

	$\mathbf{x}^N$	$\mathbf{x}^C$
$\frac{\partial}{\partial x_i} W^F(\mathbf{x})$	+[b]	+
$\frac{\partial}{\partial x_i} W^S(\mathbf{x})$	+[c]	+

[a] This requires (47) and (48) for $0 < \zeta < \frac{1}{2}$.
[b] This holds for $n = 2$ or $(3 - \sqrt{7})/4 < \zeta < \frac{1}{2}$ or $(\{0 < \zeta < (3 - \sqrt{7})/4$ and $n > n^*(\zeta)\})$.
[c] This holds for $n = 2$ or $d(\zeta) \leqslant 0$ or $\{d(\zeta) > 0$ and $n > n^{**}(\zeta)\}$.

The comparison between Tables 8 and 9 yields several policy-relevant conclusions.

First, comparing the first and second rows in each table, we may assert that the qualitative conclusions remain the same even when one uses the second-best welfare criterion instead of the first-best welfare criterion. Note, however, that the policy relevance of these conclusions is quite substantially increased by the use of the second-best welfare criterion.

Second, comparing the first and second columns in Table 8, we can assert that, in the presence of large R&D spillovers, not only the non-cooperative equilibrium R&D level but also the co-operative equilibrium R&D level is socially insufficient at the margin, so that the technology policy that facilitates further investment in R&D is marginally welfare-improving irrespective of whether firms co-operate or not. In other words, there is no such thing as excessive competition in R&D investment in the presence of large R&D spillovers.

Third, comparing the first and second columns in Table 9, we can assert that, in the absence of R&D spillovers, while the co-operative equilibrium R&D level remains socially too small at the margin, the non-cooperative equilibrium R&D level turns out to be socially excessive at the margin. Therefore, the welfare-improving technology policy at the margin should facilitate (restrict) investment in R&D if firms co-operate (do not co-operate).

Fourth, comparing the third row in Table 8 with the corresponding row in Table 9, we are assured that an increase in R&D at the non-cooperative equilibrium increases (decreases) joint profits at the margin if R&D spillover effects are large (small).

In concluding this chapter, several remarks are in order concerning directions for the future analysis of co-operative R&D.

First, as Bernstein and Nadiri (1988) and Levin and Reiss (1988) have emphasized, R&D undertaken by firms outside the industry, e.g. by material suppliers and equipment suppliers, may exert an influence on a firm's marginal cost. Such *inter-industry spillover effects* should be taken into consideration along with the *intra-industry spillover effects* in order to obtain a well balanced evaluation of the effects of R&D spillovers.

Second, one of the alleged functions of co-operative R&D is precisely to generate synergetic effects by pooling various complementary resources such as research information and experience, teams of researchers, and technological know-how. From this viewpoint, our interpretation of R&D spillovers in terms in the average variable cost function, *which remains the same irrespective of whether firms co-operate or not*, may be seriously inadequate. For fuller analysis, we should presumably endogenize the spillover function by making the cost-reducing technology dependent on the extent to which firms pool their complementary R&D resources.

Third, the potential benefits of co-operative R&D are often related to an acceleration in the speed of invention and innovation by risk-spreading and risk-pooling. In discussing cost-reducing R&D, therefore, we should introduce an element of uncertainty into the analysis.

Fourth, our concentration on the second-stage quantity game and the assumption of symmetric equilibria are likely to restrict the generality of our conclusions. In particular, it may well be worth while selecting a subgroup of co-operating firms and letting this subgroup conduct R&D exclusively—subject to the cost-sharing agreements among all member firms—since the group as a whole can thereby save on the fixed cost of equipment installation and avoid any unnecessary duplication of R&D efforts.

The policy implications of our results should be interpreted carefully in the light of these qualifying observations. Nevertheless, it is hoped that our results, partial though they are, and the method of analysis that has been developed *en route*, will be of some help in deepening understanding of the complex issue of co-operative R&D.[5]

NOTES TO CHAPTER 6

1. Several salient features of co-operative research activities are analysed by d'Aspremont and Jacquemin (1988), Dutta and Suzumura (1993), Hayashi *et al.* (1989), Itoh *et al.* (1991: ch. 20), Jacquemin (1988), Kamien *et al.* (1992), Katz (1986), Katz and Ordover (1990), Okimoto *et al.* (1984), Okimoto (1989), Ordover and Willig (1985), Peck (1986), Suzumura (1992), Suzumura and Goto (1993), and Suzumura and Yanagawa (1993), among many others. Needless to say, there are several relevant features of co-operative research activities that we had to leave out of this chapter, but in the concluding remarks we shall point out several directions in which the present analysis should be further developed.
2. Our definition of large R&D spillovers in terms of the sign of $\theta(\mathbf{x})$ is in concordance with the one adopted by d'Aspremont and Jacquemin (1988). Indeed, in their duopoly example where $0 > (\partial/\partial x_j)c(x_i; \mathbf{x}_{-i}) = -\varepsilon > -1 = (\partial/\partial x_i)c(x_i; \mathbf{x}_{-i})$ $(i \neq j;\ i, j = 1, 2)$, $f(Q) = a - bQ$, $a > 0$, and $b > 0$, we may compute that $\theta(\mathbf{x}) = (2\varepsilon - 1)/3$, which is positive if and only if $\varepsilon > 1/2$, i.e. if and only if the R&D spillovers are 'sufficiently large' in the sense of the term used by d'Aspremont and Jacquemin.
3. One may also add that, by participating in co-operative R&D association, firms can save on the fixed costs of R&D equipment and administration.
4. By the single-peakedness of a function $f(\mathbf{x})$, where $\mathbf{x} = (x_1, \ldots, x_i, \ldots, x_n)$, we here mean that $f(x_i; \mathbf{x}_{-i})$ has a unique local, hence global, maximum with respect to x_i for any specified value of $\mathbf{x}_{-i} = (x_1, \ldots, x_{i-1}, x_{i+1}, \ldots, x_n)$ $(i = 1, 2, \ldots, n)$. Note that, in the duopoly example analysed by d'Aspremont and Jacquemin (1988), we are assured that the first-best welfare function as well as the joint profit function is concave, hence single-peaked.
5. In Appendix B at the end of this monograph, an in-depth overview is provided of Japanese collaborative R&D, including a brief discussion on the Antimonopoly Act Guideline which was recently published by the Fair Trade Commission of Japan. Some of the policy issues just mentioned will be examined in more detail with special reference to the postwar experience in Japan.

III

Generalizations and Qualifications

Mess. Gracious Madam,
I that do bring the news made not the match.
Cleo. Say 'tis not so, a province I will give thee,
And make thy fortunes proud: the blow thou hadst
Shall make thy peace for moving me to rage,
And I will boot thee with what gift beside
Thy modesty can beg.

William Shakespeare, *Anthony and Cleopatra*

In this monograph, we have identified several situations of oligopolistic interactions where the spontaneous outcome of competitive forces turns out to be socially excessive. Note that our verdict is based on a well defined welfare criterion which is commonly used in several distinct branches of standard welfare economics. Part I centred around the competitive forces in the long run, whereas Part II examined the competitive forces in the shorter run where the analytical focus was on the strategic moves of oligopolistic competitors. The task of Part III is twofold. First, we will synthesize the excess entry theorem in Part I and the excess investment theorem in Part II, thereby crystallizing the analytical results of these two parts. Second, we will introduce alternative specifications of oligopolistic interactions with the purpose of examining the robustness of our preceding theoretical results on oligopolistic competition and economic welfare.

More concretely, the plan of Part III is as follows. Chapter 7 constructs a three-stage model of oligopolistic competition. In the first stage, each firm decides whether to enter into, or stay out of, the industry. In the second stage, each firm that has entered decides on the level of strategic commitment with R&D investment. In the third stage, firms compete in terms of output, their cost functions being determined by the R&D commitment made in the previous stage. We examine whether the excess entry result holds in this generalized situation of oligopolistic interactions. Chapter 8 examines how the results of Parts I and II are affected (1) if firms are profit-constrained sales-maximizers or profit-sharing income-per-employee-maximizers rather than profit-maximizers pure and simple, (2) if firms form conjectures about the response of rival firms other than the simple Cournot conjecture, (3) if firms produce differentiated products and consumers have preference for product diversity, and (4) if firms compete in terms of prices rather than quantities. Finally, Chapter 9 dispenses with the basic assumption of identical firms and symmetric equilibria and demonstrates that there still remains a basic message which can be carried over from our preceding analyses based on the simplifying assumptions of identical firms and symmetric equilibria.

7 Entry, Commitment, and Welfare: A Synthesis

1. INTRODUCTION

In Parts I and II, we established two basic theorems on the symmetric Cournot oligopoly equilibrium and economic welfare which go squarely counter to 'a widespread belief that increasing competition will increase welfare' (Stiglitz 1981: 184). The first theorem, which is established in Chapters 1 and 2, maintains that the equilibrium number of firms in the homogeneous output Cournot oligopoly is socially excessive at the margin in the sense that a marginal *decrease* in the number of firms unambiguously *increases* social welfare. The second theorem, which is established in Chapter 4 and generalized and qualified in Chapter 6 in the presence of R&D spillovers, asserts that R&D commitment at the subgame-perfect equilibrium of the two-stage symmetric Cournot oligopoly is socially excessive at the margin if the number of firms is sufficiently large. Besides, the critical number of firms for this theorem to hold remains consistently small for a wide range of oligopoly models.

In this chapter, by allowing endogenous change in the number of firms within a symmetric Cournot oligopoly model where incumbent firms compete in two stages, we will synthesize these theorems and establish that the excess entry theorem basically remains true in a symmetric Cournot oligopoly even in the presence of R&D commitment prior to competition in the homogeneous product market. In view of the crucial role of strategic commitment in oligopolistic interactions, this extension of the excess entry theorem seems to enhance the relevance of our theorem rather substantially.

The plan of the chapter is as follows. In Section 2, our model of three-stage oligopolistic competition with endogenous change in the number of firms is introduced. In Section 3, our excess entry theorem in the presence of strategic commitment is presented. Section 4 contains all proofs, and Section 5 concludes with several clarifying observations.

2. OLIGOPOLY MODEL WITH STRATEGIC COMMITMENT AND ENDOGENOUS ENTRY

2.1. Basic structure and equilibrium concepts

We consider oligopolistic competition in a homogeneous product industry played out in three stages. In the first stage firms decide simultaneously whether or not to enter the market. In the second stage firms make an irrevocable commitment to R&D investments, which affect production costs in the third stage, where firms compete in quantities. Since R&D investment is a fixed commitment made in advance, firms' investment decisions are affected by strategic considerations. The purpose of our analysis is to explore the welfare performance of a symmetric subgame-perfect equilibrium of this three-stage game.

Clearly, the second- and third-stage games, where the number of firms is predetermined, are basically the same as the two-stage game analysed in Chapter 4. Therefore, our decomposition of the welfare effect of an additional R&D investment into the *commitment effect* and the *distortion effect* will play an integral part in the analysis of the fully fledged three-stage game.

In this chapter we will utilize three different equilibrium concepts. Given any arbitrary number of firms and R&D investment profile, the *third-stage Cournot–Nash equilibrium* is defined. Given an arbitrary number of firms, the *second-stage subgame-perfect equilibrium* is defined when the relevant game is specified by the second and third stages of the entire game. Finally, the *first-stage free-entry equilibrium* is defined as a subgame-perfect equilibrium of the entire game. The focus of our analysis is the welfare performance of the first-stage free-entry equilibrium.

2.2. *Basic assumptions*

The inverse demand function for the product is $p = f(Q)$, where p is price and Q is industry output. The cost-reducing R&D and the output level of firm i are denoted by x_i and q_i, respectively, and the variable cost function of firm i is represented by $c(x_i)q_i$, where the function $c(x)$ is assumed to be identical for all firms.

For each specified number of firms n, where $2 \leqslant n < \infty$, and for each specified R&D profile $\mathbf{x} = (x_1, \ldots, x_i, \ldots, x_n)$, the third-stage payoff function of firm i is defined by

$$\pi_i(q_i, Q_{-i}; x_i; n) := [f(Q) - c(x_i)]q_i - x_i, \tag{1}$$

where $Q = q_i + Q_{-i}$. As usual, we are assuming that the R&D investment is measured by the fixed cost of equipment installations. Let $\mathbf{q}^N(\mathbf{x}; n) = (q_1^N(\mathbf{x}; n), \ldots, q_i^N(\mathbf{x}; n), \ldots, q_n^N(\mathbf{x}; n))$ denote the Cournot–Nash equilibrium of the third- stage game corresponding to the prescribed $(\mathbf{x}; n)$. We assume that $\mathbf{q}^N(\mathbf{x}; n)$ is symmetric and positive if the R&D profile $\mathbf{x}$ is symmetric and positive. In this chapter we assume the following.

A1: $f(Q)$ is twice continuously differentiable with $f'(Q) < 0$ for all $Q \geqslant 0$ such that $f(Q) > 0$. Furthermore, the elasticity

$$\delta(Q) := \frac{Qf''(Q)}{f'(Q)} \tag{2}$$

is constant.

A2: $c(x)$ is twice continuously differentiable and satisfies $c(x) > 0$, $c'(x) < 0$ and $c''(x) > 0$ for all $x > 0$.

As noted in Chapter 5, the second half of A1 implies that the admissible inverse demand functions must be in the following class:

$$f(Q) = \begin{cases} a - bQ^{\varepsilon} & \text{if } \varepsilon = \delta + 1 \neq 0 \\ a - b \log Q & \text{if } \delta = -1 \end{cases}, \tag{3}$$

where a is a non-negative constant and b is another constant such that $b > 0$ ($b < 0$) if $\delta \geqslant -1$ ($\delta < -1$). Since (3) includes linear demand functions ($\varepsilon = 1$) as well as constantly elastic demand functions ($a = 0$), it is clear that A1 accommodates a wide class of 'normal' inverse demand functions.

For any R&D profile $\mathbf{x} = (x_1, \ldots, x_i, \ldots, x_n)$ and the number of firms n, let us define

$$\alpha_i(q_i, Q_{-i}; \mathbf{x}; n) := \frac{\partial^2}{\partial q_i^2} \pi_i(q_i, Q_{-i}; x_i; n)$$

and

$$\beta_{ij}(q_i, Q_{-i}; \mathbf{x}; n) := \frac{\partial^2}{\partial q_i \partial q_j} \pi_i(q_i, Q_{-i}; x_i; n), \qquad (i \neq j;\ i, j = 1, 2, \ldots, n)$$

Since the strategic variables that firms use in the third-stage competition in the product market are quantities, it is quite natural that we assume the following.

A3: The third-stage strategies are strategic substitutes; that is, we have $\beta_{ij}(q_i, Q_{-i}; \mathbf{x}; n) < 0$ for any $(q_i, Q_{-i}; \mathbf{x}; n)$ $(i \neq j;\ i, j = 1, 2, \ldots, n)$.

Recollect that

$$\alpha_i(q_i^N(\mathbf{x}; n), Q_{-i}^N(\mathbf{x}; n); \mathbf{x}; n) = 2f'(Q^N(\mathbf{x}; n)) + q_i^N(\mathbf{x}; n)f''(Q^N(\mathbf{x}; n)) \tag{4}$$

and

$$\beta_{ij}(q_i^N(\mathbf{x}; n), Q_{-i}^N(\mathbf{x}; n); \mathbf{x}; n) = f'(Q^N(\mathbf{x}; n)) + q_i^N(\mathbf{x}; n)f''(Q^N(\mathbf{x}; n)) \tag{5}$$

hold, where $Q^N(\mathbf{x}; n) = q_i^N(\mathbf{x}; n) + Q_{-i}^N(\mathbf{x}; n)$. Thanks to the assumption of symmetry, (4) and (5) can be reduced to

$$\alpha(\mathbf{x}; n) = n^{-1}(2(n + \delta)f'(Q^N(\mathbf{x}; n)) \tag{6}$$

and

$$\beta(\mathbf{x}; n) = n^{-1}(n + \delta)f'(Q^N(\mathbf{x}; n)), \tag{7}$$

where $\alpha(\mathbf{x}; n) := \alpha_i(q_i^N(\mathbf{x}; n), Q_{-i}^N(\mathbf{x}; n); \mathbf{x}; n)$ and $\beta(\mathbf{x}; n) := \beta_{ij}(q_i^N(\mathbf{x}; n), Q_{-i}^N(\mathbf{x}; n); \mathbf{x}; n)$ for short. In view of (7) and invoking A1, it follows from A3 that

$$n + \delta > 0 \tag{8}$$

holds for any specified n, where $2 \leqslant n < +\infty$. Note in passing that (6) and (7) imply $\alpha(\mathbf{x}; n) < \beta(\mathbf{x}; n)$ for any $(\mathbf{x}; n)$.

2.3. *Third-stage Cournot–Nash equilibrium*

Given the assumption of interior optimum and second-order conditions, the third-stage Cournot–Nash equilibrium $\mathbf{q}^N(\mathbf{x}; n)$ is characterized by

$$f(Q^N(\mathbf{x}; n)) + q_i^N(\mathbf{x}; n)f'(Q^N(\mathbf{x}; n)) = c(x_i) \qquad (i = 1, 2, \ldots, n). \tag{9}$$

We assume throughout that $\mathbf{q}^N(\mathbf{x}; n)$ is unique, symmetric, and positive if $\mathbf{x}$ is symmetric and positive. Let us examine how $q_i^N(\mathbf{x}; n)$ behaves in response to a change in x_i, x_j $(i \neq j)$ and n. Defining $\omega(\mathbf{x}; n) := (\partial/\partial x_i)q_i^N(\mathbf{x}; n)$ and $\theta(\mathbf{x}; n) := (\partial/\partial x_i)q_j^N(\mathbf{x}; n)$ $(i \neq j)$ as in Part II, we can verify through tedious but straightforward computation that the following properties hold, where the signs of these expressions are determined by A2 and $\alpha(\mathbf{x}; n) < \beta(\mathbf{x}; n) < 0$.

LEMMA 1. For each symmetric $\mathbf{x}$ and n,

$$\frac{\partial}{\partial n} q_i^N(\mathbf{x}; n) = -\frac{q_i^N(\mathbf{x}; n)\beta(\mathbf{x}; n)}{\alpha(\mathbf{x}; n) + (n-1)\beta(\mathbf{x}; n)} < 0, \tag{10}$$

$$\omega(\mathbf{x}; n) = \frac{c'(x_i)}{\Delta(\mathbf{x}; n)} [\alpha(\mathbf{x}; n) + (n-2)\beta(\mathbf{x}; n)] > 0, \tag{11}$$

and

$$\theta(\mathbf{x}; n) = -\frac{c'(x_i)}{\Delta(\mathbf{x}; n)} \beta(\mathbf{x}; n) < 0 \tag{12}$$

hold, where

$$\Delta(\mathbf{x}; n) := [\alpha(\mathbf{x}; n) - \beta(\mathbf{x}; n)]\,[\alpha(\mathbf{x}; n) + (n-1)\beta(\mathbf{x}; n)] > 0. \tag{13}$$

2.4. *Second-stage subgame-perfect equilibrium*

Let us now focus on the second-stage game. For each specified n, the second-stage payoff function of firm i is defined by

$$\Pi_i(\mathbf{x}; n) := \pi_i(q_i^N(\mathbf{x}; n), Q_{-i}^N(\mathbf{x}; n); x_i; n). \tag{14}$$

The Cournot–Nash equilibrium of the second-stage game is represented by $\mathbf{x}^N(n)$. It is clear that $\{\mathbf{x}^N(n), \mathbf{q}^N(\mathbf{x}^N(n); n)\}$ is nothing but the second-stage subgame-perfect equilibrium among n firms. We assume throughout that $\mathbf{x}^N(n)$ is unique, symmetric, and positive for each specified n. Assuming interior optimum and second-order conditions, $\mathbf{x}^N(n)$ can be characterized by

$$[f(Q^N(\mathbf{x}^N(n); n)) - c(x_i^N(n))]\,\omega(\mathbf{x}^N(n); n)$$
$$+ q_i^N(\mathbf{x}^N(n); n)\,[f'(Q^N(\mathbf{x}^N(n); n))\,\Psi(\mathbf{x}^N(n); n) - c'(x_i^N(n))] - 1 = 0$$
$$(i = 1, 2, \ldots, n), \qquad (15)$$

where $\Psi(\mathbf{x}^N(n); n) := \omega(\mathbf{x}^N(n); n) + (n-1)\,\theta(\mathbf{x}^N(n); n)$. Invoking (9) for $\mathbf{x} = \mathbf{x}^N(n)$, (15) can be reduced to

$$- q_i^N(\mathbf{x}^N(n); n)c'(x_i^N(n)) - 1$$
$$= (n-1)\,\theta(\mathbf{x}^N(n); n)[f(Q^N(\mathbf{x}^N(n); n)) - c(x_i^N(n))] \qquad (i = 1, 2, \ldots, n), \qquad (16)$$

which proves to be crucially important in what follows.

2.5. *First-stage free-entry equilibrium*

Consider the classical entry/exit dynamics, according to which the number of firms will increase (decrease) when the profits $\Pi_i(\mathbf{x}^N(n); n)$ earned by firm i at the second-stage subgame-perfect equilibrium $\{\mathbf{x}^N(n), \mathbf{q}^N(\mathbf{x}^N(n); n)\}$ among n firms is positive (negative). We may represent this adjustment process by the following differential equation:

$$\dot{n} = \kappa \Pi_i(\mathbf{x}^N(n); n), \qquad (17)$$

where $\dot{n}$ stands for the time derivative of n, and $\kappa > 0$ denotes the adjustment coefficient.

Let the *equilibrium number of firms*, n_e, be defined as the stationary point of the dynamic process described by (17). By definition, we have

$$\Pi_i(\mathbf{x}^N(n_e); n_e) = 0 \qquad (i = 1, 2, \ldots, n_e). \qquad (18)$$

Then the triplet $\{n_e, \mathbf{x}^N(n_e), \mathbf{q}^N(\mathbf{x}^N(n_e); n_e)\}$ denotes what we call the *first-stage free-entry equilibrium*.

2.6. *Welfare criteria*

As in the previous two Parts, we gauge the welfare performance of the industry by the *net market surplus function*:

$$W(n; \mathbf{x}; \mathbf{q}) = \int_0^Q f(Z)\mathrm{d}Z - \sum_{j=1}^{n} [c(x_j)q_j + x_j], \qquad (19)$$

where $Q = \Sigma_{j=1}^n q_j$. The welfare performance of the first-stage free-entry equilibrium $\{n_e, \mathbf{x}^N(n_e), \mathbf{q}^N(\mathbf{x}^N(n_e); n_e)\}$ may be evaluated with reference to several criteria which are introduced in terms of $W(n; \mathbf{x}; \mathbf{q})$.

If the government is able to control this industry in its entirety from the viewpoint of social welfare, it will impose the socially first-best R&D $x^F(n)$ and the socially first-best output $q^F(n)$ to each firm, when these are defined by

$$f(nq^F(n)) - c(x^F(n)) = 0 \tag{20}$$

and

$$-q^F(n)c'(x^F(n)) - 1 = 0, \tag{21}$$

and choose the *socially first-best number of firms*,

$$n_f := \arg\max_{n \geqslant 1} W(n; \mathbf{x}^F(n); \mathbf{q}^F(n)). \tag{22}$$

Realistically speaking, however, such a first-best policy is hard for anyone to pursue, since it means that incumbent firms will be forced to produce incurring deficits. If the government cannot control firms' competitive strategies, however, the best that can be aspired is to choose the *socially second-best number of firms*,

$$n_s := \arg\max_{n \geqslant 1} W(n; \mathbf{x}^N(n); \mathbf{q}^N(\mathbf{x}^N(n); n)), \tag{23}$$

and let n_s firms compete without interference to establish the second-stage subgame-perfect equilibrium $\{\mathbf{x}^N(n_s), \mathbf{q}^N(\mathbf{x}^N(n_s); n_s)\}$. Despite its obvious relevance and appeal, such a second-best policy may still be difficult to realize. Because of uncertainty over the precise nature of the functions involved, it may be prohibitively difficult for the government to identify exactly where n_s is located. What is required is a policy prescription which does not presuppose the availability of detailed knowledge on the nature of demand and cost functions involved. This is precisely what we hope to find in the next section.

3. EXCESS ENTRY THEOREMS AT THE MARGIN

3.1. First-best excess entry theorem

Left unfettered by government intervention, the first-stage free-entry equilibrium $\{n_e, \mathbf{x}^N(n_e), \mathbf{q}^N(\mathbf{x}^N(n_e); n_e)\}$ will be established. Our purpose is to show that the welfare performance of this spontaneous outcome turns out to be socially excessive.

If the government can enforce the socially optimal marginal cost principle and R&D cost minimization, we may verify that the welfare performance can be improved by restricting the number of firms and imposing the marginal cost principle and R&D cost minimization on the remaining firms. Indeed, in this case of the first-best regulation on incumbent firms, the following theorem holds true.

THEOREM 1 (FIRST- BEST EXCESS ENTRY THEOREM AT THE MARGIN). Assume that A1, A2, and A3 hold. Then a small reduction in the number of firms unambiguously improves first-best social welfare in the sense that

$$(\mathrm{d}/\mathrm{d}n)\, W(n;\, \mathbf{x}^F(n);\, \mathbf{q}^F(n)) < 0 \tag{24}$$

holds as long as $n \geqslant 2$.

It is worth while emphasizing that the assertion of Theorem 1 is true for all $n \geqslant 2$, and not just for n_e, so that the sole candidate for n_f defined by (22) is exactly 1. Therefore, to the extent that the active existence of the industry in question is worth while in the first place, the socially first-best number of firms is just 1, which is exactly the opposite of the classical maxim of Adam Smith cited in Preface: '[i]n general, if any branch of trade, or any division of labour, be advantageous to the public, the freer and more general the competition, it will always be the more so' (see Smith 1904: i. 312).

3.2. Second-best excess entry theorem

Since the enforcement of the marginal cost principle is far beyond the reach of the actual down-to-earth government anyway, the relevance of Theorem 1 may well be doubted. In answer to this possible criticism, let us now examine how the second-best welfare function, $W(n;\, \mathbf{x}^N(n);\, \mathbf{q}^N(\mathbf{x}^N(n);\, n))$, will be affected when the number of firms undergoes a marginal change from n_e.

By differentiating $W(n;\, \mathbf{x}^N(n);\, \mathbf{q}^N(\mathbf{x}^N(n);\, n))$ totally with respect to n, we obtain

$$\begin{aligned}(\mathrm{d}/\mathrm{d}n)\, W(n;\, \mathbf{x}^N(n);\, \mathbf{q}^N(\mathbf{x}^N(n);\, n)) &= \Pi_i(\mathbf{x}^N(n);\, n)\\ &+ n\,[f(Q^N(\mathbf{x}^N(n);\, n)) - c(x_i^N(n))]\,(\partial/\partial n)\, q_i^N(\mathbf{x}^N(n);\, n)\\ &+ n\,[\gamma_i(n) + \delta_i(n)](\mathrm{d}/\mathrm{d}n)\, x_i^N(n),\end{aligned} \tag{25}$$

where

$$\gamma_i(n) := -q_i^N(\mathbf{x}^N(n);\, n)\, c'(x_i^N(n)) - 1 \tag{26}$$

and

$$\delta_i(n) := [f(Q^N(\mathbf{x}^N(n);\, n)) - c(x_i^N(n))]\, \Psi(\mathbf{x}^N(n);\, n). \tag{27}$$

Note that the first term in the RHS of (25) is zero when it is evaluated at $n = n_e$ by virtue of the definition (18) of n_e, whereas the second term in (25), evaluated at $n = n_e$, i.e.

$$n_e\,[f(Q^N(\mathbf{x}^N(n_e);\, n_e) - c(x_i^N(n_e))]\,(\partial/\partial n)\, q_i^N(\mathbf{x}^N(n_e);\, n_e), \tag{28}$$

is always negative by virtue of A1, (9) for $\mathbf{x} = \mathbf{x}^N(n_e)$, and Lemma 1. Note also that (28) is the same expression that played a central role in our analysis in Part I above. Finally, the third term in the RHS of (25) is specific to the oligopoly models with strategic commitment. Indeed, $\gamma_i(n)$ ($\delta_i(n)$) is nothing other than the commitment effect (distortion effect) which was introduced in Chapter 4.

As in Chapter 4, $\gamma_i(n_e)$ can be rewritten as

$$\gamma_i(n_e) = (n_e - 1)\,\theta(\mathbf{x}^N(n_e); n_e)\,[f(Q^N(\mathbf{x}^N(n_e); n_e)) - c(x_i^N(n_e))], \tag{29}$$

by virtue of (16) for $n = n_e$. It is clear from A1, (9) for $\mathbf{x} = \mathbf{x}^N(n_e)$, and Lemma 1 that $\gamma_i(n_e) < 0$ and $\delta_i(n_e) > 0$. Therefore, the presence of strategic commitment may seem to introduce some ambiguity in determining the sign of (25). Nevertheless, we can in fact establish the following quite unambiguous result.

THEOREM 2 (SECOND-BEST EXCESS ENTRY THEOREM AT THE MARGIN). *Assume that* A1, A2, *and* A3 *hold. Then a small reduction in the number of firms at the first-stage free-entry equilibrium unambiguously improves second-best social welfare in the sense that*

$$(\mathrm{d}/\mathrm{d}n)\,W(n_e; \mathbf{x}^N(n_e); \mathbf{q}^N(\mathbf{x}^N(n_e); n_e)) < 0 \tag{30}$$

holds as long as $n_e \geqslant 1 - \delta$.

Thanks to Theorem 2, we can be assured that the exit of an incumbent firm at the first-stage free-entry equilibrium is definitely welfare-improving at the margin in the second-best sense even if we do not know exactly where n_f and n_s are located. Note also that the crucial inequality $n_e \geqslant 1 - \delta$ is obviously satisfied if the inverse demand function is concave, hence $\delta \geqslant 0$.

4. PROOFS

4.1. *Proof of Lemma 1*

By differentiating (9) with respect to n and rearranging terms using $\alpha(\mathbf{x}; n)$ and $\beta(\mathbf{x}; n)$, we obtain

$$[\alpha(\mathbf{x}; n) + (n-1)\beta(\mathbf{x}; n)](\partial/\partial n)q_i^N(\mathbf{x}; n) = -\,\beta(\mathbf{x}; n)q_i^N(\mathbf{x}; n), \tag{31}$$

which yields (10). The negative sign of $(\partial/\partial n)q_i^N(\mathbf{x}; n)$ is due to A1 and A3.

To prove (11) and (12), we differentiate (9) with respect to x_i and x_j ($i \neq j$), respectively, and rearrange terms using $\omega(\mathbf{x}; n)$ and $\theta(\mathbf{x}; n)$ to obtain

$$\alpha(\mathbf{x}; n)\,\omega(\mathbf{x}; n) + (n-1)\beta(\mathbf{x}; n)\,\theta(\mathbf{x}; n) = c'(x_i) \tag{32}$$

and

$$\beta(\mathbf{x}; n)\,\omega(\mathbf{x}; n) + [\alpha(\mathbf{x}; n) + (n-2)\beta(\mathbf{x}; n)]\,\theta(\mathbf{x}; n) = 0. \tag{33}$$

Solving (32) and (33) for $\omega(\mathbf{x}; n)$ and $\theta(\mathbf{x}; n)$, we may obtain (11) and (12). The signs of $\omega(\mathbf{x}; n)$, $\theta(\mathbf{x}; n)$, and $\Delta(\mathbf{x}; n)$ are determined by A3, (6), and (7). □

4.2. *Proof of Theorem 1*

By differentiating $W(n; \mathbf{x}^F(n); \mathbf{q}^F(n))$ totally with respect to n, we obtain

$$(\mathrm{d}/\mathrm{d}n)W(n; \mathbf{x}^F(n); \mathbf{q}^F(n)) = -x^F(n) + [f(nq^F(n)) - c(x^F(n))][q^F(n) + n(\mathrm{d}/\mathrm{d}n)q^F(n)] + n(\mathrm{d}/\mathrm{d}n)x^F(n)[-q^F(n)c'(x^F(n)) - 1]. \tag{34}$$

Invoking (20) and (21), we are then led to conclude that

$$(\mathrm{d}/\mathrm{d}n)W(n; \mathbf{x}^F(n); \mathbf{q}^F(n)) = -x^F(n), \tag{35}$$

which is always negative as long as $x^F(n) > 0$, as we set out to show. □

4.3. *Proof of Theorem 2*

Step 1. By virtue of A1, (9) for $\mathbf{x} = \mathbf{x}^N(n_e)$, (18), and (29), it can easily be verified that the sign of (25) coincides with that of

$$\Lambda(n) := (\partial/\partial n)q_i^N(\mathbf{x}^N(n); n) + [\omega(\mathbf{x}^N(n); n) + 2(n-1)\theta(\mathbf{x}^N(n); n)](\mathrm{d}/\mathrm{d}n)x_i^N(n) \tag{36}$$

at $n = n_e$. Invoking Lemma 1, $\Lambda(n)$ can be further reduced to

$$\Lambda(n) = \frac{1}{\alpha^N(n) + (n-1)\beta^N(n)}\left\{-q_i^N(\mathbf{x}^N(n); n)\beta^N(n) + \frac{c'(x_i^N(n))}{\alpha^N(n) - \beta^N(n)}[\alpha^N(n) - n\beta^N(n)](\mathrm{d}/\mathrm{d}n)x_i^N(n)\right\}, \tag{37}$$

where $\alpha^N(n) := \alpha(\mathbf{x}^N(n); n)$ and $\beta^N(n) := \beta(\mathbf{x}^N(n); n)$ for short. By virtue of (6) and (7) for $\mathbf{x} = \mathbf{x}^N(n)$ and A3, it follows that

$$\operatorname{sgn}\Lambda(n) = \operatorname{sgn}\{(n+\delta)q_i^N(\mathbf{x}^N(n); n)f'(Q^N(\mathbf{x}^N(n); n)) + c'(x_i^N(n))[n(n-2) + \delta(n-1)](\mathrm{d}/\mathrm{d}n)x_i^N(n)\} \tag{38}$$

holds.

Step 2. Let us examine some properties of the first-stage payoff function $\Pi_i(\mathbf{x}; n)$ with the purpose of evaluating $(\mathrm{d}/\mathrm{d}n)x_i^N(n)$ which appears in (38). To begin with, we can establish by elementary yet rather complicated computation that

$$\Pi_{i,i}(\mathbf{x}; n) := \frac{\partial}{\partial x_i} \Pi_i(\mathbf{x}; n)$$
$$= -q_i^N(\mathbf{x}; n) c'(x_i) \eta(n) - 1 \tag{39}$$

holds, where

$$\eta(n) := 1 + \frac{n-1}{n} \frac{n+\delta}{1+n+\delta} \tag{40}$$

and use is made of (2), (4), (5), and Lemma 1.

By differentiating (39) partially with respect to x_i and x_j ($i \neq j$), respectively, we obtain

$$\Pi_{i,ii}(\mathbf{x}; n) := \frac{\partial^2}{\partial x_i^2} \Pi_i(\mathbf{x}; n)$$
$$= -\eta(n)[q_i^N(\mathbf{x}; n) c''(x_i) + c'(x_i) \omega(\mathbf{x}; n)] \tag{41}$$

and

$$\Pi_{i,ij}(\mathbf{x}; n) := \frac{\partial^2}{\partial x_i \, \partial x_j} \Pi_i(\mathbf{x}; n) = -\eta(n) c'(x_i) \theta(\mathbf{x}; n) \quad (i \neq j). \tag{42}$$

Note that the second-order conditions for profit maximization at the first-stage game require that $\Pi_{i,ii}(\mathbf{x}^N(n); n) < 0$ holds. In view of A3, (40), and (41), we then obtain

$$c''(x_i^N(n)) q_i^N(\mathbf{x}^N(n); n) + c'(x_i^N(n)) \omega(\mathbf{x}^N(n); n) > 0. \tag{43}$$

Applying (11) and (13) to (43) and invoking (4) and (5), (43) can be reduced to

$$\chi(n) := c''(x_i^N(n)) q_i^N(\mathbf{x}^N(n); n)$$
$$+ [c'(x_i^N(n))]^2 \frac{n + \delta(n-1)/n}{f'(Q^N(\mathbf{x}^N(n); n))(1+n+\delta)} > 0, \tag{44}$$

which is of substantial importance in what follows.

Note in passing that A2, Lemma 1, and (42) ensure that $\Pi_{i,ij}(\mathbf{x}; n) < 0$ ($i \neq j$) holds for any $(\mathbf{x}; n)$. Therefore, *the first-stage strategies are warranted to be strategic substitutes if the second-stage strategies are.*[1]

By differentiating (39) partially with respect to n and noting that

$$\eta'(n) = \frac{2n^2 + 2\delta n + \delta(\delta+1)}{n^2(1+n+\delta)^2} \tag{45}$$

follows from (40), we can finally obtain

$$\frac{\partial}{\partial n} \Pi_{i,i}(\mathbf{x}^N(n); n) = c'(x_i^N(n)) q_i^N(\mathbf{x}^N(n); n) \frac{(n-1)[2(n+\delta)^2 + \delta]}{n^2(1+n+\delta)^2}. \tag{46}$$

Step 3. By definition, $\mathbf{x}^N(n)$ is characterized by

$$\Pi_{i,\,i}(\mathbf{x}^N(n); n) = 0 \qquad (i = 1, 2, \ldots, n). \tag{47}$$

By differentiating (47) totally with respect to n and invoking symmetry, we obtain

$$\frac{\mathrm{d}}{\mathrm{d}n} x_i^N(n) = -\frac{(\partial/\partial n)\Pi_{i,\,i}(\mathbf{x}^N(n); n)}{\Pi_{i,\,ii}(\mathbf{x}^N(n); n) + (n-1)\Pi_{i,\,ij}(\mathbf{x}^N(n); n)}. \tag{48}$$

By virtue of Lemma 1, (41), (42), and (46), we can reduce (48) to

$$\frac{\mathrm{d}}{\mathrm{d}n} x_i^N(n) = \frac{(n-1)[2(n+\delta)^2 + \delta]c'(x_i^N(n))q_i^N(\mathbf{x}^N(n); n)}{n^2(1+n+\delta)^2\eta(n)\zeta(n)}, \tag{49}$$

where

$$\zeta(n) := c''(x_i^N(n))q_i^N(\mathbf{x}^N(n); n) + \frac{[c'(x_i^N(n))]^2}{f'(Q^N(\mathbf{x}^N(n); n))\,(1+n+\delta)}. \tag{50}$$

Substituting (49) for $(\mathrm{d}/\mathrm{d}n)x_i^N(n)$ in (38) and rearranging terms, we can verify that $\operatorname{sgn}\Lambda(n)$ is determined by the sign of

$$(n+\delta)f'(Q^N(\mathbf{x}^N(n); n)) + [c'(x_i^N(n))]^2\,\frac{(n-1)[n(n-2)+\delta(n-1)]\,[2(n+\delta)^2+\delta]}{n^2(1+n+\delta)^2\eta(n)\zeta(n)}. \tag{51}$$

Note, however, that

$$\zeta(n) - \chi(n) = \frac{-(n-1)(1+\delta/n)[c'(x_i^N(n))]^2}{f'(Q^N(\mathbf{x}^N(n); n))\,(1+n+\delta)} > 0$$

holds, so that (44) guarantees that $\zeta(n) > 0$. Coupled with (51), this implies that $\operatorname{sgn}\Lambda(n)$ is dictated by the sign of

$$(n+\delta)f'(Q^N(\mathbf{x}^N(n); n))n^2(1+n+\delta)^2\eta(n)\zeta(n) + (n-1)[c'(x_i^N(n))]^2\phi_\delta(n), \tag{52}$$

where

$$\phi_\delta(n) := -4n^3 - 8\delta n^2 - \delta(5\delta+2)n - \delta^2(\delta+1). \tag{53}$$

It is clear that the first term in (52) is negative under A1 and A3.

Step 4. The proof of Theorem 2 is complete if we can show that $\phi_\delta(n) < 0$ as long as $n \geqslant 1-\delta$. Since $\phi_\delta(n) < 0$ holds for all $n \geqslant 1$ if $\delta \geqslant 0$, we have only to examine the case where $\delta < 0$. With this goal in mind, let $n^*(\delta)$ stand for the largest real root of the cubic equation $\phi_\delta(n) = 0$. Since the coefficient of the highest-order term of this cubic equation is negative, we have $1-\delta > n^*(\delta)$ if all of $\phi_\delta(n)$, $\phi_\delta{}'(n)$, and $\phi_\delta{}''(n)$ are negative at $n = 1-\delta$. (See Fig. 13 for geometric intuition behind this reasoning.) By computing $\phi_\delta{}'(n)$ and $\phi_\delta''(n)$ from (53), and substituting $n = 1-\delta$, we can easily verify that

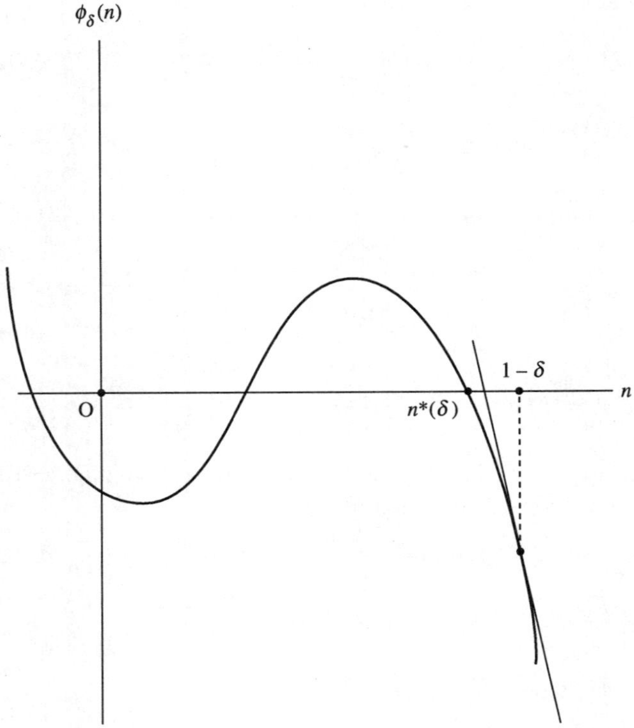

Fig. 13 Local concavity of $\phi_\delta(n)$ at $n = 1 - \delta$

$$\phi_\delta(1-\delta) = 2(\delta - 2) < 0 \qquad \text{for } \delta < 0,$$

$$\phi_\delta'(1-\delta) = -\delta^2 + 6\delta - 12 < 0 \qquad \text{for } \delta < 0,$$

and

$$\phi_\delta''(1-\delta) = -8(3-\delta) < 0 \qquad \text{for } \delta < 0.$$

If $n \geqslant 1 - \delta$, we have $n > n^*(\delta)$, so that we have $\phi_\delta(n) < 0$, which suffices to establish our theorem. □

5. CONCLUDING REMARKS

The excess entry theorem, which we have proved in this chapter in the presence of strategic commitment, is based on three explicit assumptions. The first is on the admissible class of inverse demand functions. Despite its restrictive nature, we should note that the admissible class is too wide to be ignored, as it accommodates *all* linear inverse demand functions as well as *all* constantly elastic inverse demand functions. The second assumption is on the nature of cost-reducing technology, but this seems to be a safe assumption. The third assumption is on the nature of strategic relatedness of competitive measures. Within a model of quantity competition, the assumed strategic substitutability seems to be widely recognized as the norm. Despite its rather paradoxical implications, therefore, the excess entry theorem cannot be simply discarded as pathological. Indeed, the fact that the theorem holds even in the presence of strategic commitment seems to enhance its relevance rather substantially.

It goes without saying that there are other implicit assumptions on which the theorem hinges. To cite just a few, profit maximization pure and simple, quantity competition rather than price competition, exclusive focus on the symmetric equilibria, no uncertainty in cost-reducing R&D, and no product differentiation are all involved in our excess entry theorem. It is almost certain, and in some cases demonstrably certain, that the robustness and relevance of the theorem are severely limited by these underlying assumptions.

The purpose of the succeeding two chapters is to examine how our excess entry/investment theorems are affected if we discard some of the above-mentioned implicit assumptions. However, the basic fact remains that the arena where the excess entry/investment theorems do have their relevance is in no sense negligible, and we are in need of more careful analyses of the role of competition as an efficient allocator of resources. The purpose of this monograph will have been served if it succeeds in bringing this simple point home.

NOTE TO CHAPTER 7

1. It is the latter half of A1 that is responsible for the validity of this neat property. In general, it does not necessarily hold. See Chs. 5 and 6.

8 Alternative Firm Objectives and Strategies

1. INTRODUCTION

One crucial, if not explicit, assumption behind the excess entry theorem and excess investment theorem is that firms are profit-maximizers pure and simple, which use quantities as their strategic variables when they compete in the product market. It is also assumed that firms form a Cournot conjecture as to the way their competitors would respond to their own strategic moves. Furthermore, the oligopolistic industry we analyse is assumed to have a single homogeneous product, which assumes away any room for product differentiation. These simplifying assumptions have been commonly adopted in the literature on oligopolistic competition and economic welfare. In this sense, our foregoing analyses have not focused on the pathological situations at all. Nevertheless, the question naturally arises of whether these seemingly innocuous assumptions are primarily responsible for the theorems whose implications are somewhat unconventional.

In an attempt to answer this important question, our first aim in this chapter is to eliminate the assumption of simple profit maximization and to examine how the validity of the excess entry theorem and/or the excess investment theorem will be thereby affected. From among several alternative hypotheses that have been propounded in the literature, in Section 2 we select and examine the hypothesis that 'oligopolists typically seek to maximize their *sales* subject to a minimum profit constraint' (Baumol 1958: 187) in the context of the excess entry theorem. The second hypothesis of interest, which we select and examine in Sections 3 and 4 in the context of the excess entry theorem and the excess investment theorem, respectively, claims that the organizational characteristics of some modern firms can be more appropriately captured by profit-sharing among stockholders and employees than by profit maximization pure and simple.

In order to divide our task into manageable pieces, and also to isolate the effect of each variation of our basic assumptions, we shall retain in Sections 2, 3, and 4 the assumptions of quantity strategies in the product market competition, and of Cournot conjecture. In Section 5 we return to the case of simple profit maximization and assume, instead, that firms form quasi-Cournot conjecture *à la* Seade (1980*b*). Our analytical focus in this arena is the verification of the degree to which collusion among firms will affect the validity of the excess entry theorem.

Section 6 examines the welfare effects of product differentiation with the purpose of verifying whether or not the validity of the excess entry theorem will be thereby affected. This is a particularly interesting question, as the entry of a new firm entails the increased diversity of the product range, which may well have an independent appeal to consumers who prefer product diversity.

In Section 7 we return to the two-stage model of oligopolistic competition. However, in contrast with the analyses in Part II as well as in Section 4 of this chapter, we assume that firms compete in the second stage of the entire game in terms of price strategies rather than quantity strategies with the purpose of examining how this change in strategies in the second-stage game affects the validity of the excess investment theorem.

It should be clear by now that our analyses in this chapter are conducted selectively rather than exhaustively. Needless to say, we could easily explore several other combinations of the novel features introduced in this chapter in the context of the two types of theorems, or could introduce yet another factor that our previous analyses have assumed away. In order to keep the length of the chapter within reasonable bounds, however, we will not explore these further avenues and so leave many cases of interest for our readers' own exploration. Section 8 concludes the chapter with a brief summary of the main results and their implications.

2. QUANTITY COMPETITION AMONG SALES-MAXIMIZING FIRMS

2.1. *Motivation*

In establishing the excess entry theorems in an oligopolistic economy, it has been assumed that the oligopolistic firms are profit-maximizers pure and simple.[1] In view of the many alternative hypotheses on sustainable firm objectives that are proposed and vigorously discussed in the literature, it is clearly worth while investigating whether the central message of excess entry theorems can be maintained even if firms are not simply maximizing profits.

Let us begin this investigation with the case where oligopolistic firms are profit-constrained sales maximizers *à la* Baumol (1958; 1959), and Portes (1968).[2] It will be shown that there are non-trivial cases where excess entry theorems are indeed in need of some qualifications if firms are not simply maximizing profits.

2.2. *Oligopolistic competition among profit-constrained sales-maximizers*

Consider an industry producing a single homogeneous output. The inverse demand function for the product is denoted by $p = f(Q)$, where p is price and Q is industry output. As in Chapter 1, the following will be assumed.

A1: $f(Q)$ is twice continuously differentiable and $f'(Q) < 0$ holds for all $Q \geqslant 0$ such that $f(Q) > 0$.

There are n firms, where $2 \leqslant n < +\infty$, in this industry, and profits of firm i are denoted by

$$\pi_i(q_i, Q_{-i}) := q_i f(Q) - C(q_i) \qquad (i = 1, 2, \ldots, n), \tag{1}$$

where $Q = q_i + Q_{-i}$, and $C(q_i)$ is the cost function which is assumed to be common for all firms. As in Chapter 1, we assume the following.

A2: $C(q)$ is twice continuously differentiable and satisfies $C'(q) > 0$ as well as $C''(q) > 0$ for all $q > 0$.

Following Baumol (1958; 1959), we will assume that each firm i tries to maximize its sales revenue $R_i(q_i, Q_{-i}) := f(Q)q_i$ subject to the minimum profit constraint $\pi_i(q_i, Q_{-i}) \geqslant \pi_0$, where $\pi_0 \geqslant 0$ denotes the minimum permissible level of profits. We assume that π_0 is common for all firms. Under the assumption of Cournot conjecture, interior optimum, and second-order conditions, the first-order conditions for profit-constrained sales maximization are given by

$$f(Q) + f'(Q)q_i + \lambda(\partial/\partial q_i)\pi_i(q_i, Q_{-i}) = 0 \qquad (i = 1, 2, \ldots, n) \tag{2}$$

and

$$\pi_i(q_i, Q_{-i}) = \pi_0 \qquad (i = 1, 2, \ldots, n), \tag{3}$$

where λ_i denotes the Lagrange multiplier for firm i.

Assuming the existence of an interior symmetric Cournot–Nash equilibrium, let $q^N(n; \pi_0)$ be the equilibrium output of each firm when the number of firms is n and the minimum permissible level of profits is π_0. By virtue of the assumed symmetry, all firms produce the same amount of output at equilibrium. Let $\lambda^N(n; \pi_0) := (\partial/\partial \pi_0) R_i(q^N(n; \pi_0), Q^N_{-i}(n; \pi_0))$ be the Lagrange multiplier at the symmetric Cournot–Nash equilibrium $\mathbf{q}^N(n; \pi_0)$, all of whose components are denoted by $q^N(n; \pi_0)$. Assuming that $\lambda^N(n; \pi_0) > 0$, it is easy to verify that $\mathbf{q}^N(n; \pi_0)$ can be characterized by the first-order conditions

$$f(Q^N(n; \pi_0)) + q^N(n; \pi_0) f'(Q^N(n; \pi_0)) = \Lambda^N(n; \pi_0) C'(q^N(n; \pi_0)) \tag{4}$$

and

$$\pi_i(q^N(n; \pi_0), Q^N_{-i}(n; \pi_0)) = \pi_0, \tag{5}$$

where $Q^N(n; \pi_0) = nq^N(n; \pi_0)$ denotes the equilibrium industry output and $\Lambda^N(n; \pi_0) := \lambda^N(n; \pi_0)/[1 + \lambda^N(n; \pi_0)]$.

To gauge the welfare performance of this industry, we invoke the usual market surplus function $W(n, \mathbf{q})$ where $\mathbf{q} = (q_1, \ldots, q_i, \ldots, q_n)$ which is defined by

$$W(n, \mathbf{q}) := \int_0^Q f(Z)\mathrm{d}Z - nC(q). \tag{6}$$

Without further ado, let us determine the sign of $(\mathrm{d}/\mathrm{d}n)W(n, \mathbf{q}^N(n; \pi_0))$. It is easy to verify that

$$(\mathrm{d}/\mathrm{d}n)W(n, \mathbf{q}^N(n; \pi_0)) = \pi_0 + n(\partial/\partial n)q^N(n; \pi_0)\,[f(Q^N(n; \pi_0)) - C'(q^N(n; \pi_0))] \tag{7}$$

holds, where we have made use of (5). It is clear from (7) that the marginal welfare verdict will hinge squarely on the signs of the two terms, i.e. $(\partial/\partial n)q^N(n; \pi_0)$ and $\mu^N(n; \pi_0) := f(Q^N(n; \pi_0)) - C'(q^N(n; \pi_0))$.

To get necessary information on the first term, i.e. $(\partial/\partial n)q^N(n; \pi_0)$, we differentiate (5) with respect to n and invoke (4) to obtain

$$(\partial/\partial n)q^N(n; \pi_0) = -\frac{1}{\Gamma(n; \pi_0)} f'(Q^N(n; \pi_0))\,[q^N(n; \pi_0)]^2, \tag{8}$$

where

$$\Gamma(n; \pi_0) := (n-1)q^N(n; \pi_0)f'(Q^N(n; \pi_0)) - \frac{C'(q^N(n; \pi_0))}{1 + \lambda^N(n; \pi_0)} < 0. \tag{9}$$

It is clear from (8) and (9) that $(\partial/\partial n)q^N(n; \pi_0) < 0$ under A1 and A2. We have thus established the following theorem.

THEOREM 1. Suppose that A1 and A2 are satisfied. Then:

(*a*) If $\mu^N(n; \pi_0) < 0$ holds, so that price is less than marginal cost at the Cournot–Nash equilibrium $\mathbf{q}^N(n; \pi_0)$, then $(\mathrm{d}/\mathrm{d}n)W(n, \mathbf{q}^N(n; \pi_0))$ is definitely positive. Therefore, it is welfare-improving to increase the number of firms n marginally.

(*b*) If $\mu^N(n; \pi_0) > 0$ holds, so that price exceeds marginal cost at the Cournot–Nash equilibrium $\mathbf{q}^N(n; \pi_0)$, then the marginal welfare verdict is ambiguous in general. However, if the minimum permissible level of profits π_0 is very small, say $\pi_0 = 0$, then it is the case that $(\mathrm{d}/\mathrm{d}n)W(n, \mathbf{q}^N(n; \pi_0)) < 0$ holds. Thus, it is welfare-improving to decrease the number of firms n at the margin.

In order to understand the message of this theorem as clearly as possible, it is useful to examine how the equilibrium industry output $Q^N(n; \pi_0)$ will behave in response to a change in the number of firms n. By differentiating $Q^N(n; \pi_0)$ with respect to n, we obtain

$$(\partial/\partial n)Q^N(n; \pi_0) = \frac{q^N(n; \pi_0)}{\Gamma(n; \pi_0)}\,[f(Q^N(n; \pi_0)) - C'(q^N(n; \pi_0))]. \tag{10}$$

It follows from (9) and (10) that $(\partial/\partial n)Q^N(n; \pi_0) > 0$ (<) 0 if and only if $\mu^N(n; \pi_0) <$ (>) 0.

Once this fact is confirmed, the message of Theorem 1 is quite easy to understand intuitively. If price is less than (more than) marginal cost, so that $\mu^N(n; \pi_0) < (>) 0$, the addition of a new firm increases (decreases) industry output. Since the inverse demand function is downward-sloping by virtue of A1, price goes down (goes up), with a result that consumer's surplus increases (decreases). The minimal permissible profit constraint being binding before and after the entry of a new firm, each firm earns π_0, so that the entry of an additional firm increases the producer's surplus just by π_0. Hence an unambiguous increase of the market surplus occurs in the case where $\mu^N(n; \pi_0) < 0$. If $\mu^N(n; \pi_0) > 0$ and $\pi_0 = 0$, on the other hand, a deletion of one incumbent firm increases the consumer's surplus, keeping the producer's surplus at the previous level of zero. Once again, an unambiguous increase of the market surplus obtains. This is what our Theorem 1 in fact asserts.

It only remains to see if indeed we can have a situation where $\mu^N(n; \pi_0) < 0$. Figs. 14 and 15 exemplify that, depending on the demand and cost functions as well as the level of π_0, we can in fact obtain the Cournot–Nash equilibrium where $\mu^N(n; \pi_0)$ is positive or negative.

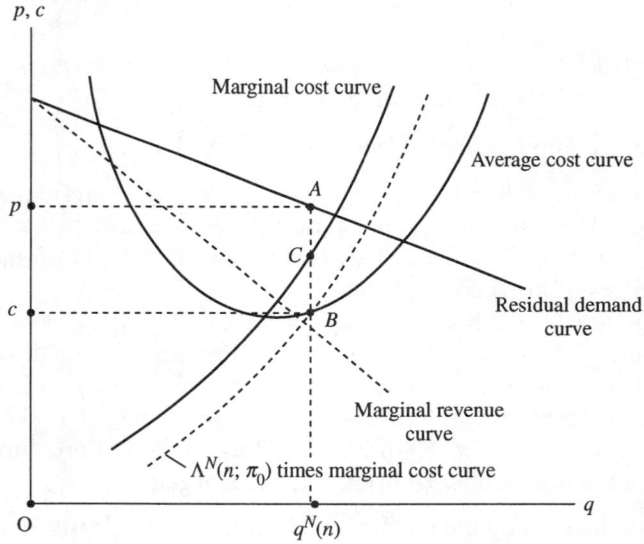

The area $ApcB = \pi_0$ and $\mu^N(n; \pi_0) = AC > 0$

Fig. 14 The case where $\mu^N(n; \pi_0) > 0$

Recollect that excess entry theorems were originally established with the purpose of casting serious doubts on the *universal* validity of a widespread belief in the role of competition as an efficient allocator of resources. This being the case, the mere fact that the theorem does not necessarily hold in

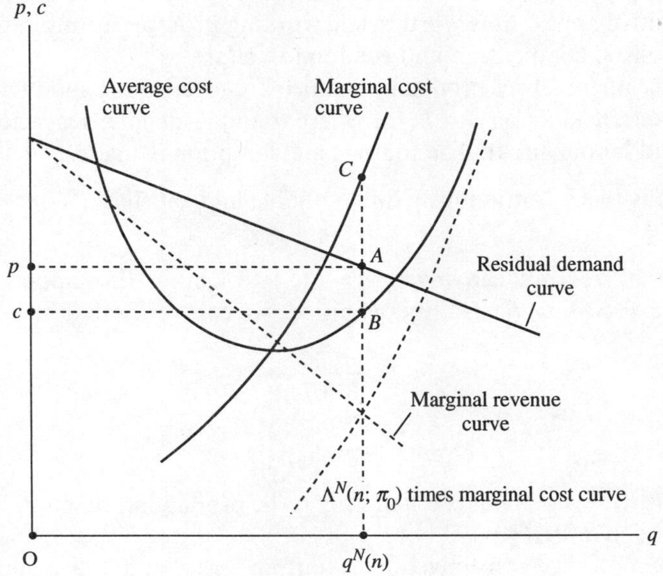

The area $ApcB = \pi_0$ and $\mu^N(n; \pi_0) = -CA > 0$

Fig. 15 The case where $\mu^N(n; \pi_0) < 0$

some situations where firms are profit-constrained sales-maximizers need not deprive the theorem of its basic thrust altogether. At the very least, however, it calls for more systematic exploration of the relation between alternative firm objectives and the welfare effects of oligopolistic competition. With this observation in mind, let us now turn to yet another alternative firm objective, the implication of which is our focus in the next two sections.

3. QUANTITY COMPETITION AMONG PROFIT-SHARING FIRMS: EXCESS ENTRY THEOREM

3.1. Model of a profit-sharing firm

The second alternative firm objective with which we replace the standard profit maximization hypothesis is that firm's profits are shared by stockholders and employees, and the firm organizes its production so as to maximize the income per employee. It is often claimed, e.g. by Komiya (1987), that the organizational characteristics of some modern firms can be better approximated by profit-sharing and income-per-employee maximization rather than by simple profit maximization. To the extent that this claim has some intuitive appeal, it is worth while working its implications in the arena of oligopolistic competition and economic welfare.

Consider, then, a firm producing a single homogeneous good by means of the production function $q = F(L)$, where q and L denote, respectively, the output and labour input. The following assumption is made.

A3: $F(L)$ is twice continuously differentiable and satisfies $F'(L) > 0$ for all $L > 0$.

By virtue of A3, we can invert $q = F(L)$ to obtain the labour demand function $L = G(q) := F^{-1}(q)$. By definition, we can verify that

$$G'(q) = \frac{1}{F'(G(q))} > 0 \tag{11}$$

and

$$G''(q) = -F''(G(q))\,[G'(q)]^3 \tag{12}$$

hold. Thus, $G''(q) > 0$ holds if and only if the production function is strictly concave, i.e. if $F''(G(q)) < 0$ holds.

Let p and w be, respectively, the output price and the competitively determined supply price of labour in the rest of the economy. The profits earned by the firm are defined by

$$\pi(q; p, w) := pq - wG(q) - K, \tag{13}$$

which are distributed among employees and stockholders, where $K > 0$ denotes the reward to the unspecified fixed factor of production.

Let ξ and $1 - \xi$ be, respectively, the share of profits accruing to employees and stockholders, where ξ is a constant which satisfies $0 < \xi < 1$. Then the income per employee can be denoted by

$$y(q; p, w) := \frac{wG(q) + \xi\pi(q; p, w)}{G(q)} = (1 - \xi)w + \xi\sigma(q; p), \tag{14}$$

where $\sigma(q; p) := (pq - K)/G(q)$. It is clear, then, that

$$\arg\max_{q>0} y(q; p, w) = \arg\max_{q>0} \sigma(q; p) \tag{15}$$

holds. Thus, a profit-sharing firm that maximizes income per employee is behaviourally indistinguishable from a firm that maximizes $\sigma(q; p)$.

3.2. Oligopolistic competition among profit-sharing firms

Suppose that there are n (where $2 \leqslant n < +\infty$) identical profit-sharing firms producing the same homogeneous output, which are engaging in the Cournot–Nash quantity competition. Let $p = f(Q)$ be the inverse demand function for this product, where $Q = \Sigma_{i=1}^{n} q_i$ is industry output, which is assumed to satisfy A1 above. The payoff function of firm i is specified by

$$\sigma_i(\mathbf{q}) := \frac{f(Q)q_i - K}{G(q_i)} \qquad (i = 1, 2, \ldots, n). \tag{16}$$

Assuming interior optimum, Cournot conjecture and second-order conditions, the first-order condition for payoff maximization is given by[3]

$$\frac{\partial}{\partial q_i}\sigma_i(\mathbf{q}) = \frac{G(q_i)\,[f(Q) + q_i f'(Q)] - G'(q_i)[f(Q)q_i - K]}{[G(q_i)]^2} = 0, \tag{17}$$

so that the symmetric Cournot–Nash equilibrium of the game among n profit-sharing firms, to be denoted by $\mathbf{q}^N(n)$, all of whose n components are $q^N(n)$, can be characterized by

$$G(q^N(n))\,[f(Q^N(n)) + q^N(n)f'(Q^N(n))] = G'(q^N(n))\,[f(Q^N(n))q^N(n) - K], \tag{18}$$

where $Q^N(n) = nq^N(n)$.

As an auxiliary step in analysing the properties of $\mathbf{q}^N(n)$, let us define

$$\alpha_i(\mathbf{q}) := \frac{\partial^2}{\partial q_i^2}\sigma_i(\mathbf{q}) = \frac{G(q_i)\,[2f'(Q) + q_i f''(Q)] - G''(q_i)\,[f(Q)q_i - K]}{[G(q_i)]^2} \tag{19}$$

and

$$\beta_{ij}(\mathbf{q}) := \frac{\partial^2}{\partial q_i\,\partial q_j}\sigma_i(\mathbf{q}) = \frac{G(q_i)\,[f'(Q) + f''(Q)q_i] - G'(q_i)f'(Q)q_i}{[G(q_i)]^2}, \tag{20}$$

where use is made of (17). Evaluating (19) and (20) at $\mathbf{q} = \mathbf{q}^N(n)$, we can define $\alpha^N(n) := \alpha_i(\mathbf{q}^N(n))$ and $\beta^N(n) := \beta_{ij}(\mathbf{q}^N(n))$.

Consider the following dynamic adjustment process through which firm i adjusts its output:

$$\dot{q}_i = \tau\frac{\partial}{\partial q_i}\sigma_i(\mathbf{q}) \qquad (i = 1, 2, \ldots, n), \tag{21}$$

where $\dot{q}_i$ denotes the time derivative of q_i and $\tau > 0$ denotes the adjustment coefficient. Clearly, the stationary point of the process (21) is nothing other than the Cournot–Nash equilibrium $\mathbf{q}^N(n)$. As in our analysis of the profit-maximizing firms in Chapter 1, $\mathbf{q}^N(n)$ is locally stable with respect to the process (21) if the following stability condition is satisfied:

A4: $\alpha^N(n) + (k - 1)\beta^N(n) < 0$ holds for all $k = 0, 1, \ldots, n$.

We are now in the stage of examining the long-run adjustment of the number of firms. Let n_e be the *equilibrium number of firms*, which is defined by

$$f(Q^N(n_e))q^N(n_e) - wG(q^N(n_e)) - K = 0. \tag{22}$$

Left undisturbed by government intervention or any other impediments, the spontaneous competitive forces will establish the Cournot–Nash equilibrium corresponding to the equilibrium number of firms, i.e. $\mathbf{q}^N(n_e)$. To see how the equilibrium outcome $\mathbf{q}^N(n_e)$ fares *vis-à-vis* the socially optimal outcome in some well defined sense, we invoke the *second-best market surplus function*:

$$W^N(n) := \int_0^{Q^N(n)} f(Z)\mathrm{d}Z - n\,[wG(q^N(n)) + K]. \tag{23}$$

Differentiating (23) with respect to n, we may obtain

$$(\mathrm{d}/\mathrm{d}n)\,W^N(n) = f(Q^N(n))q^N(n) - wG(q^N(n)) - K$$
$$+\, n(\mathrm{d}/\mathrm{d}n)q^N(n)\,[f(Q^N(n)) - wG'(q^N(n))]. \tag{24}$$

If we evaluate (24) at $n = n_e$ and invoke (22), we may verify that

$$\frac{\mathrm{d}}{\mathrm{d}n}\,W^N(n_e) = n\,\frac{\mathrm{d}}{\mathrm{d}n}\,q^N(n_e)\left\{f(Q^N(n_e)) - \frac{G'(q^N(n_e))}{G(q^N(n_e))}\,[f(Q^N(n_e))q^N(n_e) - K]\right\} \tag{25}$$

holds, which can further be reduced to

$$(\mathrm{d}/\mathrm{d}n)\,W^N(n_e) = -f'(Q^N(n_e))\,Q^N(n_e)(\mathrm{d}/\mathrm{d}n)q^N(n_e), \tag{26}$$

where use is made of (18) at $n = n_e$. In view of A1 above, it follows from (26) that

$$\mathrm{sgn}\;(\mathrm{d}/\mathrm{d}n)\,W^N(n_e) = \mathrm{sgn}\;(\mathrm{d}/\mathrm{d}n)q^N(n_e). \tag{27}$$

With the purpose of evaluating the crucial term $(\mathrm{d}/\mathrm{d}n)q^N(n_e)$ in (27), we differentiate the first-order condition $(\partial/\partial q_i)\,\sigma_i(\mathbf{q}^N(n)) = 0$, which is defined by (17) at $\mathbf{q} = \mathbf{q}^N(n)$, with respect to n, to obtain the following expression for $(\mathrm{d}/\mathrm{d}n)q^N(n)$:

$$\frac{\mathrm{d}}{\mathrm{d}n}q^N(n) = -q^N(n)\,\frac{\beta^N(n)}{\alpha^N(n) + (n-1)\beta^N(n)}. \tag{28}$$

Invoking assumption A4 for $k = n$, it follows from (27) and (28) for $n = n_e$ that

$$\mathrm{sgn}(\mathrm{d}/\mathrm{d}n)\,W^N(n_e) = \mathrm{sgn}\,\beta^N(n_e). \tag{29}$$

To summarize our reasoning so far, we have established the following.

THEOREM 2. Suppose that A1, A3, and A4 are satisfied. Then the equilibrium number of profit-sharing firms is socially excessive (insufficient) at the margin if and only if $\beta^N(n_e) < (>)\ 0$ holds.

Note that $\beta^N(n_e) < (>)\ 0$ holds if and only if the strategies of profit-sharing firms are strategic substitutes (complements) with reference to the payoff functions (16). This being the case, there exists a prima-facie similarity between Theorem 3 in Chapter 1, which applies to the oligopolistic competition among profit-maximizing firms, and Theorem 2 above which we have just established for oligopolistically competitive profit-sharing firms. It is very important to recognize, however, that the strategic substitutability assumption on profit-maximizing firms and that on profit-sharing firms are two quite distinct assumptions if they are expressed in terms of the more basic characteristics of the economy.

With the purpose of bringing this important point into clear relief, let us rewrite $\beta^N(n)$ as follows:

$$\beta^N(n) = \frac{f''(Q^N(n))q^N(n) + f'(Q^N(n))\,[1 - \varepsilon_G(q^N(n))]}{G(q^N(n))} \tag{30}$$

where

$$\varepsilon_G(q^N(n)) = G'(q^N(n))\,\frac{q^N(n)}{G(q^N(n))} \tag{31}$$

denotes the elasticity of labour demand at the Cournot–Nash equilibrium $\mathbf{q}^N(n)$.[4]

Recollect that the strategic substitutability assumption on profit-maximizing firms is always satisfied if inverse demand function $p = f(Q)$ is linear, say, $f(Q) = a - bQ$ with $a > 0$ and $b > 0$. It follows from (30), however, that $\operatorname{sgn}\beta^N(n) = \operatorname{sgn}[\varepsilon_G(q^N(n)) - 1]$ holds for linear inverse demand function. Thus, even when inverse demand function is linear, $\beta^N(n) < (>)\ 0$ holds if and only if $\varepsilon_G(q^N(n)) < (>)\ 1$.

To summarize, we have identified a set of non-trivial assumptions under which the excess (insufficient) entry theorem at the margin holds for the oligopolistic competition among profit-sharing firms. This set of assumptions is substantially different from the one that supports the validity of the excess (insufficient) entry theorem at the margin when firms are profit-maximizers pure and simple. In particular, the excess entry theorem at the margin fails to hold here if the elasticity of labour demand exceeds unity at equilibrium and the inverse demand function satisfies weak convexity. A sharp contrast with the case of profit-maximizing firms is quite obvious.

4. QUANTITY COMPETITION AMONG PROFIT-SHARING FIRMS: THE EXCESS INVESTMENT THEOREM

4.1. A two-stage model of oligopolistic competition among profit-sharing firms

In order to gauge the robustness of the sharp contast we have just identified between the welfare effect of competition among profit-maximizing firms and that of competition among profit-sharing firms, let us examine how profit-sharing firms fare in the different arena of two-stage competition with strategic commitment. As in Part II, each profit-sharing firm is now assumed to make a strategic commitment to efficiency-improving R&D investment in full anticipation of the equilibrium in the later stage, when firms compete in terms of quantities.

Concerning the demand side of the economy, we assume that the inverse demand function $p = f(Q)$ satisfies A1 above. With regard to the supply side, let the production function of each firm be specified by $q = F(\phi(x)L)$, where q is output, L is labour input, and x is efficiency-improving R&D investment. The following is assumed.

A5: $F(z)$ is twice continuously differentiable and satisfies $F(z) > 0$ and $F'(z) > 0$ for all $z > 0$, whereas $\phi(x)$ is twice continuously differentiable and satisfies $\phi(x) > 0$, $\phi'(x) > 0$, and $\phi''(x) < 0$ for all $x > 0$.

By virtue of this assumption, we can invert $q = F(\phi(x)L)$ to obtain $G(q) := F^{-1}(q) = \phi(x)L$, which enables us to derive

$$G'(q) = \frac{1}{F'(G(q))} \tag{32}$$

and

$$G''(q) = -F''(G(q))\,[G'(q)]^3, \tag{33}$$

where $G''(q) > (<)\ 0$ if and only if $F''(G(q)) < (>)\ 0$, i.e. if and only if $F(z)$ is concave (convex).

Suppose that there are n (where $2 \leqslant n < +\infty$) identical profit-sharing firms which compete with each other in two stages. In the first stage each firm i chooses the level of efficiency-improving R&D investment x_i, whereas in the second stage it chooses the output level q_i. Capitalizing on our analysis in Section 3, we can identify the second-stage payoff function of firm i as

$$\sigma_i(\mathbf{q};\, x_i) := \frac{\phi(x_i)\,[f(Q)q_i - x_i]}{G(q_i)} \qquad (i = 1, 2, \ldots, n). \tag{34}$$

Let $\mathbf{q}^N(\mathbf{x}) = (q_1^N(\mathbf{x}), \ldots, q_i^N(\mathbf{x}), \ldots, q_n^N(\mathbf{x}))$ be the symmetric Cournot–Nash equilibrium of the second-stage game corresponding to the specified symmetric R&D profile $\mathbf{x} = (x_1, \ldots, x_i, \ldots, x_n)$. Assuming interior optimum and second-order conditions, the Cournot–Nash equilibrium $\mathbf{q}^N(\mathbf{x})$ can be characterized by $(\partial/\partial q_i)\sigma_i\,(\mathbf{q}^N(\mathbf{x});\, x_i) = 0$ $(i = 1, 2, \ldots, n)$; i.e.,

$$f(Q^N(\mathbf{x})) + q_i^N(\mathbf{x})f'(Q^N(\mathbf{x})) = \frac{G'(q_i^N(\mathbf{x}))}{G(q_i^N(\mathbf{x}))}\,[f(Q^N(\mathbf{x}))q_i^N(\mathbf{x}) - x_i] \qquad (i = 1, 2, \ldots, n), \tag{35}$$

where $Q^N(\mathbf{x}) = \Sigma_{j=1}^n\, q_j^N(\mathbf{x})$.

Turning to the first-stage game, the payoff function of firm i can be defined by

$$\hat{\sigma}_i^N(\mathbf{x}) := \sigma_i(\mathbf{q}^N(\mathbf{x}); x_i) \qquad (i = 1, 2, \ldots, n), \tag{36}$$

so that the Nash equilibrium of the first-stage game, to be denoted by $\mathbf{x}^N = (x_1^N, \ldots, x_i^N, \ldots, x_n^N)$, can be characterized by $(\partial/\partial x_i)\hat{\sigma}_i^N(\mathbf{x}^N) = 0$; i.e.

$$\begin{aligned} G'(q_i^N(\mathbf{x}^N))\,[f(Q^N(\mathbf{x}^N))q_i^N(\mathbf{x}^N) - x_i^N]\,\frac{\partial}{\partial x_i}\,q_i^N(\mathbf{x}^N) \\ = G(q_i^N(\mathbf{x}^N))\left\{\frac{\phi'(x_i^N)}{\phi(x_i^N)}\,[f(Q^N(\mathbf{x}^N))q_i^N(\mathbf{x}^N) - x_i^N]\right. \\ \left. + \; q_i^N(\mathbf{x}^N)f'(Q^N(\mathbf{x}^N))\,\frac{\partial}{\partial x_i}\,Q^N(\mathbf{x}^N) + f(Q^N(\mathbf{x}^N))\,\frac{\partial}{\partial x_i}\,q_i^N(\mathbf{x}^N) - 1\right\} \\ (i = 1, 2, \ldots, n). \end{aligned} \tag{37}$$

Invoking (35) evaluated at $\mathbf{x} = \mathbf{x}^N$, (37) can be reduced to

$$\frac{\phi'(x_i^N)}{\phi(x_i^N)}\,[f(Q^N(\mathbf{x}^N))q_i^N(\mathbf{x}^N) - x_i^N] + q_i^N(\mathbf{x}^N)f'(Q^N(\mathbf{x}^N))\sum_{j\neq i}\frac{\partial}{\partial x_i}\,q_j^N(\mathbf{x}^N) - 1 = 0 \qquad (i = 1, 2, \ldots, n). \tag{38}$$

In what follows, our focus will be on the welfare performance of the subgame-perfect equilibrium of our two-stage game, i.e. $\{\mathbf{x}^N, \mathbf{q}^N(\mathbf{x}^N)\}$.

4.2. *Second-best excess investment theorem at the margin*

Let the second-best market surplus function be defined by

$$W^N(\mathbf{x}) := \int_0^{Q^N(\mathbf{x})} f(Z)\mathrm{d}Z - \sum_{j=1}^{n}\left[\frac{wG(q_j^N(\mathbf{x}))}{\phi(x_j)} + x_j\right]. \tag{39}$$

Our eventual task in this section is to evaluate $(\partial/\partial x_i)W^N(\mathbf{x})$ at $\mathbf{x} = \mathbf{x}^N$, where

$$\begin{aligned} \frac{\partial}{\partial x_i}\,W^N(\mathbf{x}) &= f(Q^N(\mathbf{x}))\,\frac{\partial}{\partial x_i}\,Q^N(\mathbf{x}) \\ &\quad - \frac{w}{[\phi(x_i)]^2}\left[\phi(x_i)G'(q_i^N(\mathbf{x}))\,\frac{\partial}{\partial x_i}\,q_i^N(\mathbf{x}) - \phi'(x_i)G(q_i^N(\mathbf{x}))\right] \\ &\quad - 1 - \sum_{j\neq i}\frac{wG'(q_j^N(\mathbf{x}))}{\phi(x_j)}\,\frac{\partial}{\partial x_i}\,q_j^N(\mathbf{x}) \qquad (i = 1, 2, \ldots, n). \end{aligned} \tag{40}$$

In order to make further progress in evaluating (40) at $\mathbf{x} = \mathbf{x}^N$, let us suppose that the number of firms is at the equilibrium level, i.e. $n = n_e$, so that the level of profits at the subgame-perfect equilibrium $\{\mathbf{x}^N, \mathbf{q}^N(\mathbf{x}^N)\}$ is zero:

$$f(Q^N(\mathbf{x}^N))q_i^N(\mathbf{x}^N) - \frac{wG(q_i^N(\mathbf{x}^N))}{\phi(x_i^N)} - x_i^N = 0 \qquad (i = 1, 2, \ldots, n_e). \tag{41}$$

It follows from (35) and (41) that

$$\frac{wG'(q_i^N(\mathbf{x}^N))}{\phi(x_i^N)} = f(Q^N(\mathbf{x}^N)) + q_i^N(\mathbf{x}^N)f'(Q^N(\mathbf{x}^N)), \tag{42}$$

which enables us to reduce (40) at $\mathbf{x} = \mathbf{x}^N$ into

$$\frac{\partial}{\partial x_i} W^N(\mathbf{x}^N) = - q_i^N(\mathbf{x}^N)f'(Q^N(\mathbf{x}^N))\left[\frac{\partial}{\partial x_i} Q^N(\mathbf{x}^N) + \sum_{j \neq i} \frac{\partial}{\partial x_i} q_j^N(\mathbf{x}^N)\right], \tag{43}$$

where use is also made of (38).

Let us define $\omega^N(\mathbf{x}) := (\partial/\partial x_i)q_i^N(\mathbf{x})$ and $\theta^N(\mathbf{x}) := (\partial/\partial x_i)q_j^N(\mathbf{x})(i \neq j)$ for any symmetric R&D profile $\mathbf{x}$. Differentiating the first-order condition $(\partial/\partial q_i)\sigma_i(\mathbf{q}^N(\mathbf{x}); x_i) = 0$ with respect to x_i and x_h $(h \neq i)$, respectively, and using the short-hand notation $\alpha^N(\mathbf{x}) := (\partial^2/\partial q_i^2)\sigma_i(\mathbf{q}^N(\mathbf{x}); x_i)$, $\beta^N(\mathbf{x}) := (\partial^2/\partial q_i\, \partial q_j)\sigma_i(\mathbf{q}^N(\mathbf{x}); x_i)$, and $\nu^N(\mathbf{x}) := (\partial^2/\partial x_i\, \partial q_i)\sigma_i(\mathbf{q}^N(\mathbf{x}); x_i)$, we obtain the following simultaneous equations for $\omega^N(\mathbf{x})$ and $\theta^N(\mathbf{x})$:

$$\begin{bmatrix} \alpha^N(\mathbf{x}) & (n_e - 1)\beta^N(\mathbf{x}) \\ \beta^N(\mathbf{x}) & \alpha^N(\mathbf{x}) + (n_e - 2)\beta^N(\mathbf{x}) \end{bmatrix} \begin{bmatrix} \omega^N(\mathbf{x}) \\ \theta^N(\mathbf{x}) \end{bmatrix} = \begin{bmatrix} -\nu^N(\mathbf{x}) \\ 0 \end{bmatrix}. \tag{44}$$

Solving (44), we obtain

$$\omega^N(\mathbf{x}) = \frac{-\nu^N(\mathbf{x})}{\Delta^N(\mathbf{x})}\left[\alpha^N(\mathbf{x}) + (n_e - 2)\beta^N(\mathbf{x})\right] \tag{45}$$

and

$$\theta^N(\mathbf{x}) = \frac{\beta^N(\mathbf{x})\gamma(\mathbf{x})}{\Delta^N(\mathbf{x})}, \tag{46}$$

where $\Delta^N(\mathbf{x}) := [\alpha^N(\mathbf{x}) - \beta^N(\mathbf{x})]\,[\alpha^N(\mathbf{x}) + (n_e - 1)\beta^N(\mathbf{x})]$. It follows from (45) and (46) that

$$\frac{\partial}{\partial x_i} Q^N(\mathbf{x}) = \omega^N(\mathbf{x}) + (n - 1)\,\theta^N(\mathbf{x}) = -\frac{\nu^N(\mathbf{x})}{\Delta^N(\mathbf{x})}\left[\alpha^N(\mathbf{x}) - \beta^N(\mathbf{x})\right], \tag{47}$$

so that (43) can be finally boiled down to

$$\frac{\partial}{\partial x_i} W^N(\mathbf{x}^N) = \frac{-\nu^N(\mathbf{x}^N)q_i^N(\mathbf{x}^N)f'(Q^N(\mathbf{x}^N))}{\Delta^N(\mathbf{x}^N)}\left[n_e\beta^N(\mathbf{x}^N) - \alpha^N(\mathbf{x}^N)\right]. \tag{48}$$

At this juncture of our reasoning, note that the crucial terms $\alpha^N(\mathbf{x})$, $\beta^N(\mathbf{x})$ and $\nu^N(\mathbf{x})$ for any symmetric R&D profile $\mathbf{x}$ can be computed as follows:

$$\alpha^N(\mathbf{x}) = \frac{\phi(x_i)}{[G(q_i^N(\mathbf{x}))]^2} \{G(q_i^N(\mathbf{x}))\,[2f'(Q^N(\mathbf{x})) + q_i^N(\mathbf{x})f''(Q^N(\mathbf{x}))]$$
$$- G''(q_i^N(\mathbf{x}))\,[f(Q^N(\mathbf{x}))q_i^N(\mathbf{x}) - x_i]\}, \tag{49}$$

$$\beta^N(\mathbf{x}) = \frac{\phi(x_i)}{[G(q_i^N(\mathbf{x}))]^2} \{G(q_i^N(\mathbf{x}))\,[f'(Q^N(\mathbf{x})) + q_i^N(\mathbf{x})f''(Q^N(\mathbf{x}))]$$
$$- G'(q_i^N(\mathbf{x}))f'(Q^N(\mathbf{x}))q_i^N(\mathbf{x})\}, \tag{50}$$

and

$$\nu^N(\mathbf{x}) = \frac{G'(q_i^N(\mathbf{x}))\phi(x_i)}{[G(q_i^N(\mathbf{x}))]^2} > 0, \tag{51}$$

where use is made of (35). Note further that the following assumption (A6) is enough to guarantee the local stability of the dynamic adjustment process, i.e. $\dot{q}_i = \tau(\partial/\partial q_i)\sigma_i(\mathbf{q}; x_i)$ $(i = 1, 2, \ldots, n)$, where $\dot{q}_i$ is the time derivative of q_i, $\tau > 0$ is the adjustment coefficient, and $\mathbf{x} = (x_1, \ldots, x_i, \ldots, x_n)$ denotes any symmetric R&D profile.

A6: $\alpha^N(\mathbf{x}) + (k-1)\beta^N(\mathbf{x}) < 0$ holds for all $k = 0, 1, \ldots, n_e$.

It follows from A6, for $k = 0, 1, 2, n_e - 1$, and n_e, that $\Delta^N(\mathbf{x}^N) > 0$, $\omega^N(\mathbf{x}^N) > 0$ and $\theta^N(\mathbf{x}^N) < (>)\, 0$ if and only if $\beta^N(\mathbf{x}^N) < (>)\, 0$, $(\partial/\partial x_i)Q^N(\mathbf{x}^N) > 0$, and $\alpha^N(\mathbf{x}^N) < 0$. Finally, it follows from (48) that

$$\text{sgn}\,\frac{\partial}{\partial x_i} W^N(\mathbf{x}^N) = \text{sgn}\,[n_e\beta^N(\mathbf{x}^N) - \alpha^N(\mathbf{x}^N)], \tag{52}$$

which is the basic equation for welfare change.[5] Note, in particular, that $(\partial/\partial x_i)W^N(\mathbf{x}^N) > 0$ is unambiguously the case if $\beta^N(\mathbf{x}^N) > 0$, i.e. if outputs are strategic complements. Since $\beta^N(\mathbf{x}^N)$ holds if and only if

$$q_i^N(\mathbf{x}^N)f''(Q^N(\mathbf{x}^N) + f'(Q^N(\mathbf{x}^N))\,[1 - \varepsilon_G(q_i^N(\mathbf{x}^N))] > (<)\, 0, \tag{53}$$

where $\varepsilon_G(q_i^N(\mathbf{x}^N)) := G'(q_i^N(\mathbf{x}^N))q_i^N(\mathbf{x}^N)/G(q_i^N(\mathbf{x}^N))$ denotes the elasticity of effective labour demand, $(\partial/\partial x_i)W^N(\mathbf{x}^N) > 0$ holds if $f''(Q^N(\mathbf{x}^N)) \geqslant 0$ and $\varepsilon_G(q_i^N(\mathbf{x}^N)) > 1$. In other words, *the efficiency-improving R&D investment is socially insufficient at the margin if inverse demand function is weakly convex and the elasticity of effective labour demand exceeds unity.*[6]

The conclusion of our analysis in this section is basically parallel to that in the previous section. We have identified a set of non-trivial assumptions under which the excess (or insufficient) investment theorem at the margin holds for the oligopolistic competition among profit-sharing firms. Despite its apparent formal similarity with the case for profit-maximizing firms, the real contents of these assumptions are substantially different. In particular, the excess investment theorem at the margin fails to hold in this arena if the inverse demand function is weakly convex and the elasticity of effective labour demand exceeds unity.

5. QUASI-COURNOT CONJECTURE AND EXCESS ENTRY THEOREMS

5.1. Motivation

It goes without saying that Cournot conjecture, whereby an oligopolistic competitor expects that rival firms will *not* adjust their strategies in response to a change in its own strategies, is a great simplifier of the analysis of oligopolistic competition and economic welfare. It is clear that our analyses in this monograph have extensively utilized the services rendered by this simplification. Unfortunately, however, Cournot conjecture is self-defeating out of equilibrium, as it just implies that firms keep on expecting that other firms will not respond when they are in fact changing their strategic variables throughout the process of adjustment towards equilibrium. We should also add that the assumption of Cournot conjecture prevents us from examining the welfare effects of collusion among oligopolistic firms. The purpose of this section is to verify how the validity of excess entry theorems will be affected if we relax the Cournot conjecture assumption into somewhat more general 'quasi-Cournot' conjecture *à la* Seade (1980*b*).

5.2. Welfare effects of entry under quasi-Cournot conjecture

According to the quasi-Cournot hypothesis on conjectures, 'firms may have a certain degree of "collusion," that is, awareness of their interdependence *via* the equilibrium effects of their individual actions, provided these effects are well defined and well predicted by producers' (Seade 1980*b*: 480).[7]

In order to embody this hypothesis into our analysis, we assume that the inverse demand function $p = f(Q)$ satisfies A1 above. There are n identical firms in the industry, where $2 \leqslant n < +\infty$, and the cost function $C(q)$ of each firm is assumed to satisfy A2. The profits of firm i are represented by $\pi_i(\mathbf{q}) := f(Q)q_i - C(q_i)$ $(i = 1, 2, \ldots, n)$, where $Q = \Sigma_{j=1}^{n} q_j$. Assuming interior optimum and second-order conditions, the first-order condition for profit maximization requires

$$f(Q) + \mu(n)q_i f'(Q) - C'(q_i) = 0 \qquad (i = 1, 2, \ldots, n), \tag{54}$$

where $\mu(n) := \partial Q/\partial q_i = 1 + \partial Q_{-i}/\partial q_i$ and $Q_{-i} = \Sigma_{j \neq i} q_j$. It is this function $\mu(n)$, which represents the conjectural change in total output Q relative to a small change in a firm's output, that plays a crucial role in the following analysis. What is important is the existence of a well defined function $\mu(n)$ such that each firm can predict correctly the effect of its change of strategy on the industry output. Notice also that the conjectural variation function $\mu(n)$ is assumed to depend on the number of firms n, 'as the greater ease of communication amongst firms or of enforcement of (explicit or tacit) agreements when they are few may facilitate more collusive policies to be pursued' (Seade 1980*b*: 488).

Concerning the values that the conjectural variation function $\mu(n)$ takes on, the reasonable range seems to be $[0, n]$, where $\mu(n) \in [0, 1)$ corresponds to the situation of 'struggle', whereas $\mu(n) \in (1, n]$ corresponds to that of 'collusion', with $\mu(n) = 1$ denoting the watershed situation of Cournot conjecture.

The story of 'struggle' and 'collusion' may go as follows.[8] A firm whose conjectural variation $\mu(n)$ lies in $[0, 1)$ expects that, were it to reduce its output in the pursuit of moving up along its perceived demand curve, rival firms would expand their output with the purpose of taking part of its market share, whereas a firm whose conjectural variation $\mu(n)$ lies in $(1, n]$ expects that any 'profitable' move it makes would be matched at least partly by similar moves of its rivals, with $\mu(n) = n$ corresponding to the situation of full collusion of all firms in the industry. Given this interpretation, it makes natural sense to regard $m(n) := n/\mu(n)$ as the number of 'effective' firms in the industry. Indeed, if $\mu(n) = 1$ and there exists no collusion, it is reasonable to say that the market has n 'effective' firms, whereas if $\mu(n) = n$ and there exists full collusion of all firms, it is natural to say that the market involves only one 'effective' firm. In the limiting case, where a firm expects that a change in its individual output will exert no influence on market price, hence $\mu(n) = 0$, the number of 'effective' firms becomes infinite, so that the market is perfectly competitive.

Let $q^N(n)$ be the output of each profit-maximizing firm at the symmetric Cournot–Nash equilibrium among n firms.[9] In view of (54), $q^N(n)$ can be characterized by

$$f(Q^N(n)) + \mu(n)q^N(n)f'(Q^N(n)) - C'(q^N(n)) = 0, \tag{55}$$

where $Q^N(n) = nq^N(n)$. Differentiating (55) with respect to n, we obtain

$$\frac{\mathrm{d}}{\mathrm{d}n} q^N(n) = \frac{q^N(n)}{\Delta^N(n)} [\beta^N(n) + \mu(n)\mu'(n)f'(Q^N(n))], \tag{56}$$

where

$$\begin{aligned}\Delta^N(n) := {} & \alpha^N(n) + (n-1)\beta^N(n) \\ & + [\mu(n) - 1]\,[\mu(n)f''(Q^N(n)) - C''(q^N(n))],\end{aligned} \tag{57}$$

$$\alpha^N(n) := (\partial^2/\partial q_i^2)\, \pi_i(\mathbf{q}^N(n))$$
$$= 2\mu(n)f'(Q^N(n)) + q^N(n)[\mu(n)]^2 f''(Q^N(n)) - C''(q^N(n)), \tag{58}$$

and

$$\beta^N(n) := (\partial^2/\partial q_i\, \partial q_j)\pi_i(\mathbf{q}^N(n))$$
$$= \mu(n)\, [f'(Q^N(n)) + q^N(n)\mu(n)f''(Q^N(n))] \quad (i \neq j). \tag{59}$$

Since we have reverted to the competition among profit-maximizing firms, it is natural to make the following assumption.

A7: The strategic substitutability prevails; i.e. $\beta^N(n) < 0$ holds.

As in the model of oligopoly with Cournot conjecture, we may verify that the quasi-Cournot–Nash equilibrium $\mathbf{q}^N(n)$, all of whose elements are given by $q^N(n)$, is stable with respect to the adjustment process $\dot{q}_i = \tau(\partial/\partial q_i)\pi_i(\mathbf{q})$, where $\dot{q}_i$ denotes the time derivative of q_i and $\tau > 0$ denotes the adjustment coefficient, if the following stability condition is satisfied.

A8: $\alpha^N(n) + (k-1)\beta^N(n) < 0$ holds for all $k = 0, 1, \ldots, n$.

It is also easy to verify that the excess entry theorem at the margin holds if and only if $(d/dn)q^N(n) < 0$ holds. With the purpose of knowing when in fact this crucial inequality obtains, we define:[10]

$$\varepsilon := \inf_{n>0} \left[\frac{\beta^N(n)}{\mu(n)f'(Q^N(n))}\right] \geqslant 0. \tag{60}$$

We may then assert the following.

Theorem 3. Suppose that A1, A2, A7, and A8 hold. Then the equilibrium number of firms n_e is socially excessive at the margin if $\mu'(n_e) > -\varepsilon$ holds.

Proof. To begin with, A8 for $k = 0$ enables us to obtain

$$\mu(n)f'(Q^N(n)) - C''(q^N(n)) = \alpha^N(n) - \beta^N(n) < 0, \tag{61}$$

where use is made of (58) and (59). It follows from (57) and (61) that

$$\Delta^N(n) = n\beta^N(n) + \mu(n)\,[\alpha^N(n) - \beta^N(n)] < 0, \tag{62}$$

where use is made of A7 and $\mu(n) > 0$.

Next, by virtue of (60), the inequality $\mu'(n_e) > -\varepsilon$ implies

$$-\mu'(n_e) < \varepsilon \leqslant \frac{\beta^N(n_e)}{\mu(n_e)f'(Q^N(n_e))}, \tag{63}$$

which, in its turn, implies

$$\beta^N(n_e) + \mu'(n_e)\mu(n_e)f'(Q^N(n_e)) < 0, \tag{64}$$

where use is made of $\mu(n_e) > 0$ and $f'(Q^N(n_e)) < 0$. Coupled with (56) and (62), (64) implies that $(\mathrm{d}/\mathrm{d}n)q^N(n_e) < 0$. This is precisely what we set out to show. □

In the case of Cournot conjecture where $\mu(n) = 1$ holds for all n, the crucial inequality $\mu'(n_e) > -\varepsilon$ is trivially satisfied. In this sense, the second-best excess entry theorem at the margin under Cournot conjecture, i.e. Theorem 3(*b*) in Chapter 1, is nothing other than a special case of the Theorem 3 that we have just established.

It only remains to see what is involved in the condition $\mu'(n_e) > -\varepsilon$. Roughly speaking, this condition, if violated, implies that $\mu'(n_e)$ is a sufficiently large negative number. This is tantamount to saying that, when we decrease the number of firms marginally from n_e to n, the increase in $\mu(n)$ is quite large, and the effective number of firms decreases rather sharply. The situation is illustrated in Fig. 16. The upshot of our analysis is that the exception to the excess entry theorem occurs if the degree of collusion among firms sharply increases when the number of firms is decreased. Interpreted in this way, the message of Theorem 3 seems to be quite natural and reasonable.

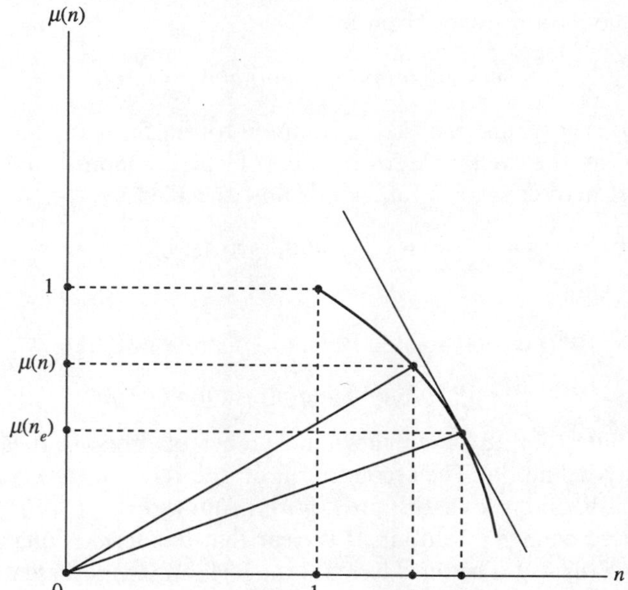

Fig. 16 Conjectural variation function and effective number of firms

6. WELFARE EFFECTS OF PRODUCT DIFFERENTIATION[11]

We are now at the stage of exploring the effects of product differentiation on the welfare impact of marginal firm entry. The gist of the problem is that the entry of a new firm producing a differentiated product enhances product diversity, so that the welfare of consumers who prefer diversity will be thereby positively affected.

In order to capture this product diversification effect of new entry as simply as possible, let us specify gross consumer benefit function by

$$B(q_1, \ldots, q_i, \ldots) := V\left[\sum_{i=1}^{\infty} v(q_i)\right], \tag{65}$$

where q_i is firm i's output, $v(0) = 0$, $v'(q) > 0$, and $v''(q) < 0$ for all $q \geqslant 0$, and $V'(z) > 0$ and $V''(z) < 0$ for all $z \geqslant 0$. We are thus assuming that consumers indeed prefer product variety and that the outputs of firms are substitutes for each other.

Assuming that firms are identical save for the fact that the products are differentiated in the perception of consumers, we consider the oligopolistic equilibrium among n firms. Since consumers maximize their gross benefits, each firm's product price is equal to $V'[nv(q(n))]v'(q(n))$ in equilibrium, where $q(n)$ denotes the equilibrium output of each firm. Thus, the equilibrium profits of a firm are given by

$$\pi(n) = V'[nv(q(n))]\, v'(q(n))q(n) - C(q(n)), \tag{66}$$

where $C(q)$ is cost function that is common for all firms.

Turning to the welfare performance of this economy, note that the second-best market surplus function is now specified by

$$W(n) = V[nv(q(n))] - nC(q(n)), \tag{67}$$

so that we obtain

$$\begin{aligned} W'(n) = \pi(n) + nq'(n)\left\{V'[nv(q(n))]v'(q(n)) - C'(q(n))\right\} \\ + V'[nv(q(n))]\,[v(q(n)) - q(n)v'(q(n))]. \end{aligned} \tag{68}$$

If we evaluate (68) at the equilibrium number of firms n_e, it is clear that $\pi(n_e) = 0$ by definition. The second term on the RHS of (68) is familiar to us, i.e. the oligopolistic distortion $V[nv(q(n))]v'(q(n)) - C'(q(n))$ times the entry-induced change in output. It is clear that this term is unambiguously negative if $q'(n) < 0$. The third term on the RHS of (68) represents the novel effect of product diversity, which is clearly positive by virtue of the strict concavity of $v(q)$.[12] When consumers have preference for product diversity, therefore, the crucial expression $W'(n_e)$ consists of two terms that have different signs. Hence the sign of $W'(n_e)$ remains ambiguous in general. However, if consumers have a strong preference for product diversity, the negative distortion effect may well be dominated by the positive diversification effect. Thus, the exception to the excess entry theorem is likely to emerge if consumers have a strong preference for product diversity, whereas the degree of scale economies is of lesser importance.

7. PRICE COMPETITION WITH STRATEGIC COMMITMENT

7.1 Motivation

Throughout our analyses in Part II above, where we examined the welfare effects of strategic commitment in terms of a two-stage model of oligopolistic competition, it was commonly assumed that the strategic variables in the second-stage competition in the product market are strategic substitutes. Needless to say, it is quite natural to make this assumption in the context where firms compete in terms of quantities, as it corresponds to the downward-sloping reaction curves in the quantity space. In a model with product differentiation where firms compete in terms of prices, however, the normal strategic assumption should be such that the strategic variables in the second-stage game are strategic complements.[13] The purpose of this section is to determine how the policy-relevant conclusions that we have obtained in Chapter 6 are affected if firms compete in terms of prices rather than quantities in the product market. In so doing, it will be shown that the method of analysis developed in Part II for the Cournot–Nash quantity competition can be applied, *mutatis mutandis*, to the Bertrand–Nash price competition as well. This fact may be of some interest in view of the recent concerns over the normative and positive contrast between the Cournot quantity competition and the Bertrand price competition.[14]

7.2. A two-stage model with price strategies

Consider an industry involving n firms, where $2 \leqslant n < +\infty$, which produce differentiated products. Let $q_i = f^i(\mathbf{p})$, where $\mathbf{p} = (p_1, \ldots, p_i, \ldots, p_n)$, be the demand function for the ith product, where q_i and p_i denote output and price of the ith product, respectively ($i = 1, 2, \ldots, n$). The cost of producing the ith product, and the cost of cost-reducing R&D incurred by firm i, are assumed to be $c(x_i; \mathbf{x}_{-i})q_i$ and x_i, respectively, where $\mathbf{x}_{-i} = (x_1, \ldots, x_{i-1}, x_{i+1}, \ldots, x_n)$ is the profile of R&D expenditures by all firms other than i.

Throughout this section the following assumptions are made.

A9: $f^i(\mathbf{p})$ is twice continuously differentiable on the price space $\mathbf{P} := \{\mathbf{p} \in \mathbf{R}^n_+ \mid f^j(\mathbf{p}) > 0 \ (j = 1, 2, \ldots, n)\}$, with

(*a*) $f_i^i(\mathbf{p}) := (\partial/\partial p_i) f^i(\mathbf{p}) < 0$,
(*b*) $f_j^i(\mathbf{p}) := (\partial/\partial p_j) f^i(\mathbf{p}) > 0 \ (i \neq j)$,
(*c*) $\Sigma_{j=1}^n f_j^i(\mathbf{p}) < 0$, and
(*d*) $f^i(\mathbf{p})$, $f_i^i(\mathbf{p})$, and $f_j^i(\mathbf{p})$ are independent of firm indices for any symmetric price profile $\mathbf{p} \in \mathbf{P}$.[15]

A10: The average variable cost function $c(x_i; \mathbf{x}_{-i})$ is defined on $\mathbf{R}_+^n$ and twice continuously differentiable on the space of R&D profiles $\mathbf{X} = \{\mathbf{x} \in \mathbf{R}_+^n \mid c(x_j; \mathbf{x}_{-j}) > 0 \ (j = 1, 2, \ldots, n)\}$, with
(*a*) $(\partial/\partial x_i) c(x_i; \mathbf{x}_{-i}) < 0$, and $(\partial/\partial x_j) c(x_i; \mathbf{x}_{-i}) \leqslant 0 \ (i \neq j)$, and
(*b*) $(\partial/\partial x_i) c(x_i; \mathbf{x}_{-i}) < (\partial/\partial x_j) c(x_i c(x_i; \mathbf{x}_{-i}) \ (i \neq j)$ for any symmetric R&D profile $\mathbf{x} \in \mathbf{X}$.

Thus, products are ordinary substitutes and the firm's own-price effect dominates the aggregate cross-price effects. A firm's R&D is cost-reducing and can exert beneficial impact on other firms without payment. However, it is assumed that the cost-reducing effect of a firm's own R&D outweighs the benefits accruing freely from other firms when all firms are spending the same amount on R&D.

Firms engage in a two-stage competition. In the first stage firms make an irrevocable commitment to a level of R&D, whereas in the second stage they compete by choosing prices. To characterize the second-stage Bertrand–Nash equilibrium, let the payoff function of firm i in the second-stage game be

$$\pi_i(\mathbf{p}; \mathbf{x}) := [p_i - c(x_i; \mathbf{x}_{-i})] \, f^i(\mathbf{p}) - x_i, \tag{69}$$

where $\mathbf{p} = (p_1, \ldots, p_i, \ldots, p_n) \in \mathbf{P}$ and $\mathbf{x} = (x_1, \ldots, x_i, \ldots, x_n) \in \mathbf{X}$. In what follows, $\mathbf{p}^N(\mathbf{x}) = (p_1^N(\mathbf{x}), \ldots, p_i^N(\mathbf{x}), \ldots, p_n^N(\mathbf{x}))$ denotes the Bertrand–Nash equilibrium of the second-stage game corresponding to the specified R&D profile $\mathbf{x} \in \mathbf{X}$. Thus:

$$p_i^N(\mathbf{x}) := \arg \max_{p_i > 0} \pi_i \, ((p_i, \mathbf{p}_{-i}^N(\mathbf{x})); \mathbf{x}) \qquad (i = 1, 2, \ldots, n), \tag{70}$$

where $\mathbf{p}_{-i}^N(\mathbf{x}) = (p_1^N(\mathbf{x}), \ldots, p_{i-1}^N(\mathbf{x}), p_{i+1}^N(\mathbf{x}), \ldots, p_n^N(\mathbf{x}))$.

Assuming interior optimum and second-order conditions, $\mathbf{p}^N(\mathbf{x})$ can be characterized by the first-order conditions $(\partial/\partial p_i) \pi_i(\mathbf{p}^N(\mathbf{x}); \mathbf{x}) = 0$:

$$f^i(\mathbf{p}^N(\mathbf{x})) + [p_i^N(\mathbf{x}) - c(x_i; \mathbf{x}_{-i})] \, f_i^i(\mathbf{p}^N(\mathbf{x})) = 0 \qquad (i = 1, 2, \ldots, n). \tag{71}$$

In what follows, $\mathbf{p}^N(\mathbf{x})$ is assumed to be symmetric for any symmetric $\mathbf{x} \in \mathbf{X}$.

As an auxiliary step in introducing our crucial strategic assumption, let us now define $\alpha_i(\mathbf{p}; \mathbf{x}) := (\partial^2/\partial p_i^2) \pi_i(\mathbf{p}; \mathbf{x})$ and $\beta_{ij}(\mathbf{p}; \mathbf{x}) := (\partial^2/\partial p_i \, \partial p_j) \pi_i(\mathbf{p}; \mathbf{x})$ $(i \neq j; \, i, j = 1, 2, \ldots, n)$. Since our second-stage game is played by using prices rather than quantities as strategic variables, it is natural to require the following assumption.

A11: Firms' second-stage strategic variables are strategic complements; that is, $\beta_{ij}(\mathbf{p}; \mathbf{x}) > 0$ $(i \neq j;\ i, j = 1, 2, \ldots, n)$ holds for any price–R&D profile $(\mathbf{p}; \mathbf{x}) \in \mathbf{P} \times \mathbf{X}$.

By carrying out required second-order differentiation, we can obtain

$$\alpha_i(\mathbf{p}; \mathbf{x}) = 2f_i^i(\mathbf{p}) + [p_i - c(x_i; \mathbf{x}_{-i})]\, f_{ii}^i(\mathbf{p}) \tag{72}$$

and

$$\beta_{ij}(\mathbf{p}; \mathbf{x}) = f_j^i(\mathbf{p}) + [p_i - c(x_i; \mathbf{x}_{-i})]\, f_{ij}^i(\mathbf{p}), \tag{73}$$

where $f_{ii}^i(\mathbf{p}) := (\partial^2/\partial p_i^2) f^i(\mathbf{p})$ and $f_{ij}^i(\mathbf{p}) := (\partial^2/\partial p_i\, \partial p_j) f^i(\mathbf{p})$ $(i \neq j)$.

The following assumption ensures that the Bertrand reaction mappings are contractions, so that the existence, uniqueness, and stability of the Bertrand–Nash equilibrium are thereby warranted.[16]

A12: $\alpha_i(\mathbf{p}; \mathbf{x}) + \Sigma_{j \neq i}\, \beta_{ij}(\mathbf{p}; \mathbf{x}) < 0$ holds for any price–R&D profile $(\mathbf{p}; \mathbf{x}) \in \mathbf{P} \times \mathbf{X}$ $(i = 1, 2, \ldots, n)$.

Turning to the first stage of our game, let the first-stage payoff function of firm i be defined by

$$\begin{aligned} \Pi_i(\mathbf{x}) &:= \pi_i(\mathbf{p}^N(\mathbf{x}); \mathbf{x}) \\ &= [p_i^N(\mathbf{x}) - c(x_i; \mathbf{x}_{-i})]\, f^i(\mathbf{p}^N(\mathbf{x})) - x_i \qquad (i = 1, 2, \ldots, n). \end{aligned} \tag{74}$$

In the context of the first-stage game, we examine two equilibrium concepts as in Chapter 6. The first concept is the non-co-operative equilibrium *à la* Nash, denoted by $\mathbf{x}^N = (x_1^N, \ldots, x_i^N, \ldots, x_n^N)$ and characterized under the assumption of interior optimum and second-order conditions by the first-order conditions $(\partial/\partial x_i)\Pi_i(\mathbf{x}^N) = 0$ $(i = 1, 2, \ldots, n)$. The equilibrium pair $\{\mathbf{x}^N, \mathbf{p}^N(\mathbf{x}^N)\}$, then, is nothing other than the subgame-perfect equilibrium of the entire (two-stage) game. The second concept is the co-operative equilibrium where firms co-ordinate their R&D levels in order to maximize their joint profits. Under the assumption of interior optimum and second-order conditions, the co-operative equilibrium $\mathbf{x}^C = (x_1^C, \ldots, x_i^C, \ldots, x_n^C)$ can be characterized by the first-order conditions $(\partial/\partial x_i)\, \Sigma_{j=1}^n\, \Pi_i(\mathbf{x}^C) = 0$ $(i = 1, 2, \ldots, n)$, with the proviso that $x_1 = x_2 = \ldots = x_n$. In what follows, we assume that $\mathbf{x}^N$ as well as $\mathbf{x}^C$ is symmetric, so that $\mathbf{p}^N(\mathbf{x}^N)$ as well as $\mathbf{p}^N(\mathbf{x}^C)$ is also symmetric.

It can be verified that $\mathbf{x}^N$ is characterized by

$$- f^i(\mathbf{p}^N(\mathbf{x}^N))\, \frac{\partial}{\partial x_i}\, c(x_i^N; \mathbf{x}_{-i}^N) - 1$$

$$+ (n-1) f_j^i(\mathbf{p}^N(\mathbf{x}^N)) \, [p_i^N(\mathbf{x}^N) - c(x_i^N; \mathbf{x}_{-i}^N)] \frac{\partial}{\partial x_i} p_j^N(\mathbf{x}^N) = 0$$

$$(i \neq j;\ i, j = 1, 2, \ldots, n), \qquad (75)$$

where use is made of (71) for $\mathbf{x} = \mathbf{x}^N$, whereas $\mathbf{x}^C$ is characterized by

$$- f^j(\mathbf{p}^N(\mathbf{x}^C)) \frac{\partial}{\partial x_j} c(x_j^C; \mathbf{x}_{-j}^C) - 1 - (n-1) f^j(\mathbf{p}^N(\mathbf{x}^C)) \frac{\partial}{\partial x_i} c(x_j^C; \mathbf{x}_j^C)$$

$$+ (n-1) \frac{\partial}{\partial p_i} \pi_j(\mathbf{p}^N(\mathbf{x}^C); \mathbf{x}^C) \left[\frac{\partial}{\partial x_i} p_i^N(\mathbf{x}^C) + (n-1) \frac{\partial}{\partial x_i} p_j^N(\mathbf{x}^C) \right] = 0$$

$$(i \neq j;\ i, j = 1, 2, \ldots, n). \qquad (76)$$

For expositional simplicity, the verification of these characterizations will be relegated to section 7.5 below.

7.3. Displacement of the second-stage equilibrium

As an auxiliary step in carrying out our welfare analysis, let us look at how the Bertrand–Nash equilibrium price $\mathbf{p}^N(\mathbf{x})$ reacts to a change in a firm's R&D expenditure. For any symmetric R&D profile $\mathbf{x} \in \mathbf{X}$, let us define $\omega^B(\mathbf{x}) := (\partial/\partial x_i) p_i^N(\mathbf{x})$ and $\theta^B(\mathbf{x}) := (\partial/\partial x_i) p_j^N(\mathbf{x})$ $(i \neq j;\ i, j = 1, 2, \ldots, n)$. It is shown in 7.5 below that

$$\omega^B(\mathbf{x}) = \frac{f_i^i(\mathbf{p}^N(\mathbf{x}))}{\Delta^B(\mathbf{x})} \left\{ [\alpha^B(\mathbf{x}) + (n-2)\, \beta^B(\mathbf{x})] \frac{\partial}{\partial x_i} c(x_i; \mathbf{x}_{-i}) \right.$$

$$\left. - (n-1) \beta^B(\mathbf{x}) \frac{\partial}{\partial x_j} c(x_i; \mathbf{x}_{-i}) \right\} < 0 \qquad (77)$$

and

$$\theta_B(\mathbf{x}) = \frac{f_i^i(\mathbf{p}(\mathbf{x}))}{\Delta^B(\mathbf{x})} \left[\alpha^B(\mathbf{x}) \frac{\partial}{\partial x_j} c(x_i; \mathbf{x}_{-i}) - \beta^B(\mathbf{x}) \frac{\partial}{\partial x_i} c(x_i; \mathbf{x}_{-i}) \right] \qquad (78)$$

$$< 0$$

hold, where $\alpha^B(\mathbf{x}) := \alpha_i(\mathbf{p}^N(\mathbf{x}); \mathbf{x})$, $\beta^B(\mathbf{x}) := \beta_{ij}(\mathbf{p}^N(\mathbf{x}); \mathbf{x})$ and

$$\Delta^B(\mathbf{x}) := [\alpha^B(\mathbf{x}) + (n-1)\beta^B(\mathbf{x})]\, [\alpha^B(\mathbf{x}) - \beta^B(\mathbf{x})] > 0. \qquad (79)$$

Therefore, *an increase in a firm's cost-reducing R&D unambiguously decreases the equilibrium price of all firms, irrespective of whether the R&D spillovers are large or small.*

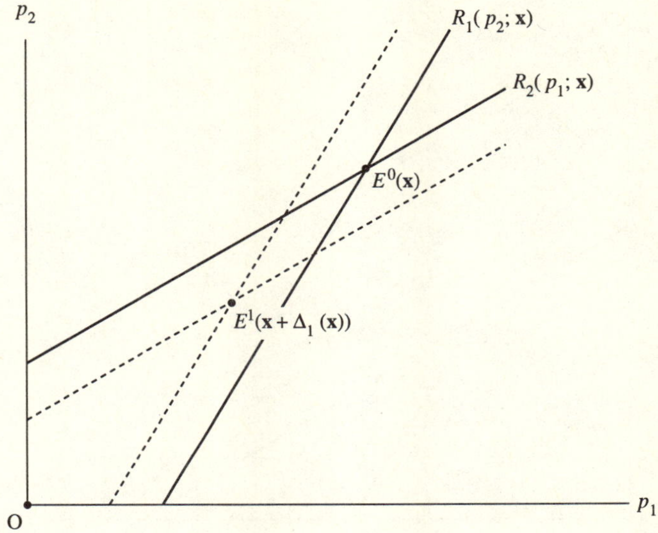

Fig. 17 Bertrand–Nash duopoly equilibrium

To highlight the crucial implication of strategic complementarity *vis-à-vis* strategic substitutability, Figs. 17 and 18 describe the displacement of Bertrand–Nash duopoly equilibrium and that of Cournot–Nash duopoly equilibrium, respectively, in response to a change in the R&D expenditure by firm 1. In Fig. 17 (Fig. 18), $R_i(p_j;\ \mathbf{x})$ ($R_j(q_j;\ \mathbf{x})$) ($i \neq j$) denotes the Bertrand (Cournot) reaction curve of firm i ($i = 1, 2$) when the R&D profile $\mathbf{x}$ prevails. The second-stage Bertrand–Nash equilibrium (Cournot–Nash equilibrium) is represented by point $E^0(\mathbf{x})$ where the two reaction curves intersect. Because the R&D expenditure is cost-reducing, an increase in x_1 by $\varepsilon > 0$ shifts up $R_1(p_2;\ \mathbf{x})$ as well as $R_1(q_2;\ \mathbf{x})$, but it also shifts up $R_2(p_1;\ \mathbf{x})$ as well as $R_2(q_1;\ \mathbf{x})$ through spillovers of the cost-reducing benefits. In the case of Fig. 17, the Bertrand–Nash equilibrium changes from $E^0(\mathbf{x})$ to $E^1(\mathbf{x} + \Delta_1(\mathbf{x}))$, where $\Delta_1(\mathbf{x}) = (\varepsilon, 0)$. It is clear from this figure that the equilibrium price is lower at $E^1(\mathbf{x} + \Delta_1(\mathbf{x}))$ than at $E^0(\mathbf{x})$ for both products, irrespective of the extent of R&D spillovers. In the case of Fig. 18, however, the Cournot–Nash equilibrium changes from $E^0(\mathbf{x})$ to either $E^1(\mathbf{x} + \Delta_1(\mathbf{x}))$ or $E^2(\mathbf{x} + \Delta_1(\mathbf{x}))$ depending on the extent of R&D spillovers, so that the equilibrium output of firm 2 increases (decreases) if R&D spillovers are sufficiently large (small) in the sense described in Chapter 6. It is this sharp contrast between the implications of strategic complementarity and strategic substitutability that is reflected in the contrasting welfare implications. These will be developed below.

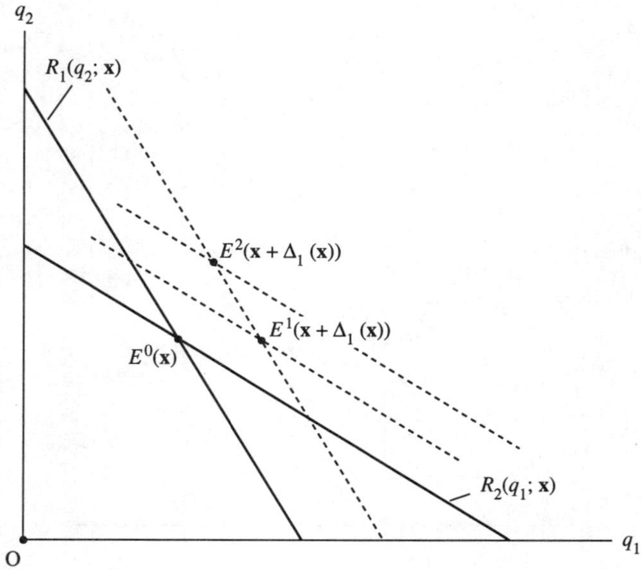

Fig. 18 Cournot–Nash duopoly equilibrium

7.4 Welfare verdicts on co-operative and non-cooperative R&D

With the purpose of gauging the welfare performance of $\{\mathbf{x}^C, \mathbf{p}^N(\mathbf{x}^C)\}$ *vis-à-vis* $\{\mathbf{x}^N, \mathbf{p}^N(\mathbf{x}^N)\}$, we introduce the market surplus function $W(\mathbf{x}, \mathbf{q})$ by

$$W(\mathbf{x}, \mathbf{q}) := V(\mathbf{q}) - \sum_{j=1}^{n} [c(x_j, \mathbf{x}_{-j})q_j + x_j], \tag{80}$$

where $V(\mathbf{q})$ is the gross benefit function of the representative consumer. Let $\mathbf{q}^N(\mathbf{x}) = (q_1^N(\mathbf{x}), \ldots, q_i^N(\mathbf{x}), \ldots, q_n^N(\mathbf{x}))$ and $\mathbf{q}^F(\mathbf{x}) = (q_1^F(\mathbf{x}), \ldots, q_i^F(\mathbf{x}), \ldots, q_n^F(\mathbf{x}))$ be defined, respectively, by $q_i^N(\mathbf{x}) := f^i(\mathbf{p}^N(\mathbf{x}))$ and $q_i^F(\mathbf{x}) := f^i(\mathbf{c}(\mathbf{x}))$, where $\mathbf{c}(\mathbf{x}) := (c(x_1; \mathbf{x}_{-1}), \ldots, c(x_i; \mathbf{x}_{-i}), \ldots, c(x_n; \mathbf{x}_{-n}))$ is the profile of marginal costs. Then the *first-best welfare function* $W^F(\mathbf{x})$ and the second-best welfare function $W^S(\mathbf{x})$ are defined, respectively, by

$$W^F(\mathbf{x}) := W(\mathbf{x}, \mathbf{q}^F(\mathbf{x})) \tag{81}$$

and

$$W^S(\mathbf{x}) := W(\mathbf{x}, \mathbf{q}^N(\mathbf{x})). \tag{82}$$

To simplify our notation, let us now introduce the following conventions:

$$p_j^\tau(\mathbf{x}) := \begin{cases} c(x_j; \mathbf{x}_{-j}) & \text{if } \tau = F \\ p_j^N(\mathbf{x}) & \text{if } \tau = S \end{cases} \qquad (j = 1, 2, \ldots, n) \tag{83}$$

and $\mathbf{q}^S(\mathbf{x}) := \mathbf{q}^N(\mathbf{x})$. Differentiating $W^\tau(\mathbf{x})$ ($\tau = F, S$) partially with respect to x_i and invoking $(\partial/\partial q_i)V(\mathbf{q}^\tau(\mathbf{x})) = p_j^\tau(\mathbf{x})$ ($j = 1, 2, \ldots, n$), we obtain

$$\frac{\partial}{\partial x_i} W^\tau(\mathbf{x}) = \gamma^\tau(\mathbf{x}) + \delta^\tau(\mathbf{x}) + \sigma^\tau(\mathbf{x}), \tag{84}$$

where

$$\gamma^\tau(\mathbf{x}) := -q_i^\tau(\mathbf{x})\,(\partial/\partial x_i)c(x_i; \mathbf{x}_{-i}) - 1, \tag{85}$$

$$\delta^\tau(\mathbf{x}) := \sum_{j=1}^{n}\left[p_j^\tau(\mathbf{x}) - c(x_j; \mathbf{x}_{-j})\right]\frac{\partial}{\partial x_i} q_j^\tau(\mathbf{x}), \tag{86}$$

and

$$\sigma^\tau(\mathbf{x}) := -\sum_{j \neq i} q_j^\tau(\mathbf{x})\frac{\partial}{\partial x_i} c(x_j; \mathbf{x}_{-j}). \tag{87}$$

As in Chapter 6, $\gamma^\tau(\mathbf{x})$, $\delta^\tau(\mathbf{x})$, and $\sigma^\tau(\mathbf{x})$ may be called the *commitment effect*, the *distortion effect*, and the *spillover effect*, respectively. Our next task is to evaluate (84) for $\tau = F$ and S, and $\mathbf{x} = \mathbf{x}^N$ and $\mathbf{x}^C$.

To start with, let us invoke the first-best welfare criterion $W^F(\mathbf{x})$. By virtue of (83), it follows from (86) that $\sigma^F(\mathbf{x}) = 0$, whereas A10 yields $\sigma^F(\mathbf{x}) \geqslant 0$. Furthermore, note that $\gamma^F(\mathbf{x})$ can be rewritten as follows:

$$\begin{aligned}\gamma^F(\mathbf{x}) &= -q_i^F(\mathbf{x})(\partial/\partial x_i)c(x_i; \mathbf{x}_{-i}) - 1\\ &= \gamma^S(\mathbf{x}) - [q_i^F(\mathbf{x}) - q_i^N(\mathbf{x})](\partial/\partial x_i)c(x_i; \mathbf{x}_{-i}).\end{aligned} \tag{88}$$

Invoking (75), we can verify that

$$\gamma^S(\mathbf{x}^N) = -(n-1)\,\theta(\mathbf{x}^N)f_j^i(\mathbf{p}^N(\mathbf{x}^N))\,[p_i^N(\mathbf{x}^N) - c(x_i^N; \mathbf{x}_{-i}^N)] > 0 \tag{89}$$

holds, where use is made of A9 and (78). Furthermore, there exists a number $\zeta(\mathbf{x})$, $0 < \zeta(\mathbf{x}) < 1$ such that

$$q_i^F(\mathbf{x}) - q_i^N(\mathbf{x}) = -\left[p_i^N(\mathbf{x}) - c(x_i; \mathbf{x}_{-i})\right]\sum_{j=1}^{n} f_j^i\,\{\zeta(\mathbf{x})\mathbf{p}^N(\mathbf{x}) + [1 - \zeta(\mathbf{x})]\mathbf{c}(\mathbf{x})\} > 0, \tag{90}$$

where use is made of the mean value theorem and A9. Invoking A10, we can now assert, on the basis of (88), (89), and (90), that $\gamma^F(\mathbf{x}^N) > 0$. This, in its turn, ensures that $(\partial/\partial x_i)W^F(\mathbf{x}^N) > 0$.

To see how the co-operative equilibrium $\mathbf{x}^C$ fares in this arena, we now invoke (76) to obtain

$$\begin{aligned}\gamma^S(\mathbf{x}^C) &= (n-1)q_j^N(\mathbf{x}^C)\frac{\partial}{\partial x_i}c(x_i^C; \mathbf{x}_{-j}^C)\\ &\quad - (n-1)\,[p_j^N(\mathbf{x}^C) - c(x_j^C; \mathbf{x}_{-j}^C)]\,f_i^j(\mathbf{p}^N(\mathbf{x}^C))\,\Psi^B(\mathbf{x}^C),\end{aligned} \tag{91}$$

where $\Psi^B(\mathbf{x}^C) := \omega^B(\mathbf{x}^C) + (n-1)\theta^B(\mathbf{x}^C) < 0$ by virtue of (77) and (78). It follows from (84), $\delta^F(\mathbf{x}^C) = 0$, (87), (88), and (91) that

$$(\partial/\partial x_i) W^F(\mathbf{x}^C) = -(n-1)\Big\{[p_j^N(\mathbf{x}^C) - c(x_j^C; \mathbf{x}_{-j}^C)]\, f_i^j(\mathbf{p}^N(\mathbf{x}^C))\, \Psi^B(\mathbf{x}^C) + [q_j^F(\mathbf{x}^C) - q_j^N(\mathbf{x}^C)](\partial/\partial x_i) c(x_j^C; \mathbf{x}_{-j}^C)\Big\} > 0 \tag{92}$$

where use is also made of (90), for $\mathbf{x} = \mathbf{x}^C$.

We have thus obtained the first main result in this section.

THEOREM 4. Suppose that A9, A10, A11, and A12 hold. Then the non-cooperative equilibrium R&D level, as well as the co-operative equilibrium R&D level, is socially insufficient at the margin in terms of the first-best welfare criterion.

Let us now turn to the second-best welfare criterion, $W^S(\mathbf{x})$. Note that (89) already ensures that $\gamma^S(\mathbf{x}^N) > 0$, whereas $\sigma^S(\mathbf{x}^N) \geqslant 0$ holds in view of A10. In sharp contrast with the first-best case, however, the distortion effect $\delta^S(\mathbf{x})$ does not vanish in the second-best case, which can be evaluated as follows:

$$\delta^S(\mathbf{x}) = [p_i^N(\mathbf{x}) - c(x_i; \mathbf{x}_{-i})]\,[f_i^i(\mathbf{p}^N(\mathbf{x})) + (n-1) f_j^i(\mathbf{p}^N(\mathbf{x}))]\, \Psi^B(\mathbf{x}) > 0, \tag{93}$$

where use is made of A9 and $\Psi^B(\mathbf{x}) < 0$. We have thus verified the crucial inequality $(\partial/\partial x_i) W^S(\mathbf{x}^N) > 0$.

Turning to the second-best performance of the co-operative R&D, we note that the first term in the RHS of (91) cancels with $\sigma^S(\mathbf{x}^C)$, whereas the second term thereof is unambiguously positive. Coupled with $\sigma^S(\mathbf{x}^C) > 0$, which follows from (92) for $\mathbf{x} = \mathbf{x}^C$, we may assert that $(\partial/\partial x_i) W^S(\mathbf{x}^C) > 0$.

We have thus established the second main result in this section.

THEOREM 5. Suppose that A9, A10, A11, and A12 hold. Then the non-cooperative equilibrium R&D level, as well as the co-operative equilibrium R&D level, is socially insufficient at the margin in terms of the second-best welfare criterion.

Comparing Theorems 1 and 2 with the conclusions we have obtained in Chapter 6 in the context of the Cournot–Nash quantity competition in the second-stage game, it clearly stands out that, unlike the case of Bertrand–Nash price competition in the second-stage game, the marginal welfare verdicts in the case of the Cournot–Nash quantity competition hinge squarely on the extent of R&D spillovers. Furthermore, the marginal welfare verdicts also depend crucially on the number of firms if firms compete in terms of quantities. It is this sharp contrast between quantity competition and price competition in the second-stage game that we wish to emphasize and call readers' attention to. More specifically, this contrast should be kept in mind in designing the welfare-improving technology policy in an oligopolistic economy.

7.5. *Proofs*

Derivation of the first-order condition for $\mathbf{x}^C$. Differentiating $\Sigma_{j=1}^{n} \pi_j(\mathbf{p}^N(\mathbf{x}); \mathbf{x})$ with respect to x_i and noting that all firms co-ordinate their R&D symmetrically, we obtain

$$\sum_{j=1}^{n}\left\{\sum_{k=1}^{n}\frac{\partial}{\partial p_k}\pi_j(\mathbf{p}^N(\mathbf{x});\mathbf{x})\frac{\partial}{\partial x_j}p_k^N(\mathbf{x})+\frac{\partial}{\partial x_j}\pi_j(\mathbf{p}^N(\mathbf{x});(\mathbf{x})\right.$$

$$\left.+\sum_{h\neq j}\left[\sum_{k=1}^{n}\frac{\partial}{\partial p_k}\pi_j(\mathbf{p}^N(\mathbf{x});\mathbf{x})\frac{\partial}{\partial x_h}p_k^N(\mathbf{x})+\frac{\partial}{\partial x_h}\pi_j(\mathbf{p}^N(\mathbf{x});\mathbf{x})\right]\right\}=0. \qquad (94)$$

Note that $(\partial/\partial p_i)\pi_i(\mathbf{p}^N(\mathbf{x}); \mathbf{x}) = 0$ holds by the second-stage payoff maximization. Furthermore, $(\partial/\partial x_j)\pi_j(\mathbf{p}^N(\mathbf{x}); \mathbf{x}) = -q_j^N(\mathbf{x})(\partial/\partial x_j)c(x_j; \mathbf{x}_{-j}) - 1$ and $(\partial/\partial x_h)\pi_j(\mathbf{p}^N(\mathbf{x}); \mathbf{x}) = -q_j^N(\mathbf{x})(\partial/\partial x_h)c(x_j; \mathbf{x}_{-j})$ $(h \neq j)$ hold. Putting all these pieces together, (94) can be reduced to (76). □

Derivation of the formulas for $\omega^B(\mathbf{x})$ *and* $\theta^B(\mathbf{x})$. Differentiating the first-order condition (71), which characterizes $\mathbf{p}^N(\mathbf{x})$, with respect to x_i and x_h $(h \neq i;\ h, i = 1, 2, \ldots, n)$, we obtain the following simultaneous equations for $\omega^B(\mathbf{x})$ and $\theta^B(\mathbf{x})$:

$$\begin{bmatrix}\alpha^B(\mathbf{x}) & (n-1)\beta^B(\mathbf{x})\\ \beta^B(\mathbf{x}) & \alpha^B(\mathbf{x})+(n-2)\beta^B(\mathbf{x})\end{bmatrix}\begin{bmatrix}\omega^B(\mathbf{x})\\ \theta^B(\mathbf{x})\end{bmatrix}=f_i^i(\mathbf{p}^N(\mathbf{x}))\begin{bmatrix}(\partial/\partial x_i)c(x_i;\mathbf{x}_{-i})\\ (\partial/\partial x_h)c(x_i;\mathbf{x}_{-i})\end{bmatrix},$$

which can be solved for $\omega^B(\mathbf{x})$ and $\theta^B(\mathbf{x})$ to obtain (77) and (78). The sign of $\omega^B(\mathbf{x})$, $\theta^B(\mathbf{x})$, and $\Delta^B(\mathbf{x})$ is determined by virtue of A9, A10, A11, and A12.

8. CONCLUDING REMARKS

In this chapter we have examined the robustness of excess entry and/or investment theorems by introducing firms' objectives other than profit maximization pure and simple as well as by relaxing the exacting Cournot conjecture into a quasi-Cournot conjecture *à la* Seade (1980*b*). The alternative firm objectives that we have actually explored are profit-constrained sales maximization *à la* Baumol (1958, 1959), and net-income-per-employee maximization by profit-sharing firms. We have also examined the welfare effects of product differentiation and of using prices rather than quantities in the second-stage product market competition within the context of a two-stage model of competition with strategic commitment.

The main results of this chapter can be summarized as follows.

1. When firms are profit-constrained sales-maximizers (profit-sharing net-income-per-employee-maximizers), we have identified the conditions under which excess entry (investment) theorems at the margin hold. It is worth emphasizing that the conditions thus identified have quite remarkable formal similarity with those for profit-maximizing firms. Nevertheless, the real substance thereof in terms of the basic characteristics of the economy is in sharp contrast with that for profit-maximizing firms. Furthermore, there are situations, which are not at all pathological, where competition among profit-maximizing firms generates excess entry (excess investment) at equilibrium, whereas the competition among profit-sharing firms generates insufficient entry (investment) at equilibrium.

2. When Cournot conjecture is replaced by quasi-Cournot conjecture and the possibility of collusion among firms is thereby introduced, we obtain an interesting generalization of the excess entry theorem at the margin. In simple words, it asserts that, unless a marginal decrease in the number of firms abruptly precipitates collusion among the remaining firms, an increase in technical efficiency induced by the decreasing number of firms overcompensates the concomitant worsening of allocative efficiency, and the validity of the excess entry theorem at the margin is vindicated.

3. If we dispense with the assumption of homogeneous product, the entry of a new firm accompanies a totally new effect of promoting product diversification along with the effects on scale economies and allocative efficiency. If consumers have a strong preference in favour of product diversity, this new effect may well overturn the tendency towards excess entry which dominates in the absence of product differentiation.

4. The welfare verdicts on the two-stage model of strategic competition with R&D commitment are found to be strictly contingent on the strategies firms invoke in the second stage game where firms compete in the product market. When firms compete in terms of quantities, there is a distinct possibility of overcommitment with non-cooperative R&D in the presence of small R&D spillover effects. In sharp contrast, if firms compete in terms of prices, not only co-operative but also non-cooperative R&D is socially insufficient at the margin irrespective of the extent of R&D spillovers. In designing technology policy in the pursuit of social welfare improvement, it seems to be of crucial importance to recognize this sharply contrasting implication of price competition and quantity competition in the context of oligopolistic competition with strategic commitment.

In concluding this chapter, it deserves emphasis that we have still retained one of the most restrictive assumptions, upon which our preceding analyses hinge. This is the assumption that all firms are identical, both in technology and in behaviour, which motivated us to focus exclusively on symmetric equilibria. It is all too natural to ask whether or not the main message of our analyses based on the simplifying assumption of identical firms can be kept intact at least to some reasonable extent. We now turn to this important question.

NOTES TO CHAPTER 8

1. This is quite explicit in the analyses of Konishi *et al.* (1990), Suzumura and Kiyono (1987), Vickers (1989), and Part I above. In contrast, Mankiw and Whinston (1986) made an assumption to the effect that, for any number of firms, the resulting equilibrium price exceeds marginal cost, which is guaranteed if firms are profit-maximizers and inverse demand function is downward-sloping, but not otherwise.
2. According to Baumol (1958: 187), 'the typical large corporatiton in the United States seeks to maximise not its profits but its total revenues which the businessman calls his sales. That is, once his profits exceed some vaguely defined minimum level, he is prepared to sacrifice further increases in profits if he can thereby obtain larger revenues.' Even when the profit-constrained sales maximization hypothesis is not accepted *in toto* as a fully fledged alternative to the profit maximization hypothesis, it is commonly invoked whenever some deviations from the pure and simple profit maximization are discussed in the literature. See e.g. Fershtman and Judd (1987) and Vickers (1985*b*).
3. It is easy to check that condition (17) means that *the average net-output-per-employee must be equal to the marginal net-output-per-employee*, where the net output is specified by $f(Q)q_i - K$.
4. Going further back to the basic production function $q = F(L)$, $\varepsilon_G(q^N(n))$ can be rewritten as follows:

$$\varepsilon_G(q^N(n)) = \frac{1}{\varepsilon_F(G(q^N(n)))},$$

where $\varepsilon_F(G(q^N(n))) := G(q^N(n))F'(G(q^N(n)))/F(G(q^N(n)))$.
5. It is worth pointing out that equation (45) in Chapter 4 entails

$$\text{sgn}\,\frac{\partial}{\partial x_i}\,W^N(\mathbf{x}^N) = \text{sgn}\,[n\beta(\mathbf{x}^N) - \alpha(\mathbf{x}^N)],$$

which has a noticeable resemblance to (52).
6. More generally, $(\partial/\partial x_i)\,W^N(\mathbf{x}^N) < (>)\ 0$ holds if and only if

$$G(q_i^N(\mathbf{x}^N))f'(Q^N(\mathbf{x}^N))\left\{\frac{n_e - 1}{n_e}\,\delta(Q^N(\mathbf{x})) + n_e\,[1 - \varepsilon_G(q_i^N(\mathbf{x}^N))] - 2\right\}$$

$$+ G''(q_i^N(\mathbf{x}^N))\,[f(Q^N(\mathbf{x}^N))q_i^N(\mathbf{x}^N) - x_i^N] < (>)\ 0,$$

where $\delta(Q^N(\mathbf{x}^N)) := Q^N(\mathbf{x}^N)f''(Q^N(\mathbf{x}^N))/f'(Q^N(\mathbf{x}^N))$.

7. Despite its formal generality *vis-à-vis* the Cournot conjecture, there are papers in the theoretical literature that suggest that static conjectural variations models are inherently flawed; see, among many others, Tirole (1988: 244–5) and Ulph (1983). Since this is an issue that is beyond the scope of this short section, we will confine ourselves to deriving the implication of static conjectural variations models in the present context.
8. This story is essentially due to Seade (1980*b*).
9. It goes without saying that the welfare effects of quasi-Cournot conjecture can be examined in the alternative context of competition among profit-constrained sales-maximizers and/or competition among profit-sharing firms. It is simply for the purpose of keeping the length of this chapter within reasonable bounds that we focus exclusively on the case of competition among profit-maximizing firms.
10. In what follows, we assume throughout that $\mu(n) > 0$ for all n.
11. Our discussion in this section owes much to Mankiw and Whinston (1986) and Spence (1976*b*).
12. Note that $V'[nv(q(n))]v(q(n))$ stands for the contribution of a marginal entrant to the gross social benefit, whereas $V'[nv(q(n))]v'(q(n))q(n)$ is the revenue that accrues to the marginal entrant. As far as $v(q)$ is strictly concave, i.e. as far as $v''(q) < 0$ holds for any $q > 0$, we obtain $v(q) - qv'(q) > 0$ for any $q > 0$. Therefore, the social benefit of marginal entry outweighs the private gain captured by the marginal entrant.
13. Those who need to be reminded of these basic strategic assumptions are referred back to the Prologue.
14. See e.g. Singh and Vives (1984), and Vives (1985).
15. This assumption is satisfied by the linear demand function defined by $q_i = a - bp_i + c\Sigma_{j \neq i}p_j$ $(i = 1, 2, \ldots, n)$ if the parameters a, b, and c satisfy $a > 0$, $b > 0$, $c > 0$, and $b > (n - 1)c$.
16. Readers are referred to Friedman (1977: 72) and Vives (1985) for further discussion on the rationale of this assumption.

9 Non-Symmetric Equilibria

1. INTRODUCTION

Other things being equal, simplicity is a virtue rather than a vice. However, in the context of excess entry and excess investment theorems, which lie at the heart of this monograph, the simplifying assumption of identical firms and symmetric equilibria may seem to be so drastically unrealistic that the theorems whose validity hinges squarely on the simplification rendered thereby may be regarded as suspect. Nevertheless, the crucial fact remains that it is not at all clear how we can verify the truth or falsity of the excess entry and/or excess investment theorems when firms are not identical. Indeed, not even the way these theorems should be expressed is clear. The task of this final chapter is to develop a method of coping with these difficulties and to establish a generalized excess entry theorem and a generalized excess investment theorem respectively in a well defined sense.

Section 2 analyses the generalized excess entry theorem for a Cournot–Nash oligopoly model where differences in cost functions among firms are properly admitted. We assume that there exists an identical number of firms in each category of conceivable cost functions, and we let the number of firms increase uniformly over all categories whenever we talk about the entry of new firms. This approach, which was first introduced by Okuguchi (1973) in the related context of quasi-competitiveness of Cournot oligopoly equilibrium, is modelled after the seminal analysis of Debreu and Scarf (1963) on the equivalence of core and the set of competitive equilibria in a pure exchange economy.[1] It will be shown that the second-best excess entry theorem holds within this generalized model of Cournot–Nash oligopoly.

Section 3 establishes the generalized excess investment theorem at the margin for a Cournot–Nash oligopoly model with interfirm differences in cost functions. More precisely, it will be demonstrated that a marginal decrease in the R&D investment by the least efficient firm at the subgame-perfect equilibrium unambiguously improves the second-best social welfare if the number of firms is sufficiently large.

Finally, Section 4 concludes by summarizing some of the main messages of this monograph in the light of the generalized excess entry and excess investment theorems established in this chapter.

2. EXCESS ENTRY THEOREMS WITH INTERFIRM DIFFERENCES IN COST FUNCTIONS

2.1. A generalized model of Cournot–Nash oligopoly

Consider an industry producing a single homogeneous product. There are m categories of conceivable cost functions and n firms within each category, where $2 \leqslant m, n < +\infty$, so that the total number of firms is given by $m \times n$. Let (i, j) be the index of the jth firm having the ith cost function. For each $i \in M := \{1, 2, \ldots, m\}$, the cost function $C_{ij}(q_{ij})$ of the firm (i, j) is the same for all $j \in N := \{1, 2, \ldots, n\}$, so that we have

$$C_{ij}(q_{ij}) = C_i(q_{ij}) \qquad \text{for all } (i, j) \in M \times N, \tag{1}$$

where q_{ij} denotes the output of the firm (i, j). We make the following assumption.

A1: $C_i(q)$ is twice continuously differentiable with $C_i(q) > 0$, $C_i'(q) > 0$, and $C_i''(q) > 0$ for all $q > 0$ and $i \in M$.

Let $p = f(Q)$ be inverse demand function for the product of this industry, where p is price and $Q = \Sigma_{i=1}^{m}\Sigma_{j=1}^{n} q_{ij}$ is industry output. As in Chapter 1, we assume the following.

A2: $f(Q)$ is twice continuously differentiable and $f'(Q) < 0$ holds for all $Q \geqslant 0$ with $f(Q) > 0$.

The profit function of the firm $(i, j) \in M \times N$ is defined by

$$\pi_{ij}(\mathbf{q}) := q_{ij} f(Q) - C_i(q_{ij}), \tag{2}$$

where $\mathbf{q} = (q_{11}, \ldots, q_{ij}, \ldots, q_{mn})$. Throughout this chapter, firms are assumed to be profit-maximizers pure and simple, which use quantities as their strategic variables when they compete in the product market. Let $\mathbf{q}^N(n) = (q_{11}^N(n), \ldots, q_{ij}^N(n), \ldots, q_{mn}^N(n))$ be the Cournot–Nash equilibrium among $m \times n$ firms, which is characterized by $(\partial/\partial q_{ij})\pi_{ij}(\mathbf{q}^N(n))) = 0$; that is,

$$f(Q^N(n)) + q_{ij}^N(n) f'(Q^N(n)) - C_i'(q_{ij}^N(n)) = 0 \qquad \text{for all } (i, j) \in M \times N \tag{3}$$

under the assumption of interior optimum and second-order conditions, where $Q^N(n) = \Sigma_{i=1}^{m}\Sigma_{j=1}^{n} q_{ij}^N(n)$.

To prepare for the introduction of our strategic assumption, we define

$$\alpha_{ij}(\mathbf{q}) := \frac{\partial^2}{\partial q_{ij}^2}\pi_{ij}(\mathbf{q}) = 2f'(Q) + q_{ij} f''(Q) - C_i''(q_{ij}) \tag{4}$$

and

$$\beta_{ij,\,hk}(\mathbf{q}) := \frac{\partial^2}{\partial q_{hk}\,\partial q_{ij}}\,\pi_{ij}(\mathbf{q}) := f'(Q) + q_{ij} f''(Q), \tag{5}$$

where $h, i \in M$ and $j, k \in N$. In these terms, we can introduce the following standard assumption.

A3: $\beta_{ij,\,hk}(\mathbf{q}) < 0$ holds for each $\mathbf{q} = (q_{11}, \ldots, q_{ij}, \ldots, q_{mn})$ and for all (i, j), $(h, k) \in M \times N$.

Note that A3 is nothing other than the familiar condition of strategic substitutability of quantity strategies. Note also that A3 ensures that $\alpha_{ij}(\mathbf{q}) < 0$ holds for all $\mathbf{q} = (q_{11}, \ldots, q_{ij}, \ldots, q_{mn})$ and $(i, j) \in M \times N$ in the presence of A1 and A2, i.e. the second-order conditions for profit maximization are satisfied. Furthermore, it can easily be verified that A3 guarantees the local stability of the Cournot–Nash equilibrium $\mathbf{q}^N(n)$ with respect to the adjustment process defined by $\dot{q}_{ij} = \sigma(\partial/\partial q_{ij})\pi_{ij}(\mathbf{q})$ for all $(i, j) \in M \times N$, where $\sigma > 0$ denotes the adjustment coefficient. It is assumed that the Cournot–Nash equilibrium $\mathbf{q}^N(n)$ uniquely exists.[2]

Throughout our analysis in this section, the following lemma renders a great service in simplifying our subsequent reasoning.

LEMMA 1 (Equal Treatment Property). Under A1, A2, and A3, $q^N_{ij}(n) = q^N_{ik}(n)$ holds for all (i, j) $(i, k) \in M \times N$.

Proof. By definition of $\mathbf{q}^N(n)$, we have

$$f(Q^N(n)) + q^N_{ij}(n) f'(Q^N(n)) - C'_i(q^N_{ij}(n)) = 0 \tag{6}$$

and

$$f(Q^N(n)) + q^N_{ik}(n) f'(Q^N(n)) - C'_i(q^N_{ik}(n)) = 0 \tag{7}$$

for any (i, j), $(i, k) \in M \times N$. If $q^N_{ij}(n) \neq q^N_{ik}(n)$ holds, there exists a θ, $0 < \theta < 1$ such that

$$[q^N_{ij}(n) - q^N_{ik}(n)]\, f'(Q^N(n) = C'_i(q^N_{ij}(n)) - C'_i(q^N_{ik}(n))$$

$$= [q^N_{ij}(n) - q^N_{ik}(n)]\, C''_i[\theta q^N_{ij}(n) + (1 - \theta) q^N_{ik}(n)] \tag{8}$$

holds by virtue of the mean value theorem, which implies that we should have $[q^N_{ij}(n) - q^N_{ik}(n)]\,\{f'(Q^N(n)) - C''_i[\theta q^N_{ij}(n) + (1 - \theta) q^N_{ik}(n)]\} = 0$. But this is impossible to sustain in view of A1 and A2. Therefore, it must be the case that $q^N_{ij}(n) = q^N_{ik}(n)$ for all (i, j), $(i, k) \in M \times N$. □

The message of Lemma 1 is very simple as well as intuitive. Consider any two firms having a cost function of the same category. Then, according to Lemma 1, they must produce the same amount of output at the Cournot–Nash equilibrium $\mathbf{q}^N(n)$. Thanks to this useful property, the equilibrium output of firms having a cost function of the same category i can be simply written as $q_i^N(n)$, i.e. $q_{ij}^N(n) = q_i^N(n)$ for all $(i, j) \in M \times N$. Thus, the Cournot–Nash equilibrium $\mathbf{q}^N(n)$ can be neatly characterized by

$$f(Q^N(n)) + q_i^N(n)f'(Q^N(n)) - C_i'(q_i^N(n)) = 0 \qquad \text{for all } i \in M \tag{9}$$

and

$$Q^N(n) = n \sum_{i=1}^{m} q_i^N(n). \tag{10}$$

2.2. *Displacement of the Cournot–Nash equilibrium*

The number of firms competing in the generalized Cournot oligopoly will be endogenously determined in accordance with the classical entry/exit dynamics. As an auxiliary step in examining the welfare implication of this long-run competitive mechanism, let us ask how the Cournot–Nash equilibrium output $q_i^N(n)$ responds to an exogenous change in the number of firms. With this task in mind, we differentiate (9) and (10) with respect to n and obtain the following system of simultaneous equations for $(\mathrm{d}/\mathrm{d}n)q_i^N(n)$:

$$\mathbf{A}(\mathrm{d}/\mathrm{d}n)\mathbf{q}^N(n) = -[Q^N(n)/n^2]\mathbf{b}, \tag{11}$$

where $\mathbf{A} = [a_{ij}]$ is an $m \times m$ matrix whose elements are specified by

$$a_{ii} = a_i = f'(Q^N(n)) - C_i''(q_i^N(n)) + n[f'(Q^N(n)) + q_i^N(n)f''(Q^N(n))] \tag{12}$$

and

$$a_{ij} = b_i = n\,[f'(Q^N(n)) + q_i^N(n)f''(Q^N(n))] \qquad (i \neq j) \tag{13}$$

for $i, j \in M$, $(\mathrm{d}/\mathrm{d}n)\mathbf{q}^N(n)$ is an m-vector whose ith element is given by $(\mathrm{d}/\mathrm{d}n)q_i^N(n)$, and $\mathbf{b}$ is an m-vector whose ith element is given by b_i, which in turn is defined by (13). It is easy to verify that a_i and b_i can be related to $\alpha_i(n) := \alpha_{ij}(\mathbf{q}^N(n))$ and $\beta_i(n) := \beta_{ij,\,hk}(\mathbf{q}^N(n))$ as follows:

$$a_i = \alpha_i(n) + (n-1)\beta_i(n) \tag{14}$$

and

$$b_i = n\beta_i(n) \tag{15}$$

Since $\alpha_i(n) < 0$ and $\beta_i(n) < 0$ follow from A3 for $\mathbf{q} = \mathbf{q}^N(n)$, we have $a_i < 0$ and $b_i < 0$ from (14) and (15). Besides, (12) and (13) entail that

$$a_i - b_i = f'(Q^N(n)) - C_i''(q_i^N(n)) < 0, \tag{16}$$

where we have invoked A1 and A2. It is also useful to note the following.

LEMMA 2

$$\det \mathbf{A} = \prod_{j=1}^{m}(a_j - b_j) + \sum_{i=1}^{m} b_i \prod_{\substack{j \neq i \\ j=1}}^{m} (a_j - b_j). \tag{17}$$

Proof. When $m = 2$, $\det \mathbf{A} = a_1 a_2 - b_1 b_2 = (a_1 - b_1)(a_2 - b_2) + b_1(a_2 - b_2) + b_2(a_1 - b_1)$, so that (17) holds. Assume that (17) is true for $m = s - 1$, and consider the case where $m = s$. Multiplying the sth column of det **A** by -1 and adding the result to all other columns of det **A**, we obtain

$$\det \mathbf{A} = \det \begin{bmatrix} a_1 - b_1 & 0 & \dots & 0 & b_1 \\ 0 & a_2 - b_2 & \dots & 0 & b_2 \\ \vdots & \vdots & & \vdots & \vdots \\ 0 & 0 & \dots & a_{s-1} - b_{s-1} & b_{s-1} \\ b_s - a_s & b_s - a_s & \dots & b_s - a_s & a_s \end{bmatrix}$$

$$= (a_1 - b_1) \det \begin{bmatrix} a_2 - b_2 & \dots & 0 & b_2 \\ 0 & \dots & 0 & b_3 \\ \vdots & & \vdots & \vdots \\ b_s - a_s & \dots & b_s - a_s & a_s \end{bmatrix}$$

$$+ (-1)^{s-1}(b_s - a_s) \det \begin{bmatrix} 0 & 0 & \dots & 0 & b_1 \\ a_2 - b_2 & 0 & \dots & 0 & b_2 \\ \vdots & \vdots & & \vdots & \vdots \\ 0 & 0 & \dots & a_{s-1} - b_{s-1} & b_{s-1} \end{bmatrix}$$

$$= (a_1 - b_1)\left[\prod_{j=2}^{s} (a_j - b_j) + \sum_{\substack{j \neq i \\ j=2}}^{s} (a_j - b_j)\right] + b_1 \prod_{j=2}^{s} (a_j - b_j)$$

$$= \prod_{j=1}^{s} (a_j - b_j) + \sum_{i=1}^{s} b_i \prod_{\substack{j \neq i \\ j=1}}^{s} (a_j - b_j), \tag{18}$$

where the third equality is due to the induction hypothesis. □

We can now solve (11) for $(\mathrm{d}/\mathrm{d}n)q_i^N(n)$ by applying Cramer's rule to obtain the following:

$$\frac{\mathrm{d}}{\mathrm{d}n} q_i^N(n) = -\frac{Q^N(n)}{n^2 \det \mathbf{A}} \det \begin{bmatrix} a_1 & \dots & \overset{(i)}{b_1} & \dots & b_1 \\ \vdots & & \vdots & & \vdots \\ b_i & \dots & b_i & \dots & b_i \\ \vdots & & \vdots & & \vdots \\ b_m & \dots & b_m & \dots & a_m \end{bmatrix}$$

$$= -\frac{b_i Q^N(n)}{n^2 \det \mathbf{A}} \prod_{j \neq i} (a_j - b_j)$$

$$< 0, \tag{19}$$

where the sign of $(\mathrm{d}/\mathrm{d}n)q_i^N(n)$ is due to (16) and (18). Furthermore, it follows from (10) and (19) that

$$\frac{\mathrm{d}}{\mathrm{d}n} Q^N(n) = \sum_{j=1}^{m} q_j^N(n) + n \sum_{j=1}^{m} \frac{\mathrm{d}}{\mathrm{d}n} q_j^N(n) = \frac{Q^N(n)}{n \det \mathbf{A}} \prod_{j=1}^{m} (a_j - b_j) \tag{20}$$

$$> 0.$$

Therefore, a uniform increase in the number of firms within each category of cost function entails a decrease in the equilibrium output of each and every firm, and an increase in the equilibrium output of the Cournot market as a whole.[3]

We are now ready to define the equilibrium number of firms. Let the *average* profits at the Cournot–Nash equilibrium $\mathbf{q}^N(n)$ be defined by

$$\pi^N(n) := \frac{1}{m} \sum_{i=1}^{m} [q_i^N(n) f(Q^N(n)) - C_i(q_i^N(n))], \tag{21}$$

which enables us to define the *equilibrium number of firms* n_e by $\pi^N(n_e) = 0$.

A natural question may suggest itself as to why firms should be at all interested in the *average* profits in deciding whether to enter into or stay away from the industry. Indeed, if each firm knows for certain its own type among the spectrum of cost functions, it will certainly be interested in knowing whether the incumbent firms of the same type are earning positive or negative profits and will base its entry/exit decision on this information. In contrast, if firms are unaware of their position in the spectrum of cost functions and if they are risk-neutral, they will base their entry/exit decision on how incumbent firms are doing *on average*. This latter situation is what we are assuming in this section.

Since we have

$$\frac{\mathrm{d}}{\mathrm{d}n} \pi^N(n) = \frac{1}{m} \sum_{i=1}^{m} \{f'(Q^N(n)) q_i^N(n) \frac{\mathrm{d}}{\mathrm{d}n} Q^N(n)$$

$$+ [f(Q^N(n)) - C_i'(q_i^N(n))] \frac{\mathrm{d}}{\mathrm{d}n} q_i^N(n)\}$$

$$< 0 \tag{22}$$

by virtue of (19) and (20), it is clear that the equilibrium number of firms n_e must be unique.

2.3. *First-best welfare performance*

Let the net market surplus function in our present context be defined by

$$W(n, \mathbf{q}) := \int_0^Q f(Z)\mathrm{d}Z - \sum_{i=1}^{m}\sum_{j=1}^{n} C_i(q_{ij}), \tag{23}$$

where $Q = \Sigma_{i=1}^m \Sigma_{j=1}^n q_{ij}$. For each $n > 0$, let $\mathbf{q}^F(n) = (q_{11}^F(n), \ldots, q_{ij}^F(n), \ldots, q_{mn}^F(n))$ denote the *first-best output profile*, which is defined by

$$\mathbf{q}^F(n) := \arg\max_{\mathbf{q}>0} W(n, \mathbf{q}). \tag{24}$$

Under the assumption of interior optimum and second-order conditions, $\mathbf{q}^F(n)$ may be characterized by

$$(\partial/\partial q_{ij})\, W(n, \mathbf{q}^F(n)) = f(Q^F(n)) - C_i'(q_{ij}^F(n)) = 0 \tag{25}$$

where $(i, j) \in M \times N$ and $Q^F(n) = \Sigma_{i=1}^m \Sigma_{j=1}^n q_{ij}^F(n)$. Suppose that it happens to be $q_{ij}^F(n) \neq q_{ik}^F(n)$ for some (i, j), $(i, k) \in M \times N$. It then follows from $f(Q^F(n)) = C_i'(q_{ij}^F(n)) = C_i'(q_{ik}^F(n))$ that

$$C_i''[\theta q_{ij}^F(n) + (1-\theta) q_{ik}^F(n)]\,[q_{ij}^F(n) - q_{ik}^F(n)] = 0 \tag{26}$$

for some θ, $0 < \theta < 1$ by virtue of the mean value theorem. Since (26) is impossible to sustain in the presence of A1, we may conclude that $q_{ij}^F(n) = q_{ik}^F(n)$ holds for all (i, j), $(i, k) \in M \times N$; i.e. all firms having the same cost function must produce the same output, say $q_i^F(n)$ $(i \in M)$, at the first-best output profile.

Paying due attention to this useful property of $\mathbf{q}^F(n)$, we may now define the *first-best welfare criterion* by

$$W^F(n) := W(n, \mathbf{q}^F(n)) = \int_0^{Q^F(n)} f(Z)\mathrm{d}Z - n\sum_{i=1}^{m} C_i(q_i^F(n)), \tag{27}$$

where $Q^F(n) = n\, \Sigma_{i=1}^m q_i^F(n)$. In order to identify the optimum optimorum of our economy, let us define the *first-best number of firms*, n_f,[4] by

$$n_f := \arg\max_{n>0} W^F(n). \tag{28}$$

Under the assumption of interior-optimum and second-order conditions, n_f can be characterized by $(\mathrm{d}/\mathrm{d}n)\, W^F(n_f) = 0$, that is,

$$\sum_{i=1}^{m} [f(Q^F(n_f))q_i^F(n_f) - C_i(q_i^F(n_f))] = 0, \tag{29}$$

where we have made use of (25). It is clear that $\{n_f, \mathbf{q}^F(n_f)\}$, i.e. the situation where n_f firms of each category $i \in M$ are producing $q_i^F(n_f)$ each, is the optimum optimorum of our economy.

As an auxiliary step in examining the performance of long-run Cournot–Nash equilibrium $\{n_e, \mathbf{q}^N(n_e)\}$ *vis-à-vis* $\{n_f, \mathbf{q}^F(n_f)\}$ in terms of social welfare, we investigate how $q_i^F(n)$ and $Q^F(n)$ behave when n undergoes a change, as well as how $q_i^F(n)$ $(Q^F(n))$ compares with $q_i^F(n)$ $(Q^N(n))$ for each $n > 0$. Our answer to the first question can be summarized as follows.

LEMMA 3. Under A1 and A2,

$$\frac{\mathrm{d}}{\mathrm{d}n} q_i^F(n) = \frac{(-1)^m Q^F(n) f'(Q^F(n))}{n \det \mathbf{B}} \prod_{h \neq i} C_h''(q_h^F(n)) \tag{30}$$

for all $i \in M$ and

$$\frac{\mathrm{d}}{\mathrm{d}n} Q^F(n) = \frac{(-1)^m Q^F(n)}{n \det \mathbf{B}} \prod_{h=1}^{m} C_h''(q_h^F(n))$$

$$> 0 \tag{31}$$

hold, where

$$\det \mathbf{B} = (-1)^m \prod_{h=1}^{m} C_h''(q_h^F(n))$$

$$+ (-1)^{m-1} n f'(Q^F(n)) \sum_{i=1}^{m} \prod_{h \neq i} C_h''(q_h^F(n)). \tag{32}$$

Proof. Differentiating $f(Q^F(n)) = C_i'(q_i^F(n))$ and $Q^F(n) = n \sum_{i=1}^m q_i^F(n)$ with respect to n, we may obtain the following simultaneous equations for $(\mathrm{d}/\mathrm{d}n)q_i^F(n)$ with $i \in M$:

$$\mathbf{B}(\mathrm{d}/\mathrm{d}n)\mathbf{q}^F(n) = -[Q^F(n) f(Q^F(n))/n]\mathbf{e}, \tag{33}$$

where $\mathbf{B} = [b_{ij}]$ is an $m \times m$ matrix whose elements are given by $b_{ii} = a_i^* := nf'(Q^F(n)) - C_i''(q_i^F(n))$ $(i \in M)$ and $b_{ij} = b^* = nf'(Q^F(n))$ $(i \neq j;\ i, j \in M)$, $(\mathrm{d}/\mathrm{d}n)\mathbf{q}^F(n)$ is an m-vector whose ith element is $(\mathrm{d}/\mathrm{d}n)q_i^F(n)$, and $\mathbf{e}$ is an m-vector all of whose elements are 1. By making use of Lemma 2, we may verify that $\det \mathbf{B}$ can be written as (32), and we have the solution for $(\mathrm{d}/\mathrm{d}n)q_i^F(n)$ in the form of (30) by invoking Cramer's rule. Finally, (31) follows from $(\mathrm{d}/\mathrm{d}n)Q^F(n) = \sum_{i=1}^m q_i^F(n) + n \sum_{i=1}^m (\mathrm{d}/\mathrm{d}n)q_i^F(n)$ and (30). □

Turning to the second question, i.e. the comparison between $q_i^F(n)$ $(Q^F(n))$ and $q_i^N(n)$ $(Q^N(n))$, the best we can generally assert is that

$$Q^F(n) > Q^N(n) \text{ for all } n > 0. \tag{34}$$

Suppose to the contrary that $Q^F(n) \leqslant Q^N(n)$ holds for some $n > 0$. Then $q_i^F(n) \leqslant q_i^N(n)$ must be the case for some $i \in M$. It follows from A2 that $f(Q^F(n)) \geqslant f(Q^N(n)) > f(Q^N(n)) + q_i^N(n)f'(Q^N(n))$, which then yields $C_i'(q_i^F(n)) > C_i'(q_i^N(n))$ by virtue of (9) and (25). Under A1, however, this last inequality contradicts the original inequality that $q_i^F(n) \leqslant q_i^N(n)$.

Clearly, (34) falls substantially short of the assertion of Lemma 3 in Chapter 1; that is, we cannot assert in general that $q_i^F(n) > q_i^N(n)$ holds for all $i \in M$ in our generalized Cournot–Nash oligopoly model. To see that this ambiguity is unavoidable, let us consider the following example.

Example. Suppose that there are two categories of cost functions $i = H, L$, such that $C_i(q) = K_i + (c_i/2)q^2$ with $K_H > K_L > 0$ and $c_H > c_L > 0$. Suppose also that the inverse demand function is given by $f(Q) = 1 - Q$. When there are n firms within each category, we can easily verify that

$$q_i^F(n) = \frac{1}{c_i} \frac{1}{1 + n\left(\dfrac{1}{c_H} + \dfrac{1}{c_L}\right)} \quad (i = H, L), \tag{35}$$

$$Q^F(n) = \frac{n\left(\dfrac{1}{c_H} + \dfrac{1}{c_L}\right)}{1 + n\left(\dfrac{1}{c_H} + \dfrac{1}{c_L}\right)}, \tag{36}$$

$$q_i^N(n) = \frac{1}{1 + c_i} \frac{1}{1 + n\left(\dfrac{1}{1 + c_H} + \dfrac{1}{1 + c_L}\right)} \quad (i = H, L), \tag{37}$$

and

$$Q^N(n) = \frac{n\left(\dfrac{1}{1 + c_H} + \dfrac{1}{1 + c_L}\right)}{1 + n\left(\dfrac{1}{1 + c_H} + \dfrac{1}{1 + c_L}\right)}. \tag{38}$$

It is easy to ascertain that (36) and (38) yield

$$\begin{aligned} \operatorname{sgn}\,[Q^F(n) - Q^N(n)] &= \operatorname{sgn} \sum_{i = H, L} \left(\frac{1}{c_j} - \frac{1}{1 + c_j}\right) \\ &> 0 \end{aligned} \tag{39}$$

in conformity with the general assertion (34). However, it follows from (35) and (37) that

$$\operatorname{sgn}\,[q_i^F(n) - q_i^N(n)] = \operatorname{sgn}\begin{cases} \dfrac{1}{n} + \dfrac{1}{1+c_H}\left(1 - \dfrac{c_L}{c_H}\right) > 0 & \text{if } i = L \\[2ex] \dfrac{1}{n} + \dfrac{1}{c_L}\left(1 - \dfrac{c_H}{c_L}\right) \gtreqless 0 & \text{if } i = H. \end{cases} \tag{40}$$

Note that the RHS for $i = H$ turns out to be negative if, for instance, $c_H = 2c_L$ and $n > 1 + c_L$. □

Since the counterpart of Lemma 3 in Chapter 1 is not available in our present context of the generalized Cournot–Nash oligopoly model, we cannot establish the first-best excess entry theorem along the lines of which we proved Theorem 1 in Chapter 1. Note, however, that we can compute the values of n_f and n_e in the case of the above example by solving the quadratic equations

$$\frac{\dfrac{1}{c_H} + \dfrac{1}{c_L}}{2\left[1 + n_f\left(\dfrac{1}{c_H} + \dfrac{1}{c_L}\right)\right]^2} = K_H + K_L \tag{41}$$

and

$$\frac{\dfrac{1}{c_H} + \dfrac{1}{c_L}}{2\left[1 + n_e\left(\dfrac{1}{1+c_H} + \dfrac{1}{1+c_L}\right)\right]^2} = K_H + K_L, \tag{42}$$

respectively. We have indeed computed the values of (n_f, n_e) thus defined for the specified values of (c_H, c_L, K_H, K_L). A few representative cases are summarized in Table 11. Note that this table (and all other computations that we have conducted sufficiently many times) is fully consistent with the assertion of the first-best excess entry theorem to the effect that $n_e > n_f$ holds as long as $n_f \geqslant 1$.

2.4. *Second-best welfare performance*

Turning to the second-best welfare analysis on the generalized Cournot–Nash equilibrium $\mathbf{q}^N(n)$, let us define the *second-best welfare criterion* by

$$W^S(n) := \int_0^{Q^N(n)} f(Z)\mathrm{d}Z - n\sum_{i=1}^{m} C_i\,(q_i^N(n)). \tag{43}$$

It can be easily verified that

Table 11. (n_f, n_e) for alternative values of (c_H, c_L, K)

(c_L, K)	0.01	0.02	0.03	0.04	0.05
Case 1: $c_H = 2c_L$					
1.0	(7.50, 11.91)	(5.11, 8.07)	(4.05, 6.37)	(3.42, 5.36)	(2.98, 4.67)
2.0	(10.21, 13.64)	(6.83, 9.09)	(5.33, 7.08)	(4.44, 5.88)	(3.83, 5.06
3.0	(12.14, 15.01)	(8.00, 9.87)	(6.16, 7.59)	(5.07, 6.23)	(4.32, 5.30)
4.0	(13.66, 16.16)	(8.88, 10.49)	(6.76, 7.97)	(5.50, 6.47)	(4.64, 5.45)
5.0	(14.92, 17.15)	(9.58, 10.99)	(7.21, 8.26)	(5.80, 6.64)	(4.83, 5.53)
Case 2: $c_H = 3c_L$					
1.0	(7.91, 12.41)	(5.37, 8.38)	(4.25, 6.60)	(3.58, 5.53)	(3.12, 4.81)
2.0	(10.75, 14.27)	(7.16, 9.48)	(5.57, 7.35)	(4.62, 6.09)	(3.98, 5.22)
3.0	(12.75, 15.71)	(8.36, 10.27)	(6.41, 7.87)	(5.25, 6.43)	(4.46, 5.45)
4.0	(14.32, 16.91)	(9.25, 10.90)	(7.00, 8.23)	(5.66, 6.45)	(4.75, 5.56)
5.0	(15.61, 17.92)	(9.94, 11.40)	(7.43, 8.50)	(5.93, 6.78)	(4.91, 5.60)
Case 3: $c_H = 4c_L$					
1.0	(8.14, 12.79)	(5.52, 8.62)	(4.36, 6.78)	(3.67, 5.68)	(3.20, 4.93)
2.0	(11.05, 14.71)	(7.34, 9.74)	(5.70, 7.54)	(4.72, 6.23)	(4.06, 5.33)
3.0	(13.09, 16.17)	(8.55, 10.54)	(6.54, 8.05)	(5.35, 6.56)	(4.53, 5.54)
4.0	(14.69, 17.38)	(9.45, 11.16)	(7.13, 8.40)	(5.74, 6.76)	(4.80, 5.64)
5.0	(16.00, 18.40)	(10.14, 11.64)	(7.55, 8.65)	(6.00, 6.87)	(4.94, 5.65)
Case 4: $c_H = 5c_L$					
1.0	(8.30, 13.08)	(5.62, 8.81)	(4.44, 6.92)	(3.73, 5.79)	(3.25, 5.02)
2.0	(11.24, 15.02)	(7.46, 9.93)	(5.79, 7.68)	(4.79, 6.33)	(4.11, 5.42)
3.0	(13.31, 16.50)	(8.68, 10.73)	(6.63, 8.17)	(5.41, 6.65)	(4.57, 5.61)
4.0	(14.92, 17.71)	(9.58, 11.34)	(7.21, 8.52)	(5.80, 6.83)	(4.83, 5.69)
5.0	(16.25, 18.73)	(10.27, 11.81)	(7.62, 8.75)	(6.04, 6.93)	(4.96, 5.68)

$$\frac{\mathrm{d}}{\mathrm{d}n} W^S(n) = m\pi^N(n) + n \sum_{i=1}^{m} [f(Q^N(n)) - C_i'(q_i^N(n))] \frac{\mathrm{d}}{\mathrm{d}n} q_i^N(n). \tag{44}$$

Evaluating (44) at $n = n_e$, and invoking $\pi^N(n_e) = 0$ and (19), we obtain $(\mathrm{d}/\mathrm{d}n) W^S(n_e) < 0$. Thus, we have established the following theorem.

THEOREM 1 (GENERALIZED SECOND-BEST EXCESS ENTRY THEOREM AT THE MARGIN). Suppose that A1, A2, and A3 hold. Then the equilibrium number of firms n_e is socially excessive at the margin in terms of the second-best welfare criterion.

The message of Theorem 1 can be strengthened by introducing the *second-best number of firms*, n_s, which is defined by

$$n_s := \arg\max_{n>0} W^S(n). \tag{45}$$

Under the assumption of interior optimum and second-order conditions, n_s is characterized by $(\mathrm{d}/\mathrm{d}n)\, W^S(n_s) = 0$; i.e.

$$m\pi^N(n_s) + n_s \sum_{i=1}^{m} [f(Q^N(n_s)) - C_i'(q_i^N(n_s))] \frac{\mathrm{d}}{\mathrm{d}n} q_i^N(n_s) = 0. \tag{46}$$

Invoking $n = n_s$, (46) may be reduced to

$$\pi^N(n_s) = \frac{n_s}{m} f'(Q^N(n_s)) \sum_{i=1}^{m} q_i^N(n_s) \frac{\mathrm{d}}{\mathrm{d}n} q_i^N(n_s), \tag{47}$$

which is positive by virtue of A2 and (19). Invoking (22), we can conclude from $\pi^N(n_s) > 0 = \pi^N(n_e)$ that $n_s < n_e$. Thus, we have established the following theorem.

THEOREM 2 (GENERALIZED SECOND-BEST EXCESS ENTRY THEOREM). Under A1, A2, and A3, the equilibrium number of firms n_e must exceed the second-best number of firms n_s.

We have thus demonstrated that the substance of second-best excess entry theorems can be essentially preserved even when we discard the restrictive assumptions of identical firms and symmetric equilibria as long as product homogeneity, quantity competition, and profit maximization are retained.

3. EXCESS INVESTMENT THEOREM WITH INTERFIRM DIFFERENCES IN COST FUNCTIONS

3.1. A generalized model of two-stage competition

Let us now turn to the oligopolistic competition with strategic commitment among m firms, where $2 \leqslant m < +\infty$, producing a single homogeneous output using different cost functions. As in Part II, these firms compete in two stages. Let x_i denote the level of R&D commitment by firm i in the first stage, which affects the variable cost function $C_i(q_i; x_i) := c_i(x_i)q_i$ in the second stage, where q_i is output of firm i. As in Chapter 4, we make the following assumption.

A4: $c_i(x)$ is twice continuously differentiable with $c_i(x) > 0$ and $c_i'(x) < 0$ for all $x > 0$ and $i \in M$.

Let $p = f(Q)$ be the inverse demand function for the product of this industry, where p is price and $Q = \Sigma_{i=1}^m q_i$ is industry output. As in Chapter 4, the following assumption is made.

A5: $f(Q)$ is twice continuously differentiable and $f'(Q) < 0$ holds for all $Q \geqslant 0$ with $f(Q) > 0$. Furthermore, there exists a constant $\delta_0 > -\infty$

such that $\delta(Q) := Qf''(Q)/f'(Q) \geq \delta_0$ holds for all $Q \geq 0$ with $f(Q) > 0$.

Given an R&D profile $\mathbf{x} = (x_1, \ldots, x_i, \ldots, x_m)$ chosen in the first-stage game, the second-stage payoff function of the profit-maximizing firm i is defined by[5]

$$\pi_i(\mathbf{q}; x_i) := [f(Q) - c_i(x_i)]q_i - x_i \tag{48}$$

for all $i \in M$. Let $\mathbf{q}^N(\mathbf{x}) = (q_1^N(\mathbf{x}), \ldots, q_i^N(\mathbf{x}), \ldots, q_m^N(\mathbf{x}))$ be the Cournot–Nash equilibrium of the second-stage game, which is characterized by

$$f(Q^N(\mathbf{x})) + q_i^N(\mathbf{x})f'(Q^N(\mathbf{x})) - c_i(x_i) = 0 \tag{49}$$

for all $i \in M$ under the assumption of interior optimum and second-order conditions. In terms of $\mathbf{q}^N(\mathbf{x})$, the first-stage payoff function of firm i is defined by

$$\Pi_i(\mathbf{x}) := \pi_i(\mathbf{q}^N(\mathbf{x}); x_i) \tag{50}$$

for all $i \in M$. Let $\mathbf{x}^N = (x_1^N, \ldots, x_i^N, \ldots, x_m^N)$ be the Cournot–Nash equilibrium of the first-stage game, which is characterized by

$$\sum_{j=1}^{m} (\partial/\partial q_i)\pi_i(\mathbf{q}^N(\mathbf{x}^N); x_i^N)(\partial/\partial x_i)q_j^N(\mathbf{x}^N) + (\partial/\partial x_i)\pi_i(\mathbf{q}^N(\mathbf{x}^N); x_i^N) = 0 \tag{51}$$

for all $i \in M$ under the assumption of interior optimum and second-order conditions. By paying due attention to

$$(\partial/\partial x_i)\pi_i(\mathbf{q}^N(\mathbf{x}^N); x_i^N) = -q_i^N(\mathbf{x}^N)c_i'(x_i^N) - 1 \tag{52}$$

and

$$(\partial/\partial x_j)\pi_i(\mathbf{q}^N(\mathbf{x}^N); x_i^N) = f'(Q^N(\mathbf{x}^N))q_i^N(\mathbf{x}^N) \qquad (i \neq j;\ i, j \in M), \tag{53}$$

which follow from (48), we can reduce (51) to

$$[f(Q^N(\mathbf{x}^N)) - c_i(x_i^N)] \sum_{j=1}^{m} (\partial/\partial x_i)q_j^N(\mathbf{x}^N) = -\, q_i^N(\mathbf{x}^N)c_i'(x_i^N) - 1 \tag{54}$$

for all $i \in M$, where use is also made of (49) at $\mathbf{x} = \mathbf{x}^N$.

In the subsequent analysis, we will focus on the welfare performance of the subgame perfect equilibrium $\{\mathbf{x}^N, \mathbf{q}^N(\mathbf{x}^N)\}$.

3.2. Displacement of the second-stage Cournot–Nash equilibrium

As is customary in our analysis, our first task is to see how the second-stage Cournot–Nash equilibrium $\mathbf{q}^N(\mathbf{x})$ will respond to a change in x_i for each

$i \in M$. Differentiating the first-order condition characterizing $\mathbf{q}^N(\mathbf{x})$, i.e. $(\partial/\partial q_i)\pi_i(\mathbf{q}^N(\mathbf{x}); x_i) = 0$, with respect to x_i and x_h $(h \neq i)$, we obtain

$$\alpha_i(\mathbf{x})\,\omega_i(\mathbf{x}) + \beta_i(\mathbf{x}) \sum_{j \neq i} \theta_{ji}(\mathbf{x}) = c_i'(x_i^N) \qquad (i \in M) \tag{55}$$

and

$$\alpha_i(\mathbf{x})\,\theta_{ih}(\mathbf{x}) + \beta_i(\mathbf{x})\,\omega_h(\mathbf{x}) + \beta_i(\mathbf{x}) \sum_{j \neq h,\, i} \theta_{jh}(\mathbf{x}) = 0 \qquad (h \neq i;\ h,\, i \in M) \tag{56}$$

respectively, where

$$\alpha_i(\mathbf{x}) := \frac{\partial^2}{\partial q_i^2}\,\pi_i(\mathbf{q}^N(\mathbf{x}); x_i), \tag{57}$$

$$\beta_i(\mathbf{x}) := \frac{\partial^2}{\partial q_i\,\partial q_j}\,\pi_i(\mathbf{q}^N(\mathbf{x}); x_i) \qquad (i \neq j), \tag{58}$$

$$\omega_i(\mathbf{x}) := \frac{\partial}{\partial x_i}\, q_i^N(\mathbf{x}), \tag{59}$$

and

$$\theta_{ji}(\mathbf{x}) := \frac{\partial}{\partial x_i}\, q_j^N(\mathbf{x}) \qquad (i \neq j), \tag{60}$$

where $i, j \in M$. Whenever it is useful in simplifying our expression, we will also use the convention of writing $\theta_{ii}(\mathbf{x}) := \omega_i(\mathbf{x})$ for each and every $i \in M$.

Let us now define an $m \times m$ matrix $\mathbf{A}(\mathbf{x}) = [a_{ij}(\mathbf{x})]$ and an m-dimensional vector $\theta^i(\mathbf{x}) = [\theta_j^i(\mathbf{x})]$ for each $i \in M$ and each R&D profile $\mathbf{x}$ by $a_{ii}(\mathbf{x}) = \alpha_i(\mathbf{x})$, $a_{ij}(\mathbf{x}) = \beta_i(\mathbf{x})$ $(i \neq j)$ and $\theta_j^i(\mathbf{x}) = \theta_{ji}(\mathbf{x})$, where $i, j \in M$. It is important to note that the system of simultaneous equations (55) and (56) for $\theta_{ji}(\mathbf{x})$, where $i, j \in M$, can be neatly decomposed into the m sub-systems as follows:

$$\mathbf{A}(\mathbf{x})\,\theta^i(\mathbf{x}) = \begin{bmatrix} 0 \\ \vdots \\ c_i'(x_i) \\ \vdots \\ 0 \end{bmatrix} \ (i), \tag{61}$$

where $i \in M$. Applying Lemma 2 to $\mathbf{A}(\mathbf{x})$, we can compute $\det \mathbf{A}(\mathbf{x})$ as follows:

$$\det \mathbf{A}(\mathbf{x}) = \prod_{j=1}^{m} [\alpha_j(\mathbf{x}) - \beta_j(\mathbf{x})] + \sum_{i=1}^{m} \beta_i(\mathbf{x}) \prod_{\substack{j \neq i \\ j=1}}^{m} [\alpha_j(\mathbf{x}) - \beta_j(\mathbf{x})]. \tag{62}$$

Solving (61), and remembering that $\omega_i(\mathbf{x}) = \theta_{ii}(\mathbf{x})$, we obtain

$$\omega_i(\mathbf{x}) = \frac{c_i'(x_i)}{\det \mathbf{A}(\mathbf{x})} \left\{ \prod_{j \neq i} [\alpha_j(\mathbf{x}) - \beta_j(\mathbf{x})] + \sum_{k \neq i} \beta_k(\mathbf{x}) \prod_{j \neq i,\, k} [\alpha_j(\mathbf{x}) - \beta_j(\mathbf{x})] \right\} \tag{63}$$

and

$$\theta_{ji}(\mathbf{x}) = -\frac{c_i'(x_i)}{\det \mathbf{A}(\mathbf{x})} \prod_{k \neq i, j} [\alpha_k(\mathbf{x}) - \beta_k(\mathbf{x})] \qquad (i \neq j), \tag{64}$$

where $i, j \in M$. It follows from (63) and (64) that

$$\begin{aligned} \frac{\partial}{\partial x_i} Q^N(\mathbf{x}) &= \omega_i(\mathbf{x}) + \sum_{j \neq i} \theta_{ji}(\mathbf{x}) \\ &= \frac{c_i'(x_i)}{\det \mathbf{A}(\mathbf{x})} \prod_{j \neq i} [\alpha_j(\mathbf{x}) - \beta_j(\mathbf{x})]. \end{aligned} \tag{65}$$

At this juncture of our analysis, let us introduce the following standard assumption of strategic substitutability.

A6: $\beta_i(\mathbf{x}) < 0$ holds for all $\mathbf{x} > 0$ and $i \in M$.

It should be noted that (57) and (58) imply

$$\begin{aligned} \alpha_i(\mathbf{x}) &= 2f'(Q^N(\mathbf{x})) + q_i^N(\mathbf{x})f''(Q^N(\mathbf{x})) < f'(Q^N(\mathbf{x})) + q_i^N(\mathbf{x})f''(Q^N(\mathbf{x})) \\ &= \beta_i(\mathbf{x}) \end{aligned} \tag{66}$$

in view of A5, so that A6 guarantees that the second-order condition for payoff maximization in the second stage, i.e. $\alpha_i(\mathbf{x}) < 0$, is satisfied. It is also useful to remember that, coupled with (66), A6 guarantees the local stability of the second-stage Cournot–Nash equilibrium $\mathbf{q}^N(\mathbf{x})$ with respect to the adjustment process defined by $\dot{q}_i = \sigma(\partial/\partial q_i)\pi_i(\mathbf{q}; x_i)$ for all $i \in M$, where $\sigma > 0$ denotes the adjustment coefficient.

Back, then, to (63), (64), and (65). It is clear from A4, A6, and (66) that $\omega_i(\mathbf{x}) > 0$, $\theta_{ji}(\mathbf{x}) < 0$, and $(\partial/\partial x_i)Q^N(\mathbf{x}) > 0$ $(i \neq j;\ i, j \in M)$ hold for any $\mathbf{x} > 0$. The economic implication of these results is so familiar to us by now that we may safely skip the explanation thereof.

3.3. *Second-best excess investment theorem at the margin*

In order to gauge the welfare performance of the subgame-perfect equilibrium $\{\mathbf{x}^N, \mathbf{q}^N(\mathbf{x}^N)\}$, let us introduce the second-best welfare criterion by

$$W^S(\mathbf{x}) := \int_0^{Q^N(\mathbf{x})} f(Z)\mathrm{d}Z - \sum_{j=1}^{m} [c_j(x_j)q_j^N(\mathbf{x}) + x_j]. \tag{67}$$

As usual, our analytical focus will be on whether $(\partial/\partial x_i)W^S(\mathbf{x}^S)$ is positive or negative. By differentiating (67) with respect to x_i, we obtain

$$\frac{\partial}{\partial x_i} W^S(\mathbf{x}) = -q_i^N(\mathbf{x})c_i'(x_i) - 1 + \sum_{j=1}^{m} [f(Q^N(\mathbf{x})) - c_j(x_j)] \frac{\partial}{\partial x_i} q_j^N(\mathbf{x}). \tag{68}$$

Evaluating (68) at $\mathbf{x} = \mathbf{x}^N$ and taking (54) into consideration, we may obtain

$$\frac{\partial}{\partial x_i} W^S(\mathbf{x}^N) = [f(Q^N(\mathbf{x}^N)) - c_i(x_i^N)] \frac{\partial}{\partial x_i} Q^N(\mathbf{x}^N)$$

$$+ \sum_{j \neq i} [f(Q^N(\mathbf{x}^N)) - c_j(x_j^N)] \frac{\partial}{\partial x_i} q_i^N(\mathbf{x}^N). \tag{69}$$

Let i_0 be the index of a firm which is defined by

$$i_0 := \arg \min_{i \leq i \leq m} [f(Q^N(\mathbf{x}^N)) - c_i(x_i^N)], \tag{70}$$

which is nothing other than the index of the least efficient firm at the subgame-perfect equilibrium $\{\mathbf{x}^N, \mathbf{q}^N(\mathbf{x}^N)\}$.[6] Noting that $\theta_{ji}(\mathbf{x}) < 0$ for all $i, j \in M$ such that $i \neq j$, it follows from (69) that

$$\frac{\partial}{\partial x_{i_0}} W^S(\mathbf{x}^N) \leq [f(Q^N(\mathbf{x}^N)) - c_{i_0}(x_{i_0}^N)] \Psi_{i_0}(\mathbf{x}^N) \left[1 - \sum_{j \neq i_0} - \theta_{ji_0} - \frac{\theta_{ji_0}(\mathbf{x}^N)}{\Psi_{i_0}(\mathbf{x}^N)}\right], \tag{71}$$

where $\Psi_{i_0}(\mathbf{x}^N) := (\partial/\partial x_{i_0}) Q^N(\mathbf{x}^N) > 0$ and use is made of A5 and (49). Since $-\theta_{ji_0}(\mathbf{x}^N)/\Psi_{i_0}(\mathbf{x}^N) = -(\partial/\partial x_{i_0}) q_i^N(\mathbf{x}^N)/(\partial/\partial x_{i_0}) Q^N(\mathbf{x}^N)$ is nothing other than the slope of the cumulative reaction curve of firm j, *which is independent of the number of firms* m, the RHS of (71) tends to be negative as m becomes large.

To make matters even clearer, note that (60), (64), (65), and (66) entail

$$1 - \sum_{j \neq i_0} \frac{-\theta_{ji_0}(\mathbf{x}^N)}{\Psi_{i_0}(\mathbf{x}^N)} = 1 - \sum_{j \neq i_0} \frac{f'(Q^N(\mathbf{x}^N)) + q_j^N(\mathbf{x}^N) f''(Q^N(\mathbf{x}^N))}{f'(Q^N(\mathbf{x}^N))}$$

$$= 1 - \left[(m-1) + \frac{\Sigma_{j \neq i_0} q_j^N(\mathbf{x}^N)}{Q^N(\mathbf{x}^N)} \frac{Q^N(\mathbf{x}^N) f''(Q^N(\mathbf{x}^N))}{f'(Q^N(\mathbf{x}^N))}\right]$$

$$\leq 1 - \left\{(m-1) + \delta_0 \left[1 - \frac{q_{i_0}^N(\mathbf{x}^N)}{Q^N(\mathbf{x}^N)}\right]\right\}, \tag{72}$$

where use is made of A5. It should be clear that the extreme RHS of the inequality (72) becomes negative as m becomes large. Therefore, (71) and (72) establish the following theorem.

THEOREM 3 (GENERALIZED EXCESS INVESTMENT THEOREM AT THE MARGIN). Suppose that A4, A5, and A6 hold. Then the subgame-perfect level of R&D by the least efficient firm is socially excessive at the margin, i.e. $(\partial/\partial x_{i_0}) W^S(\mathbf{x}^N)$ is negative, if the number of firms is large enough.

We have thus demonstrated that the substance of second-best excess investment theorem at the margin can be essentially preserved even when we discard the restrictive assumption of identical firms and symmetric equilibria as long as product homogeneity, quantity competition, and profit maximization are retained.

4. CONCLUDING REMARKS

This completes our long and winding study on oligopolistic competition and economic welfare. Putting to one side some digressions, in the course of which we explored the simple general equilibrium analysis of oligopoly, taxation and welfare (Chapter 3), the welfare effects of excise tax and subsidy on oligopolistic producers with strategic commitment (Chapter 5), and the contrasts in terms of social welfare between the non-cooperative R&D and the co-operative R&D with spillovers (Chapter 6), there are two types of theorems that have been the central focus of our attention throughout this monograph: the excess entry theorem, and the excess investment theorem.

Despite their somewhat unorthodox nature, we have verified in Parts I and II that these theorems are quite robust as long as the following three basic assumptions are satisfied:

1. The oligopolistic competitors are profit-maximizers pure and simple.
2. The oligopolistic industry produces a single homogeneous product.
3. The strategic variables that oligopolists use in the product market competition are strategic substitutes.

In Part III we have also shown that the excess entry theorem remains true even in the presence of strategic commitment (Chapter 7), and that the basic message of these theorems is preserved even when competitors are not identical in the sense of their having different cost functions and when the equilibrium is non-symmetric (Chapter 9).

Another task we have tried to accomplish is to locate the precise boundaries that these theorems cannot trespass. Indeed, we have shown in Chapter 8 that

1. if oligopolistic firms are profit-constrained sales-maximizers or profit-sharing income-per-employee-maximizers, we can identify a set of conditions under which the excess entry theorem and/or the excess investment theorem do not hold;
2. if products are differentiated and consumers have a strong preference for product diversity, the entry of a new firm exerts an additional welfare-improving effect of widening product spectrum with a result that the excess entry theorem may be invalidated;

3. if firms compete by choosing prices rather than quantities, the nature of strategic interactions among oligopolistic firms undergoes a fundamental change, which modifies the qualitative nature of the effect of a change in strategic commitment, hence the welfare effect of oligopolistic competition, quite substantially.

As far as the theoretical purpose of this monograph is concerned, it is well served if we have succeeded in bringing these points home. Concerning the policy implications of our theoretical analysis, however, we still have several relevant observations to make; these are relegated to the Epilogue.

NOTES TO CHAPTER 9

1. A Cournot–Nash oligopoly without product differentiation is said to be *quasi-competitive* if the equilibrium industry output increases, and the equilibrium market price decreases, when the number of firms in the industry increases. See, among many others, Frank (1965), Okuguchi (1973), Ruffin (1971), and Seade (1980*b*).
2. For the conditions that guarantee the uniqueness of the Cournot–Nash equilibrium, readers are referred back to Section 3 of the Prologue. See also Friedman (1977), Kolstad and Mathiesen (1987), Okuguchi and Suzumura (1971), Suzumura (1971), and Szidarovszky and Yakowitz (1977).
3. Thanks to A1, we are assured that the Cournot–Nash equilibrium price $p^N(n) := f(Q^N(n))$ satisfies $(\mathrm{d}/\mathrm{d}n)p^N(n) = f'(Q^N(n))(\mathrm{d}/\mathrm{d}n)Q^N(n) < 0$. This means in effect that the generalized Cournot–Nash oligopoly model developed in this chapter is quasi-competitive in the sense defined in n. 1.
4. Strictly speaking, it is not correct to call n_f the first-best number of firms, since the actual number of firms, when each category of firms is replicated n_f times, is in fact $m \times n_f$. It is for the purpose of avoiding awkward and lengthy circumlocution that we will stick to this slight misuse of a word. The same caveat applies to the equilibrium number of firms n_e and the second-best number of firms n_s, to be introduced shortly.
5. As in Part II above, we are measuring the level of R&D by the expenditure for equipment installations.
6. If (70) does not determine a unique i_0, the following analysis applies to any one of such firm indices.

Epilogue

> The man who never alters his opinion is like standing water, and breeds reptiles of the mind.
>
> William Blake, 'A Memorable Fancy', from *The Marriage of Heaven and Hell*

1. WHITHER NOW?

The major part of this monograph has been devoted to re-examining the widely held belief that increasing competition improves social welfare. In sharp contrast with this conventional wisdom, it has been shown that, in oligopolistic industries with economies of scale and homogeneous products, where these products are strategic substitutes, the long-run free-entry equilibrium number of firms persistently exceeds the welfare-maximizing (first-best as well as second-best) number of firms. It follows that the restriction of new entry so as to prevent the number of firms from exceeding the welfare-maximizing number, rather than intensifying competition through the new entry of firms, can *in principle* improve social welfare. It has also been shown that the strategic commitment with cost-reducing R&D investment can be socially excessive in oligopolistic industries with homogeneous products, where these products are strategic substitutes. The larger the number of firms, the greater is the likelihood of the strategic commitment being socially excessive. In this arena, too, the restriction of competition for the purpose of preventing the socially excessive strategic commitment can *in principle* lead to an increase in social welfare.[1]

In view of these robust results, it seems an unavoidable conclusion that reasonable doubts exist on the unexceptional validity of the traditional belief in the welfare-improving effects of increasing competition. In other words, our reasoned answer to the first basic question posed in the Prologue cannot but be in the affirmative. However, this should not be construed to mean that regulating competition, rather than allowing free competition, should be the guideline of economic policy whenever 'excessive competition' in the identified sense surfaces. To put it differently, our reasoned answer to the second basic question posed in the Prologue is not unconditionally in the affirmative. It is important to understand why this should be so.

There are three distinct considerations behind this plea for caution in interpreting the message of the two basic theorems. Of these considerations, the first, which is explained in the remainder of this section, is related to the rather insidious nature of these results.

Recollect that the two basic theorems are obtained by using the welfare criterion of net market surplus function, which is nothing more than the simple sum of consumer's surplus and producer's surplus. It is all too clear that this welfare criterion is fundamentally insensitive to any distributional considerations.[2] Thus, an economic change may well be justified on the basis of this simple welfare criterion, even when it hurts one party quite substantially, inasmuch as the loss on the part of one involved party is overcompensated by the large gain on the part of the other involved party.

A clear example of this potential defect of our welfare criterion may be found in the demonstration of the second-best excess entry theorem established in Chapter 1. To see this, let us decompose the second-best welfare criterion $W^S(n)$, which is defined by (38) in Chapter 1, into the producer's surplus function,

$$PS^N(n) := n\pi^N(n) = n[q^N(n)f(Q^N(n)) - C(q^N(n))], \tag{1}$$

and the consumer's surplus function,

$$CS^N(n) := \int_0^{Q^N(n)} f(Z)\,\mathrm{d}Z - Q^N(n)f(Q^N(n)). \tag{2}$$

Differentiating (1) and (2) with respect to n and evaluating the outcome at the equilibrium number of firms $n = n_e$, our standard set of assumptions ensures that

$$(\mathrm{d}/\mathrm{d}n)PS^N(n_e) = n_e(\mathrm{d}/\mathrm{d}n)\pi^N(n_e) < 0 \tag{3}$$

and

$$(\mathrm{d}/\mathrm{d}n)CS^N(n_e) = -Q^N(n_e)f'(Q^N(n_e))(\mathrm{d}/\mathrm{d}n)Q^N(n_e) > 0 \tag{4}$$

hold. It is clear that consumer and producer benefits are diametrically opposed to each other with respect to a change in the number of firms at $n = n_e$. Indeed, $PS^N(n)$ will increase (decrease) when n is marginally less (more) than n_e, whereas $CS^N(n)$ will increase (decrease) when n is marginally more (less) than n_e. However, the absolute magnitude of $(\mathrm{d}/\mathrm{d}n)PS^N(n_e)$ dominates that of $(\mathrm{d}/\mathrm{d}n)CS^N(n_e)$; hence we have an unambiguous result to the effect that $(\mathrm{d}/\mathrm{d}n)W^S(n_e) < 0$. This is what lies at the heart of the second-best excess entry theorem at the margin.[3]

Once this insidious feature is clearly understood, a natural doubt comes to the fore. It is true that a welfare improvement in the aggregate may result from the marginal decrease in the number of firms at the free-entry Cournot–Nash equilibrium by virtue of the greater exploitation of scale economies thereby entailed. However, unless we are blind believers in the hypothetical compensation criteria *à la* Kaldor, Hicks, and Scitovsky, it is not at all obvious that we should actually follow the signal of the second-best excess entry theorem and head straight towards entry regulation in the name of keeping excessive competition under due control.[4]

2. FIRST-BEST AND SECOND-BEST GOVERNMENT INTERVENTIONS

The second reservation on the policy implications of the excess entry and excess investment theorems is based on the limited capability of the actual government. To crystallize our point as neatly as possible, let us suppose that a market failure arising from 'excessive competition' somehow emerges, and let us ask the following question: what are the conditions that are necessary for the government to be able to remove this functional impediment of the market mechanism and improve social welfare? It seems to me that there are at least three important conditions to be satisfied.

First, the government must be capable of gathering accurate information concerning the part of the economy in which market failure occurs, as well as the cause and the extent of the functional impediments thereby created. This is the condition required for the proper diagnosis of the functional impediments arising from market failure. Second, the government must be endowed with sufficient jurisdiction, as well as political support, to enable it to take effective and efficient measures to cope with the functional impediments thus identified. This condition is required in order that the government can apply the appropriate remedy for the diagnosed market failure. Third, the government must be endowed with the capability to look far beyond the direct and immediate effects of current policy interventions, to recognize their indirect and long-term consequences, and to prepare for any side-effects of the adopted policy measures on other parts of the economy as well as on the future course of the economy. This condition will enable it to prepare for any long-term side-effects of the remedial policies adopted.

Needless to say, these conditions are extremely stringent. The first condition requires that the government be in the position to gather accurate information on technology, preferences, and resources, information that is widely dispersed and privately owned. It is likely that the original owners of such private information may have no incentive to submit this information voluntarily to the government. To make matters even more complex and intractable, the original owners of such information themselves may be unable to describe it in the well-coded as well as interpersonally transferable format that is suitable for accurate and timely transmission to other economic agents, including the government. Thus, it may be difficult, if not impossible, for a government to gather such widely dispersed private information in order to identify accurately and diagnose properly each instance of market failure as it occurs.

The second condition relates to the actual implementability of a policy designed to cope with the identified instance of market failures. Note that it is not enough that the government be endowed with powerful administrative authority to invoke effective and efficient policy measures; it is also of crucial importance that the policy of this government be supported, or at least not objected to, by those who form the political backbone of the country.

The third condition requires the government to be able to see through the complex and subtle causal linkages and into a future veiled by uncertainty. Needless to say, this is a very demanding condition indeed.

Let us call the all-knowing and all-powerful government that satisfies these stringent conditions the 'first-best government', and the policy interventions against market failures that are implemented by such a government the 'first-best government interventions'. It is clear that the first-best government interventions are the ideal measures against market failure. However, the real-world government is hardly ever the first-best government in this sense, and such first-best government interventions are not actually implementable. This being the case, even when first-best government interventions can successfully rectify any instance of market dysfunction, it does not follow automatically that the interventions pursued by an actual government will be rationalized. On the contrary: a clumsy intervention by an imperfect government in the name of resolving the market failure may in fact make social welfare deteriorate, rather than improve. The situation is similar to the one where an ideal arbiter can settle a bitter dispute nicely to the satisfaction of all the parties involved, yet an imperfect and inconsiderate arbiter may aggravate the dispute, to the bitter disappointment of all.

In examining the appropriateness of administrative interventions in the competitive market mechanism, allowance should be made for the fact that a real-world government is not all-knowing and all-powerful, and must of necessity be subject to the severe informational, physical, institutional, political, and international constraints. Because of these constraints, the government interventions that can in practice be made in the competitive market mechanism need not guarantee a welfare improvement in the face of excessive competition. Only when the interventions by the 'second-best government' are effective in improving the welfare performance of competitive market mechanism will such intervention qualify as a serious contender to free competition in the market.[5]

3. INTRINSIC VALUE OF COMPETITION

Our third and last qualification on the policy implications of excessive competition, which drives a sharp wedge between the theoretical verdicts on whether competition can ever be excessive (the first basic question in the Prologue) and the policy prescription on whether competition should be regulated (the second basic question), is deeply rooted in the intrinsic, rather than instrumental, value of competition.

Up to this point, the roles of market competition mentioned in this book have all been construed as instrumental in promoting something of intrinsic value. Let us briefly recapitulate these instrumental roles of competition in order to bring this point into clear relief.

To begin with, competition abhors waste, just as nature abhors a vacuum. If the current state of resource allocation contains some waste of scarce resources, this fact sends an unambiguous signal that there are unexploited profit opportunities. In response to this signal, and in the absence of any interference, free competition among efficient firms will soon drive out such waste. Thus, free and vigorous competition plays an instrumental role in promoting the intrinsic value of economic efficiency.

Secondly, competition can serve as a spontaneous mechanism through which new innovations are introduced by firms into the decentralized economic system for competitive survival and success. Thus, free competition plays an instrumental role in promoting the intrinsic value of long-run economic progress.

Thirdly, competition serves as a spontaneous discovery mechanism through which dispersed private information on such basic economic data as technology, preference, and resources are discovered not by order or coercion, but by voluntary and spontaneous acts of profit-seeking firms, thus enabling society to make an efficient and effective use of initially dispersed private information. In this sense, free competition plays an instrumental role in promoting the intrinsic value of privacy-respecting decentralized decision-making.

In addition to these important instrumental roles, it must be emphasized that competition has an intrinsic value of its own as a unique social mechanism through which each agent can try out his own life chance on his own initiative and risk. There is no doubt that this process can be cruel as well as wasteful in weaning out the winners from the losers,[6] but it is a unique process which provides each agent with an equal opportunity to pursue his own aspirations in life.[7]

If we regulate competition so as to keep the social excessiveness thereof under due public control, not only should we design some alternative social process which can shoulder the task hitherto performed by market competition, but also we should be ready to let the intrinsic value of competition go. The social cost of depriving private agents of the opportunity to act on their own initiative and to bear risk seems to be quite high indeed. The existence of this social cost is precisely the third and last qualification we mentioned at the outset.

Putting all these pieces together, we can conclude that, although there may well be some situations where competition can be socially excessive in the welfare-theoretic sense, this should not precipitate us into accepting the policy prescriptions that suppress the free working of the competitive process. As was aptly observed by Hayek,

> We can probably still learn more about the real significance of competition by studying the results which regularly occur where competition is deliberately suppressed than by concentrating on the shortcomings of actual competition compared with an ideal which is irrelevant for the given facts . . . The evils which experience has shown to be the regular consequence of a suppression of competition are on a different plane from those which the imperfection of competition may cause. (Hayek 1948: 105)

It is with this classic warning by Hayek, which has an acute relevance even now, that I wish to close this monograph on the welfare-improving effects of increasing competition.

NOTES TO EPILOGUE

1. In postwar Japan, allusion to the danger of excessive competition has been made quite frequently with the purpose of motivating government interventions into the free-market forces; see App. A for a brief overview of the anti-competitive policy measures that have been persistently invoked.
2. Recollect that our analysis of excessive competition in the presence of general equilibrium interactions (Ch. 2) invoked the welfare criterion that is apparently focused exclusively on the consumer's welfare, i.e. the indirect utility function of the representative consumer. Note, however, that the representative consumer is the sole receiver of all factor incomes—profits and wages alike—so that this welfare function is again somewhat lacking in its total insensitivity to the distributional issues.
3. Fig. 5 above (Ch. 1) illustrates this point clearly. A marginal decrease in the number of firms at the free-entry Cournot–Nash equilibrium increases profits from zero to the area of $Ap^N(n)c^N(n)D$, whereas there is a decrease in the consumer's surplus by the area of $Ap^N(n)p^N(n_e)B$. Thus, the net change in welfare is the area $Cp^N(n_e)c^N(n)D$ minus the area ACB, which is clearly positive. What is involved in this exercise is that a loss in consumer's surplus induced by a decrease in n is more than compensated by the accompanied increase in producer's surplus.
4. The policy prescriptions recommending entry and/or investment regulation on the basis of the excess entry theorem and/or excess investment theorem pose another serious problem of equity. According to these recommendations, it is welfare-improving to decrease the number of firms at the free-entry Cournot–Nash equilibrium; it is also welfare-improving to restrict strategic commitment

with R&D investment at the subgame-perfect equilibrium. However, to the extent that all firms are symmetrically positioned, there exists no rational reason to favour some firms at the expense of the others. If such a discrimination is somehow made, the basis of discrimination cannot but be unfair to the firm(s) called upon to exit or to refrain from making strategic commitment with R&D investment.

5. To design an implementable second-best government policy in the face of excessive competition identified in this monograph is an interesting as well as important research subject. However, I must relegate extensive work along this line to the future.
6. Suppose that an agent A, participating in a free and competitive society, has actually realized a state x by trying out her life chance on her own initiative. As a counterfactual exercise, suppose that A is assigned the same state x by an external authority. In terms of the state of life, these two situations provide A with exactly the same state: x. Note, however, that the first situation provides A with complete freedom in trying her own life chance on her own initiative and settles with x by her own choice, whereas the second situation provides A with no such chance of trying something else other than just accepting x. Even when x happens to be the best conceivable state of life for A, it seems that there still exists a huge difference between these two situations, and the difference in question boils down to what we are calling the intrinsic value of competition.
7. Once we recognize the intrinsic value of competition as such, a totally new insight into the message of the two basic theorems can be obtained. In effect, what they imply is that the pursuit of social welfare and the realization of freedom to compete are two social values of intrinsic importance, which are in general incompatible. In order to improve social welfare you may have to restrict the freedom of competition, whereas if you want to realize freedom of competition you must be ready to sacrifice some potential welfare gain. Viewed in this way, the two basic theorems can be construed as the variants of the *impossibility of a Paretian liberal*, which Sen (1970*a*, *b*, 1976, 1983, 1992) presented in the framework of social choice theory. For the discussion of this paradigmatic paradox in social choice theory, those who are interested should refer to Gaertner *et al.* (1992), Gärdenfors (1980), Gibbard (1974), Nozick (1974), Suzumura (1978, 1980, 1983, 1990*a*), and Wriglesworth (1985), among many others.

APPENDIX A

*Exemption Systems from Anti-Monopoly Law and Other Anti-Competitive Measures in Japan: Overview and Evaluation**

1. INTRODUCTION

The original Anti-Monopoly Law (AML hereafter) in Japan, which was enacted in 1947 as an integral part of the economic democratization policy pursued by the Occupation Forces and modelled after the American anti-trust laws, was quite rigorous in its pro-competitive nature. Not only was a *per se* illegal standard for cartels applied, but also, stringent control over mergers and acquisitions was imposed. As time went on, however, a rigorous competition policy based on the original AML came to be recognized as unrealistic, and several amendments to the AML were introduced with the purpose of relaxing major provisions of the law. As early as 1953, for example, the *per se* illegality of cartels was modified to a prohibition of cartels only if they restrained competition substantially against the public interest, and recession cartels and rationalization cartels were exempted from the AML under some conditions. In addition, several other laws were introduced; these exempted certain anti-competitive agreements among firms from the application of the AML and allowed anti-competitive agreements in such areas as the export/import industry, small enterprises, marine transport, fire and marine insurance, and certain specific areas such as coal and fertilizers.

In addition to these laws and provisions which explicitly legalized some anti-competitive practices, administrative guidance has been sought by the Japanese government, the Ministry of International Trade and Industry (MITI hereafter) in particular, as an informal means of achieving industrial policy objectives. In pursuit of these objectives, MITI often gave private firms administrative guidance to forming a cartel and consolidating private resources and facilities. Such administrative guidance has been applied even when no exempting provision has existed, which occasionally has ignited debates on whether cartels are unlawful even if they are based on MITI's administrative guidance.

* This appendix was written while I was participating in the Competition Policy Workshop organized by the Institute for International Economics. I am grateful to the members of this project for their helpful comments and discussions on an early draft.

Furthermore, there existed several other measures which could be invoked by the government to regulate competition, e.g. laws restricting entry, stipulating various qualifications for starting businesses, and controlling prices. These laws, which include public utility regulation, licensing for maintaining health and safety standards, and protection of a specific industry such as agriculture, enabled the government to interfere directly in an industry by entry and/or price regulation.

In view of these anti-competitive measures in Japan, which were not only wide-ranging in coverage but also complicated in their stipulations, we are naturally led to wonder why there should be so many channels through which the free working of the competitive market mechanism could be interfered with, despite the deeply rooted and widely held belief among orthodox economists on the welfare-enhancing effects of increasing competition. The purpose of this appendix is to present a succinct overview and evaluation of the exemption systems from the AML and other anti-competitive measures in postwar Japan. In so doing, our purpose is to provide an empirical background of the basic questions examined in the main text of this monograph.

The plan of the appendix is as follows. Section 2 shows that the answer to the question as to whether there is a room for rationalizable interference in the free working of the competitive market mechanism hinges squarely on which criterion we use from among consumers' surplus, producers' surplus, and the social welfare in terms of net market surplus. This is useful in understanding the nature and relevance of the different stances taken by MITI, the Fair Trade Commission of Japan (JFTC hereafter), the business community at large, and the Supreme Court in the context of whether, and to what extent, competition should be regulated in the name of promoting public interest. Section 3 gives a succinct summary of the exemption systems from the AML and other exempting laws. Section 4 exemplifies the problem inherent in entry regulation in terms of administrative guidance by using the Large-Scale Retail Store Law and its erosion as a case study. In Section 5 we turn our attention to the telecommunications industry following the 1985 Telecommunications Reform, whereby competition has been handcuffed by the Ministry of Posts and Telecommunications even after the industry was liberalized and the Nippon Telegraph and Telephone Public Corporation was privatized by the reform. Section 6 concludes.

2. IS THERE RATIONALIZABLE INTERFERENCE IN MARKET COMPETITION?

2.1. Socially excessive firm entry under private incentives

Capitalizing on our analysis in Part I, let us begin by summarizing the welfare effects of firm entry. Consider an industry where n firms are producing a single homogeneous commodity, where $2 \leqslant n < +\infty$. The inverse demand function and the cost function of each firm are $p = f(Q)$ and $C(q_i)$, respectively, where p is output price, q_i is output of firm i, and $Q = \Sigma_{j=1}^{n} q_j$ is industry output. It is assumed that firms are identical, that $f(Q)$ is twice continuously differentiable with $f'(Q) < 0$ for all $Q \geqslant 0$ such that $f(Q) > 0$, and that $C(q_i)$ is twice continuously differentiable with $C(q_i) > 0$, $C'(q_i) > 0$, and $C''(q_i) > 0$ for all $q_i \geqslant 0$.

Consider a game G defined by a set of players $N = \{1, 2, \ldots, n\}$ and a profile of payoff functions $\{\pi^i(\cdot) \mid i \in N\}$, where $\pi^i(\cdot)$ is defined by $\pi^i(\mathbf{q}) = q_i f(q_i + Q_{-i}) - C(q_i)$, $\mathbf{q} = (q_1, q_2, \ldots, q_n)$, and $Q_{-i} = Q - q_i = \Sigma_{j \neq i} q_j$. Let $\mathbf{q}^N(n) = (q_1^N(n), q_2^N(n), \ldots, q_n^N(n))$ be the Cournot–Nash equilibrium of the game G, which is characterized by

$$f(Q^N(n)) + q_i^N(n) f'(Q^N(n)) - C'(q_i^N(n)) = 0, \tag{A1}$$

where $Q^N(n) = q_i^N(n) + Q_{-i}^N(n) = \Sigma_{j=1}^{n} q_j^N(n)$. Assuming that firms are identical, we focus on the symmetric Cournot–Nash equilibrium, so that we have $q_i^N(n) = q^N(n)$, say, for all $i \in N$. Throughout this appendix, we assume that the strategic substitutability prevails, i.e. that $\beta^N(n) < 0$ holds, where $\beta^N(n) = (\partial^2/\partial q_i\, \partial q_j)\pi^i(\mathbf{q}^N(n))$ $(i \neq j)$. In Section 3.2 in Chapter 1, we saw that this assumption may guarantee that $(\mathrm{d}/\mathrm{d}n) q^N(n) < 0$ and $(\mathrm{d}/\mathrm{d}n) Q^N(n) > 0$ hold.

Let $\pi^N(n)$ be the profits earned by each firm at $\mathbf{q}^N(n)$; i.e.

$$\pi^N(n) = q^N(n) f(Q^N(n)) - C(q^N(n)). \tag{A2}$$

Since $\pi^N(n) > (<)$ induces new entry of potential competitors (exit of incumbent firms), a long-run equilibrium will be attained only if the number of firms reaches the equilibrium value, n_e, which is defined by $\pi^N(n_e) = 0$.

Let $CS^N(n)$ and $PS^N(n)$ stand for the consumers' surplus and the producers' surplus, respectively, which are defined by

$$CS^N(n) = \int_0^{Q^N(n)} f(Z)\,\mathrm{d}Z - Q^N(n) f(Q^N(n)) \tag{A3}$$

and

$$PS^N(n) = \sum_{i=1}^{n} [q_i^N(n) f(Q^N(n)) - C(q_i^N(n))]. \tag{A4}$$

By adding up $CS^N(n)$ and $PS^N(n)$, we obtain a social welfare measure in terms of net market surplus, i.e. $W^N(n) = CS^N(n) + PS^N(n)$.

To see how these criteria will be affected by an exogenous change in n, we differentiate $CS^N(n)$, $PS^N(n)$, and $W^N(n)$ with respect to n to obtain

$$(\mathrm{d}/\mathrm{d}n) CS^N(n) = -Q^N(n) f'(Q^N(n)) (\mathrm{d}/\mathrm{d}n) Q^N(n), \tag{A5}$$

$$(\mathrm{d}/\mathrm{d}n)PS^N(n) = \pi^N(n) + Q^N(n)f'(Q^N(n))[(\mathrm{d}/\mathrm{d}n)Q^N(n) - (\mathrm{d}/\mathrm{d}n)q^N(n)], \quad \text{(A6)}$$

and

$$(\mathrm{d}/\mathrm{d}n)W^N(n) = \pi^N(n) - Q^N(n)f'(Q^N(n))(\mathrm{d}/\mathrm{d}n)q^N(n). \quad \text{(A7)}$$

It follows from (A5) that $(\mathrm{d}/\mathrm{d}n)CS^N(n) > 0$ holds for all n, so that it is always to the benefit of consumers to *increase* the number of firms within the class of models we are envisaging. On the other hand, it follows from (A6), as well as from $(\mathrm{d}/\mathrm{d}n)q^N(n) < 0$, $(\mathrm{d}/\mathrm{d}n)Q^N(n) > 0$, and $(\mathrm{d}/\mathrm{d}n)\pi^N(n) < 0$ (which were established in Section 2.4 in Chapter 1), that $(\mathrm{d}/\mathrm{d}n)PS^N(n)$ consists of two terms that have opposite signs as long as n is less than n_e; however, it becomes unambiguously negative when $n = n_e$, as the first term in (A6) will be zero at $n = n_e$. Thus, it is to the benefit of producers to *decrease* the number of firms from $n = n_e$. In fact, the negative effect of $(\mathrm{d}/\mathrm{d}n)PS^N(n_e)$ is so overwhelming *vis-à-vis* the effect of $(\mathrm{d}/\mathrm{d}n)CS^N(n_e)$ that $(\mathrm{d}/\mathrm{d}n)W^N(n_e)$ becomes unambiguously negative. This implies that the social welfare measured in terms of net market surplus is improved by a marginal *decrease* in the number of firms from its equilibrium value. Thus, it is in society's interest for the government to interfere with the free competitive forces so as to keep the number of firms less than its equilibrium value as long as it is willing to compensate a loss in consumers' surplus by the concomitant gain in producers' surplus.

2.2. Socially excessive capacity investment under private incentives

Capitalizing on our analysis in Part II, let us briefly summarize the welfare effects of strategic commitment to cost-reducing R&D. Consider an industry with n firms producing a single homogeneous commodity, where $2 \leqslant n < +\infty$. Firms compete in two stages. In the first stage, each firm makes a strategic commitment to R&D investment in full anticipation of the equilibrium in the second stage, where firms compete in terms of quantities.

Let x_i and q_i be the R&D investment and the output of firm i, chosen, respectively, in the first and the second stages. The second-stage variable cost function of firm i is $c(x_i)q_i$, where $c(x_i) > 0$ and $c'(x_i) < 0$ for all $x_i > 0$. Given a profile $\mathbf{x} = (x_1, x_2, \ldots, x_n)$ of R&D investments, let $G(\mathbf{x})$ be a game defined by a set of players $N = \{1, 2, \ldots, n\}$ and a profile of payoff functions $\{\pi^i(\cdot; x_i) \mid i \in N\}$, where $\pi^i(\cdot; x_i)$ is defined by $\pi^i(\mathbf{q}; x_i) = [f(Q) - c(x_i)]q_i - x_i$, $\mathbf{q} = (q_1, q_2, \ldots, q_n)$ and $Q = \Sigma_{j=1}^n q_j$. Let $\mathbf{q}^N(\mathbf{x}) = (q_1^N(\mathbf{x}), \ldots, q_i^N(\mathbf{x}), \ldots, q_n^N(\mathbf{x}))$ be the Cournot–Nash equilibrium of the game $G(\mathbf{x})$. Assuming interior optimum, $\mathbf{q}^N(\mathbf{x})$ is characterized by

$$f(Q^N(\mathbf{x})) + q_i^N(\mathbf{x})f'(Q^N(\mathbf{x})) = c(x_i), \quad \text{(A8)}$$

where $Q^N(\mathbf{x}) = \Sigma_{j=1}^n q_j^N(\mathbf{x})$.

Let G be a game defined by a set of players $N = \{1, 2, \ldots, n\}$ and a profile of payoff functions $\{\Pi^i(\cdot) \mid i \in N\}$, where $\Pi^i(\cdot)$ is defined by $\Pi^i(\mathbf{x}) = \Pi^i(\mathbf{q}^N(\mathbf{x}); x_i)$. Let $\mathbf{x}^N$ be the Nash equilibrium of the game G, which may be characterized by

$$\sum_{j=1}^{n} \frac{\partial}{\partial q_j} \pi^i(\mathbf{q}^N(\mathbf{x}^N); x_i^N) \frac{\partial}{\partial x_i} q_i^N(\mathbf{x}^N) + \frac{\partial}{\partial x_i} \pi^i(\mathbf{q}^N(\mathbf{x}^N); x_i^N) = 0 \qquad \text{(A9)}$$

under the assumption of interior optimum. The equilibrium path $\{\mathbf{x}^N, \mathbf{q}^N(\mathbf{x}^N)\}$ is the subgame-perfect equilibrium of our two-stage game.

Throughout this appendix, we assume that the second-stage Cournot–Nash equilibrium $\mathbf{q}^N(\mathbf{x})$ is symmetric for any symmetric R&D profile $\mathbf{x}$, i.e. that $q_i^N(\mathbf{x}) = q^N(\mathbf{x})$, say, for all $i \in N$ if $\mathbf{x}$ is symmetric. We also assume that the first-stage Nash equilibrium $\mathbf{x}^N$ is symmetric, i.e. that $x_i^N = x^N$, say, for all $i \in N$.

To see whether or not there is any room for rationalizable interference in this arena, we introduce the consumers' surplus $CS^N(\mathbf{x})$, the producers' surplus $PS^N(\mathbf{x})$, and the social welfare in terms of the net market surplus $W^N(\mathbf{x})$ by

$$CS^N(\mathbf{x}) = \int_0^{Q^N(\mathbf{x})} f(Z)\mathrm{d}Z - Q^N(\mathbf{x}) f(Q^N(\mathbf{x})), \qquad \text{(A10)}$$

$$PS^N(\mathbf{x}) = \sum_{i=1}^{n} [q_i^N(\mathbf{x}) f(Q^N(\mathbf{x})) - c(x_i) q_i^N(\mathbf{x}) - x_i] \qquad \text{(A11)}$$

and

$$W^N(\mathbf{x}) = CS^N(\mathbf{x}) + PS^N(\mathbf{x}) \qquad \text{(A12)}$$

Differentiating $CS^N(\mathbf{x})$ and $PS^N(\mathbf{x})$ with respect to x_i, we obtain

$$\frac{\partial}{\partial x_i} CS^N(\mathbf{x}) = -Q^N(\mathbf{x}) f'(Q^N(\mathbf{x})) \frac{\partial}{\partial x_i} Q^N(\mathbf{x}) \qquad \text{(A13)}$$

and

$$\frac{\partial}{\partial x_i} PS^N(\mathbf{x}) = [f(Q^N(\mathbf{x})) + Q^N(\mathbf{x}) f'(Q^N(\mathbf{x}))] \frac{\partial}{\partial x_i} Q^N(\mathbf{x})$$

$$- \sum_{j \neq i} c(x_j) \frac{\partial}{\partial x_i} q_j^N(\mathbf{x}) - c'(x_i) q_i^N(\mathbf{x}) - 1. \qquad \text{(A14)}$$

At this stage of our analysis, we assume that the second-order condition for payoff maximization in the game $G(\mathbf{x})$ is satisfied at $\mathbf{q}^N(\mathbf{x})$, i.e. that $\alpha^N(\mathbf{x}) = (\partial^2/\partial q_i^2)\pi^i(\mathbf{q}^N(\mathbf{x}); x_i) < 0$ holds. It is also assumed that the strategic substitutability holds at $\mathbf{q}^N(\mathbf{x})$, i.e. that $\beta^N(\mathbf{x}) = (\partial^2/\partial q_i\, \partial q_j)\pi^i(\mathbf{q}^N(\mathbf{x}); x_i) < 0$ $(i \neq j)$ is satisfied. As Section 2.4 in Chapter 4 shows, under these assumptions, $(\partial/\partial x_i) q_i^N(\mathbf{x}) > 0$, $(\partial/\partial x_i) q_j^N(\mathbf{x}) < 0$ $(i \neq j)$, and $(\partial/\partial x_i)\ Q^N(\mathbf{x}) > 0$

hold. It follows from (A13) that $(\partial/\partial x_i)CS^N(\mathbf{x}) > 0$ holds for any $\mathbf{x}$. Thus, the strategic R&D investment is always insufficient from the point of view of consumers; hence promotion rather than restriction of competition in R&D commitment should be the rational policy prescription from the exclusive viewpoint of consumers' welfare. On the other hand, it follows from (A14) that the sign of $(\partial/\partial x_i)PS^N(\mathbf{x})$ is ambiguous in general. However, it may be verified by virtue of (A8) and (A9) that

$$\frac{\partial}{\partial x_i} PS^N(\mathbf{x}^N) = (n-1)q_i^N(\mathbf{x}^N)f'(Q^N(\mathbf{x}^N))\left[\frac{\partial}{\partial x_i} Q^N(\mathbf{x}^N) - \frac{\partial}{\partial x_i} q_j^N(\mathbf{x}^N)\right] < 0 \qquad \text{(A15)}$$

holds at the subgame-perfect equilibrium $\{\mathbf{x}^N, \mathbf{q}^N(\mathbf{x}^N)\}$. It follows that the strategic R&D investment is excessive at the subgame-perfect equilibrium; hence restriction rather than promotion of strategic R&D competition should be the rational policy prescription from the exclusive point of view of producers' benefit.

Turning to the point of view of social welfare defined by the net market surplus, and putting (A13) at $\mathbf{x}^N$ and (A15) together, we obtain

$$\frac{\partial}{\partial x_i} W^N(\mathbf{x}^N) = -q_i^N(\mathbf{x}^N)f'(Q^N(\mathbf{x}^N))\left[\frac{\partial}{\partial x_i} Q^N(\mathbf{x}^N) + (n-1)\frac{\partial}{\partial x_i} q_i^N(\mathbf{x}^N)\right], \qquad \text{(A16)}$$

which is in general of indeterminate sign. However, it was shown in Section 4.3 in Chapter 4 that $(\partial/\partial x_i)W^N(\mathbf{x}^N) < 0$ unambiguously holds if the number of firms n is sufficiently large, which implies that the strategic R&D investment is marginally excessive at the subgame-perfect equilibrium. Thus, restriction rather than promotion of competition in terms of R&D commitment should be the rational policy prescription from the point of view of social welfare defined by the net market surplus.

2.3. *Empirical relevance*

In postwar Japan, interfirm competition has been consistently keen and has played a major role in promoting rapid growth by embodying new technology through extensive investment in plant and equipment. So keen has it been that a dysfunction of the market mechanism has allegedly developed from time to time, and government intervention has been applied in the name of keeping 'excessive competition' in investments under due control. However, hardly anyone has ever defined the meaning of 'excessive competition' within the standard conceptual framework of microeconomic theory. Indeed, most of the common arguments on 'excessive competition' boil down to the assertion that the market competition is so keen that some of the incumbent firms are forced to retreat from the competitive arena. If this is all what can be meant by 'excessive competition', there is no real social substance to this esoteric term. In order to gauge the real relevance of alternative stances taken by the industrial policy authorities represented by MITI, the competition policy authorities represented by JFTC, and the Supreme Court in the context of competition versus regulation, our first order of business is to explore the theoretical meaning, if there is any, of 'excessive competition'. Recollect in this context that the 'excessive competion in investment . . . tends to develop in industries characterized by heavy overhead capital, homogeneous products, and oligopoly. Examples are iron and steel, petroleum refining, petrochemicals, certain other chemicals, cement, paper and pulp, and suger refining' (Komiya 1975: 213–14). It is in response to this acute observation that the two models briefly summarized in this section were developed in the main text of this monograph by embodying the three crucial features identified by Komiya.

According to our analyses, we may clearly identify several situations in which 'excessive competition' in the welfare-theoretic sense does or does not surface.

(*a*) There is no such phenomenon as 'excessive competition' if we evaluate the performance of competition exclusively in terms of consumers' surplus.

(*b*) If we measure the performance of competition exclusively in terms of producers' surplus, the competitive equilibrium number of firms (the subgame-perfect equilibrium level of R&D investment) is excessive at the margin, in the sense that a marginal decrease in the number of firms from its long-run equilibrium value (a marginal decrease in the R&D investment from its subgame-perfect equilibrium level) improves the performance of the industry at the margin.

(*c*) If we measure the performance of competition exclusively in terms of net market surplus, the competitive equilibrium number of firms (the subgame-perfect equilibrium level of R&D investment) is excessive at the margin in that a marginal decrease in the number of firms from its long-run equilibrium value (a marginal decrease in the R&D investment from its subgame-perfect equilibrium level) improves the industry performance at the margin.

It is worth emphasizing that the three performance criteria we have referred to are of crucial empirical relevance in the Japanese context. According to Article 2–5 (private monopolization) and Article 2–6 (cartels) of the AML, a monopolization or a cartel is unlawful if and only if it restrains competition substantially in a particular field of trade 'contrary to the public interest'. As Matsushita and Davis (1990: 16–20) have aptly observed, however, the crucial expression 'contrary to the public interest' admits several alternative interpretations, and the choice made among them may dictate the rigour with which we are ready to apply the AML to a private monopolization and/or a cartel. The following three views on the issue of interpretation can be identified with a sharp contrast in their respective policy implications.[1]

The view taken by JFTC. According to JFTC, the so-called 'public interest' means nothing other than 'free competition', so that the expression 'contrary to the public interest' simply implies that there is a lack of free competition. This view can be traced back directly to the basic objective of the AML which is stipulated in Article 1 thereof, according to which the law is designed to 'promote fair and free competition. . .'. If we subscribe to this view held by JFTC, there is no room for an independent performance criterion other than free competition itself in judging whether or not we should interfere in the working of market competition.

The view held by business community. The business community in general, and the Federation of Economic Organizations in particular, maintain the view that the 'public interest' should be construed to mean something far broader than free competition alone, and should pay due attention to a balanced development of the national economy, consumers' welfare, and co-operation with foreign countries. In other words, rigorous application of the AML should not be construed as an end in itself, and an interference in the working of free competition may be rationalized if it contributes to an enhancement of a suitably defined measure of social welfare, i.e. 'public interest'.

The view of the Supreme Court in the oil cartel decision. In the context of the 1984 decision in one of the oil cartel cases, the Supreme Court took an intermediate view which struck a balance between the view of JFTC and the view held by the business community. According to the Supreme Court, the 'public interest' should in principle mean nothing other than free competition, and, under normal circumstances, an anti-competitive agreement among firms should be deemed contrary to the 'public interest'. However, this view admits that there are exceptional circumstances under which an anti-competitive agreement may be justified if the disadvantage of interfering in free competition may be overcompensated by the social advantage secured only by an anti-competitive agreement among firms. Inasmuch as the circumscription of the so-called 'exceptional circumstances' is left unclear, the extent to which this view diverges from the JFTC view is also left opaque. It is worth emphasizing, however, that the real importance of this view lies in the fact that it admits the existence of the areas in which a comparison, in terms of social welfare, between free competition and anti-competitive regulation should be made before we decide on the application of the AML.

This completes our preliminary observations. We can now begin to describe the exemption systems laid down by the AML and other anti-competitive policy measures in Japan.

3. OVERVIEW OF THE EXEMPTION SYSTEMS FROM THE AML IN JAPAN

3.1. Current status of the exemption systems

The exemption systems from the AML in Japan, which are designed for the exceptional exemption of anti-competitive agreements (cartels) and the like by firms and trade associations from the prohibitive provisions of the AML, are quite extensive, to say the least. In June 1991 there existed 68 exemption systems under 42 laws, of which 56 exempted cartel systems under 37 laws accounted for the vast majority.

Among these, 30 exemption systems under 15 laws were administered with the authorization by JFTC, or by the competent Cabinet Minister after having obtained the consent of, or having consulted with, or notified, JFTC. The number of cartels under these systems has been decreasing, and some of the exempted cartel systems have been dormant for a long period—some have never been implemented since their introduction. To convey the numerical order of magnitude, there were 1,079 exempted cartels at the end of March 1966, of which 72% involved small and medium enterprise associations, 21% involved foreign trade, and the remainder involved coastal shipping and other associations of various kinds. The number of exempted cartels was reduced to 505 at the end of March 1982, the most dramatic decrease having occurred in the areas of foreign trade (from 225 to 69) and small and medium enterprise associations (from 781 to 461). In June 1991 there were 247 active cartels under 6 laws, of which 170 involved small and medium enterprise associations, 34 involved foreign trade, 37 involved hairdressing, and the remaining 6 involved coastal shipping and fisheries.[2]

3.2. Exempting laws currently in effect

Given the large number of exemption systems and laws, it is too cumbersome to enumerate all of them. Instead, we refer only to those laws that are typical as well as of substantial importance.

Some exemptions are based on the AML itself or the Law Concerning Exemption (etc.), from the AML, whereas others are provided for in other laws. In the first category are included the following:

(*a*) natural monopolies (Article 21);
(*b*) intellectural property rights (Article 23);

(*c*) certain activities of co-operatives (Article 24);
(*d*) resale price maintenance (Article 24–2);
(*e*) recession cartels (Article 24–3);
(*f*) rationalization cartels (Article 24–4).

Table A1 lists the cartels that were exempted from the AML by Article 24–3 (recession cartels) and Article 24–4 (rationalization cartels) in order to show their historical pattern.

The second category includes the following:

(*g*) the exemption of legitimate acts performed under laws and regulations including the Land Traffic Enterprise Co-ordination Law and the Food Control Law, or orders under such laws and regulations;
(*h*) the exemption of organizations, etc., established under specific laws from Article 8 of the AML.

The third category can be illustrated by the following:

(*i*) the Marine Transportation Law, which exempts shipping conferences from the AML application;
(*j*) the Insurance Business Law, which authorizes rates fixed by fire and marine insurance companies;
(*k*) the Road Transportation Law, which exempts trucking, bus, and taxi companies from the AML;
(*l*) the Aviation Law, which allows Japanese airline companies to join the international aviation cartels;
(*m*) the Export/Import Transactions Law, which authorizes export and import cartels;
(*n*) the Small and Medium Business Organizations Law, which allows small enterprises to organize cartels.

3.3. Exempting laws of historical importance

In addition to the above-mentioned laws currently in effect, it is worth referring to some exempting laws of historical importance, although they are no longer in effect. The following laws, stipulated on behalf of several manufacturing industries as 'of strategic importance', may well illustrate the nature of such laws:

(*o*) Law on Temporary Measures for Structural Improvement of Specified Industries (May 1978–June 1988);
(*p*) Machine Industries Law (June 1956–March 1971);
(*q*) Electronics Industry Law (June 1957–March 1971);
(*r*) Law on Temporary Measures for the Promotion of Specified Electronics Industries and Specified Machinery Industries (April 1971–March 1978);

(*s*) Law on Temporary Measures for the Promotion of Specified Machinery and Information Industries (July 1978–June 1985)

Table A1. Cartels that are exempted from Anti-Monopoly Law (1)

	Exempting laws	
	AML Article 24–3	AML Article 24–4
1954	0	0
1955	0	0
1956	0	4
1957	1	6
1958	1	6
1959	5	8
1960	4	9
1961	3	9
1962	0	11
1963	1	11
1964	2	14
1965	2	14
1966	16	14
1967	1	13
1968	0	13
1969	0	12
1970	0	10
1971	0	13
1972	9	10
1973	2	10
1974	0	9
1975	2	0
1976	1	0
1977	1	0
1978	6	1
1979	4	0
1980	1	1
1981	1	1
1982	3	0
1983	2	0
1984	0	0
1985	0	0
1986	0	0
1987	0	0
1988	2	0
1989	2	0
1990	0	0
1991	0	0
1992	0	0

Source: Fair Trade Commission of Japan, Annual Report 1992, Tokyo: Fair Trade Association (1993, Attached Materials: 58–9).

Table A2 shows the historical pattern of cartels that were exempted from the AML by the exempting laws (*o*)–(*s*). Note that all these laws had ceased to be effective by June 1988.

Table A2. Cartels that are exempted from Anti-Monopoly Law (2)

	Exempting laws				
	(*a*)	(*b*)	(*c*)	(*d*)	(*e*)
1957	—	0	—	—	—
1958	—	0	0	—	—
1959	—	0	0	—	—
1960	—	1	0	—	—
1961	—	1	0	—	—
1962	—	5	0	—	—
1963	—	6	0	—	—
1964	—	14	0	—	—
1965	—	14	1	—	—
1966	—	9	1	—	—
1967	—	6	1	—	—
1968	—	8	0	—	—
1969	—	17	0	—	—
1970	—	16	1	—	—
1971	—	17	2	—	—
1972	—	—	—	0	—
1973	—	—	—	13	—
1974	—	—	—	15	—
1975	—	—	—	17	—
1976	—	—	—	16	—
1977	—	—	—	15	—
1978	—	—	—	9	—
1979	5	—	—	—	1
1980	8	—	—	—	1
1981	8	—	—	—	2
1982	4	—	—	—	1
1983	4	—	—	—	1
1984	5	—	—	—	1
1985	7	—	—	—	1
1986	6	—	—	—	—
1987	5	—	—	—	—
1988	2	—	—	—	—

(*a*) Law on Temporary Measures for Structural Improvement of Specified Industries: May 1978–June 1988.

(*b*) Law on Special Measures for the Promotion of Machinery Industry: June 1956–March 1971.

(*c*) Law on Special Measures for the Promotion of Electronics Industry: June 1957–March 1971.

(*d*) Law on Temporary Measures for the Promotion of Specified Electronics Industries and Specified Machinery Industries: April 1971–March 1978.

(*e*) Law on Temporary Measures for the Promotion of Specified Machinery and Information Industries: July 1978–June 1985.

Source: Fair Trade Commission of Japan, Annual Report 1992, Tokyo: Fair Trade Association (1993, Attached Materials: 58–61).

3.4. Evaluations

Most of the modifications of the original pro-competitive AML were brought in through the tension between MITI and JFTC, which started soon after the enactment of the AML. The first government-organized cartel was introduced in February 1952 when MITI issued an administrative guidance to ten large cotton spinners to reduce production by 40%. To enforce the quotas assigned by MITI, it was informally suggested that MITI-controlled foreign currency assignments for the following month's supply of raw cotton might be unavailable to those who rejected the quotas. Such cartels, organized as well as enforced by MITI, have proliferated since then, despite the accusation by JFTC that MITI's administrative guidance was illegal. To strengthen MITI's legal position *vis-à-vis* the AML, MITI soon submitted to the Diet the Law on Special Measures for the Stabilization of Designated Medium and Small Enterprises and the Exports Transactions Law, which authorized MITI to create cartels among small businesses without their being constrained by the AML.

This movement towards securing a safeguard against AML accusations was not confined to medium and small enterprises. Indeed, the Steel Federation, as well as the Federation of Economic Organizations, petitioned the Diet in 1953 to permit recession cartels and rationalization cartels. MITI also asked for the power to approve not only recession and rationalization cartels, but also other co-operative behaviour adopted to restrict production and sales. It was against this background that the Diet amended the AML in September 1953 to approve recession and rationalization cartels.

Furthermore, beginning with the Law on Special Measures for the Equipment of the Textile Industry in 1956, the Law on Special Measures for the Promotion of the Machinery Industry in 1956, and the Law on Special Measures for the Promotion of the Electronics Industry in 1957, MITI began to implement a long series of industry laws which secured exemptions from the AML for the designated industries.

MITI's persistent attempts towards securing powerful institutional devices for anti-competitive market interventions culminated in its plan in 1958 for a 'public sales system' for the steel industry, which was, quite surprisingly, approved by JFTC. The widely held perception that JFTC would approve anything that MITI claimed necessary for Japan seems to be deeply rooted in this dark period of competition policy in Japan.

In view of this historical background of the exemption systems from the AML and other anti-competitive measures, the evaluation of institutional anti-competitive devices becomes almost tantamount to the evaluation of the Japanese industrial policy. Leaving this larger task to much more extensive studies such as Itoh *et al.* (1991), C. Johnson (1982),

Komiya *et al.* (1988), and Okimoto (1989), I shall make only two brief observations.

First, there is very little solid proof, if any, that MITI's protective intervention into the mechanism of free competition was indispensable for the recovery, rationalization, rapid growth, and adjustment to external shocks in the postwar Japanese economy. Indeed, the effectiveness of the government sanctioned cartels has been strongly doubted. For example, in his analysis on the competitive consequences of Japan's export cartel associations, Dick (1992: 280) concluded that 'Japanese export cartels appear to have had no statistically significant effect upon either export prices or quantities' and suggested that 'several seemingly anti-competitive provisions of Japanese antitrust law, including the limited antitrust exemption for resale price maintenance and the exemption for private depression cartels, appear in practice to have allowed efficient forms of competition to emerge' (Dick 1992: 291). To cite a more recent study, Weinstein's (1993) evaluation of the administrative guidance and cartels in Japan concluded that 'MITI's guidance and cartel policies seem to have had rather small impacts on firm behavior' and that, 'in comparison to the favorable tax treatment, subsidies, protection, and low interest loans that some sectors received, exemptions from the virtually defunct Anti-Monopoly Law seem like relatively mild forms of government intervention'.

Secondly, it can hardly be denied that MITI had often outmanœuvred JFTC at least until the early 1970s. However, there were two changes in the late 1970s and thereafter that are worth mentioning. In the first place, there was a sharp and outright confrontation between MITI and JFTC when in February 1974 JFTC charged the Petroleum Association of Japan and twelve petroleum companies with operating an illegal price cartel. The case was turned over to the Tokyo High Public Prosecutor's Office. What was unique to this case was that the petroleum companies pleaded not guilty by saying that whatever they had done collectively had been done in accordance with MITI's administrative guidance. Although MITI was not charged in this context, neither was MITI's administrative guidance openly referred to in the indictment; the very fact that MITI's administrative guidance underlay the first criminal prosecution for a violation of the AML clearly indicated that the day had long passed when MITI could impose its anti-competitive measures on JFTC without much challenge. In the second place, the lenient nature of the AML in Japan has recently become one of the focal issues of the US–Japan Debates on Structural Impediments Initiatives. In response to this external pressure, JFTC has recently reviewed and re-evaluated exemption systems to the AML in Japan. It seems to be safe to surmise that, whatever impact one may associate with the current exemption systems and other anti-competitive measures, these systems and measures are in the process of being curtailed, if not actually extinguished.

4. CASE STUDY I: ENTRY REGULATION IN THE JAPANESE RETAIL INDUSTRY

4.1. Formal structure of the Large-Scale Retail Store Law

Since large firms tend to be technically more efficient than small firms, substantial social conflict occurs whenever a few large firms come to compete with many small firms in a segmented market. From the point of view of technical efficiency, it may well be better to have fewer and larger firms rather than more and smaller ones. However, quite apart from the problem that a larger proportion of overall market power would then be held by these larger firms, there are at least two countervailing considerations. First, more often than not, larger firms are newcomers to the segmented ('local') market, in which smaller firms have been engaged in business over many years or even generations; hence the arrival of larger rivals may be viewed as eradicating fair and rightful business opportunities for those who have been totally dependent on the local market. Secondly, smaller firms, being predominant in number, are capable of exerting strong political pressure over the government, which may well result in some governmental measures being taken to regulate, if not blockade, the new entry of technically superior and larger firms into a local market. We can best illustrate how these considerations interact, and how they tend to generate a complex and informal system of entry regulation, by examining the local retail markets.

I shall begin by describing the formal system of entry regulation in local retail markets which existed until the recent reform, and will then explain the huge divergence that subsequently developed between this lawful framework and the actual *modus operandi* of entry regulation in this industry.[3] It is hoped that this case study will illustrate the difficulties that must be faced in attempting to design and implement a welfare-enhancing entry regulation, and also that it will suggest how great the social cost of less-than-ideal anti-competitive market intervention can be.

The formal structure of the Law Concerning the Adjustment of Retail Activities by Large-Scale Retail Stores, enacted in 1974 (Large-Scale Retail Store Law for short), is fairly simple and straightforward. According to Article 1, the purpose of this law is to keep retail activities by large-scale stores under due control, thereby securing fair business opportunities for local small and medium-sized retailers, and to maintain the well-balanced development of retail industry in the local area without sacrificing consumers' benefits.[4]

Whenever a large-scale retailer intends to start a new store whose size exceeds 500 square metres in a local retail market, it must follow the accommodation procedure stipulated by the Law.[5] In the first place, those who intend to build the large-scale retail store in question must notify MITI of their construction plans through the local municipality. This is known as the Article 3 notification. After this notification is filed, MITI should make it known to those who are likely to be affected by the proposed entry that a formal process of accommodation in accordance with the law is about to start. After this first formal step is completed, the second notification to MITI, known as the Article 5 notification, must be filed through the local municipality by those who are going to engage in retail business activities in the proposed large-scale retail store at least five months before the start of their activities. This second notification has to contain such information as opening date, total floor space, frequency of discount sales, and so on.

If MITI feels that opening of the proposed store may adversely affect the business opportunities of small local retailers beyond a reasonable limit, it is within MITI's jurisdiction to recommend that the potential entrant delay the opening of the store, or reduce the planned floor space, or both. This recommendation should be made within four months after the Article 5 notification is filed. Furthermore, MITI should consult the Large-Scale Retail Store Council, which is an advisory council under MITI's jurisdiction, for its opinion concerning the necessity of a recommendation. The Council, being rather distant from the local circumstances and opinions, will consult the Local Chamber of Commerce for its opinion; the latter in turn will organize the Council to Accommodate Commerce Activities (CACA for short), whose function is to hold discussions to accommodate local interest groups. It is noteworthy that the formal members of CACA consist of local business representatives *excluding* those who are directly affected by the large-scale retail store in question, plus consumer representatives and neutral third parties including informed academics.[6]

The maximum allowable length of time for this accommodation process is obviously limited by the maximum length allowed between the Article 5 notification and MITI's lawful recommendation. As a matter of fact, MITI's administrative guidance recommended that the length be restricted to two months. Therefore, it should be possible under the law to open a new large-scale retail store within as little as seven months of filing the Article 3 notification, as long as the original entry plan is duly modified in accordance with any MITI recommendation. If MITI's recommendation is not voluntarily followed, then it can issue a legal order to enforce its lawful recommendation.

This formal accommodation procedure is briefly summarized in Fig. A1. It should be clear that the Large-Scale Retail Store Law empowers no one, not even MITI officials and local municipalities, to *reject* new entry into a local retail market, as long as the two lawful notifications are filed in time and MITI's lawful recommendation based on the formal procedure is carefully observed.

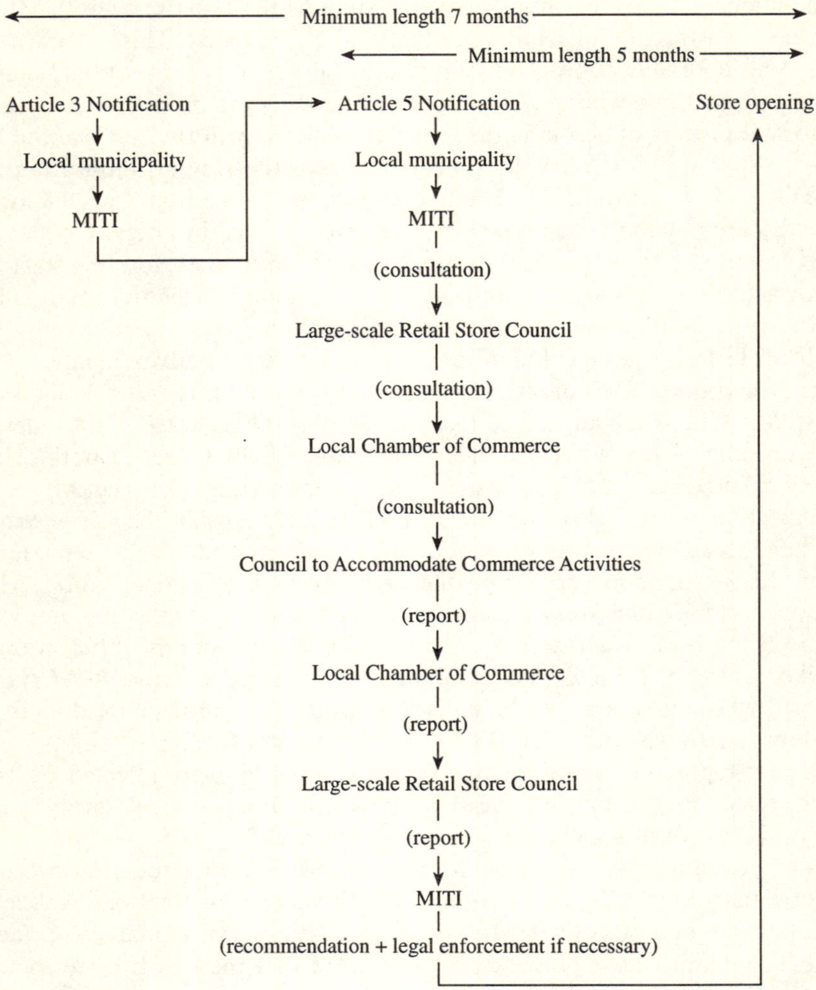

Fig. A1 Formal accommodation procedure in accordance with the law

4.2. Actual working of the system of entry accommodation

In reality, however, actual accommodation procedure has been quite different from what has been described so far. In some cases, the formal accommodation procedure can begin only after quite lengthy and unofficial *ex ante* negotiations with local interest groups have been successfully carried out, which sometimes can last for as long as five years. In view of this prolonged and painful process of accommodation, which is obviously costly to those wanting to enter a local retail market, there have been cases where attempted entry plans were abandoned or shifted away to another area. A natural question suggests itself as to how this could ever happen.

There seem to be at least two reasons, one involving MITI's administrative guidance and bureaucratic conventions, another involving additional local regulations brought in by local municipalities.

The first step in the erosion of the official accommodation procedure is that it soon became a bureaucratic convention that MITI consulted the opinion of the local Chamber of Commerce in between the two lawful notifications, the reason presumably being to facilitate better reflection of local opinions in the final settlement. Since the official CACA is formed only *after* the Article 5 notification is filed and the Large-Scale Retail Store Council has consulted the opinion of the local Chamber of Commerce, it was necessary to introduce another informal council, without any lawful status whatsoever, which dealt with the substantial matter of accommodation consisting of floor space, opening date, holidays, and opening hours. This informal council came to be called the Prior CACA, and it lies completely outside the lawful accommodation procedure, with two regrettable consequences. First, unlike the official CACA, there was absolutely no time limit on the accommodation within the Prior CACA; nor was there any accountable restriction on its membership. Second, this informal council in effect pre-empted the formal accommodation procedure as laid down in the Large-Scale Retail Store Law. It was inevitable that much time was thereby wasted; but the more serious problem was that the lawful accommodation procedure was deprived of its substance. That the official CACA came to be dubbed the Confirmation CACA is symbolic of the extent to which it was undermined by the unofficial Prior CACA.

To rectify this situation, in May 1979 MITI introduced an administrative guidance to the effect that the length of time between the Article 3 and Article 5 notifications should not exceed eight months. This, in effect, set an upper limit of eight months on the allowable length of accommodation within the Prior CACA. In response to this administrative guidance, however, a bizarre practice came into being. The Preliminary Explanation by the potential entrant to the local interest groups, which was also introduced by MITI's administrative guidance as a prerequisite for officially filing the Article 3 notification, transformed itself into the Prior *Prior* CACA, within which the whole substance of the accommodation procedure was in effect completed. As this Preliminary Explanation had to be completed before filing the Article 3 notification, there were no legal stipulations on the membership of the Prior Prior CACA; nor was there any constraint on the content and length of negotiations within it.

Along with this erosion of the entry regulation system administered by the central government, many local municipalities introduced additional entry regulations which made the entry accommodation procedures even more opaque and inefficient. On the one hand, some local municipalities required that the agreement concluded in the Prior Prior CACA should be appended to the Article 3 notification. Needless to say, this administrative practice has no legal foundation in the Law itself.[7] On the other hand, many local municipalities extended the scope of entry regulations based on the Large-Scale Retail Store Law so as to cover retail stores with floor space far less than 500 square metres.[8] In extreme cases, local entry regulation was applied to retail stores whose floor space exceeded just 1 square metre when the store was funded by someone residing outside the municipality in question. Fig. A2 summarizes the actual entry regulation system in local retail markets schematically.[9]

Given this labyrinth of informal entry regulations, it is all too common for many large-scale retail stores to be effectively blocked from entering local markets, or 'voluntarily' to shift away from local markets known for

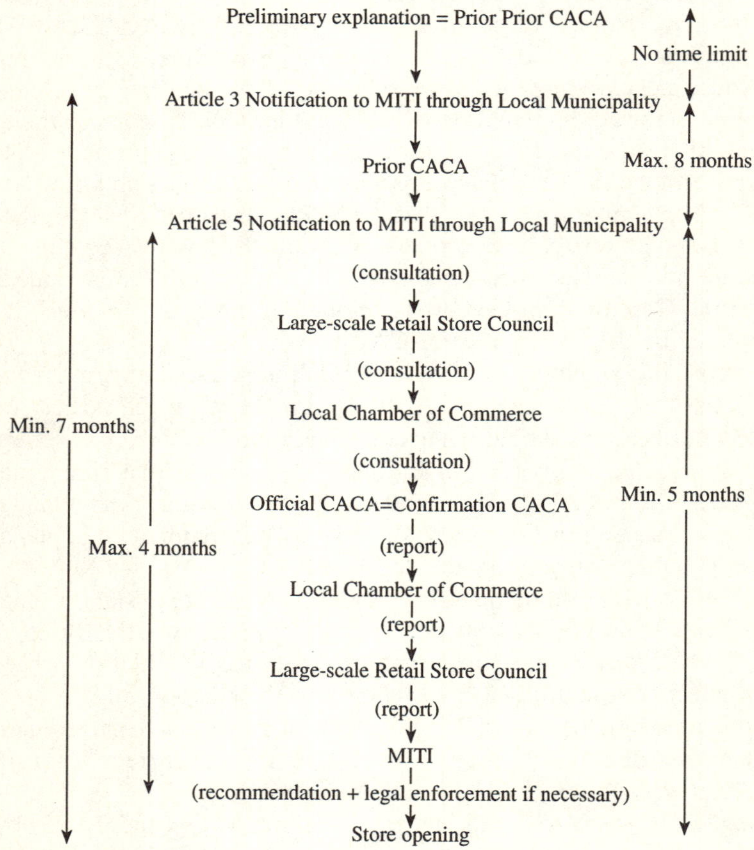

Fig. A2 The informal accommodation procedure that subsequently developed

their vigorous entry-preventive activities, to the clear detriment of local consumers. If and when an attempted entry does prove successful, the entry 'fee', in the form of forgone imputed rent on the prospective store site, the cost of lengthy negotiations, and pecuniary or non-pecuniary compensations paid out to local retailers, is ultimately passed on to the consumers residing in that municipality.

The story told thus far should not be thought to suggest that large-scale retailers have been exploited by incumbent small and medium-sized retailers through the informal mechanism of entry regulations. Since most large-scale retailers repeatedly played this game, even when pressed to pay compensation for their attempts to enter a local market, the same mechanism would effectively protect them from future attempts at entry by their rivals. It follows that the initial entry fee, which is shifted to customers after entry anyway, is in fact considered money well spent from their point of view. Thus, not only small and medium-sized retailers, but also the large-scale retailers themselves are beneficiaries of this informal mechanism of entry regulations. This is one of the crucial reasons why the mechanism has been so robustly preserved, despite its obvious inefficiency, unfairness, and lack of transparency.

4.3. Prospects for regulatory reform in the Japanese retail industry

Entry regulations in the retail industry became the symbolic focus of the US–Japan Debates on Structural Impediments Initiatives. In response to the criticisms raised by the US representatives against the firm-oriented nature of administrative practices in Japan, several important steps have been taken to improve both administrative practices and the formal structure of entry regulations.

The initial step was taken in May 1990, when MITI issued a circular to all municipalities and Chambers of Commerce. This circular requested that the total length of accommodation be shortened to eighteen months in total, and that the improper use of the Preliminary Explanation as the Prior Prior CACA be terminated. The Law itself was revised in May 1991 and became effective nine months later. The revised law stipulated that the total length of accommodation should be less than one year; it also simplified the accommodation procedure by placing accommodation-related activities exclusively in the hands of the Large-Scale Retail Store Council. It is worth emphasizing that neither the Prior CACA, nor the official CACA itself, has any role whatsoever in the newly revised procedure.

The immediate response to these revisions was quite remarkable. Within one month of MITI's circular in May 1990, more than 1,500 large-scale retail stores announced their intention either to open a new store or to upgrade their existing store/s. This figure was three times larger than the total number of Article 3 notifications filed in 1989. It spoke eloquently to the severity of the entry regulations, and indicated how many potential entries had had to remain latent.

Although the implementation of this regulatory reform may not be easy for various reasons, the shift towards more transparent and consumer-oriented entry accommodation mechanisms should be welcomed. Note, however, that the Large-Scale Retail Store Council has to face a prodigious task in view of the number of proposed new entries. It is not clear how the Council will cope with this tremendous task. In addition, it is not clear how the extended use of entry regulations by local municipalities, which was one of the major reasons for the failure of the former accommodation procedure, can be effectively contained without violating the important principle of local autonomy.

In concluding this case study, a general remark seems to be in order. Even when the formal system of market intervention is straightforward, it may be made complex and internally inconsistent by a sequence of administrative guidances which, by their very nature, are based on no clear and logical procedural principles. The situation is even worse when the formal system itself contains some internal inconsistencies. Indeed, what underlies the quagmire of entry regulations in the Japanese retail industry is a conflict between two basic requirements on social policy: efficiency of industry performance, and protection of the 'rights' of those who have been engaged in local business long before the proposed entry of their rivals.[10] Once we agree that the 'right' in question is worth social protection, the concomitant loss in social efficiency should be regarded as a cost to be borne collectively. Even in this case, however, we can design a much more efficient and straightforward mechanism for protecting this 'right' than leaving the issue to be settled through the complex procedure of endless negotiations and compensations. On the other hand, if the general validity of such a 'right' is not generally agreed on, the *raison d'être* of the tangled negotiation procedure will be that much less.

5. CASE STUDY II: TELECOMMUNICATIONS REFORM AND HANDCUFFED COMPETITION

5.1. Telecommunications reform of 1985

The telecommunications industry has been under the jurisdiction of the Ministry of Posts and Telecommunications (MPT hereafter). In 1985, MPT introduced an extensive telecommunications reform which is pro-competitive in nature. Before the implementation of this important reform, Nippon Telegraph and Telephone Public Corporation had legally monopolized domestic telecommunications in Japan. Our second case study is focused on the nature and aftermath of this reform, with special emphasis on the public decision-making mechanism that led to this reform.[11]

The origin of the 1985 reform can be traced back to the Third Report of the Second Ad Hoc Commission on Administrative Reform which was submitted to the Prime Minister in 1982. A brief account of the nature of this Ad Hoc Commission may not be out of order. Historically speaking, it was the Occupation authorities who encouraged participatory democracy in order to reduce and rectify the arbitrary nature of the prewar administration. With the implementation of the National Administrative Organization Law in 1949, the ministries began to establish advisory bodies on the levels of their cabinet ministers, bureau chiefs, and section chiefs. These advisory bodies are classified into 'consultative bodies', which deliberate on policies, and 'examining bodies', which, by participating in administrative decision-making, ensure that the laws are fairly administered. A report submitted by a consultative body is not legally binding, whereas the resolution of an examining body can act as a constraint on bureaucracy. Thus, examining bodies are far stronger administrative committees than consultative bodies in terms of their degree of independent authority, and they are grounded in Article 3 of the National Administrative Organization Law. Although the Second Ad Hoc Commission was a consultative body grounded in Article 8 of the National Administrative Organization Law, its reports were widely considered to be close to legally binding, owing to the fact that the Prime Minister publicly promised the chairman of the Second Ad Hoc Commission that his government would faithfully implement its recommendations.

Concerning the telecommunications industry, the Third Report made the following recommendations: (*a*) Nippon Telegraph and Telephone Public Corporation should be privatized. (*b*) This public corporation should be divided into a central corporation, which would manage the long-distance network, and the local corporations, which would manage the local networks in their respectively designated areas. (*c*) The telecommunications industry should be liberalized and new entry into the long-distance market should be encouraged.[12]

Of these recommendations, (*a*) and (*c*) were indeed implemented by the 1985 Telecommunications Reform Act. The Nippon Telegraph and Telephone Public Corporation was transformed into a special government-controlled private company called NTT. In addition, in 1987 three New Common Carriers (NCCs hereafter) selectively entered the long-distance market and started telecommunications services in the most profitable market segment. Concerning recommendation (*b*), however, no firm commitment to its implementation was made in the 1985 reform. It was simply announced that the performance of the new organization of the telecommunications industry in general, and the performance of NTT in particular, would be reviewed after five years with the purpose of deciding what further steps should be taken. At the time of the 1985 reform, therefore, NTT remained a consolidated common carrier and continued to monopolize the local telecommunications market.

The 1984 pro-competitive reform notwithstanding, the telecommunications industry has remained highly regulated, and the nascent competition between the privatized NTT and the newly arrived NCCs has been hampered by MPT's incessant interference. Not only NTT, but also the NCCs have been subject to MPT's price and service regulations, which seem to have been guided by MPT's industrial policy aimed at promoting the NCCs as an effective countervailing power against the bottleneck monopolist, i.e. NTT. Indeed, at least up to June 1992, there had always been 20% price difference between NTT's and the NCCs' long-distance telephone services in the NCCs' favour, which sufficed to bring about a rapid shift in the long-distance telephone market from NTT to the NCCs.[13]

Not only the entry of potential firms into this industry, but also the exit of incumbent firms from the industry is under the strict surveillance of MPT. Since NTT was not divested in the 1985 reform but retained its integrated network, a fundamental asymmetry persists between NTT and the NCCs. Thus, each NCC can complete its long-distance telecommunications service only by being smoothly connected with NTT's local network, whereas NTT can provide a self-contained telecommunications service. Given this structural asymmetry between NTT and NCCs, it makes sense that there should remain an asymmetric regulation in order to keep the potential danger of NTT's bottleneck monopoly under proper control. However, the current intervention by MPT would seem to go far beyond such rule-oriented and pro-competitive regulation and to interfere with the choice of competitive strategies by market participants. The current method of price regulation, which remains the classical rate-of-return regulation, is not really pro-competitive either. Besides, MPT has never allowed NTT to revise its rates structure, with a result that the local telephone charge has remained absolutely fixed ever since the 1985 reform, in the face of a sharp decrease in the long-distance telephone charges arising from the introduction of controlled competition in this segment of the market.[14]

In 1988, MPT sought the opinion of the Telecommunications Deliberation Council, the advisory body at MPT level, on further measures to be adopted with the purpose of improving NTT's performance. In March 1990 the Council submitted a report to the Minister of Posts and Telecommunications on several possible measures that could be taken, including the vertical divestiture of NTT into two parts, the Long-Distance Network Corporation and the Local Network Corporation. However, this report was unable to elicit support from other ministries, including MITI and the

Ministry of Finance—nor from the ruling Liberal Democratic Party, for that matter—and the implementation of recommendation (*b*) of the Second Ad Hoc Commission had to be postponed for another five years.

5.2. Public decision-making process of the 1985 reform

In Japan, there exists a traditional one-to-one correspondence between an industry and the ministerial bureau, division, or section under whose jurisdiction the industry in question falls. Whenever there is a new development which disrupts or blurs this finely balanced relationship, an inevitable jurisdictional dispute breaks out. This was indeed the case in the 1970s and early 1980s, when MPT and MITI had a jurisdictional dispute over data processing. MITI's concern was not to lose its influence in data processing and information services. On top of this, some large corporations under MITI's jurisdiction complained that they were being prevented from setting up nationwide, Value Added Network or VAN between companies; nor were they satisfied by the high cost of long-distance calls and the lack of customized billing. It is true that the Second Ad Hoc Commission on Administrative Reform took a clear initiative in designing NTT's privatization and divestiture, but MITI's strong concern also played an undeniable role throughout the public debates on the liberalization of telecommunications in general, and of data communications in particular.

Although jurisdictional disputes such as this are often viewed cynically, there is a positive side of the coin. This can be clearly illustrated by looking at the process through which further measures for improving NTT's performance were discussed in 1988–90. NTT being within MPT's jurisdiction, it was the Telecommunications Deliberation Council that came to the fore at this time. As is always the case, the deliberation process within the Council was closed to the public, and those who testified in the Council's meeting were strongly requested not to disclose any information outside the Council. If it were not for other organs, such as the other ministries or business organizations which expressed strong concern and publicized alternative opinions and scenarios, the general public would not have known what was really at stake. As an imperfect, yet workable, mechanism for checks and balances—the expressed interest of the concerned ministries combined with concomitant jurisdictional disputes—may play some positive role in such a situation by bringing the real policy issues under debate to public awareness.

5.3. What's wrong with controlled competition?

In view of the fact that competition has been kept keen in the long-distance telecommunications market and that customers are gaining from lower long-distance telephone charges without being required to pay higher local telephone charges, a devoted consequentialist may ask: what's wrong with handcuffed competition? But it seems to me that such competition is indeed wrong, for at least two reasons.

First of all, by controlling long-distance telephone charges in such a way that the NCCs can always maintain a substantial competitive edge against NTT, the authority in charge of handcuffed competition is in fact depriving the NCCs of any incentive to compete in terms of strategies other than controlled prices. A regrettable consequence is that customers miss out on the opportunity to choose from a wider range of services which would be competitively provided were it not for artificially maintained differentials in long-distance telephone charges.

Secondly, by maintaining artificially low local telephone charges, the authority in charge of handcuffed competition is foreclosing on the potential entry of the NCCs into the local telecommunications market where NTT is still maintaining a virtual bottleneck monopoly. If it were not for the prohibition on revising local telephone charges, there might well be a spontaneous growth of competitive power in the local telecommunications market.

It cannot be denied that unfettered competition may well be downright wasteful, but handcuffed competition may also be wasteful by suppressing spontaneous development which only free-market competition can nourish. It is not at all clear which is the lesser of the two 'evils'.

6. CONCLUDING REMARKS

This appendix has provided an overview of anti-competitive policy measures in Japan, starting with the exemption systems from the Anti-Monopoly Law. In conclusion, let us recapitulate two simple observations that have been made *en route*.

First, any reasonable overview of anti-competitive measures should not confine itself to the explicit policy measures based on the exempting laws. It is also relevant to examine some informal measures of industrial policy pursued by government ministries, such as administrative guidance, whose legal foundation has never been made explicit.

Secondly, it should be kept in mind that these anti-competitive measures have been rationalized by claiming that they help to promote the 'public interest'. However, the very sense in which this crucial term is used differs substantially from person to person. Since the extent to which people are lenient about anti-competitive measures hinges squarely on the way 'public interest' is perceived, we are in danger of having each cancel the other out if we are not careful.

NOTES TO APPENDIX A

1. The following discussion of the three interpretations on 'contrary to the public interest' is owed substantially to Matsushita and Davis (1990).
2. Detailed historical and factual information on the exemption systems in Japan may be found in Fair Trade Commission of Japan (1977; 1991), and Uesugi (1986).
3. This section is based essentially on Suzumura (1990*c*). See also Kusano (1992) and Tsuruta and Yahagi (1991).
4. It should be noted that this declared purpose of the law seems to contain some possibilities of internal inconsistency. In particular, it is not at all clear how one can protect the 'fair' business opportunities of local small retailers by the entry regulation of large-scale stores which are more efficient and more capable of providing a wider product range to consumers without sacrificing consumers' benefit.
5. According to the original 1974 law, a large-scale retail store is one whose total shop area exceeds 1,500 m^2. This stipulation only induced an increase in the number of retail stores whose total areas were 1,500 $m^2 - \varepsilon$. Partly in response to this induced tendency and partly in response to the additional regulations introduced by local municipalities which covered retail stores with total areas less than 1,500 m^2, the law was modified in 1979 so as to define a large-scale retail store as one whose total area exceeds 500 m^2. This definition lasted until January 1992, when the law was again modified in response to the US–Japan Debates on Structural Impediments Initiatives. In order to facilitate new entry of large retailers, the critical total area of retail stores was enlarged to 3,000 m^2. For more factual details about the history and content of the Large-Scale Retail Store Law, see Suzumura (1990*b*) and Kusano (1992).
6. To be precise, there is no explicit stipulation in the law concerning the role of the Council to Accommodate Commerce Activities. It was MITI's administrative guidance that first introduced this council. Its role was made more official in the 1982 revision, but was never been formally included in the law itself.
7. In March 1989 there were 117 local municipalities which had their own entry regulations on large-scale retail stores in addition to the regulations based on the Large-Scale Retail Store Law; see Kusano (1992: 28).
8. In March 1989 there were 1,014 local municipalities regulating the entry of retail stores with floor space less than 500 m^2; see Kusano (1992: 28).
9. This scheme persisted until May 1990. It was in response to the US criticism on this grotesque scheme that the first step was taken to make it more efficient and more accountable; see S. 4.3 below.
10. This basic conflict reflects itself in art. 1 of the law; see n. 4 above.
11. The following explanation greatly simplifies matters for brevity. See Suzumura (1990*a*) and Okuno-Fujiwara *et al.* (1993) for a more detailed account and analysis of the 1985 telecommunications reform.
12. The background of these radical recommendations seems to be threefold. First, under the legal monopoly by Nippon Telegraph and Telephone Public Corporation, the telecommunications industry in Japan was not responsive enough to

rapidly expanding and diversifying customer needs. Second, the extent of internal inefficiencies of the state monopoly seemed to have far exceeded the limit of public tolerance. Third, owing to the innovations in communications technology, the traditional reason for state monopoly, i.e. natural monopoly, seemed to have disappeared as far as the long-distance telecommunications were concerned.

13. The share of NCCs in the long-distance telephone services between Tokyo and Osaka via Nagoya was already as high as 40% in 1990, and came close to 60% in 1992. Given that the NCCs started their service only in 1987, this drastic shift in market share is truly remarkable.
14. In February 1988, shortly after the NCCs first started their long-distance telephone services, NTT's charge for the longest-distance telephone service (3 minutes, daytime) was ¥360, whereas the corresponding charge by NCCs was ¥300. The charges were lowered to ¥330 v. ¥280 in February 1989, ¥280 v. ¥240 in March 1990, and ¥240 v. ¥200 in March 1991. During and after this period, NTT's charge for local telephone service (3 minutes, day or night) remained absolutely fixed at ¥10.

APPENDIX B

*Collaborative Research and Development: Economic Analysis in the Light of Japanese Experience**

1. INTRODUCTION

From the time of Adam Smith to the present, a common belief strenuously persists, according to which collusion on prices and quantities among competing firms is detrimental to social welfare in competitive market economies. This being the case, it seems rather odd that economists and policy-makers alike are now becoming quite enthusiastic about collaborative R&D, whereby otherwise competing firms collude on R&D activities and share the costs as well as the benefits thereof. There would seem to be at least two reasons behind this recent upsurge of enthusiasm.

In the first place, one of the crucial features of R&D is the rapid diffusion of knowledge once generated, sometimes without compensation, hence the limited appropriability of R&D benefits. As such, collaborative R&D agreements seem to be a natural institutional arrangement which may be effective in coping with the perennial problem of free-riders. Besides, collaborative R&D agreements enable member-firms to avoid wasteful duplication of fixed costs, thereby improving the efficiency of resource allocation. Thus, from the point of view of the economics of information-sharing and organizational design, it is quite natural that collaborative R&D has become a subject of serious theoretical research.

In the second place, it is widely presumed that the success of Japanese firms in the technology-intensive industries is due at least partly to the widespread collaboration among otherwise competing Japanese firms on R&D activities. Various joint R&D projects, of which the very large-scale integrated circuit (VLSI) joint R&D project is a typical example, are not infrequently cited to be the principal vehicle that enabled Japanese computer and semiconductor manufacturers to join the leaders in the world arena. Partly inspired by the Japanese experience, other countries and regions are becoming eager to encourage collaborative R&D among domestic

* This appendix is based essentially on Suzumura and Goto (1993), which was prepared while we were participating in the Project on Competition Policy in a Global Economy organized by Professors William Comanor, Akira Goto, and Leonard Waverman. Thanks are due to Professor Akira Goto and other participants of the project.

firms. Thus, it is of crucial importance to de-mystify the mechanism of joint R&D projects in Japan and their presumed efficiency.

The purpose of this appendix is to examine the role and the limitations of R&D collaboration in accordance with the following plan. In Section 2, various types of collaborative R&D in Japan are succinctly overviewed, capitalizing on the 1982 Fair Trade Commission of Japan (JFTC) Survey. Section 3 focuses on one particular type of collaborative R&D, which is known as the technological research association and is construed to be unique to Japan in several important respects. Section 4 summarizes the theoretical properties of collaborative R&D, capitalizing partly on Part II of this monograph. In so doing, the focus of the examination will be twofold. First, we ask whether the existence of R&D spillovers can justify R&D collaborations among oligopolistic competitors universally. Second, we ask whether private incentives can sustain R&D collaborations by themselves. Section 5 examines the policy implications of collaborative R&D with special reference to industrial and competition policies. Finally, Section 6 concludes with some clarifying observations.

2. COLLABORATIVE R&D IN JAPAN: AN OVERVIEW

In 1982, the Fair Trade Commission of Japan conducted an extensive survey of collaborative R&D activities among manufacturing firms, which provides us with a succinct overview of how Japanese firms collaborate in their pursuit of R&D projects.[1] According to the 1982 JFTC survey, collaborative R&D can be classified into the following three types:

Type A: signing a collaborative research contract with other firms or research institutions, and concomitantly spending R&D funds;
Type B: establishing a joint venture with other firms to carry out R&D;
Type C: participating in a research association organized under the Law on Technological Research Associations in Mining and Manufacturing Industries.

It should be noted that collaborative R&D activities of firms with their own subsidiaries, which are defined as firms whose parent company owns at least 10% of their total stocks, are excluded from this survey. The reason for this exclusion is presumably that the survey was intended to identify only those collaborative R&D activities that were conducted among independent firms.

The firms surveyed are large and medium-sized ones chosen from four broad categories of industries:

1. Electronics and Communications;
2. Automobiles and Auto Parts;

3. Chemicals;
4. Other Materials (which consist of metals and stone, clay, and glass).

It is clear that the first two industries consist essentially of assemblers of complex final goods using a large number of parts, whereas the remaining two industries consist of manufacturers of intermediate materials using large-scale processing plants.

According to the JFTC survey, collaborative R&D activities of type A amounted to 94.2% of all collaborative R&D activities as of 1982. Firms that participate in R&D collaboration of this type usually sign a contract which specifies how each firm will share the cost of collaborative R&D, how the R&D fruits are to be divided, and so on. Most R&D collaborations among vertically related firms—for example, collaborative R&D between a ceramics manufacturer and an automobile manufacturer with the purpose of developing a ceramic engine—belonged to this type. The actual R&D activities were carried out at the respective laboratories of participating firms.

Collaborative R&D activities of type B, where participating firms initiate a joint venture for the purpose of conducting R&D, accounted for only 0.3% of all R&D collaborations as of 1982. They included Sumitomo Ocean Development, established by firms belonging to the Sumitomo group; Mitsubishi Atomic, established by firms belonging to the Mitsubishi group; and Toyota Central Research, established by firms belonging to the Toyota group. In contrast with these projects, which were established by firms belonging to the same corporate group, a joint venture to develop a jet engine was initiated by a collection of firms which were either members of different corporate groupings, or were not associated with any particular group.

Although the share of collaborative R&D belonging to the B type was small at the time of the 1982 JFTC survey, it has recently increased in number and now encompasses new arrangements and features. A notable category of recent R&D joint ventures is one in which collaborative agreements are established by firms and the Key Technology Development Centre. This institution, which is attached to the Ministry of International Trade and Industry (MITI hereafter) and the Ministry of Posts and Telecommunications (MPT hereafter), invests in high-technology start-up joint ventures, and usually owns between 50% to 70% of the total stocks of these newly created joint ventures. The rest of the stocks are owned by the participating firms.[2] The Optoelectronics Technology Research Corporation is among the joint ventures established under this scheme.

Collaborative R&D activities of type C, where participating firms form a research association for the purpose of pursuing collaborative R&D, accounted for only 5.5% of all R&D collaborations covered by the 1982 JFTC survey. However, the importance of this type of R&D collaboration should not be underestimated just because of its numerical paucity.[3] On the one hand, whenever the number of firms involved is large, the organizational form of R&D collaboration is usually of this type. On the other, while the first two types of R&D collaboration are quite common, not only in Japan but also in many other countries, the type C collaborations, which are fairly recent in origin, are quite unique to Japan. The VLSI joint R&D project is presumably the best-known example of research associations in Japan. In view of its importance, we will examine this special type of R&D collaboration in more detail in Section 3.

Table B1 summarizes the findings of the JFTC survey on R&D collaborations. Around half of all responding firms were engaged in some type of collaborative R&D. On average, each firm was conducting 8.7 R&D collaborations, and firms belonging to the materials industries were found to be more active in collaborative R&D than assembly industries.

Table B1. Collaborative research (CR) in selected industries in Japan, 1982

	No. of firms responded	No. of firms with CR	Total no. of CR contracts
Electronics and Communications	70	36	261
Automobile and Parts	34	16	120
Chemicals	71	39	389
Other Materials	62	39	363
TOTAL	237	130	1,133

Note: Other materials include Stone, Clay and Glass, Iron and Steel, and Nonferrous Metals.

Source: Rokuhara (1985).

Table B2. Number of partners in collaborative research, 1982

	No. of partners		
	1 (%)	2–4 (%)	5 and over (%)
Electronics and Communications	87.4	7.4	5.1
Automobile and Parts	88.3	10.4	1.7
Chemicals	83.9	9.5	6.7
Other Materials	85.4	7.7	6.8
TOTAL	85.8	8.5	5.8

Note: See Note to Table B1.

Source: Rokuhara (1985).

Table B2 lists the number of partners in R&D collaborations. In most cases there was a single partner, so that most R&D collaborations involved only two firms. It is also apparent from this table that firms in the materials industries had more partners in their R&D collaborations than their counterparts in the assembly industries.

According to Table B3, the majority of R&D collaborations did not involve firms that were competing in the same industry. Relatively speaking, the percentage of R&D collaborations involving competitive firms was higher in the automobile industry than anywhere else. Note, however, that this feature may be due mainly to the way in which the industries were classified. Assemblers of automobiles and auto parts manufacturers, who often collaborate on R&D, were grouped together. Likewise, other industries were classified rather broadly, so that R&D collaborations that are labelled as involving firms in the same industry do not necessarily mean that firms competing in the same specific market are involved. Indeed, according to Rokuhara (1985), the majority of R&D collaborations occurred among vertically related firms (e.g. materials and intermediate goods manufacturers) and parts and equipment manufacturers on the one hand, and users and assembly firms on the other. Nevertheless, it is still noteworthy that R&D collaborations involving firms in the same broad category of industries were not uncommon.

Table B3. Ratio of collaborative research involving firms in the same industry, 1982

	%
Electronics and Communications	13.6
Automobile and Parts	44.8
Chemicals	27.7
Other Materials	10.0
TOTAL	19.1

Note: In the Electronics and the Communications industry, 13.6% of collaborative projects involved more than two firms in the same industry.

Source: Rokuhara (1985).

The kind of research carried out as collaborative R&D projects differed rather sharply from those conducted by the industries in general. According to the 1982 JFTC survey, 13.6% of the collaborative R&D expenditures were spent on basic research, 32.1% on applied research, and 54.3% on development research. In contrast, the corresponding figures for the industries in general were 5.5% on basic research, 21.9% on applied research, and 72.6% on development research. It is conspicuous that the percentage of expenditures on development research was much lower, while that on basic research much higher, in collaborative R&D projects than in independently conducted ones. This seems to be consistent with the often asserted view that R&D collaborations are most suitable for the pre-competitive stage of basic research. Nevertheless, it deserves to be emphasized that the majority of collaborative research expenditure was spent on development research.

3. COLLABORATIVE R&D IN THE FORM OF RESEARCH ASSOCIATIONS

It was in 1961 that the Law on Technological Research Associations in Mining and Manufacturing was enacted. This formally introduced a particular type of R&D collaboration formed under the auspices of MITI. The formal name of this collaborative R&D organization is the *Technological Research Association in Mining and Manufacturing*, but it is quite commonly called the *Research Association*. It is useful to understand the background of this formal system of organizing R&D collaborations.[4]

Before the introduction of this law, most collaborative R&D projects were launched either by the signing of contracts among participating firms, or by the creation of a loose form of organization within which participating firms shared the costs, the activities, and the fruits of R&D collaboration. In the latter case, these collaborative R&D organizations were also called 'research associations'. They were established in the automobile parts, camera, and chemical industries. In the case of the first two industries, industry associations played a major role in establishing and running their respective research associations. But the last project included not only firms from the chemical industry, but also firms from the machinery and steel industries. In a project like this, where the role of the industrial association, if any, is limited, because firms from various industries are involved, a new organization was needed that could function as the core of the collaborative research activities. One obvious candidate that would have been capable of taking on such a role was government laboratories.[5] However, even if government laboratories could help private firms to organize R&D collaboration, they could not run the projects of private firms. Thus, there was a growing recognition among firms as well as MITI officials that it would be easier to create an independent entity for the purpose of managing collaborative R&D. After all, it was too costly and cumbersome for member-firms to negotiate and manage assets and workers employed for collaborative research, and to administer the patent rights generated by it. Accounting and coping with various legal issues concerning collaborative R&D placed further burdens on each firm. It was in response to these needs that the 1961 Law was proposed so as to promote collaborative R&D by allowing participating firms to create an independent organization to co-ordinate it, thereby reducing the transaction costs associated with starting and managing such efforts.

The second important event in the background of the 1961 Law is the announcement of a major trade liberalization plan in 1960. As the Japanese economy recovered from the devastation of the Second World War and began to grow rapidly, Japan was urged by her trading partners to liberalize her trade and capital transactions. In 1955, when Japan joined GATT, only 16% of imports (not in terms of value but in terms of the number of tax codes) were automatically approved and a wide class of remaining commodities were subject to stringent import restrictions such as import quotas. The 1960 plan stated that by 1963 80% of imports should be automatically approved. As a matter of fact, trade liberalization proceeded more quickly than was originally planned, and the automatic approval rate already exceeded 90% of all imports by August 1963. Although imports of manufactured goods had not increased very rapidly, the prospect of competition with foreign firms in the domestic market urged Japanese firms to upgrade their technology as quickly as possible. On its part, the Japanese government was strongly apprehensive that trade liberalization was going to take place while some of the domestic industries were still in the stage of 'infancy'. In this context, the 1961 Law can be seen as a policy measure to warn domestic industries and urge them to prepare for trade liberalization.

Although the 1961 Law used the pre-existing research association system in the UK as its prototype, there are two salient and noteworthy differences between the original UK model and the Japanese version.[6]

The first is that, while the original research associations in the UK were established on an industry-wide basis, the Japanese research associations were organized to solve certain specific technological problems. In other words, the UK research association system was designed to establish joint research institutions mostly in traditional industries, which were comprised of small firms incapable of carrying out research otherwise. In sharp contrast, member-firms of the Japanese research associations were, especially after the 1970s, mostly large firms trying to enhance their technology base, or to explore the possibility of tackling long-range, risky research subjects. In many cases, member-firms came from different industries, with a prevalence of firms from user and supplier industries.

The second salient feature of the Japanese version of research associations that is distinct from the UK prototype is that the Japanese research associations were designed to be dissolved after the completion of specific research targets. It is worth emphasizing that 'completion' in this context does not necessarily mean that the original research target is achieved. In most cases, they were dissolved when it became clear that their missions were impossible to achieve within a reasonable time frame. Whether successful or not, these R&D activities usually lasted for several years. This feature of Japanese research associations is important because participants are thereby assured that they need not commit their resources to the project for an indefinite time period. Of 114 research associations established through fiscal 1990, 45 associations were already dissolved, or in the process of being dissolved.

The actual research at research associations in Japan (JRAs hereafter) was carried out mainly in two ways. In the first alternative, a JRA established a joint research laboratory of its own, and research was carried out at this laboratory. In the second alternative, the research subject of the collaborative project was divided into several sub-themes and these sub-themes were assigned to member-firms. The member-firms carried out their assigned sub-themes in their own research laboratories and met occasionally during the course of collaboration to exchange research outcomes.

Not many JRAs had their own joint research laboratories. Indeed, only 12 out of the 114 JRAs that were established by the end of fiscal 1990 had their own joint research laboratories or some sort of joint research facilities. The case of the VLSI Research Association, whose joint research laboratory has attracted wide attention, was truly exceptional, while the vast majority of JRAs were managed by dividing their respective research theme into several sub-themes and assigning them to member-firms. Even in the rare cases where JRAs actually established joint research laboratories, most of the research was allocated to member-firms and was carried out separately at their respective laboratories.[7] Thus, it was quite exceptional for researchers from various and often competing firms to get together and conduct joint research as a team under the JRA system.

The resources of JRAs, the researchers and research funds, were procured in the following way. As far as researchers were concerned, the situation depended upon whether or not the JRA in question had its own laboratory. When a JRA did not have a laboratory of its own, the situation was simple enough. Some of the researchers of member-firms were assigned to certain research subjects which coincided with the collaborative research topic. In the case where a JRA had its own laboratory, the staff of the joint laboratory was made up of researchers on loan from member-firms; no researchers were hired directly by the JRA. In addition, some researchers were dispatched from national laboratories. In the two well-known cases where JRAs had joint laboratories of their own, i.e. VLSI RA and Optoelectronics RA, the heads of the joint laboratories were both from national research laboratories.

Research funds and operating costs of JRAs were basically shared by member-firms. However, there exists no standardized rule to specify the manner in which collaborative R&D costs were divided among member-firms. In some cases they were divided evenly, whereas in other cases they were allocated to member-firms in proportion to their sales. The portion of the research that was carried out at each member-firm's laboratory was financed independently, except for cases in which equipment was bought on the JRA's account.

Government subsidies were or were not granted, depending on how important the subjects of collaborative research were from the viewpoint of national policy objectives. When government subsidies, contingent loans, and/or national research contracts were nevertheless granted, they proved to be an important source of funds for the JRAs. However, there is no specific government subsidy programme linked with the JRA system. Instead, various existing R&D subsidy programmes were tapped, including the Basic Technologies for Future Industries Programme, the Large-Scale Project Programme, and the Programme to Promote Computer and Information Processing. In 1963 there were 9 JRAs, and they spent 21% of total government R&D subsidies. In 1983, 44 JRAs were active in research, and they spent ¥64.4 billion, which was about 1.5% of total R&D spending in Japan that year. Government subsidies amounted to ¥32.8 billion, or 51% of JRA R&D spending. The subsidies to JRAs accounted for 46.9% of total government R&D subsidies. To apply for these major subsidy programmes, often firms had to form a new JRA or join an existing one. If a firm was denied membership in a JRA financed by government subsidies, it meant in effect that the firm would be unable to procure any financial assistance from the government. Thus, JRAs were often dubbed the 'receptacles' of government subsidies. Special tax breaks, including a scheme of accelerated depreciation, were also provided to JRA member-firms and to JRAs themselves.

The number of JRAs established each year, as well as their purposes and backgrounds, differed significantly. For example, as is shown in Table B4, 12 JRAs were established by 1965. These JRAs, which came into being only four years after the 1961 law was enacted, can be classified into three groups.

JRAs in the first group were established with the focused purpose of developing a standardized testing method for their industry, thereby promoting the improvement of product quality. This group included the Optical Industry Technological Research Association, which tried to develop methods of testing lenses, and the Creeping Characteristics Testing Technological Association, which aimed at establishing a method to test the creeping characteristics of steel.

JRAs in the second group sought more explicitly to promote manufacturing technologies in industries that were widely recognized to be lagging behind their US and European counterparts. This group included JRAs in the petrochemical industry and the computer industry. Their purpose was to further develop the basic production technology behind the major products of these industries such as ethylene, acetylene, alcohol, or large-scale mainframe computers. Thus, it is fair to say that their emphasis was on the enhancement of the technological competitiveness of Japanese firms that lagged far behind their US and European rivals, rather than on the promotion of basic, pre-competitive technology.

Table B4. Number of research associations established in Japan, by industry and year

	1961–65	1966–70	1971–75	1976–80	1981–85	1986–90	Total
Chemicals and Petroleum Refinery	2		2	4	9		17
Textile	2				2	1	5
Iron and Steel	3		2		1	2	8
Nonferrous Metals and New Materials	1		1		5		7
Computer and Information	1		9	3	2	1	16
General Machinery and Precision Machinery	1		2	3	5	3	14
Transportation Machinery			2	3		1	6
Paper and Pulp					1		1
Others	2		1	2	8	9	22
TOTAL	12		19	15	33	17	96

Source: Forum of Technological Research Association in Mining and Manufacturing (1991).

JRAs in the third group were designed to help small firms in traditional industries, such as textile, packing materials, casting, and lime. This type of JRA was similar to that of the UK prototype model, and was most commonly adopted at the early stage of the development of Japanese research associations.

No new JRAs were established during 1966–70. Apparently, the experience of JRAs in the early 1960s failed to generate enthusiasm among private firms. The search for a standardized testing method could have been carried out by existing national laboratories or trade associations, and establishing JRAs just for this purpose might have been regarded as redundant effort. Besides, in full awareness of the prospective liberalization of trade and foreign direct investment in Japan, and the accompanying expectation of increased competition from foreign multinationals, private firms began to increase their R&D efforts quite rapidly through their own initiatives. Indeed, R&D expenditures by industry grew 27% annually from 1966 to 1970, and in the same period payments for imported technologies more than doubled. Throughout this period, the major concern of Japanese firms was to upgrade their technology for the sake of competitive survival in the face of foreign competition; and, apparently, the system of JRAs was not recognized as an appropriate arrangement to achieve this end.

During the 1970s, however, the number of newly established JRAs increased, despite the fact that the urgency of Japanese firms to upgrade their technological capabilities in the face of domestic and foreign competition was continuing or, if anything, even increasing. From 1970 to 1979, 30 new JRAs were established. One immediate reason for this upsurge is that various government programmes to subsidize and promote R&D had started to use JRAs as the focal organization through which to administer the programme and pool government funds. The JRA on auto safety, emission control, and energy efficiency, established in 1971, was the first JRA created to run these government programmes. This JRA received subsidies in accordance with the Subsidy Programme for Research and Development in Mining and Manufacturing Industries to Develop Important Industries. It is true that this programme was established in 1955, but it was linked to a JRA for the first time in connection with this project of the automobile industry.

Several government programmes, including the Large-Scale Industrial Technology Research and Development System (started in 1966) and the Subsidy Programme to Promote the Development of Computers (started in 1972), were initiated around 1970 against the backdrop of trade and foreign investment liberalization. Three JRAs on computer technology were established in 1972, all of which were subsidized under the Subsidy Programme to Promote the Development of Computers. A JRA on the nuclear steel-making process was established in 1973 and designated as one of the Large-Scale Projects under the 1966 system. Among the 30 JRAs established during the 1970s, 16 were linked to these government programmes, while no JRAs were linked to them in the 1960s. Apparently, the government decision to use JRAs as the organization through which to run government subsidized programmes (especially the Large-Scale Project System) was one of the major reasons for their proliferation in the 1970s.

Not only did JRAs increase in number, but the size of their budgets also increased during this period. In the 1960s, except for the two very large JRAs related to the camera and computer industries with budgets exceeding ¥1 billion, the budgets of JRAs ranged from several million yen to several hundred million yen, with the median being ¥181 million. In the 1970s, however, there were three exceptionally large JRAs, all related to computers, which had budgets of more than ¥100 billion. The rest of the JRA budgets in the 1970s ranged typically from several billion yen to several hundred billion yen, and the median was ¥13.8 billion. Clearly, the size of JRAs increased tremendously in the 1970s even in real terms.

The third noteworthy feature of the JRAs in the 1970s was the large number of them related to the computer industry. There were 12 computer-related JRAs out of 30 RAs that were established in the 1970s. The four largest JRAs in terms of their budgets in that decade were all related to the computer industry. The reason for this may be attributed to the fact that trade and foreign direct investment liberalization in the computer industry proceeded more slowly than in other industries. Trade and investment in integrated circuits were liberalized in 1974, in mainframe computers in 1975, and in information-processing in 1976. At this stage, the technology base of Japanese manufacturers was far behind that of their US counterparts, most notably IBM. The government, citing the fact that the R&D expenditure of the six Japanese manufacturers combined was less than one-fifth of that of IBM in 1970, encouraged collaborative research among Japanese computer firms and increased R&D subsidies to them. The subsidies grew from ¥6.9 billion in 1972 to ¥20.0 billion in 1973. Although the amount of subsidies was relatively small in comparison with the industry's total R&D expenditure (4.2% in 1972 and 10.3% in 1973), it is worth noting that a significant percentage of these subsidies was granted to the firms through JRAs.[8] The government even created three JRAs in order to consolidate Japanese computer manufacturers into three groups along those lines.

Thus, in the 1970s a substantial number of JRAs, such as those in the computer and jet engine industries, reflected in part the urgent need perceived by firms and ministry officials to upgrade existing technology and to close the gap *vis-à-vis* their US counterparts, and in part the active involvement of the government in implementing the collaborative R&D as a policy tool to promote the technology of domestic firms. It is true that most JRAs were related to social issues such as environmental protection, energy conservation, traffic control, and medical care. When examined more closely, however, some of these JRAs turn out to be related to the development and promotion of final products, such as auto parts and medical equipment.

In the 1980s, the number of newly established JRAs increased even further, but their essence seems to have changed. The focus of research has gradually shifted to more long-ranged risky research and to research closer to the basic end of the technological spectrum. There were JRAs that carried out this type of research in earlier years, such as the JRA on the direct reduction process of steel manufacturing using nuclear power, which was abandoned after the sharp rise in energy prices triggered by the oil crisis. More of this type of JRA emerged in the 1980s. Some of the long-ranged futuristic technologies extended across traditional industrial boundaries, which resulted in the increase of the number of JRAs classified as 'others' in Table B4.

The greater number of JRAs in chemicals and non-ferrous metals in the early 1980s reflects changing circumstances. These industries were among the 'structurally depressed' industries that were facing financial problems as a result of increased energy costs and depressed demand.[9] A significant number of JRAs in the chemical and non-ferrous metal industries were established to find a way to save these afflicted industries. The Japanese aluminium smelting industry was affected most severely by the steep rise in energy costs, as it used electricity generated by burning oil. In the 1970s the Japanese aluminium smelting industry was the second largest in the world, whereas by the mid-1980s, after the two oil crises, it had disappeared except for a single smelting plant. During this decline, the industry formed a JRA with the purpose of investigating the possibility of smelting aluminium using a blast furnace, with the help of a government laboratory and subsidy. A JRA of a similar type was formed in the petrochemical industry to find a way to reduce energy costs and diversify product lines. However, most of these attempts were unsuccessful, as the structurally depressed industries were neither enthusiastic nor willing to carry out rather far-fetched research at a time when their financial viability was in jeopardy. This type of JRA reflects the economic conditions of the early 1980s and the stance of public policy with respect to these conditions. As economic conditions recovered in the late 1980s, these JRAs seem to have disappeared.

Thus, the focus of research at JRAs was gradually moving towards more long-range risky research projects which were more akin to basic research. As the focus shifted in this direction, however, firms started to rely less on JRAs as a vehicle for carrying out their research. This type of research—research closer to the basic end, like super conductivity and the fifth-generation computer—was going to be conducted by jointly setting up a more permanent research institute, rather than through a JRA destined to be dissolved after a few years. At the same time, research closer to the commercialization end of the spectrum was tending to be carried out more and more by independent firms.

4. COLLABORATIVE R&D IN THE PRESENCE OF SPILLOVERS

Capitalizing on Chapter 6 above, Dutta and Suzumura (1993), and Kamien *et al.* (1992), I shall now summarize several relevant properties of R&D collaborations with special reference to their welfare performance *vis-à-vis* competitive R&D, and their sustainability through private incentives.[10] In so doing, I am going to shed light on the crucial role of R&D spillovers and information-sharing.

Throughout this section, the analysis is based on a model of oligopoly where firms producing homogeneous products compete in two stages. There are n firms, $2 \leqslant n < +\infty$, where n is fixed throughout this analysis.[11] In the first stage, firms decide on their cost-reducing R&D either collaboratively or separately. They compete in the second stage in terms of quantities produced.[12] The cost-reducing benefits of R&D can be diffused to other firms which do not engage in R&D of their own. In the presence of such R&D spillovers, there are two important questions to ask:

1. Is collaborative R&D always welfare-improving *vis-à-vis* competitive R&D?
2. Is collaborative R&D sustainable through private incentives in the sense that no single firm will obtain a higher payoff by unilaterally deviating from collaboration?

These questions are succinctly answered under the two alternative modes of R&D collaborations.

4.1. *Collaborative R&D without full information-sharing*

The first mode of R&D collaboration is pure R&D co-ordination without actual joint research which generates synergetic effects among member-firms. In this extreme polar case, member-firms simply co-ordinate their levels of R&D expenditure so as to maximize their joint profits, but they do not share R&D information fully with each other. This institutional mode of collaborative R&D seems to correspond to the model of R&D co-operation formulated by d'Aspremont and Jacquemin (1988), which is followed by Chapter 6 above.

Let the inverse demand function for the product of this industry be

$$p = f(Q) = a - bQ, \tag{B1}$$

where p is price of the product, $Q = \Sigma_{i=1}^{n} q_i$ is the aggregate output, q_i is the output of firm i, and $a > 0$ and $b > 0$ are constant parameters.[13] Let x_i denote the level of R&D expenditure by firm i and let $c(x_i; \mathbf{x}_{-i})$ be the unit cost of production of firm i, where $\mathbf{x}_{-i} := (x_1, \ldots, x_{i-1}, x_{i+1}, \ldots, x_n)$. The dependence of c on $\mathbf{x}_{-i}$ is meant to signify the existence of R&D spillovers. We assume that

$$c(x_i; \mathbf{x}_{-i}) = c - x_i - \beta \sum_{j \neq i} x_j, \tag{B2}$$

where $a > c > 0$, $0 \leqslant \beta \leqslant 1$, and $x_i + \beta \Sigma_{j \neq i} \mathbf{x}_j \leqslant c$. In this formulation, the R&D spillover effect is measured by the parameter β. Finally, the total cost of undertaking R&D at level x_i is assumed to be

$$\gamma(x_i) = \gamma \frac{x_i^2}{2} \quad \text{where } \gamma > 0. \tag{B3}$$

For any R&D profile $\mathbf{x} = (x_1, \ldots, x_i, \ldots, x_n)$, the profits of firm i in the second stage, when an output profile $\mathbf{q} = (q_1, \ldots, q_i, \ldots, q_n)$ prevails, are defined by

$$\pi_i(\mathbf{q}; x_i, \mathbf{x}_{-i}) = [f(Q) - c(x_i; \mathbf{x}_{-i})]q_i - \gamma(x_i) \qquad (i = 1, 2, \ldots, n). \tag{B4}$$

Consider a non-cooperative game $G(\mathbf{x})$ among n firms, given an R&D profile $\mathbf{x}$, where the payoff function of player i is (B4) and i's strategic variable is q_i. Let $\mathbf{q}^N(\mathbf{x}) = (q_1^N(\mathbf{x}), \ldots, q_i^N(\mathbf{x}), \ldots, q_n^N(\mathbf{x}))$ be the Cournot–Nash equilibrium of the game $G(\mathbf{x})$. We focus on the symmetric equilibrium, so that we assume $q_i^N(\mathbf{x}) = q_j^N(\mathbf{x}) = q^N(\mathbf{x})$, say, if $\mathbf{x}$ is symmetric.

Turning to the first stage of our two-stage competition, we define the first-stage payoff function of firm i by

$$\Pi_i(\mathbf{x}) := \pi_i(\mathbf{q}^N(\mathbf{x}); x_i, \mathbf{x}_{-i}) \qquad (i = 1, 2, \ldots, n), \tag{B5}$$

which allows us to define two types of equilibria.

First, if firms choose their R&D levels non-cooperatively, we have a non-cooperative game among n firms G^N where player i's payoff function is (B5) and i's strategic variable is x_i. The Nash equilibrium of this non-cooperative game G^N is denoted by $\mathbf{x}^N = (x_1^N, \ldots, x_i^N, \ldots, x_n^N)$. We focus on the symmetric Nash equilibrium, so that $x_i^N = x_j^N = x^N$, say, for all $i, j = 1, 2, \ldots, n$. The equilibrium path $\{\mathbf{x}^N, \mathbf{q}^N(\mathbf{x}^N)\}$ is nothing but the *subgame-perfect equilibrium* of the entire two-stage game.

Secondly, if firms choose their R&D levels co-operatively in full awareness that they will compete in the second stage, they will choose their R&D levels collaboratively so as to maximize $\Sigma_{j=1}^n \pi_j(\mathbf{x})$ with respect to $\mathbf{x}$ subject to the condition that $x_i = x_j$ $(i \neq j;\ i, j = 1, 2, \ldots, n)$. Let $\mathbf{x}^C$ be the solution to this constrained maximization problem. Then the pair $\{\mathbf{x}^C, \mathbf{q}^N(\mathbf{x}^C)\}$ is what we should expect to emerge from this institutional mode of R&D collaboration subject to competition in the product market.

The welfare performance of this manner of R&D collaboration may be neatly gauged by comparing $\{\mathbf{x}^N, \mathbf{q}^N(\mathbf{x}^N)\}$ with $\{\mathbf{x}^C, \mathbf{q}^N(\mathbf{x}^C)\}$ in terms of some well-defined welfare criterion. To stay within the standard conceptual framework as much as we can, the welfare criterion we invoke is specified by

$$W^S(\mathbf{x}) = W(\mathbf{x}, \mathbf{q}^N(\mathbf{x})), \tag{B6}$$

where

$$W(\mathbf{x}, \mathbf{q}) = \int_0^Q f(Z)\,\mathrm{d}Z - \sum_{j=1}^{n} [c(x_j, \mathbf{x}_{-j})q_j + \gamma(x_j)]. \tag{B7}$$

Our verdicts on the performance of collaborative R&D *vis-à-vis* competitive R&D from the welfare viewpoint hinge squarely on the extent of R&D spillovers. Recollect that, because of the existence of R&D spillovers, an increase in cost-reducing R&D by firm i exerts two conflicting effects on the equilibrium output of i's rival firm j $(i \neq j)$. On the one hand, firm i's R&D tends to increase firm j's output by bringing j's unit cost of production down through spillovers of cost-reducing benefits. On the other hand, firm i's

R&D tends to decrease firm j's output by strengthening i's competitive edge against j. We say that *the R&D spillovers are sufficiently large if the former effect outweighs the latter so that* $\theta(\mathbf{x}) := (\partial/\partial x_i)q_j^N(\mathbf{x}) > 0$ $(i \neq j)$ *holds*. Under our demand and cost specifications, we can easily confirm that $\theta(\mathbf{x}) > 0$ holds if and only if $2\beta - 1 > 0$.[14] We may now assert that *R&D collaboration along this line, where firms simply co-ordinate their R&D levels without full information-sharing, is welfare-improving*; that is, $W^S(\mathbf{x}^C) > W^S(\mathbf{x}^N)$ *holds if R&D spillovers are sufficiently large, but not necessarily so otherwise.*[15]

We now turn to the second fundamental question, i.e. the question of sustainability of R&D collaborations through private incentives. According to d'Aspremont and Jacquemin (1988: 1135, emphasis added), '[t]o the extent that profits are higher in the case of cooperative research than in the non-cooperative game, *private incentives, independently of any public policy such as subsidies, can be sufficient to lead to such a cooperation*'. This optimistic assertion notwithstanding, our verdict on the performance of collaborative R&D in the first mode cannot but be rather pessimistic in this arena.

At the outset, several definitions must be introduced.[16] A *coalition* is any subset T of the set of all firms $N = \{1, \ldots, i, \ldots, n\}$. For any R&D profile $\mathbf{x}$, let

$$\Pi_T(\mathbf{x}) = \sum_{i \in T} \Pi_i(\mathbf{x}), \tag{B8}$$

which is nothing but the joint profits of firms in coalition T when the R&D profile $\mathbf{x}$ prevails. A *coalition structure* is any partition of N. Any coalition structure $\mathbf{P} = \{T_1, \ldots, T_k, \ldots, T_K\}$ naturally induces a K-player non-cooperative game with the payoff function of player k being defined by $\Pi_T(\mathbf{x})$ $(k = 1, 2, \ldots, K)$. Given a coalition T and an R&D profile $\mathbf{x}$, an R&D profile $\mathbf{y}$ is said to be a *T-variant* of $\mathbf{x}$ if $x_i = y_i$ holds for all $i \in N - T$. We say that an R&D profile $\mathbf{x}$ is an *equilibrium relative to the coalition structure* $\mathbf{P}$ if, for all $T \in \mathbf{P}$, $\Pi_T(\mathbf{x}) \geqslant \Pi_T(\mathbf{y})$ holds for any $\mathbf{y}$ that is a T-variant of $\mathbf{x}$. Thus, an equilibrium relative to the coalition structure $\mathbf{P}$ is nothing but a Nash equilibrium of the game in which each coalition $T \in \mathbf{P}$ acts as a single agent.

We are now ready to clarify what we mean by the sustainability of an R&D collaboration. We say that an R&D collaboration is *sustainable through private incentives* if $\Pi_N(\mathbf{x_P}) \geqslant \Pi_{\{i\}}(\mathbf{x_Q})$ holds for all $i \in N$, where $\Pi_N(\mathbf{x_P})$ denotes the profit earned by each firm at the equilibrium relative to the coalition structure $\mathbf{P} = \{N\}$, and $\pi_{\{i\}}(\mathbf{x_Q})$ denotes the profit earned by firm i at the equilibrium relative to the coalition structure $\mathbf{Q} = \big\{\{i\}, N - \{i\}\big\}$. In this case, no single firm has an incentive to deviate unilaterally from the R&D collaboration, because doing so does not result in higher profits for the deviant firm.

Despite its rather satisfactory welfare performance *vis-à-vis* competitive R&D, it is unfortunately the case that R&D collaboration without full information-sharing is likely to be unsustainable through private incentives. Indeed, Dutta and Suzumura (1993: proposition 4) have shown that this mode of R&D collaboration is not sustainable for n sufficiently 'large'. Also, for this result to be relevant, n need not be unrealistically large. To exemplify this, assume that $a - c = 1$, $b = 2$ and $\gamma = 1$. It can be verified that $\Pi_N(\mathbf{x_P})$ and $\Pi_{\{i\}}(\mathbf{x_Q})$ are given by

$$\Pi_N(\mathbf{x_P}) = \frac{1}{2\{(n+1)^2 - [1 + \beta(n+1)]^2\}} \tag{B9}$$

and

$$\Pi_{\{i\}}(\mathbf{x_Q}) = \frac{8(n+1)^2}{D^2}\,\Delta(n;\beta), \tag{B10}$$

where

$$D := 4(\{(n+1)^2 - [n - \beta(n-1)]^2\}\{(n+1)^2 - [2 + \beta(n-3)]^2\}$$
$$- (n-1)(2\beta - 1)^2[2 + \beta(n-3)][n - \beta(n-1)])$$

and

$$\Delta(n;\beta) := \{(n+1)^2 - [n - \beta(n-1)]^2\}\{(n+1) - (1-\beta)[2 + \beta(n-3)]^2\}$$

Table B5 summarizes the values of $\Pi_N(\mathbf{x_P})$ and $\Pi_{\{i\}}(\mathbf{x_Q})$ for the fixed value of $n = 5$ and for various values of β, where $0.5 < \beta < 1$. It should be clear from this table that $n = 5$ is in fact 'large' enough for all values of β to lead to an improvement in welfare through R&D collaboration *vis-à-vis* competitive R&D. We have conducted quite extensive computer simulations to confirm that this is not an accidental result of special parameter combinations, but is indeed a reflection of robust characteristics of the model.

4.2. Collaborative R&D with full information-sharing

The second polar mode of R&D collaboration is the establishment of a research association within which not only full R&D co-ordination, but also full information-sharing takes place. As a result, strong synergetic effects among member-firms are generated to the extent that the benefits from R&D conducted by any member-firm accrue equally and fully to each and every other member. Non-member firms can still enjoy spillover benefits, but the extent thereof is less than that accruing to member-firms. This mode of R&D collaboration corresponds to the model of Research Joint Venture (RJV hereafter) formulated by Kamien *et al.* (1992).

Because of full information-sharing among member-firms, there will now be asymmetric R&D spillovers among them. To capture this important implication of full information-sharing as neatly as possible, let $V(s)$ be the R&D collaboration with full R&D co-ordination and full information-sharing, where s denotes the number of member firms. Then the cost-reducing benefits accruing to firm i should now be rewritten as $c(x_i; \mathbf{x}_{-i}) = c - \Sigma_{j=1}^{n} x_j$ if a research association $V(n)$ is formed; $c(x_i; \mathbf{x}_{-i}) = c - x_i - \beta\Sigma_{j \neq i} x_j$ if a grouping $V(n-1)$ is formed, to which firm i does not belong; $c(x_i; \mathbf{x}_{-i}) = c - \beta x_j - \Sigma_{h \neq j} x_h$ if a grouping $V(n-1)$ is formed, $i \in V(n-1)$ and $\{j\} = N - V(n-1)$; and so forth.

Table B5. Instability of R&D collaboration without information-sharing[a]

β	$\Pi_{\{1\}}(\mathbf{x}^*)$	$\Pi_N(\mathbf{x}_N)$
0.50	0.0185185	0.0185185
0.52	0.0188699	0.0188582
0.54	0.0192662	0.0192201
0.56	0.0197090	0.0196060
0.58	0.0201998	0.0200179
0.60	0.0207407	0.0204583
0.62	0.0213341	0.0209296
0.64	0.0219824	0.0214349
0.66	0.0226888	0.0219776
0.68	0.0234564	0.0225615
0.70	0.0242889	0.0231911
0.72	0.0251905	0.0238714
0.74	0.0261655	0.0246082
0.76	0.0272189	0.0254085
0.78	0.0283560	0.0262804
0.80	0.0295826	0.0272331
0.82	0.0309051	0.0282779
0.84	0.0323305	0.0294284
0.86	0.0338661	0.0307004
0.88	0.0355203	0.0321138
0.90	0.0373016	0.0336927
0.92	0.0392198	0.0354670
0.94	0.0412849	0.0374745
0.96	0.0435081	0.0397633
0.98	0.0459010	0.0423958
1.00	0.0484765	0.0454544

[a] $\Pi_{\{1\}}(\mathbf{x}^*)$ and $\Pi_N(\mathbf{x}_N)$ when $n = 5$, $\gamma = a - c = 1$, and $b = 2$.

Source: Dutta and Suzumura (1993).

The welfare verdict on this type of R&D collaboration with full R&D co-ordination and full information-sharing remains essentially the same as before. We may assert that *collaborative R&D along the second mode, where* *member-firms not only co-ordinate their R&D levels, but also fully share information, is welfare-improving, that is, $W^S(\mathbf{x}^C) > W^S(\mathbf{x}^N)$ holds, if R&D spillovers are sufficiently large, but not necessarily so otherwise.*[17]

It is with regards to the sustainability of R&D collaborations through private incentives that the role of full information-sharing becomes clear. After some seemingly simple yet complicated computations, we may verify that $\Pi_N(\mathbf{x_P})$ and $\Pi_{\{i\}}(\mathbf{x_Q})$ can be derived as follows if the condition for solvability $\beta > (n-1)/n$ is satisfied:

$$\Pi_N(\mathbf{x_P}) = \frac{1}{b(n+1)^2 - 2n^2} \tag{B11}$$

and

$$\Pi_{\{i\}}(\mathbf{x_Q}) = \frac{(n+1)^2}{E^2}\,\Gamma(n;\beta), \tag{B12}$$

where

$$E := E_1E_2 - 4(2-\beta)(2\beta-1)(n-1)^2\,[n-\beta(n-1)]\,[n\beta-(n-1)], \tag{B13}$$

$$E_1 := b(n+1)^2 - 2(n-1)^2(2-\beta)^2, \tag{B14}$$

$$E_2 := b(n+1)^2 - 2[n-\beta(n-1)]^2, \tag{B15}$$

and

$$\Gamma(n;\beta) := \{b(n+1)^2 - 2\,[n-\beta(n-1)]^2\}\,[b(n+1) - 2(n-1)^2(2-\beta)(1-\beta)]^2. \tag{B16}$$

It is clear that the crucial condition $\beta > (n-1)/n$ is quite stringent, which is particularly so for large n, as $0 < \beta < 1$ and $\lim_{n\to\infty}(n-1)/n = 1$. For β close enough to 1 and for small enough n, however, R&D collaboration with full information-sharing may be unsustainable through private incentives. Table B6 exemplifies this fact when n is as small as 5. For β realistically small or for n large enough, the condition for solvability is violated, which means that there exists no profitable deviation by a single firm. It is in this sense that R&D collaborations with full information-sharing, besides being clearly welfare improving *vis-à-vis* competitive R&D, are likely to be more stable institutional set-ups than R&D collaborations without information-sharing.

5. POLICY IMPLICATIONS OF COLLABORATIVE R&D

Our theoretical verdicts on collaborative R&D in the preceding section can be summarized in broad terms as follows.

1. Forming an R&D collaboration is welfare-improving *vis-à-vis* competitive R&D irrespective of whether information is fully shared among member-firms or not, as long as there are sufficiently large spillovers of cost-reducing R&D benefits.
2. Collaborative R&D without full information-sharing is vulnerable to the individual motivation to free-ride, particularly when the number of member-firms is large. In contrast, collaborative R&D with full sharing of information is more likely to be sustained through private incentives in that there exists no incentive for unilateral deviation as long as *either* the number of member firms is reasonably large, *or* the degree of R&D spillovers to non-member firms is reasonably low.

Table B6. Instability of collaborative R&D with information-sharing[a]

β	$\Pi_{\{1\}}(\mathbf{x}^*)$	$\Pi_N(\mathbf{x}_N)$
Case 1: $b = 2$ and $\beta > 0.97$		
0.98	0.046485	0.045455
0.99	0.047515	0.045455
1.00	0.048476	0.045455
Case 2: $b = 3$ and $\beta > 0.94$		
0.95	0.017497	0.017241
0.96	0.017898	0.017241
0.97	0.018284	0.017241
0.98	0.018656	0.017241
0.99	0.019014	0.017241
1.00	0.019357	0.017241
Case 3: $b = 4$ and $\beta > 0.94$		
0.95	0.010829	0.010638
0.96	0.011022	0.010638
0.97	0.011209	0.010638
0.98	0.011390	0.010638
0.99	0.011566	0.010638
1.00	0.011736	0.010638

[a] $\Pi_{\{1\}}(\mathbf{x}^*)$ and $\Pi_N(\mathbf{x}_N)$ when $n = 5$ and $\gamma = a - c = 1$.

Source: Dutta and Suzumura (1993).

In understanding the message of these verdicts, it is crucially important to bear in mind that our theoretical model presupposes that firms are fully aware that they are going to compete in the product market irrespective of whether they co-operate in the pre-competitive R&D stage or not. It is also important that our contrast between collaborative R&D and competitive R&D is focused on *full* co-operation versus *no* co-operation, in the sense that the R&D collaboration we have analysed is confined exclusively to collaboration among all firms in the industry.[18]

These theoretical verdicts are basically consistent with our intuitive expectations of the role of R&D collaboration. Indeed, the following casual observations have been made on the positive role played by R&D collaboration, which seem to underlie the widespread belief in the usefulness of such institutional arrangements for promoting R&D. They are all geared towards a central observation: that R&D collaboration makes it possible to achieve economies of scale in the pursuit of R&D by bringing the resources of several firms together, thereby reducing overhead costs and the time required to complete R&D projects.

1. If firms were to raise funds for R&D individually in imperfect capital markets, it would be necessary for them to reveal at least a portion of information concerning the project, which might negatively affect their incentive to embark on such R&D projects on their own. Collaborative R&D arrangements could overcome this barrier and lead to an increase in aggregate R&D.

2. R&D collaboration may improve R&D efficiency if member-firms can bring in expertise from different areas. By combining expertise in complementary areas, a collaborative R&D project may be completed with less time and/or funds.[19]

3. R&D competition emcompasses an important feature of rank order competition, since the firm that achieves the R&D goal ahead of its competitors reaps most of the fruits under the effective patent system. Given this feature of R&D competition, many firms may be simultaneously scurrying to accomplish the same R&D objective, resulting in a lower social rate of return on additional private R&D investment. Through R&D collaboration, this wasteful duplication of resources may be avoided.[20]

4. Forming an R&D collaboration may provide an efficient mechanism to cope with the appropriability problem, at least partially, thereby increasing aggregate R&D investment. Indeed, by internalizing R&D externalities, the member-firms of an R&D collaboration can appropriate the benefits of R&D as a group, although outsiders can still free-ride on R&D spillovers. The diffusion of technological information among member-firms can be easier and more assured under R&D collaboration than under a competitive R&D regime.

Against these alleged benefits of collaborative R&D arrangements, some of which were vindicated by our theoretical examination, there seem to be certain drawbacks, which are not captured by our theoretical model and require careful scrutiny.

1. R&D collaborations or technology cartels may lead to an excessively high price for technology by reducing competition in the technology

market. After all, a technology cartel is a cartel that is anti-competitive by nature.

2. R&D collaborations may lead to dynamic inefficiency by reducing R&D efforts collectively. This is a real danger which is exemplified by the case of the American automobile manufacturers' attempt to slow down R&D in pollution control technology.

3. Co-operative behaviour at the R&D level by otherwise competing firms may spill over to the product market; i.e., collusion on the R&D stage may pave the way to collusion in the stage of product market competition.

In the theoretical literature, these potentially negative effects of collaborative R&D are assumed away. Indeed, it is assumed that there is no market for technology, and collaboration in the R&D stage does not exert any long-run negative impact on R&D incentives. It is also assumed that there is no spillover of collusive behaviour from the pre-competitive R&D stage to the stage of product market competition. In order to design collaborative R&D policy effectively, however, it is clearly necessary to pay due attention to the above three negative effects along with the four positive effects enumerated earlier.

Using these pros and cons of R&D collaboration as our reference points, let us now evaluate the actual performance of JRAs. Since the formation of JRAs is generally recognized as an integral part of Japanese industrial policy, this exercise may be useful in understanding the role and efficacy of this class of industrial policy.

As we have already pointed out, with rather rare exceptions, JRAs did not have joint R&D facilities. Thus, active interaction among researchers from different member-firms was not as prevalent as it would have been in the presence of joint laboratories. Even when joint laboratories were in fact established, the majority of R&D activity took place in each member-firm's own laboratory by its own staff. This having been the case, the pooling of resources to achieve scale economies in R&D, or to bring together complementary resources, was in fact rarely realized by JRAs. At best, what happened was a limited exchange of information on the research outcomes of each member-firm. It is true that member-firms could still economize on resources through even this limited exchange of information, as each firm could concentrate on the narrowly circumscribed sub-themes and still have privileged access to the research results of the whole R&D project. As in the case of collaborative R&D on computers, however, it often happens that all member-firms are manufacturers of the same final product, so that they need all the technology required to manufacture the final product. In a case like this, to have access to the technology developed by the other member-firms is simply not enough, because it is difficult to codify, and therefore transmit, all the technological information. It is often necessary for each firm to actually have its own research experience over the entire R&D project if it is to try to manufacture the final product on the basis of the developed technology. In order to circumvent this problem, member-firms must, in addition, pursue research sub-themes that are not assigned to them. Thus, R&D collaboration of this type will not result in the elimination of effort duplication.

In addition, firms purposely tried on occasion to take part in R&D sub-themes where they were especially weak, rather than in those where they were strong, so as to gain a free ride on the expertise of other member firms. To the extent that such opportunism prevails, the advantage of organizing R&D collaboration is very limited, and advanced firms have very little, if any, incentive to join.

What about the potentially positive role of R&D collaboration in avoiding duplication arising from the so-called 'rush to invent'? In the case of JRAs, this argument is not necessarily relevant. Some JRAs were organized with the clear purpose of upgrading the basic technological capabilities of all manufacturers and, as such, have no recognizable relevance to the present question. Other JRAs were geared towards projects whose chances of success were very small but whose potential impact was quite large, requiring extensive R&D investments and/or long lead-times. It is clear that there was hardly anything resembling a 'rush to invent' in these cases. Indeed, most of these projects would not have been started had the government not encouraged the JRAs with funding. Thus, in both cases the role of JRAs as deterrents to duplicate investment was minimal, if any.

Was the JRA scheme effective in solving the perennial problem of imperfect appropriability? This potentially positive role of R&D collaboration is not very relevant either in the context of JRAs. Those JRAs that tried to raise the general technological level did not create any specific proprietary knowledge. On the other hand, JRAs engaged in projects with a small chance of success but profound potential impact if successful may seem to be relevant at first sight. However, most JRAs of this type are partly funded by the government as contract researchers, so that patents thereby generated would be owned by the government. These patents are subsequently licensed to all firms, domestic and foreign alike, under the same conditions. Thus, JRA member-firms of this type cannot reap any differential benefits from inventions through the patent system. Nevertheless, at least during the joint research process, member-firms can obtain valuable skills and know-how that can be retained internally, and possibly can provide a head-start on production.[21] Thus, although this is not a clear-cut case of the internalization of externalities by a group of firms, firms nevertheless may expect to reap profits through head-start production. This may well be one of the major reasons for firms to join this type of JRA.

The second policy context in which JRAs are of relevance is that of technology policy. The JRA scheme is a convenient policy tool through which the government can promote some specific industrial policy goals. An example of such policy objectives is the promotion of the technological capabilities of a domestic industry lagging far behind its American and European counterparts. The JRA scheme was indeed used as a tool to achieve this type of goal by channelling government funds to member-firms. Since there was a clear incentive on the part of private firms to upgrade their technological capabilities so as to compete effectively with their foreign rivals, this policy initiative was received positively by private firms. It seems fairly clear that the role of JRAs in administering and channelling government funds to industries where private incentives are largely consistent with policy objectives may be more important than any other conceivable role.

The third policy context in which JRAs are of relevance is that of competition policy. Since R&D collaboration may generate some negative effects, as identified above, it is clearly important that competition policy is carefully used so that these potentially detrimental effects are effectively kept under control.

In April 1993, JFTC published the Anti-Monopoly Act Guidelines Concerning Joint Research and Development and clarified its general view regarding collaborative R&D project arrangements and their implementation. The following salient features of these guidelines are particularly worth examining.

1. The guidelines are universally applicable to all attempts of collaborative R&D to the extent that they may exert an anti-competitive effect in the Japanese market, irrespective of whether the participants are domestic or foreign firms.

2. Collaborative R&D projects that would encounter problems under the Anti-Monopoly Law (AML hereafter) would be those that competing firms undertake collaboratively. There is very little likelihood for non-competing firms collaboratively to undertake R&D that would pose problems under the AML.

3. In passing judgement as to whether or not competition in the market is substantially restrained by a particular joint R&D project, the number of participating firms and their share of and position in the market are taken into account. If the combined market share of the participants is no more than 20%, it will usually present no problem under the AML. Even when the total share exceeds 20%, however, it does not automatically pose a problem. Judgement will be made by comprehensively taking matters such as the character of research, need for collaboration, range of objectives, and so on into consideration.

4. Even where the collaborative undertaking of R&D presents no problem of its own under the AML, arrangements accompanying the actual

implementation thereof may affect competition in the product market, thereby creating problems under the law. These problems may occur (*a*) if an arrangement unjustly restricts the business activities of a participating firm, thereby impeding fair competition, and (*b*) if competitive business activities relating to the price and quantity of a product are mutually restricted among participating firms. Thus, collaborative R&D presents a problem under the AML if there is a spillover of anti-competitive practices from the pre-competitive stage of R&D to the stage of product market competition.

5. In principle, under the AML participants of collaborative R&D can be required (*a*) to disclose information on technologies necessary for the collaborative R&D project, (*b*) to report on the progress of their share of the research work to other participants, and (*c*) to keep secret the information on technologies disclosed to them by other participants in connection with the collaborative R&D.

6. In principle, it does not present problems under the AML (*a*) to restrict, within a reasonable period, the marketing of products utilizing a technology that is the fruit of the collaborative R&D project to the participants or a designated firm or firms, if deemed necessary to maintain the secrecy of the resulting know-how; (*b*) to restrict, within a reasonable time, the source or sources of supply of raw materials or parts for products utilizing the technology resulting from the collaborative R&D project to other participants or to a designated firm or firms to maintain the secrecy of the resulting know-how and ensure the quality of products based on such technology.

7. Other restrictions, even those based on the propriety of one's collaboratively developed technology such as (*a*) restrictions on the production or on the territory where the product may be sold, or (*b*) restrictions on the production or on the volume of sales of the product, may fall under unfair trade practices.

8. To supplement these guidelines, a prior consultation system has been established, whereby any uncertainty about whether a specific collaborative R&D project presents any problems under the AML may be resolved. The party eligible to request prior consultation is the firm or the trade association intending to implement the collaborative R&D, irrespective of whether the firm or the trade association is a domestic or a foreign entity.

It is worth pointing out that the JFTC Guidelines were published for the purpose of facilitating pro-competitive collaborative R&D by making the legal constraints on such associations more transparent. Recently, and in a similar spirit, the anti-trust laws and the practical implementation of these laws, both in the United States and Europe, have become clearly more lenient on collaborative R&D associations with the passage of the National

Co-operative Research Act in 1984, and the Block Exemption from Article 85 in the EC for some categories of R&D agreements in 1985. It is against this background that the following observations on the JFTC Guidelines may have some relevance.

1. The first observation is quite a general one which pertains not only to the JFTC Guidelines on collaborative R&D, but also to competition policy in general. Although some recent studies in theoretical industrial organization have cast serious doubts on the universal validity of the common belief in the welfare-improving effects of increased competitiveness (see Chapter 6 above), the vestige thereof seems to persist strenuously in the JFTC Guidelines; that is, collaborative R&D is judged to present no problem under the AML only to the extent that it is pro-competitive. It seems to me that the crucial criterion for approving or not approving any co-ordinating device should be whether or not it leads to an improvement in social welfare; to be pro-competitive is neither necessary nor sufficient for this crucial criterion to be satisfied.[22]

2. The second observation pertains to the JFTC Guideline 2 above. According to this guideline, horizontal R&D collaboration among competing firms and vertical R&D collaboration among non-competing firms have strongly contrasting implications in that the former, but not the latter, has a non-trivial likelihood to pose problems under the AML. It seems to me, however, that R&D collaboration among vertically related firms—say, a ceramics manufacturer and an automobile manufacturer for the development of a ceramic engine—if successful may have quite serious impacts on competitiveness in both the ceramics industry and the automobile industry. In general, the overly sharp demarcation between horizontal and vertical R&D collaboration does not seem to be warranted.

3. The third observation pertains to the markets whose competitiveness is the focus of the JFTC Guidelines in judging whether or not R&D collaboration presents problems under the AML. We may easily verify that domestic markets are exclusively focused on in this context, even though the JFTC Guideline 1 above asserts that foreign firms are to be treated on a par with domestic firms. In other words, the effects of the membership of foreign firms in Japanese collaborative R&D groupings on the competitiveness of foreign markets play no role whatsoever in the JFTC judgement on the pro- or anti-competitiveness of R&D collaborations. This feature of the JFTC Guidelines may need further examination from the standpoint of international harmonization of anti-monopoly legislation and its implementation.

6. CONCLUDING REMARKS

Since the topics covered in this appendix are wide as well as diverse, no attempt will be made to summarize the entire discussion in all respects. Instead, I would like to conclude by crystallizing some broad implications of the above analysis.

1. Among the various modes of organizing collaborative R&D, the particular mode of establishing research associations is unique to Japan. Furthermore, these research associations provide a wealth of policy as well as theoretical implications. In particular, those research associations that have their own joint research laboratories, and in which active interactions among researchers from participating firms with complementary experience and capabilities take place, can generate strong synergetic effects. As a result, this mode of collaborative R&D may be welfare-improving *vis-à-vis* competitive R&D. Moreover, it has a greater likelihood of being sustainable through private incentives. The VLSI Research Association is a well-known example of this type of collaborative R&D in Japan. Although the 'success' of the VLSI should be largely attributed to a rare combination of favourable factors, it is worth noting that the institutional framework of the VLSI was consistent with what the theory of R&D collaboration most recommends, namely, collaborative R&D in which full information-sharing takes place.

2. However eye-catching the 'success' of the VLSI might have been, it should not be construed to suggest that it is primarily the organizational mode of a research association that determines welfare-improving and stable collaborative R&D. The vast majority of JRAs did not have research laboratories of their own and, more often than not, failed to generate socially beneficial synergetic effects. One of the major aims of this appendix was to de-mystify this mode of collaborative R&D in factual detail.

3. From the theoretical point of view, one of the topics on which more work is definitely called for is the mechanism through which R&D spillovers are generated. Recall that our theoretical formulation simply starts off by assuming some specific form of the spillover function. In reality, however, the key to the success of R&D collaboration is precisely the generation of synergetic effects among member-firms which, in turn, create socially beneficial R&D spillovers. The most crucial next step in theoretical research on collaborative R&D would seem to be to endogenize the spillover mechanisms.

4. From the policy-oriented point of view, more work is urgently needed in shedding light on the channels through which the government can assist socially beneficial R&D collaborations. How can a government distinguish between socially beneficial and socially detrimental R&D collaborations?

Supposing that this could be done, should government subsidize socially beneficial collaborative R&D? What should be the criteria for the provision of subsidies, if the answer to the previous question is in the affirmative? Should there be any modification to the Anti-Monopoly Law so as to make it more lenient to pro-competitive R&D collaboration? These are a small sample of questions awaiting careful scrutiny.

NOTES TO APPENDIX B

1. The findings of this survey are summarized in Rokuhara (1985).
2. Government funds used to create the Japan Technology Development Centre came from the dividends on government-owned stocks of the newly privatized Nippon Telegram and Telephone (NTT). The idea to promote R&D-oriented joint venture firms in high-technology industries is alleged to have been originated from the R&D Limited Partnership System in the USA. There are two similar programmes administered by the Ministry of Agriculture, Forestry and Fisheries in the case of biotechnology, and the Ministry of Health and Welfare in the case of pharmaceuticals.
3. Indeed, this type of R&D collaboration is most intriguing as well as theoretically challenging. See Ch. 6 above and S. 4 below for the economic theory of R&D collaborations.
4. Concerning the pre-history of research associations, see Forum of Technological Research Association in Mining and Manufacturing (1991).
5. In this context, it is interesting to note that one of the reasons why there were four research associations in the automobile parts industry prior to the 1961 Law was that the director of the Mechanical Engineering Laboratory (which was attached to the Agency of Industrial Science and Technology within MITI) was interested in the British research association system and became an early advocate of that system—so much that he and his laboratory helped organize research associations in this industry.
6. As to the research association system in the UK, interested readers may consult P. Johnson (1971/2).
7. For more details, see Hayashi *et al.* (1989).
8. See Wakasugi (1988).
9. Those who are interested in 'structurally depressed' industries are referred to Peck *et al.* (1987).
10. Recent theoretical works on R&D collaboration include d'Aspremont and Jacquemin (1988), Dutta and Suzumura (1993), Grossman and Shapiro (1986), Kamien *et al*. (1992), Katz (1986), Katz and Ordover (1990), Ordover and Willig (1985), Suzumura (1992), Suzumura and Yanagawa (1993), and Teece (1992). The following observations on the welfare performance of R&D collaborations and the stability thereof capitalize partly on Ch. 6 above and on Dutta and Suzumura (1993).

11. A model of oligopolistic competition with R&D commitment where the number of firms is endogenously determined is analysed by Okuno-Fujiwara and Suzumura (1993) and Ch. 7 above.
12. Those who are interested in knowing how some of the following results would be modified when firms compete in the product market in terms of prices rather than quantities are referred to Suzumura and Yanagawa (1993).
13. There are two interesting directions in which this simple model can be generalized. First, we can generalize the linear demand function (B1), which inevitably implies that outputs are strategic substitutes, into a nonlinear function $p = f(Q)$ with $f'(Q) < 0$, thereby allowing for richer analysis on strategic interrelatedness among firms. This direction was already explored by Suzumura (1992), who also allowed for more general nonlinear cost-reduction technology. Secondly, even within the linear demand structure, we can introduce a simple form of product differentiation if we replace (B1) by

$$p_i = a - b\left(q_i + \delta \sum_{j \neq i} q_j\right) \tag{B1*}$$

where p_i is the price of good produced by firm i and δ, where $0 \leqslant \delta \leqslant 1$, is the substitutability parameter. Products are perfect substitutes when $\delta = 1$, whereas each firm is a monopoly when $\delta = 0$. This possibility was already explored by Kamien *et al.* (1992), and Dutta and Suzumura (1993).
14. This definition is due originally to d'Aspremont and Jacquemin (1988). See also Suzumura (1992) and Ch. 6 above.
15. This result is due essentially to d'Aspremont and Jacquemin (1988) and Suzumura (1992). See also Kamien *et al.* (1992).
16. These concepts are due to Dutta and Suzumura (1993).
17. See Kamien *et al.* (1992).
18. In Dutta and Suzumura (1993), we also examined some properties of partial R&D collaboration.
19. For example, a ceramic manufacturer and an automobile manufacturer may develop a ceramic engine more effectively in a collaborative effort than if each of them pursued the same R&D project independently.
20. If various approaches are possible to solve the same research subject, and if each firm pursues a separate approach, then competitive R&D may make sense. However, this type of parallel R&D through competition is unlikely to materialize. The possibility of duplication is high, because each firm tries to keep its approach secret under the competitive R&D regime. If decision-making is centralized through collaborative R&D, it is possible to diversify the approach deliberately and pursue parallel development strategy intentionally, making the allocation of R&D resources more efficient.
21. Levin *et al.* (1987) show that such a head-start is more important than the patent itself as a means to appropriate innovation.
22. Needless to say, this poses many further questions of a serious nature. How should we identify social welfare in the first place? Should we focus exclusively on consumers' welfare, or should we also pay due attention to producers' surplus? If we opt for the latter alternative, what weight should we give to

producers' surplus *vis-à-vis* consumers' surplus as an index of consumers' welfare? Although these are formidable questions to tackle even in the single-country perspective, the difficulty and challenge multiply further when we attempt to talk about the international harmonization of competition policies.

REFERENCES

Al-Nowaihi, A., and Levine, P. L. (1985), 'The Stability of the Cournot Oligopoly Model: A Reassessment', *Journal of Economic Theory*, 35: 307–21.

Anderson, R., and Ballentine, J. C. (1976), 'The Incidence and Excess Burden of a Profit Tax under Imperfect Competition', *Public Finance*, 31: 159–76.

Aoki, M. (1983), 'Managerialism Revisited in the Light of Bargaining-Game Theory', *International Journal of Industrial Organization*, 1: 1–21.

Arrow, K. J. (1963), *Social Choice and Individual Values*, 2nd edn. New York: John Wiley (1st edn. 1951).

Atkinson, A. B., and Stiglitz, J. E. (1980), *Lectures on Public Economics*. New York: McGraw-Hill.

Bain, J. S. (1956), *Barriers to New Competition*. Cambridge, Mass.: Harvard University Press.

Baumol, W. J. (1958), 'On the Theory of Oligopoly', *Economica*, 25: 187–98.

—— (1959), *Business Behavior, Value and Growth*. New York: Macmillan.

—— (1965), 'Models of Economic Competition', in P. Langhoff (ed.), *Models, Measurement and Marketing*. Englewood Cliffs, NJ: Prentice-Hall, pp. 143–68.

—— (1982), 'Contestable Markets: An Uprising in the Theory of Industry Structure', *American Economic Review*, 72: 1–15.

—— Bailey, E. E., and Willig, R. D. (1977), 'Weak Invisible Hand Theorems on the Sustainability of Multiproduct Natural Monopoly', *American Economic Review*, 67: 350–65.

—— Panzar, J. C., and Willig, R. D. (1982), *Contestable Markets and the Theory of Industry Structure*. New York: Harcourt Brace Jovanovich.

Bergson, A. (1979), 'Consumer's and Producer's Surplus and General Equilibrium', in H. Greenfield *et al.* (eds.), *Theory for Economic Efficiency: Essays in Honor of A. P. Lerner*. Cambridge, Mass.: MIT Press, pp. 12–23.

Bernstein, J. I., and Nadiri, M. I. (1988), 'Interindustry R&D Spillovers, Rates of Return, and Production in High-Tech Industries', *American Economic Review: Papers and Proceedings*, 78: 429–34.

Bertrand, J. (1883), 'Review of *Théorie mathématique de la richesse sociale* and *Recherches sur les principes mathématiques de la théorie des richesses*', *Journal des Savants*, pp. 499–508. English translation in A. F. Daugherty (ed.), *Cournot Oligopoly: Characterization and Applications*. Cambridge University Press, 1988, ch. 2.

Besley, T. (1989), 'Commodity Taxation and Imperfect Competition: A Note on the Effects of Entry', *Journal of Public Economics*, 40: 359–67.

—— and Suzumura, K. (1992), 'Taxation and Welfare in an Oligopoly with Strategic Commitment', *International Economic Review*, 33: 413–31.

Bittlingmayer, G. (1982), 'Decreasing Average Cost and Competition: A New Look at the Addyston Pipe Case', *Journal of Law and Economics*, 25: 201–29.

Boadway, R., and Bruce, N. (1984), *Welfare Economics*. Oxford: Basil Blackwell.

Borda, J. (1990), 'Antitrust Law and Innovation Cooperation', *Journal of Economic Perspectives*, 4: 97–112.

Boyer, M., and Moreaux, M. (1983*a*), 'Consistent versus Non-consistent Conjectures in Duopoly Theory: Some Examples', *Journal of Industrial Economics*, 32: 97–110.

—— —— (1983*b*), 'Conjectures, Rationality and Duopoly Theory', *International Journal of Industrial Organization*, 1: 23–41.

Brander, J. A., and Eaton, J. (1984), 'Product Line Rivalry', *American Economic Review*, 74: 323–34.

—— and Spencer, B. J. (1983), 'Strategic Commitment with R&D: The Symmetric Case', *Bell Journal of Economics*, 14: 225–35.

—— (1985), 'Tacit Collusion, Free Entry and Welfare', *Journal of Industrial Economics*, 33: 277–94.

Bresnahan, T. F. (1981), 'Duopoly Models with Consistent Conjectures', *American Economic Review*, 71: 934–45.

Browning, M. J. (1982), 'Cooperation in a Fixed-Membership Labor-Managed Enterprise', *Journal of Comparative Economics*, 6: 235–47.

—— (1983), 'Efficient Decentralization with a Transferable Good', *Review of Economic Studies*, 50: 375–81.

Bruce, N. (1977), 'A Note on Consumer's Surplus, the Divisia Index, and the Measurement of Welfare Changes', *Econometrica*, 45: 1033–8.

Bulow J. I., Geanakoplos, J. D., and Klemperer, P. D. (1985), 'Multimarket Oligopoly: Strategic Substitutes and Complements', *Journal of Political Economy*, 93: 488–511.

Burke, T., Genn-Bash, A., and Haines, B. (1988), *Competition in Theory and Practice*. London: Croom Helm.

Caplin, A. S., and Nalebuff, B. J. (1986), 'Multi-Dimensional Product Differentiation and Price Competition', in D. J. Morris (ed.), *Strategic Behaviour and Industrial Competition*. Oxford: Clarendon Press, pp. 129–45.

Caves, R. E., and Williamson, P. J. (1985), 'What is Product Differentiation, Really?' *Journal of Industrial Economics*, 34: 113–32.

Chamberlin, E. H. (1953), 'The Product as an Economic Variable', *Quarterly Journal of Economics*, 67: 1–29.

—— (1962), *Theory of Monopolistic Competition*, 8th edn. Cambridge, Mass.: Harvard University Press (first edn. 1933).

Champsaur, P. (1975), 'Cooperation versus Competition', *Journal of Economic Theory*, 11: 394–417.

Chipman, J. S., and Moore, J. C. (1976), 'The Scope of Consumer's Surplus Arguments', in A. M. Westfield and J. S. Worley (eds.), *Evolution, Welfare, and Time in Economics*. Lexington, Mass.: D. C. North, pp. 69–123.

—— —— (1980), 'Compensating Variation, Consumer's Surplus, and Welfare', *American Economic Review*, 70: 933–49.

Clark, J. M. (1940), 'Toward a Concept of Workable Competition', *American Economic Review*, 30: 241–56.

Coate, M. B., and Kleit, A. N. (1991), 'Antitrust Policy for Declining Industries', *Journal of Institutional and Theoretical Economics*, 147: 477–98.

Corden, W. M. (1971), *The Theory of Protection*. Oxford University Press.

Dasgupta, P., and Maskin, E. (1987), 'The Simple Economics of Research Portfolios', *Economic Journal*, 97: 581–95.

—— and Stiglitz, J. (1980), 'Industrial Structure and the Nature of Innovative Activity', *Economic Journal*, 90: 266–93.

—— —— (1988), 'Potential Competition, Actual Competition, and Economic Welfare', *European Economic Review*, 32: 569–77.

d'Aspremont, C., and Jacquemin, A. (1988), 'Cooperative and Non-co-operative R&D in Duopoly with Spillovers', *American Economic Review*, 78: 1133–7.

—— Gabszewicz, J.-J., and Thisse, J. F. (1979), 'On Hotelling's "Stability in Competition" ', *Econometrica*, 47: 1145–50.

—— Jacquemin, A., Gabszewicz, J.-J., and Weymark, J. (1983), 'On the Stability of Collusive Price Leadership', *Canadian Journal of Economics*, 16: 17–25.

Debreu, G., and Scarf, H. (1963), 'A Limit Theorem on the Core of an Economy', *International Economic Review*, 4: 235–46.

Demsetz, H. (1982), *Economic, Legal, and Political Dimensions of Competition*. Amsterdam: North-Holland.

—— (1989), *Efficiency, Competition, and Policy*. Oxford: Basil Blackwell.

Dennis, K. D. (1977), *Competition in the History of Economic Thought*. New York: Arno Press.

Dick, A. R. (1992), 'The Competitive Consequences of Japan's Export Cartel Associations', *Journal of the Japanese and International Economies*, 6: 275–98.

Dixit, A. K. (1979), 'A Model of Duopoly Suggesting a Theory of Entry Barriers', *Bell Journal of Economics*, 10: 20–32.

—— (1980), 'The Role of Investment in Entry-Deterrence', *Economic Journal*, 90: 95–106.

—— (1986), 'Comparative Statics for Oligopoly', *International Economic Review*, 27: 107–22.

—— (1988), 'A General Model of R&D Competition and Policy', *Rand Journal of Economics*, 19: 317–26.

—— and Stern, N. H. (1982), 'Oligopoly and Welfare', *European Economic Review*, 19: 123–43.

—— and Stiglitz, J. E. (1977), 'Monopolistic Competition and Optimum Product Diversity', *American Economic Review*, 67: 297–308.

—— and Weller, P. A. (1979), 'The Three Consumer's Surpluses', *Economica*, 46: 125–35.

Donsimoni, M.-P. (1985), 'Stable Heterogeneous Cartels', *International Journal of Industrial Organization*, 3: 451–67.

—— Economides, N. S., and Polemarchakis, H. M. (1986), 'Stable Cartels', *International Economic Review*, 27: 317–27.

Dreze, J. H. (1976), 'Some Theory of Labor Management and Participation', *Econometrica*, 44: 1125–39.

Dutta, B., and Suzumura, K. (1993), 'On the Sustainability of Collaborative R&D through Private Incentives', Working Paper, Institute of Economic Research, Hitotsubashi University.

Eaton, J., and Grossman, G. M. (1986), 'Optimal Trade and Industrial Policy under Oligopoly', *Quarterly Journal of Economics*, 101: 383–406.

Fair Trade Commission of Japan (1977), 'A Thirty Year History of Japanese Antimonopoly Policy' (in Japanese). Tokyo: Secretariat of the Fair Trade Commission of Japan.

—— (1991), 'Report of the Study Group on the Review of the Exemption Systems from the Antimonopoly Act', *FTC/Japan Views,* 12: 55–73.

—— (1993), *The Antimonopoly Act Guidelines Concerning Joint Research and Development.* 20 April. Tokyo: Fair Trade Commission.

Farrell, J. (1986), 'How Effective is Potential Competition?' *Economics Letters,* 20: 67–70.

—— and Gallini, N. T. (1988), 'Second-Sourcing as a Commitment: Monopoly Incentives to Attract Competition', *Quarterly Journal of Economics,* 103: 673–94.

Fershtman, C. (1985), 'Managerial Incentives as a Strategic Variable in Duopolistic Environment', *International Journal of Industrial Organization,* 3: 245–53.

—— (1990), 'The Interdependence between Ownership Status and Market Structure: The Case of Privatization', *Economica,* 57: 319–28.

—— and Judd, K. J. (1987), 'Equilibrium Incentives in Oligopoly', *American Economic Review,* 77: 927–40.

Forum of Technological Research Association in Mining and Manufacturing (1991), 'Thirty Years of Technological Research Association in Mining and Manufacturing' (in Japanese). Tokyo: Nihon Kogyo Gijutsu Shinko Kyokai.

Frank, Jr, C. R. (1965), 'Entry in a Cournot Market', *Review of Economic Studies,* 32: 245–50.

—— and Quandt, R. E. (1963), 'On the Existence of Cournot Equilibrium', *International Economic Review,* 4: 92–6.

Friedman, J. W. (1977), *Oligopoly and the Theory of Games.* Amsterdam: North-Holland.

—— (1983), *Oligopoly Theory.* Cambridge University Press.

—— (1986), *Game Theory with Applications to Economics.* New York: Oxford University Press.

Fudenberg, D., and Tirole, J. (1984), 'The Fat-Cat Effect, the Puppy-Dog Ploy, and the Lean and Hungry Look', *American Economic Review: Papers and Proceedings,* 74: 361–6.

Furth, D. (1986), 'Stability and Instability in Oligopoly', *Journal of Economic Theory,* 40: 197–228.

Gabszewicz, J.-J., and Thisse, J. F. (1980), 'Entry (and Exit) in a Differentiated Industry', *Journal of Economic Theory,* 22: 327–38.

Gaertner, W., Pattanaik, P. K., and Suzumura, K. (1992), 'Individual Rights Revisited', *Economica,* 59: 161–77.

Gale, D. (1988), 'Price Setting and Competition in a Simple Duopoly Model', *Quarterly Journal of Economics,* 103: 729–39.

—— and Nikaido, H. (1965), 'The Jacobian Matrix and the Global Univalence of Mappings', *Mathematische Annalen,* 159: 81–93.

Gal-Or, E. (1985), 'Differentiated Industries without Entry Barriers', *Journal of Economic Theory,* 37: 310–39.

—— (1987), 'Strategic and Non-strategic Differentiation', *Canadian Journal of Economics,* 20: 340–56.

Gärdenfors, P. (1980), 'Rights, Games and Social Choice', *Nous,* 15: 341–56.

Gibbard, A. (1974), 'A Pareto-Consistent Libertarian Claim', *Journal of Economic Theory*, 7: 388–410.

Grossman, G., and Shapiro, C. (1986), 'Research Joint Ventures: An Antitrust Analysis', *Journal of Law, Economics, and Organization*, 2: 315–37.

—— —— (1987), 'Dynamic R&D Competition', *Economic Journal*, 97: 372–87.

Grossman, S. J. (1981), 'Nash Equilibrium and the Industrial Organization of Markets with Large Fixed Costs', *Econometrica*, 49: 1149–72.

Hahn, F. H. (1962), 'The Stability of the Cournot Market', *Review of Economic Studies*, 29: 329–31.

Haley, J. O. (1986), 'Administrative Guidance versus Formal Regulations: Resolving the Paradox of Industrial Policy', in G. R. Saxonhouse and K. Yamamura (eds.), *Law and Trade Issues of the Japanese Economy: American and Japanese Perspectives*. Seattle: University of Washington Press, pp. 107–28.

Harberger, A. C. (1962), 'The Incidence of the Corporation Income Tax', *Journal of Political Economy*, 70: 215–40.

—— (1971), 'Three Basic Postulates for Applied Welfare Economics: An Interpretive Essay', *Journal of Economic Literature*, 9: 785–97.

Harris, R. (1981), 'Price and Entry Regulations with Large Fixed Costs', *Quarterly Journal of Economics*, 96: 643–55.

Hartwick, J. (1984), 'Optimal R&D Levels when Firm *j* Benefits from Firm *i*'s Inventive Activity', *Economics Letters*, 16: 165–70.

Hayashi, I., Hirano, M., and Katayama, Y. (1989), 'Collaborative Semiconductor Research in Japan', *Proceedings of the IEEE*, 77: 1430–41.

Hayek, F. A. (1948), *Individualism and Economic Order*. University of Chicago Press.

—— (1978), 'Competition as a Discovery Procedure', in *New Studies in Philosophy, Politics, Economics and the History of Ideas*. London: Routledge & Kegan Paul, pp. 179–90.

Henderson, A. (1940–1), 'Consumer's Surplus and the Compensating Variation', *Review of Economic Studies*, 8: 117–21.

Hey, J. D. (1981), 'A Unified Theory of the Behaviour of Profit-Maximising, Labour Managed and Joint-Stock Firms Operating under Certainty', *Economic Journal*, 91: 364–74.

Hicks, J. R. (1943), 'The Four Consumer's Surpluses', *Review of Economic Studies*, 11: 31–41.

—— (1945–6), 'The Generalized Theory of Consumer's Surplus', *Review of Economic Studies*, 13: 68–74.

—— (1956), *A Revision of Demand Theory*. Oxford University Press.

—— (1981), *Wealth and Welfare: Collected Essays on Economic Theory*, I. Oxford: Basil Blackwell.

Hills, M., and Waterson, M. (1983), 'Labor-Managed Cournot Oligopoly and Industry Output', *Journal of Comparative Economics*, 7: 43–51.

Hindley, B. (1984), 'Empty Economics in the Case for Industrial Policy', *World Economy*, 7: 277–94.

Hotelling, H. (1929), 'Stability in Competition', *Economic Journal*, 39: 41–57.

Howrey, E. P., and Quandt, R. E. (1968), 'The Dynamics of the Number of Firms in an Industry', *Review of Economic Studies*, 35: 349–53.

Ireland, N. J. (1983), 'Monopolistic Competition and a Firm's Product Range', *International Journal of Industrial Organization*, 1: 239–52.

—— (1987), *Product Differentiation and Non-Price Competition*. Oxford: Basil Blackwell.

—— and Law, P. J. (1981), 'Efficiency, Incentives, and Individual Labor Supply in the Labor-Managed Firm', *Journal of Comparative Economics*, 5: 1–23.

Itoh, M. (1983), 'Monopoly, Product Differentiation and Economic Welfare', *Journal of Economic Theory*, 31: 88–104.

—— Kiyono, K., Okuno-Fujiwara, M., and Suzumura, K. (1991), *Economic Analysis of Industrial Policy*. New York: Academic Press.

Iyori, H. (1986), 'Antitrust and Industrial Policy in Japan: Competition and Cooperation', in G. R. Saxonhouse and K. Yamamura (eds.), *Law and Trade Issues of the Japanese Economy: American and Japanese Perspectives*. Seattle: University of Washington Press, pp. 56–82.

Jacquemin, A. (1988), 'Cooperative Agreements in R&D and European Antitrust Policy', *European Economic Review*, 32: 551–60.

—— Nambu, T., and Dewez, I. (1981), 'A Dynamic Analysis of Export Cartels: The Japanese Case', *Economic Journal*, 91: 685–96.

Johnson, C. (1982), *MITI and the Japanese Miracle: The Growth of Industrial Policy, 1925–1975*. Stanford, Calif.: Stanford University Press.

Johnson, P. (1971/2), 'The Role of Co-operative Research in British Industry', *Research Policy*, 1: 332–50.

Jones, L. E. (1987), 'Optimum Product Diversity and the Incentives for Entry in Natural Oligopolies', *Quarterly Journal of Economics*, 102: 595–613.

Jones, R. W. (1965), 'The Structure of Simple General Equilibrium Models', *Journal of Political Economy*, 73: 557–72.

—— (1968), 'Variable Returns to Scale in General Equilibrium Theory', *International Economic Review*, 9: 261–72.

Jorde, T., and Teece, D. (1990), 'Innovation and Cooperation: Implications for Competition and Antitrust', *Journal of Economic Perspectives*, 4: 75–96.

Just, R. E., Hueth, D. L., and Schmitz, A. (1982), *Applied Welfare Economics and Public Policy*. Englewood Cliffs, NJ: Prentice-Hall.

Kamien, M. I., and Schwartz, N. L. (1982), *Market Structure and Innovation*. Cambridge University Press.

—— —— (1983), 'Conjectural Variations', *Canadian Journal of Economics*, 16: 191–211.

—— Muller, E., and Zang, I. (1992), 'Research Joint Ventures and R&D Cartels', *American Economic Review*, 82: 1293–1306.

—— and Zang, I. (1993), 'Competing Research Joint Ventures', *Journal of Economics & Management Strategy*, 2: 23–40.

Katz, M. L. (1986), 'An Analysis of Cooperative Research and Development', *Rand Journal of Economics*, 17: 527–43.

—— and Ordover, J. (1990), 'R&D Cooperation and Competition', *Brookings Papers on Economic Activity: Microeconomics*, 137–203.

—— and Rosen, H. S. (1985), 'Tax Analysis in an Oligopoly Model', *Public Finance Quarterly*, 13: 3–19.

Kay, J. A., and Thompson, D. J. (1986), 'Privatisation: A Policy in Search of a Rationale', *Economic Journal*, 96: 18–32.

Kemp, M. C. (1955*a*), 'The Efficiency of Competition as an Allocator of Resources. I: External Economies of Production', *Canadian Journal of Economics and Political Science*, 21: 30–42.

—— (1955*b*), 'The Efficiency of Competition as an Allocator of Resources. II: External Economies of Consumption', *Canadian Journal of Economics and Political Science*, 21: 217–27.

Kirzner, I. M. (1984), 'Prices, the Communication of Knowledge, and the Discovery Process', in K. R. Leube and A. H. Zlabinger (eds.), *The Political Economy of Freedom: Essays in Honor of F. A. Hayek*. Munich: Philosophia Verlag, pp. 193–206.

—— (1989), *Discovery, Capitalism, and Distributive Justice*. Oxford: Basil Blackwell.

Knight, F. H. (1935), 'The Ethics of Competition', in *The Ethics of Competition, and Other Essays*, London: George Allen & Unwin, pp. 41–75.

—— (1946), 'New Frontiers in Economic Thought', *American Economic Review*, 36: 93–111.

Koenker, R. W., and Perry, M. K. (1981), 'Product Differentiation, Monopolistic Competition and Public Policy', *Bell Journal of Economics*, 12: 217–31.

Kokoski, M. F., and Smith, V. K. (1987), 'A General-Equilibrium Analysis of Partial-Equilibrium Welfare Measures: The Case of Climate Change', *American Economic Review*, 77: 331–41.

Kolstad, C. D., and Mathiesen, L. (1987), 'Necessary and Sufficient Conditions for Uniqueness of a Cournot Equilibrium', *Review of Economic Studies*, 54: 681–90.

Komiya, R. (1975), 'Planning in Japan', in M. Bornstein (ed.), *Economic Planning: East and West*. Cambridge, Mass.: Ballinger, pp. 189–227.

—— (1987), 'Japanese Firms, Chinese Firms: Problems for Economic Reforms in China', *Journal of the Japanese and International Economies*, 1: 31–61 and 229–47.

—— Okuno, M., and Suzumura, K. (eds.) (1988), *Industrial Policy of Japan*. New York: Academic Press.

Konishi, H. (1990), 'Final and Intermediate Goods Taxation in an Oligopolistic Economy with Free Entry', *Journal of Public Economics*, 42: 371–86.

—— Okuno-Fujiwara, M., and Suzumura, K. (1990), 'Oligopolistic Competition and Economic Welfare: A General Equilibrium Analysis of Entry Regulation and Tax-Subsidy Schemes', *Journal of Public Economics*, 42: 67–88.

Kreps, D. M., and Scheinkman, J. A. (1983), 'Quantity Precommitment and Bertrand Competition Yield Cournot Outcomes', *Bell Journal of Economics*, 14: 326–37. Reprinted in A. F. Daugherty (ed.), *Cournot Oligopoly: Characterization and Applications*, Cambridge University Press, 1988, ch. 9.

Kusano, A. (1992), 'Large-Scale Retail Store Law: The Structure of Economic Regulation' (in Japanese). Tokyo: Nihon-Keizai-Shinbun-sha.

Laffont, J.-J., and Moreaux, M. (1983), 'The Non-Existence of a Free Entry Cournot Equilibrium in Labor-Managed Economies', *Econometrica*, 51: 455–62.

—— and Tirole, J. (1986), 'Using Cost Observation to Regulate Firms', *Journal of Political Economy*, 94: 614–41.

Lahiri, S. and Ono, Y. (1988), 'Helping Minor Firms Reduces Welfare', *Economic Journal*, 98: 1199–202.

Laitner, J. (1980), ' "Rational" Duopoly Equilibria', *Quarterly Journal of Economics*, 95: 641–62.

Lancaster, K. (1979), *Variety, Equity and Efficiency*. New York: Columbia University Press.

Leland, H. E. (1977), 'Quality Choices and Competition', *American Economic Review*, 67: 127–37.

Levin, R. C., and Reiss, P. C. (1988), 'Cost-Reducing and Demand-Creating R&D with Spillovers', *Rand Journal of Economics*, 19: 538–56.

—— Klevorick, A. K., Nelson, R. R., and Winter, S. G. (1987), 'Appropriating the Returns from Industrial R&D', *Brookings Papers on Economic Activity*, 783–820.

Levy, J. D., and Samuels, R. J. (1991), 'Institutions and Innovation: Research Collaborations as Technology Strategy in Japan', in L. K. Mytelka (ed.), *Strategic Partnership*. London: Pinter, pp. 120–48.

MacLure, C. E. (1975), 'General Equilibrium Incidence Analysis: The Harberger Model after Ten Years', *Journal of Public Economics*, 4: 125–61.

Mankiw, N. G., and Whinston, M. D. (1986), 'Free Entry and Social Inefficiency', *Rand Journal of Economics*, 17: 48–58.

Markusen, J. R. (1976), 'Profit-Sharing, Labour Effort and Optimal Distributive Shares', *Economica*, 43: 405–10.

Marshall, A. (1890), 'Some Aspect of Competition', in R. L. Smyth (ed.), *Essays in the Economics of Socialism and Capitalism*. London: Gerald Duckworth, pp. 90–122.

Masson, R. T., and Shaanan, J. (1984), 'Social Costs of Oligopoly and the Value of Competition', *Economic Journal*, 94: 520–35.

Matsui, A. (1989), 'Consumer-Benefited Cartels under Strategic Capital Investment Competition', *International Journal of Industrial Organization*, 7: 451–70.

Matsushita, M. (1979), 'Export Control and Export Cartels in Japan', *Harvard International Law Journal*, 20: 103–25.

—— with Davis, J. D. (1990), *Introduction to Japanese Antimonopoly Law*. Tokyo: Yuhikaku.

Matthews, R. C. O. (1981), 'Morality, Competition and Efficiency', *Manchester School of Economic and Social Studies*, 49: 289–309.

—— (1985), 'Competition in Economy and Polity', in R. C. O. Matthews (ed.), *Economy and Democracy*. London: Macmillan, pp. 1–19.

McKenzie, G. W. (1983), *Measuring Economic Welfare: New Methods*. New York: Cambridge University Press.

McManus, M. (1962), 'Numbers and Size in Cournot Oligopoly', *Yorkshire Bulletin of Social and Economic Research*, 14: 14–22.

—— (1964), 'Equilibrium, Numbers and Size in Cournot Oligopoly', *Yorkshire Bulletin of Social and Economic Research*, 16: 68–75.

McNulty, P. J. (1967), 'A Note on the History of Perfect Competition', *Journal of Political Economy*, 75: 395–9.

—— (1968), 'Economic Theory and the Meaning of Competition', *Quarterly Journal of Economics*, 82: 639–56.

Meade, J. E. (1972), 'The Theory of Labour-Managed Firms and of Profit Sharing', *Economic Journal*, 82: 402–28.

—— (1974), 'Labour-Managed Firms in Conditions of Imperfect Competition', *Economic Journal*, 84: 817–24.

—— (1986), *Alternative Systems of Business Organization and of Workers' Remuneration*. London: Allen & Unwin.

Merz, J. (1986), 'The Optoelectronics Joint Research Laboratory: Light Shed on Cooperative Research in Japan', *Scientific Bulletin*, 11: 1–30.

Mieszkowski, P. M. (1969), 'Tax Incidence Theory: The Effects of Taxes on the Distribution of Income', *Journal of Economic Literature*, 7: 1103–24.

Moore, H. L. (1906), 'Paradoxes of Competition', *Quarterly Journal of Economics*, 20: 211–30.

Mussa, M., and Rosen, S. (1978), 'Monopoly and Product Quality', *Journal of Economic Theory*, 18: 301–17.

Myers, M. G., and Weintraub, E. R. (1971), 'A Dynamic Model of Firm Entry', *Review of Economic Studies*, 38: 127–9.

Nalebuff, B. J., and Stiglitz, J. E. (1983), 'Information, Competition, and Markets', *American Economic Review: Papers and Proceedings*, 73: 278–83.

Neary, H. M. (1984), 'Labor-Managed Cournot Oligopoly and Industry Output: A Comment', *Journal of Comparative Economics*, 8: 322–7.

Nikaido, H. (1968), *Convex Structures and Economic Theory*. New York: Academic Press.

Nishimura, K., and Friedman, J. (1981), 'Existence of Nash Equilibria in *n*-Person Games without Quasi-Concavity', *International Economic Review*, 22: 637–48.

Novshek, W. (1980), 'Equilibrium in Simple Spatial (or Differentiated Product) Models', *Journal of Economic Theory*, 22: 313–26.

—— (1984), 'Finding All *n*-Firm Cournot Equilibria', *International Economic Review*, 25: 61–70.

—— (1985), 'On the Existence of Cournot Equilibrium', *Review of Economic Studies*, 52: 85–98. Reprinted in A. F. Daugherty (ed.), *Cournot Oligopoly: Characterization and Applications*, Cambridge University Press, 1988, ch. 4.

Nozick, R. (1974), *Anarchy, State and Utopia*. Oxford: Basil Blackwell.

Okimoto, D. I. (1989), *Between MITI and the Market*. Stanford, Calif.: Stanford University Press.

—— Sugano, T., and Weinstein, F. B. (eds.) (1984), *Competitive Edge: The Semiconductor Industry in the US and Japan*. Stanford, Calif.: Stanford University Press.

Okuguchi, K. (1973), 'Quasi-Competitiveness and Cournot Oligopoly', *Review of Economic Studies*, 40: 145–8.

—— (1976), *Expectations and Stability in Oligopoly Models*. Berlin: Springer-Verlag.

—— (1986), 'Labor-Managed Bertrand and Cournot Oligopolies', *Journal of Economics*, 46: 115–22.

—— and Suzumura, K. (1971), 'Uniqueness of the Cournot Oligopoly Equilibrium', *Economic Studies Quarterly*, 22: 81–3.

Okuno, M., and Suzumura, K. (1986), 'The Economic Analysis of Industrial Policy: A Conceptual Framework through the Japanese Experience', in H. Mutoh,

S. Sekiguchi, K. Suzumura, and I. Yamazawa (eds.), *Industrial Policies for Pacific Economic Growth*, Sydney: Allen & Unwin, pp. 23–41.

Okuno-Fujiwara, M., and Suzumura, K. (1993), 'Symmetric Cournot Oligopoly and Economic Welfare: A Synthesis', *Economic Theory*, 3: 43–59.

—— —— and Nambu, T. (eds.) (1993). *Telecommunications in Japan: The Economics of Competition and Regulation* (in Japanese). Tokyo: Nihon-Keizai-Shinbun-sha.

Ordover, J., and Baumol, W. (1988), 'Antitrust Policy and High-Technology Industries', *Oxford Review of Economic Policy*, 4: 13–34.

—— and Willig, R. D. (1985), 'Antitrust for High-Technology Industries: Assessing Research Joint Ventures and Mergers', *Journal of Law and Economics*, 28: 311–33.

Panzar, J. C., and Willig, R. D. (1977), 'Free Entry and the Sustainability of Natural Monopoly', *Bell Journal of Economics*, 8: 1–22.

—— (1981), 'Economics of Scope', *American Economic Review: Papers and Proceedings*, 71: 268–72.

Pattanaik, P. K. (1971), *Voting and Collective Choice*. Cambridge University Press.

Peck, M. J. (1986), 'Joint R&D: The Case of Microelectronics and Computer Technology Corporation', *Research Policy*, 15: 219–31.

—— Levin, R. C., and Goto, A. (1987), 'Picking Losers: Public Policy toward Declining Industries in Japan', *Journal of Japanese Studies*, 13: 79–123.

Perry, M. K. (1984), 'Scale Economies, Imperfect Competition, and Public Policy', *Journal of Industrial Economics*, 32: 313–33.

—— and Porter, R. H. (1985), 'Oligopoly and the Incentive for Horizontal Merger', *American Economic Review*, 75: 219–27.

Portes, R. D. (1968), 'Input Demand Functions for the Profit-Constrained Sales-Maximizer: Income Effects in the Theory of the Firm', *Economica*, 35: 233–48.

Reynolds, L. G. (1940), 'Cutthroat Competition', *American Economic Review*, 30: 736–47.

Roberts, J., and Sonnenschein, H. (1976), 'On the Existence of Cournot Equilibrium without Concave Profit Functions', *Journal of Economic Theory*, 13: 112–17.

—— —— (1977), 'On the Existence of Cournot Equilibrium without Concave Profit Functions: Acknowledgement', *Journal of Economic Theory*, 16: 521.

Robinson, J. (1954), 'The Impossibility of Competition', in E. H. Chamberlin (ed.), *Monopoly and Competition and their Regulation*. London: Macmillan, pp. 245–54.

—— (1969), *The Economics of Imperfect Competition*, 2nd edn. London: Macmillan, (first edn. 1933).

Rokuhara, A. (ed.) (1985), 'R&D and Antimonopoly Policy' (in Japanese). Tokyo: Gyosei.

Rosenthal, R. W. (1980), 'A Model in which an Increase in the Number of Sellers Leads to a Higher Price', *Econometrica*, 48: 1575–9.

Rothschild, K. (1954), 'The Wastes of Competition', in E. H. Chamberlin (ed.), *Monopoly and Competition and their Regulation*. London: Macmillan, pp. 301–14.

Ruff, L. E. (1969), 'Research and Technological Progress in a Cournot Economy', *Journal of Economic Theory*, 1: 397–415.

Ruffin, R. J. (1971), 'Cournot Oligopoly and Competitive Behaviour', *Review of Economic Studies*, 38: 493–502.

Sah, R. K., and Stiglitz, J. E. (1987), 'The Invariance of Market Innovation to the Number of Firms', *Rand Journal of Economics*, 18: 98–108.

Salant, S. W., Switzer, S., and Reynolds, R. J. (1983), 'Losses from Horizontal Merger: The Effects of an Exogenous Change in Industry Structure on Cournot–Nash Equilibrium', *Quarterly Journal of Economics*, 98: 185–99. Reprinted in A. F. Daugherty (ed.), *Cournot Oligopoly: Characterization and Applications*, Cambridge University Press, 1988, ch. 16.

Salop, S. C. (1979), 'Monopolistic Competition with Outside Goods', *Bell Journal of Economics*, 10: 141–56.

Samuelson, P. A. (1947), *Foundations of Economic Analysis*. Cambridge, Mass.: Harvard University Press (enlarged ed. 1983).

—— (1960), 'An Extension of the Le-Chatelier Principle', *Econometrica*, 28: 368–79.

—— (1967), 'The Monopolistic Competition Revolution', in R. E. Kuenne (ed.), *Monopolistic Competition Theory: Studies in Impact*. New York: John Wiley, pp. 105–38.

—— (1990), 'When Deregulation Makes Things Worse Before They Get Better', in C. Moir and J. Dawson (eds.), *Competition and Markets: Essays in Honour of Margaret Hall*. London: Macmillan, pp. 11–20.

Scherer, F. M., and Ross, D. (1990), *Industrial Market Structure and Economic Performance*, 3rd edn. Boston: Houghton Mifflin.

Schmalensee, R. (1976), 'Is More Competition Necessarily Good?' *Industrial Organization Review*, 4: 120–1.

—— (1983), 'Book review: *Barriers to Entry* by C. C. von Weizsäcker', *Journal of Economic Literature*, 21: 562–4.

Seade, J. (1978), 'Consumer's Surplus and Linearity of Engel Curves', *Economic Journal*, 88: 511–23.

—— (1980*a*), 'The Stability of Cournot Revisited', *Journal of Economic Theory*, 23: 15–27.

—— (1980*b*), 'On the Effects of Entry', *Econometrica*, 48: 479–89.

—— (1985), 'Profitable Cost Increases and the Shifting of Taxation: Equilibrium Responses of Markets in Oligopoly', Warwick Economic Research Paper, University of Warwick.

Selten, R. (1975), 'Re-examination of the Perfectness Concept for Equilibrium Points in Extensive Games', *International Journal of Game Theory*, 4: 25–55.

—— (1988), *Models of Strategic Rationality*. Dordrecht: Kluwer.

Sen, A. K. (1966), 'Labour Allocation in a Cooperative Enterprise', *Review of Economic Studies*, 33: 361–71.

—— (1970*a*), *Collective Choice and Social Welfare*. San Francisco: Holden-Day.

—— (1970*b*), 'The Impossibility of a Paretian Liberal', *Journal of Political Economy*, 78: 152–7.

—— (1976), 'Liberty, Unanimity and Rights', *Economica*, 43: 217–45.

—— (1983), 'Liberty and Social Choice', *Journal of Philosophy*, 80: 5–28.

—— (1992), 'Minimal Liberty', *Economica*, 59: 139–59.

Shaked, A., and Sutton, J. (1982), 'Relaxing Price Competition through Product Differentiation', *Review of Economic Studies*, 49: 3–13.

—— —— (1983), 'Natural Oligopolies', *Econometrica*, 51: 1469–83.

Sharkey, W. W. (1982), *The Theory of Natural Monopoly*. Cambridge University Press.

Shepherd, W. (1984), ' "Contestability" vs Competition', *American Economic Review*, 74: 572–87.

Sheshinski, E. (1976), 'Price, Quality and Quantity Regulation in Monopoly Situation', *Economica*, 43: 127–37.

Shleifer, A. (1985), 'A Theory of Yardstick Competition', *Rand Journal of Economics*, 16: 319–27.

Sigurdson, J. (1986), *Industry and State Partnership in Japan: The Very Large-Scale Integrated Circuit (VLSI) Project*. Lund: Research Policy Institute.

Silberberg, E. (1972), 'Duality and the Many Consumer's Surpluses', *American Economic Review*, 62: 942–52.

Simon, L. S. (1984), 'Bertrand, the Cournot Paradigm and the Theory of Perfect Competition', *Review of Economic Studies*, 51: 209–30.

Singh, N., and Vives, X. (1984), 'Price and Quantity Competition in a Differentiated Duopoly', *Rand Journal of Economics*, 15: 546–54.

Smart, D. R. (1974), *Fixed Point Theorems*. Cambridge University Press.

Smith, A. (1904), *An Inquiry into the Nature and Causes of the Wealth of Nations*, ed. Edwin Cannan. London: Methuen (first published 1776).

Spence, A. M. (1975), 'Monopoly, Quality, and Regulation', *Bell Journal of Economics*, 6: 417–29.

—— (1976*a*), 'Product Differentiation and Welfare', *American Economic Review: Papers and Proceedings*, 66: 407–14.

—— (1976*b*), 'Product Selection, Fixed Costs, and Monopolistic Competition', *Review of Economic Studies*, 43: 217–35.

—— (1977), 'Entry, Capacity, Investment, and Oligopolistic Pricing', *Bell Journal of Economics*, 8: 534–44.

—— (1981), 'The Learning Curve and Competition', *Bell Journal of Economics*, 12: 49–70.

—— (1983), 'Contestable Market and the Theory of Industry Structure: A Review Article', *Journal of Economic Literature*, 21: 981–90.

—— (1984), 'Cost Reduction, Competition, and Industry Performance', *Econometrica*, 52: 101–21.

Spencer, B. J., and Brander, J. A. (1983), 'International R&D Rivalry and Industrial Strategy', *Review of Economic Studies*, 50: 707–22.

Spulber, D. F. (1989), *Regulation and Markets*. Cambridge, Mass.: MIT Press.

Stern, N. H. (1987), 'The Effects of Taxation, Price Control and Government Contracts in Oligopoly and Monopolistic Competition', *Journal of Public Economics*, 32: 133–58.

Stigler, G. J. (1957), 'Perfect Competition, Historically Contemplated', *Journal of Political Economy*, 65: 1–17.

—— (1972), 'Economic Competition and Political Competition', *Public Choice*, 13: 91–106.

—— (1982), 'The Ethics of Competition: The Friendly Economists', in G. J. Stigler, *The Economist as Preacher and Other Essays*. University of Chicago Press, pp. 14–54.

Stiglitz, J. E. (1981), 'Potential Competition May Reduce Welfare', *American Economic Review: Papers and Proceedings*, 71: 184–9.

—— (1987), 'Competition and the Number of Firms in a Market: Are Duopolies More Competitive than Atomistic Markets?' *Journal of Political Economy*, 95: 1041–61.

Sugden, R. (1985), 'Liberty, Preference, and Choice', *Economics and Philosophy*, 1: 213–29.

Suzumura, K. (1971), 'The Pure Theory of Trade and Growth', unpublished dissertation submitted to Hitotsubashi University in partial fulfilment of the doctoral course.

—— (1978), 'On the Consistency of Libertarian Claims', *Review of Economic Studies*, 45: 329–42; 'A Correction', *Review of Economic Studies*, 46: 743.

—— (1980), 'Liberal Paradox and the Voluntary Exchange of Rights Exercising', *Journal of Economic Theory*, 22: 409–22.

—— (1983), *Rational Choice, Collective Decisions, and Social Welfare*. New York: Cambridge University Press.

—— (1988), 'Equity, Efficiency and Incentives: Behavioural Theory of Distributive Justice Revisited', public lecture delivered at the Murphy Institute of Political Economy, Tulane University.

—— (1990*a*), 'Alternative Approaches to Libertarian Rights in the Theory of Social Choice', in K. J. Arrow (ed.), *Markets and Welfare*, vol. I of *Issues in Contemporary Economics*. London: Macmillan, pp. 215–42.

—— (1990*b*), 'Competition and Regulation in the Telecommunications Industry: Present State and Future Tasks of Telecommunications Reform 7 (in Japanese), Discussion Paper no. 224, Institute of Economic Research, Hitotsubashi University.

—— (1990*c*), 'The Economic Consequences of Entry Regulation in the Japanese Distribution Industry: Or, What's Wrong with the Large-Scale Retail Store Law?' (in Japanese), Discussion Paper no. 230, Institute of Economic Research, Hitotsubashi University.

—— (1991), 'Alternative Firm Objectives and the Welfare Effects of Entry', *Osaka Economic Papers*, 40: 194–8.

—— (1992), 'Cooperative and Non-Cooperative R&D in an Oligopoly with Spillovers', *American Economic Review*, 82: 1307–20.

—— (1993*a*), 'Oligopolistic Competition and Economic Welfare: The Effects of Ownership Structure', Working Paper, Institute of Economic Research, Hitotsubashi University.

—— (1993*b*), 'Exemption Systems from the Antimonopoly Law and Other Anti-Competitive Measures in Japan: Overview and Evaluation', Working Paper, Institute of Economic Research, Hitotsubashi University.

—— (1994*a*), 'Oligopolistic Competition and Economic Welfare: The Effects of Ownership Structures', paper presented at the Technical Symposium in New York University; forthcoming in the Conference Volume edited by R. Sato, H. Hori, and R. Ramachandran.

—— (1994*b*), 'Hal Varian on Entry and Cost Reduction', forthcoming in *Japan and the World Economy*.

—— and Goto, A. (1993), 'Collaborative Research and Development: Economic Analysis in the Light of Japanese Experience', paper presented at the Workshop on Competition Policy in a Global Economy, University of California at Santa Barbara.

Suzumura, K., and Ishikawa, J. (1993), 'Voluntary Trade Restraints and Economic Welfare', Working Paper, Institute of Economic Research, Hitotsubashi University.

—— and Kiyono, K. (1987), 'Entry Barriers and Economic Welfare', *Review of Economic Studies*, 54: 157–67.

—— and Okuno-Fujiwara, M. (1987), 'Industrial Policy in Japan: Overview and Evaluation', in R. Sato and P. Wachtel (eds.), *Trade Friction and Economic Policy*. Cambridge University Press, pp. 50–85.

—— and Yanagawa, N. (1993), 'Cooperative and Non-Cooperative R&D in an Oligopoly with Spillovers: Strategic Substitutes versus Strategic Complements', *Hitotsubashi Journal of Economics*, 34: 1–11.

Szidarovszky, F., and Yakowitz, S. (1977), 'A New Proof of the Existence and Uniqueness of the Cournot Equilibrium', *International Economic Review*, 18: 787–9.

—— —— (1982), 'Contributions to Cournot Oligopoly Theory', *Journal of Economic Theory*, 28: 51–70.

Tandon, P. (1984), 'Innovation, Market Structure, and Welfare', *American Economic Review*, 74: 394–403.

Teece, D. (1986), 'Profiting from Technological Innovation: Implications for Integration, Collaboration, Licencing and Public Policy', *Research Policy*, 15: 285–305.

—— (1992), 'Competition, Cooperation and Innovation', *Journal of Economic Behaviour and Organization*, 18: 1–25.

Telser, L. G. (1966), 'Cutthroat Competition and the Long Purse', *Journal of Law and Economics*, 9: 259–77.

—— (1985), 'Cooperation, Competition, and Efficiency', *Journal of Law and Economics*, 28: 271–95.

Thompson, A. A., Jr (1980), 'Competition as a Strategic Process', *Antitrust Bulletin*, 25: 777–803.

Tirole, J. (1988), *The Theory of Industrial Organization*. Cambridge, Mass.: MIT Press.

Tsuruta, T., and Yahagi, T. (1991), 'The System of Large-Scale Retail Store Law and its Hollowing-Out Process' (in Japanese), in K. Nishimura and Y. Miwa (eds.), *The Distributions in Japan*. University of Tokyo Press, pp. 283–324.

Uesugi, A. (1986), 'Japan's Cartel System and its Impact on International Trade', *Harvard International Law Journal*, 27 (Special Issue): 389–424.

Ulph, D. (1983), 'Rational Conjectures in the Theory of Oligopoly', *International Journal of Industrial Organization*, 1: 131–54.

Veblen, T. (1898), 'Why is Economics not an Evolutionary Science?' *Quarterly Journal of Economics*, 12: 373–97.

Veloce, W., and Zellner, A. (1984), 'Modeling a Competitive Industry with Entry (Implication for Demand and Supply Analysis)', *Economics Letters*, 16: 71–5.

Vickers, J. S. (1985*a*), 'Strategic Competition among the Few: Some Recent Developments in Oligopoly Theory', *Oxford Review of Economic Policy*, 1: 39–62.

—— (1985*b*), 'Delegation and the Theory of the Firm', *Economic Journal*, 95 (Conference Supplement): 138–47. Reprinted in A. F. Daugherty (ed.), *Cournot Oligopoly: Characterization and Applications*, Cambridge University Press, 1988, ch. 17.

—— (1989), 'The Nature of Costs and the Number of Firms at Cournot Equilibrium', *International Journal of Industrial Organization*, 7: 503–9.

—— —— and Yarrow, G. K. (1988), *Privatization: An Economic Analysis*. Cambridge, Mass.: MIT Press.

Vives, X. (1985), 'On the Efficiency of Bertrand and Cournot Equilibria with Product Differentiation', *Journal of Economic Theory*, 36: 166–75. Reprinted in A. F. Daugherty (ed.), *Cournot Oligopoly: Characterization and Applications*, Cambridge University Press, 1988, ch. 10.

—— (1990), 'Information and Comparative Advantage', *International Journal of Industrial Organization*, 8: 17–35.

von Weizsäcker, C. C. (1980*a*), 'A Welfare Analysis of Barriers to Entry', *Bell Journal of Economics*, 11: 399–420.

—— (1980*b*), *Barriers to Entry: A Theoretical Treatment*. Berlin: Springer-Verlag.

Wakasugi, R. (1988), 'Economic Analysis of Cooperative R&D' (in Japanese), *Shinshu Daigaku Keizaigaku Ronshu*, 26: 1–26.

Weinstein, D. E. (1993), 'Evaluating Administrative Guidance and Cartels in Japan (1957–1988)', Discussion Paper 1628, Harvard Institute of Economic Research, September.

Weitzman, M. L. (1982), 'Increasing Returns and the Foundations of Unemployment Theory', *Economic Journal*, 92: 787–804.

—— (1983), 'Some Macroeconomic Implications of Alternative Compensation Systems', *Economic Journal*, 93: 763–83.

—— (1984), *The Share Economy*, Cambridge, Mass.: Harvard University Press.

—— (1988), 'Consumer's Surplus as an Exact Approximation when Prices are Appropriately Deflated', *Quarterly Journal of Economics*, 103: 543–53.

Whalley, J. (1975), 'How Reliable is Partial Equilibrium Analysis?' *Review of Economics and Statistics*, 57: 299–310.

Willig, R. (1976), 'Consumer's Surplus without Apology', *American Economic Review*, 66: 589–97.

—— (1983), 'Sector-Differentiated Capital Taxation with Imperfect Competition and Inter-Industry Flows', *Journal of Public Economics*, 21: 295–316.

Wolfstetter, E. (1990), 'The Labor Managed Firm: A Duality Approach', *Journal of Institutional and Theoretical Economics*, 146: 439–44.

Wriglesworth, J. L. (1985), *Libertarian Conflicts in Social Choice*. Cambridge University Press.

Yamamura, K. (1982), 'Success that Soured: Administrative Guidance and Cartels in Japan', in K. Yamamura (ed.), *Policy and Trade Issues of the Japanese Economy: American and Japanese Perspectives*. University of Tokyo Press, pp. 77–112.

Yarrow, G. K. (1976), 'On the Predictions of Managerial Theories of the Firm', *Journal of Industrial Economics*, 24: 267–79.

—— (1985), 'Welfare Losses in Oligopoly and Monopolistic Competition', *Journal of Industrial Economics*, 33: 515–29.

AUTHOR INDEX

SUBJECT INDEX

Note: Page numbers in italics indicate references to figures or tables only and not to text.